"This is the Baptist history textbook I have been waiting for since I studied the subject in seminary. It actually makes the subject interesting! This work has been long overdue."

Daniel L. Akin, president, Southeastern Baptist Theological Seminary

"Respected church historians Anthony Chute, Nathan Finn, and Michael Haykin have served the church well with their book *The Baptist Story: From English Sect to Global Movement*. Though intended as a textbook, their fine work is accessible to most every reader, including those in nonacademic settings. For all interested in Baptist history, I heartily recommend *The Baptist Story*."

Jason K. Allen, president, Midwestern Baptist Theological Seminary

"The Baptists have grown from a small and mainly marginal body in seventeenth-century England into a strong and sometimes influential set of denominations across the world. While the core of this account of their development concentrates on the history of the two-thirds of the world's Baptists who live in the United States, there is also coverage of England, Canada, Germany, and the rest of the world. So this volume provides a concise but comprehensive summary of the course of Baptist life over the last four centuries."

David Bebbington, professor of history, University of Stirling

"The Baptist story is long and often convoluted. Numerous histories have been written over the course of their 400 years. Each new volume proffers its own interpretation of the data and furthers the cause and concern of the author. While honest, this has not always been helpful, and often fails to provide today's Baptists with a modern account of their tale that informs the mind and encourages the soul.

The Baptist Story, as told by Haykin, Chute, and Finn, changes all that. The authors give us an irenic yet thorough reading of our collective past. They admit the nuances of a faith that boldly defends and exemplifies liberty of conscience while explaining the facts. While the authors concede that their goal was not to provide *the* definitive telling of the Baptist story, they may have done just that. Haykin, Chute, and Finn are to be commended for their effort, thanked for their grace, and congratulated for their contribution to the cause of Christ and the history of the Baptist people. *The Baptist Story* always encourages, sometimes challenges, and never disappoints."

Peter Beck, associate professor of Christian studies, Charleston Southern University

"*The Baptist Story* is a masterful work by three superb Baptist historians. Tony Chute, Nathan Finn, and Michael Haykin are to be commended for providing us with an even-handed, incisive, well-organized, and accessible survey of the larger Baptist family. Readers will be introduced to both general and particular Baptists, as well as revivalists and Landmarkists, fundamentalists and liberals. In doing so, they will gain a fresh appreciation for the contributions of thoughtful theologians and practical pastors, along with faithful missionaries and martyrs. This full-orbed, carefully researched, and well-written look at the expansion and development of Baptists over the past four hundred years will certainly become a standard resource for the study of Baptist history for years to come. It is with much enthusiasm that I gladly recommend this work."

David S. Dockery, president, Trinity International University

"Being a Baptist is about more than bearing a denominational label. It's about affirming a doctrinal distinctive and embracing an identity based on historical precedent. This superb volume will help you appreciate what it means to be a Baptist and celebrate the unique contributions we have made to global Christianity. Read it with holy awe at how God has used Baptists to make a difference in his world!"

Jeff Iorg, president, Golden Gate Baptist Theological Seminary

"This textbook originates from within but expands beyond the Southern Baptist tradition to narrate the Baptist story in a way readers will understand and appreciate. Images, primary source quotations, and review questions make the book especially useful for the undergraduate or graduate classroom."

Melody Maxwell, assistant professor of Christian studies, Howard Payne University

"*The Baptist Story* reflects well on the gifts and expertise of three distinguished Baptist historians and professors. They have written an eminently readable, thorough, and well-balanced account of the Baptist past from its roots in English Separatism to the modern context where the Baptist movement has become truly global. The authors respect the diversity and complexity of Baptist history, and they judiciously avoid any partisan agendas. In addition to providing vital factual information about Baptist history, they suggest some important interpretive and analytical perspectives that enrich their narrative. This textbook should be widely adopted for use in relevant college and seminary courses, as well as in church study groups."

Jim Patterson, professor of Christian thought and tradition and associate dean, School of Theology and Missions, Union University

"*The Baptist Story* is meticulously researched, well written, and full of insight into the history of the people called Baptists. This will be the textbook in Baptist history for the next generation of conservative Baptist students and scholars."

Andrew C. Smith, assistant professor of religion and director of the Center for Baptist Studies, Carson-Newman University

The
BAPTIST
STORY

From English Sect to Global Movement

Anthony L. Chute

Nathan A. Finn

Michael A. G. Haykin

B&H
ACADEMIC

NASHVILLE, TENNESSEE

The Baptist Story: From English Sect to Global Movement
Copyright © 2015 by Anthony L. Chute, Nathan A. Finn,
and Michael A. G. Haykin

B&H Publishing Group
Nashville, Tennessee

All rights reserved

ISBN: 978-1-4336-7375-7

Dewey Decimal Classification: 286.09
Subject Heading: BAPTISTS—HISTORY \ SOUTHERN BAPTISTS
\ ANABAPTISTS \ SEPARATE BAPTISTS \ BLACK BAPTISTS

Printed in the United States of America
2 3 4 5 6 7 8 9 10 • 21 20 19 18 17

To David Bebbington, Raymond Brown, Keith Harper, Timothy George, Tom Nettles, George Rawlyk, Doug Weaver, Barrie White, and Greg Wills

These Baptist historians are Doctores Ecclesiae who have modeled for us a commitment to historical scholarship, Baptist identity, and the ministry of the Word.

CONTENTS

ACKNOWLEDGMENTS

This book has been a long time in the making, and we have incurred many debts along the way. We first began discussing a new Baptist history textbook with B&H Academic in 2009. At that time, between the three of us, we had two different ideas for a textbook. Jim Baird, Ray Clendenen, Terry Wilder, and Andreas Köstenberger—all of whom have been a part of B&H Academic at some point in recent years—helped us combine and refine our ideas, resulting in the book you now hold in your hands (or see before you on your e-reader). Chris Cowan, who joined the team at B&H Academic in 2011, has been a constant source of encouragement and advice to us; it has been a genuine pleasure to work with him. When Chris Cowan moved to a new position at B&H Reference, Chris Thompson arrived to shepherd this project through its final stages.

In addition to our friends at B&H Academic, others have offered key assistance to us. Numerous institutions helped us by providing many of the images we use in this book. We wish to thank the following for their assistance: Adam Winters of the Archives and Special Collections Department at The Southern Baptist Theological Seminary, Taffey Hall of the Southern Baptist Historical Library and Archives, Frederick J. Boehlke and Fran Decker of Eastern Baptist University, Gord Heath and Adam McCulloch of the Canadian Baptist Archives at McMaster Divinity College, Art Toalston of *Baptist Press*, Gary W. Long and Terry Wolever of Particular Baptist Press; and Jonathan Parnell of Desiring God Ministries. We also wish to thank the following individuals for giving us permission to use images in their possession: Dustin Benge, Jason Duesing, Jonathan Jones, Steve Weaver, Malcolm Yarnell, and Fred and Jim Zaspel. Two of Nathan's PhD students also assisted us in important ways: Aaron Lumpkin helped prepare the study questions for each chapter, while Shane Shaddix prepared the subject index.

We are thankful for our colleagues, including Keith Harper, Chris Morgan, Tom Nettles, Steve Weaver, Greg Wills, and Shawn Wright, who have read drafts of chapters and provided suggestions for improvement. Chris in particular graciously read an earlier draft of our entire manuscript and offered numerous helpful recommendations that have strengthened this book. We also acknowledge the assistance of the two anonymous reviewers whom B&H Academic asked to look at our manuscript. We appreciate the input from all of these scholars and take full responsibility for any errors or shortcomings that remain.

The administrations of our respective institutions have enthusiastically supported this project from the beginning. We are especially thankful for the encouragement of our respective presidents, each of whom recently celebrated milestone anniversaries at their schools: Daniel L. Akin (ten years at The Southeastern Baptist Theological Seminary), Ronald L. Ellis (twenty years at California Baptist University), and R. Albert Mohler Jr. (twenty years at Southern Baptist Theological Seminary). Nathan was blessed to receive a sabbatical from Southeastern Seminary during the spring 2014 semester. The administration at Union University was gracious enough to invite Nathan to spend his sabbatical on their campus, allowing him to devote considerable time to editing the manuscript as we all finished our respective sections of the book. He would like to thank David Dockery, Gene Fant, and the faculty of the School of Theology and Missions at Union University for taking such an interest in this textbook.

Our families have championed this project from its early days as a mere potentiality to its final fruition as a Baptist history textbook. We count our wives—Connie Chute, Leah Finn, and Alison Haykin—to be among God's most precious gifts to us. We could not have written this book without their support and, when necessary, gentle prodding. We are also grateful for the support of our children. We appreciate Amos and Joelle Chute; Georgia, Baxter, Eleanor, and Fuller Finn; and Nigel and Victoria Haykin for sharing us with Baptists from bygone eras as we worked on this book. We are each also Baptist churchmen who are vitally involved in the ministries of our respective congregations in California, North Carolina, and Ontario. We appreciate the encouragement we have received from many members in our local Baptist churches as we have sought to tell the story of which they are a part.

We are conscious of the reality that we have been fundamentally shaped by those scholars who taught us Baptist history through their classroom instruction and the various books and essays they have written. With gratitude, we wish to honor them by acknowledging their influence on us. We would not be the Baptist historians we are today were it not for their impact on each of us. Their scholarly visions inform our own, and their interpretive "echoes" can be heard on nearly every page of this book. We have grown to love Baptist history, in part, because their love of Baptist history is infectious. We are grateful to God for their ministries of teaching and scholarship. We dedicate this book to our mentors in Baptist history in the hope that it embodies the best of all that they have taught us about the Baptist story.

Anthony L. Chute
Nathan A. Finn
Michael A. G. Haykin

INTRODUCTION

When Jesse Mercer purchased *The Christian Index*, a Georgia-based Baptist newspaper, his first editorial contained the following observations:

> We now enter immediately on our duties as Editor of a religious journal, and begin to feel them of mountain weight. In the first, chief place, how to please God, the Judge of All, otherwise than by the presentment of truth, frankly and candidly expressed, according to his conscientious views of the most holy Word; he knows not: but in doing this, in the second place; how to please his Patrons (whom to please would be a high gratification to him) in their various and conflicting sentiments, in different sections are clothed, is a herculean task indeed.

Mercer's wordiness aside, of his two main concerns—pleasing God and pleasing Baptists—the latter gave him most pause. The year was 1833, and Mercer had in mind a recent separation of Baptists over the need for missions and the role of theological education. Mercer realized that Primitive Baptists had already discounted his views and those of his allies, the so-called Missionary Baptists, which were positive on the aforementioned topics. Yet he understood all too well that even Baptists who sided with him on missions and theological education might find cause to nitpick his articles in one way or another. Where two or three Baptists are gathered, it seems, three or four opinions are sometimes in the midst of them. Walter Shurden, Baptist historian and professor at Mercer University from 1983 to 2007, captured this feisty Baptist spirit across the centuries in his aptly titled book *Not a Silent People* (Smyth & Helwys, 1995).

Our attempt to produce a history of Baptists has caused us to feel a mountain of weight as well, and we are sympathetic to Mercer's depiction of it as being a herculean task. Indeed, writing such a history some 200 years after American Baptists first organized an international mission agency (the Triennial Convention) has placed us in the context of writing about more, not fewer, Baptist groups. Consequently our audience includes, but is not limited to, independent Baptists and Cooperative Baptists, Seventh Day Baptists and Southern Baptists, Free Will Baptists and Reformed Baptists, regulative principle Baptists and seeker-sensitive Baptists. Among these groups are differing views of biblical inspiration, age of baptismal recipients, elder-led churches, women pastors, sovereign decrees, and the propriety of vacation Bible school—to name only a few!

This disparity leads to a dilemma: what does it mean to be Baptist? Is it enough to call oneself a Baptist, or must one meet specific criteria to qualify as such? One may consider two titles of previous works to note how authors differ in their views of Baptist relatedness: Bill Leonard's *Baptist Ways: A History* (Judson Press, 2003) and R. Stanton Norman's *The Baptist Way: Distinctives of a Baptist Church* (B&H Academic, 2005). The former depicted Baptists as a multifaceted movement using believer's baptism and congregational polity as unifying factors, whereas the latter brought attention to biblical authority as a leading Baptist distinctive from which other matters—such as regenerate church membership and religious freedom—derive. Although Leonard wrote a historical narrative and Norman provided a theological analysis, their differing approaches to "Baptist Ways" versus "The Baptist Way" are not merely methodological. They reflect a genuine disagreement on what it means to be Baptist; and, by voicing their beliefs, they prove that Baptists are indeed not a silent people.

We realize that even the title of our book, *The Baptist Story: From English Sect to Global Movement*, raises questions regarding our understanding of Baptist history. Although our headline, *The Baptist Story*, begins with the definite article, we do not intend this to be *the* final history that replaces previous Baptist histories. To the contrary, works on Baptist history, large and small, have helped us immensely by collectively contributing to our knowledge of and appreciation for this movement.

Ours is both an individual and a collaborative effort. We divided this project according to our specialties: Michael Haykin wrote the chapters on seventeenth- and eighteenth-century Baptists, Anthony Chute authored the section on nineteenth-century Baptists, and Nathan Finn concluded with the twentieth century and beyond. However, we have each provided substantive input and editorial oversight regarding the book as a whole. This textbook is a collaborative effort at every level.

Not only have we been helped by one another's contributions, but we have also developed a greater appreciation for those who have tackled this topic on their own. Leon McBeth's *The Baptist Heritage: Four Centuries of Baptist Witness* (Broadman, 1987) remains a magisterial reference work for Baptist historians. Leonard's *Baptist Ways* and Tom Nettles's three-volume work on *The Baptists* (Mentor, 2005–2007) will each undoubtedly be used for decades to come. The broader perspective embodied in Robert Johnson's *A Global Introduction to Baptist Churches* (Cambridge University Press, 2010) and David Bebbington's *Baptists through the Centuries* (Baylor University Press, 2010) have informed our own narrative of Baptist history. Moreover, we are indebted to many scholars who have written more specialized monographs and essays, knowing that they have helped us nuance certain aspects of the Baptist story.

Our decision to write in true textbook form (incorporating a received body of knowledge using our particular perspectives) led us to conclude that widespread use of footnotes would restrict an already limited word count and could prove to be less user-friendly for students. However, we have included a bibliography at the end of each chapter in order to reflect our dependence on previous works and to direct the reader toward further research. Within our bibliographies students will encounter differing approaches to the Baptist story, such as William Brackney's *A Genetic History of Baptist Thought* (Mercer University Press, 2004) and James Leo Garrett's *Baptist Theology: A Four-Century Study* (Mercer University Press, 2009), two fine historical-theological surveys that represent masterful scholarship. This book, therefore, is not meant to replace previous histories; instead, it is a collation and updating of many stories, one that itself will need to be updated in the future.

Moreover, this is not the complete story. Through our collaborative efforts, we have offered suggestions to one another regarding the inclusion and exclusion of Baptist events, personalities, issues, and controversies. Historians who read this book may wince at the lack of space given to their favorite, perhaps nearly forgotten, Baptist heroine or hero. We too shudder to think of what we have either understated or left unsaid. Our main goal, however, has not been to write for other historians but rather to produce a work primarily for students that recognizes the global sweep of Baptists, with all of their historic and doctrinal variety. In short, we omitted some details so students who read this book will not be lost in the particulars.

We believe we have accomplished the substantive purpose of this project in presenting the reader with a historical survey of Baptists that includes not only the major organizations but the minor players and minority members as well, whose work for and among Baptists is no less important even though it may be less visible. We also believe we have stayed true to our task of presenting the Baptist story "warts and all." Baptists—or any people for that matter—are in desperate need of divine grace, and our history reflects that. Therefore, we have included elements in our narrative that make us rather uncomfortable yet are faithful to the historical record and point the reader to the faithfulness of God.

This is not the final story, and it is not the complete story, but it is a story nonetheless. We have striven to present the narrative in a way teachers can use and students can appreciate. Each of us has taught dozens of courses on Baptist history to college, seminary, and doctoral students, and we feel we have acquired an appreciation for bringing together what is important with what is interesting. We have structured several sections of this book based on questions students commonly ask, and we have included areas of personal interest we have not found in other textbooks. Moreover, we have attempted to weave as seamlessly as possible institutional and individual histories as well as integrating the global narrative with local issues. At times our focus on the width of the Baptist movement has restricted us from carefully exploring its depth. Therefore, the reader will notice, particularly in the chapters dealing with the twentieth century, the pace of the narrative becomes more brisk as the Baptist movement becomes more global.

The inclusion of pictures and information boxes within the text reflects our desire to communicate. We appreciate the fact that many students are visual learners but, even more, we want to remind readers that this narrative is not mere history. The Baptists of earlier eras who thought the ideas, made the decisions, and founded the institutions recounted in this book were as alive in previous centuries as the reader of these pages is today. Baptists do not canonize saints, but they can reflect on those whose earthly lives made a difference for generations to come. Thus, we hope our readers will be motivated to expect great things from God and attempt great things for God. Furthermore, we have included elements of personal and corporate piety as a way of reminding our readers that the Baptists who made history did so because they loved the Lord who purchased them with his own blood. Such people are to be considered as children of God first and then, as necessitated by this book, viewed as Baptists. Whether they wrote hymns, debated fine points of theology, built meetinghouses, or organized for missions, Baptists have viewed their denominational contributions within the larger context of advancing the gospel of Jesus Christ.

Our subtitle also deserves explanation. The informed historian will note that we begin the Baptist story when Baptists were an "English Sect." This notation represents our understanding that the Baptist movement does not reach back to John the Baptist in the first century, but its historical roots are in the Separatist movement that emerged from the Church of England in the first decade of the seventeenth century. Baptists have not always agreed on their own origins (again, we are not a silent people!); but the historical record, as it presently stands, confirms that the Baptist movement, as we now know it, began with John Smyth and was continued through the work of Thomas Helwys. Both were Englishmen who left the Anglican Church, convinced that it was too politicized by the Crown and too Catholic for their comfort. They later disagreed with their Separatist brethren over the issue of infant baptism and completed their search for the New Testament church by founding a congregation based on regenerate church membership and committed to believer's baptism. We concur with this history, tracing Baptist beginnings to 1609.

Yet even this assertion does not conclude the matter. John Smyth departed the Baptist movement upon discovering that Anabaptists had formed churches on exactly the same principles nearly a century earlier. His decision to apply for membership with the Waterlander Mennonites, a branch of the Anabaptist movement, has led Baptist historians to question what relationship Anabaptists have with Baptists. We join with other scholars in recognizing the spiritual kinship Baptists have with many Anabaptists, noting the common thread of a regenerate church, believer's baptism, congregational polity, and a form of church-state separation. Indeed, we recommend that our students pursue this connection further by reading William Estep's classic work, *The Anabaptist Story* (Eerdmans, 1995; 3rd ed.), and a recent work edited by Malcolm Yarnell III, *The Anabaptists and Contemporary Baptists: Restoring New Testament Christianity* (B&H Academic, 2013). In so doing, students will find that modern-day Baptists can appreciate Anabaptists of old for many of their core beliefs. Students will also discover a long list of largely forgotten Christian heroes and heroines who chose to die for their beliefs rather than surrender conscience for the sake of convenience.

However, while we concur there were some theological similarities between some early Baptists and Anabaptists, we find the movements separated by a host of other issues including the Anabaptist tendency to withdraw from society, their emphasis on pacifism, their tendency toward communalism, and their weakened position on the effects of the fall. Though Baptists are a diverse people, some of whom even share these beliefs with Anabaptists, we also note the lack of a historical thread that formally ties the Anabaptist and Baptist movements together. We distinguish, therefore, between indebtedness and connectedness. Baptists are indebted to many Christian groups throughout the history of the church, from the early church fathers with their emphasis on the full deity and humanity of Christ to the Reformation leaders with their clarion call to trust in Christ alone for salvation. However, differences in life and practice have led Baptists to distinguish themselves from other Christian groups, even those with similar names. We have therefore highlighted the primacy of history when writing this story.

The decision to follow the historical evidence in this regard underscores our conviction that Baptists should use history in a ministerial rather than a magisterial manner. In other words, history can help us see what Baptists have believed, but it should not be used to tell us what Baptists must believe. Baptists are a "people of the book," and even though they read that book differently from time to time, they understand that nothing else carries the same authority over their lives as the Bible. Whereas Baptists have sometimes used history to pressure others into conforming to a particular position, we have attempted instead to provide a history that informs the reader of how Baptists have reached their conclusions. To give one example, we believe the question of whether the first Baptists were Calvinists is a moot point because the answer is both no and yes. The successors to the Smyth-Helwys tradition were not Calvinists, but the English Baptists who emerged from the Jacob-Lathrop-Jessey Church certainly were Calvinists. History teaches us that some Baptist groups have held on to these beliefs and gone separate ways, while others have found ways to hold on to a portion of those beliefs and join together, and still others have agreed to split the difference by working together while not making the finer points of Calvinism or Arminianism an issue. The same could be said for other theological issues that tend to divide Baptists. As historians, then, we do not claim any theological superiority stemming from our assessment of Baptist beginnings.

And yet we do not want to leave the impression that we are indifferent to what Baptists believe. The three of us have similar theological convictions that shape our lives and inform our denominational and local church identity. Our concluding chapter, titled "Identity and Distinctives," is therefore more prescriptive than descriptive as we attempt to define what it means to be Baptist from our particular perspective. It is broad and inclusive, but readers will find that we have offered more of our own leanings in that section than we have earlier in the book. Since we are more prescriptive in that section, we have placed it at the end of our book instead of the beginning, placing primacy on history. We trust this placement will help our readers draw their own conclusions inductively as they reflect on the history of Baptists.

Perhaps the one aspect of our title everyone can agree on is that Baptists are a "Global Movement." On any given Sunday (or Saturday, for our Seventh Day Baptist friends and many Baptist "megachurches"), Baptists around the world voluntarily gather to worship the Triune God, offering prayer and praise to the Father, through the Son, in the power of the Holy Spirit. Whether they meet in a storefront in Tokyo or a tent in Turkmenistan, publicly outside in Newport Beach or secretly in a house church in China, with dancing in a tribal village in Africa or with reserved solemnity in London, Baptists around the world share at least two common characteristics. They have embraced the gospel of Jesus Christ, repenting of their sins and trusting in his meritorious work, and they have followed through with his command to be baptized, a visible display of death to sin and resurrection to new life. If Baptist controversies can be described with the phrase "not a silent people," the same can be said about Baptist missions. Baptists are global because their message is viral. Our prayer is that Baptists, and other Christians, will continue to share the story and not be silent so that when future histories are written, someone may rightfully say that the gospel has gone into all the world and disciples have been made of all nations, baptized, and taught to obey all of Christ's commands (Matt 28:18–20).

Section One

BAPTISTS IN THE SEVENTEENTH AND EIGHTEENTH CENTURIES

Chapter 1

BAPTIST BEGINNINGS

Beginnings are important. They set directions and give shape to journeys. The beginnings of the Baptist story in England, Holland, and America are no exception. These early years of the Baptist story highlight one of the most vital aspects of this narrative: it is a history of the intertwined lives of men and women, some of whom still loom large in this fifth century since Baptists began as a small sect in the English-speaking world—figures like John Smyth, Thomas Helwys, Henry Jessey, and Roger Williams. Baptists are now a worldwide movement, and the thoughts and achievements of these early leaders and others are still helping orient Baptist history in the twenty-first century.

Anabaptist Similarities

Many historians judge the Reformation to be the most important event in the history of Christianity since the ancient church. Protestants believe it was a time of both remarkable spiritual awakening and a rediscovery of biblical teaching on such fundamental issues as salvation, worship, and marriage. The Reformation also witnessed the division of the Church in Western Europe into Roman Catholic and Protestant. While the majority of Protestants disagreed strongly with the Roman Catholic Church over issues like the nature of salvation and the question of religious authority, both groups agreed that the state had a vital role to play in the life of the church. Most sixteenth-century Protestants could not envision a world where state and church were not working together for the cause of Christ. However, a small number of individuals refused to identify themselves with this way of thinking. These men and women by and large rejected the idea of a national church, to which every individual in the state belonged, along with its support of infant baptism. Instead they advocated churches composed solely of believers who were admitted on the basis of a personal confession of faith and believer's baptism. In the early days of the Reformation, this small group of Protestants would have been baptized as infants. When they were baptized as believers, their opponents, both Roman Catholic and Protestant, dubbed them "rebaptizers," or Anabaptists.

These Anabaptists generally baptized by pouring or sprinkling. The first Anabaptist baptism took place in Zürich on January 21, 1525, when Conrad Grebel baptized Jörg [George] Blaurock by pouring water over his head, that is, by affusion. Even though a month later Grebel did baptize Wolfgang Ulimann by immersion, this was exceptional; the usual mode of baptism among the Swiss Anabaptists was affusion. The early German Anabaptists, of whom Hans Hut is a good example, also baptized by affusion. On occasion Hut simply baptized believers by dipping his thumb in a dish of water and making a cross on the forehead of the person to be baptized, in accordance with his view that the seal mentioned in Revelation 7:3 was baptism.

For these early Anabaptists believer's baptism was the doorway to a life of ongoing transformation as they sought to live as disciples of Christ in community with like-minded believers. By and large these Anabaptists shared the conviction with Martin Luther and the French Reformer John Calvin that "faith alone makes us righteous before God," to quote the words of the German Anabaptist leader Balthasar Hubmaier. But the Anabaptists insisted this faith was an active faith, full of "all sorts of works of brotherly love toward others," to again quote Hubmaier. For Hubmaier, these fruits of faith were central to the essence of genuine faith. Sadly, because these early Anabaptists rejected the union of church and state assumed by the majority of

Balthasar Hubmaier (1480–1528)

professing Christians in Western Europe, their communities were regarded as a dire threat to the stability and security of the state. Thus, many of the Anabaptists perished at the hands of both Roman Catholics and Protestants. Hubmaier was burned at the stake in 1528 in Roman Catholic Vienna, for example, while Felix Manz, in whose house Blaurock had been baptized, was drowned in the Limmat River in Zürich by fellow Protestants.

Exacerbating the negative image of the Anabaptists in the sixteenth century was the seizure of the town of Münster in Germany by a fanatical group of Anabaptists who believed the kingdom of God could be set up by force of arms. From 1534 to 1535 the inhabitants of the town were ruled by Jan Matthys and Jan Bockelson (also known as John of Leyden). They established a theocracy with all property held in common, legalized polygamy, and punished adultery with death. Although this Anabaptist experiment was short-lived—the town fell to a Catholic army in June 1535—and was hardly representative of the main thrust of Anabaptism, the scandalous horror of Münster made the name Anabaptist a byword for fanaticism and violent anarchy well into the seventeenth century.

There are "remarkable similarities," as Paige Patterson has put it, between these European Anabaptists of the sixteenth century and the English Baptists of the following century. Moreover, Anabaptists were active in England prior to the clear emergence of the Baptists. But this does not mean there was a direct organic influence by these Anabaptists on the Baptists who emerged in the seventeenth century. First, it was possible for both groups to reach independently similar conclusions since both groups appealed to the Scriptures as the standard for church life and order. Second, if the Baptists were deeply indebted to the Anabaptists, they would have been reluctant to admit it, due to the popular image

John of Leyden (ca. 1509–1536)

of Anabaptists as violent, social revolutionaries that had developed during the sixteenth century, owing in part to the Münster incident. For example, when the first Particular Baptist churches issued a confession of faith in 1644 that outlined their theological beliefs, they stated on the title page of the confession that they were "commonly (though falsly [*sic*]) called Anabaptists." They clearly wanted to dissociate themselves totally from the specter of Anabaptism. Determining the impact of the Anabaptists in a context where any links with them is denied is virtually impossible. Third, the best explanation for the development of Baptist convictions and ideas exists in the

development of the English Separatists, who came out of the Puritan movement of the late sixteenth century and who are briefly examined below. As
English Baptist historian Barrie R. White has maintained, when an explanation for the emergence of Baptist convictions from the English context of the
Puritan-Separatist movement is readily available, the onus of proof lies on
those who argue for continental Anabaptism as having a decisive role in the
emergence of the Baptists.

Puritan Soil

Baptists are children of the Puritans, a movement with roots stretching
back to the European Reformation in the sixteenth century. In England the
initial stages of the Reformation had taken place during the reign of Henry
VIII, though not until the reign of his son Edward VI and then his daughter
Elizabeth I did it find a firm footing. Following the reign of the Catholic
monarch Mary Tudor, Elizabeth I ascended to the throne in 1558, perma-
nently securing England's place in the Protestant orbit.

The Elizabethan Church of England faced an important question: to what
extent would the Scripture be its guide in theology, worship, and church
governance? Elizabeth seemed content with a church that was Protestant
in theology but largely medieval in its pattern of worship and liturgy and in
which the monarch held the reins of power. The Puritans arose in response
to this situation, seeking to pattern the Elizabethan church after the model
of Reformed churches on the European continent, which included in their
worship only forms and practices they believed the Bible explicitly commanded. For instance, John Calvin, whose name has become synonymous
with the Reformation in Geneva, declared with regard to the worship of the
church that "nothing pleases God but what he himself has commanded us in
his Word."

Separatist Roots

In the 1580s and 1590s, some of the more radical-minded Puritans, despair-
ing of reformation within the Church of England, began to separate from
the state church and organize what historians call Separatist congregations.
Two books marked the "clarion call" of the Separatist movement: *A Treatise of Reformation Without Tarrying for Anie* and *A Booke Which Sheweth
the Life and Manners of All True Christians*. Both works were published in
1582 by Robert Browne—"Troublechurch" Browne, as one of his opponents
nicknamed him. Browne came from a family of substance and was related
to Robert Cecil, Elizabeth I's lord treasurer and chief minister. During his

undergraduate years at Cambridge University, Browne became a thorough-going Presbyterian. Within a few years, however, he came to the conviction that each local congregation had the right and responsibility to elect its own elders. By 1581, he was convinced of the necessity of planting congregations apart from the state church and its parish system.

That same year Browne established a Separatist congregation at Norwich in Norfolk. After being persecuted, the entire congregation left England the following year for the freedom of the Netherlands. What attracted Separatists like Browne to the Netherlands was its geographical proximity to England, its policy of religious toleration, its phenomenal commercial prosperity—the early seventeenth century witnessed such a flowering of Dutch literary, scientific, and artistic achievement that this period has often been called "the golden age of the Netherlands"—and the Reformed nature of its churches. From his new home Browne published his two influential Separatist treatises. In these tracts Browne set forth his views which, over the course of the next century, became common property of all the theological children of the English Separatists, including Baptists.

Browne willingly conceded the right of civil authorities to rule and to govern. However, he drew a line between their powers in society at large and their power with regard to local churches. As citizens of the state, the individual members of churches were to be subject to civil authorities, but, he emphasized, these authorities had no right "to compel religion, to plant Churches by power, and to force a submission to ecclesiastical government by laws and penalties." Browne conceived of the local church as a "gathered" church, that is, a company of Christians who had covenanted together to live under the rule of Christ, whose will was made known through his Word and his Spirit. The pastors and elders of the church, though they ultimately received their authority and offices from God, were to be appointed to office by "due consent and agreement of the church" according to "the number of the most which agree." For Browne, Christianity was ultimately a matter of personal conviction rather than public order, and the church a fellowship of believers rather than an army of conscripts.

Although Browne later recanted his views, he started a movement that could not be held in check. Browne's mantle fell to three men—John Greenwood, Henry Barrow, and John Penry—all of whom were hanged in 1593 for secession from the established church, an act the state regarded as civil disobedience. Before their respective deaths, however, their preaching and writings led a significant number of Christians in London to adopt Separatist principles. As the English Baptist historian Barrie White has noted, "For many it was but a short step from impatient Puritanism within the established Church to convinced Separatism outside it."

In an effort to curb the growth of Separatists, a law was passed in April 1593 requiring everyone over the age of sixteen to attend the church of their local parish, which comprised all who lived within a certain geographic boundary. Failure to do so for an entire month meant imprisonment. If, three months following an individual's release from prison, he still refused to conform, the person was to be given a choice of exile or death. In other words, the established church and the state were hoping to be rid of the Separatist problem by sending those who were recalcitrant into exile. Understandably, when faced with a choice of death or exile, most Separatists chose the latter. About forty of them ended up in Amsterdam, where they were later joined by their pastor, Francis Johnson.

Francis Johnson was arrested at the same time as Greenwood and Barrow. Though they were executed, he was kept in prison until 1597, when he was released on the condition that he go into exile to Canada. Johnson did not end up in Canada but rather relocated to Amsterdam, where his Separatist congregation was residing. Though the Separatists now enjoyed freedom of worship, their troubles were not over. Francis's brother George Johnson began to cause problems for the congregation by voicing complaints about certain habits of Francis's wife Thomasine: her taste for expensive clothing; her use of whalebones in her petticoats so that, according to George, her figure was accentuated and she was hindered in bearing children; the fact that she stayed in bed till nine o'clock on Sunday mornings. The latter was an issue since these Separatists met for worship in the Johnsons' house. To such criticisms George added one considerably more substantial: that his brother Francis was power hungry and was the center of power rather than the congregation. The church ultimately sided with Francis and his wife, and George Johnson, when he refused to withdraw his charges, was excommunicated around 1600.

In 1608, a second Separatist congregation arrived in Amsterdam. John Smyth was the leader of this church. Initially the two congregations held considerable similarity; both were Separatist in theology and both were composed of expatriate English men and women. Nevertheless, within a year significant differences between the two groups were evident. These differences eventually led the Smyth congregation to become the first English-speaking Baptists.

General Baptist Origins

John Smyth's exact origins are unknown, though he may have grown up at Sturton-le-Steeple in Nottinghamshire. Our first definite sight of Smyth is when he was at Christ's College, Cambridge, where he obtained a BA in

1590 and an MA in 1597. During this period Cambridge University was a nursery of Puritanism; Francis Johnson was among Smyth's tutors. Unsurprisingly, Smyth's Puritan views led to trouble a few years after his departure from Cambridge. He had been ordained as a minister in the Church of England in 1594, but within three years he was voicing strong disagreement with aspects of the Church's liturgy that he believed were unscriptural. Appointed to give Sunday afternoon lectures in the town of Lincoln by its Puritan-leaning town council in 1600, he stayed in this position till 1602. Some sermons he gave during that time—later published as *The Bright Morning Starre* (1603) and *A Paterne of True Prayer* (1605)—show a man who was Puritan in theology but still considered himself to be a loyal member of the Church of England.

By the autumn of 1607, Smyth became convinced of the Separatist position and gathered a Separatist congregation in the town of Gainsborough in Lincolnshire. The critical factor in convincing Smyth that he should leave the Church of England appears to be a series of church decrees by King James I in late 1604. King James required complete conformity of all Church of England ministers to the Thirty-Nine Articles, the doctrinal foundation of the established church, and the *Book of Common Prayer*, which set forth the worship and liturgy of the Church of England. The decrees also demanded support for episcopal polity. Smyth apparently met with a number of other Puritans to discuss what course of action they should take. Most Puritans decided to remain within the established church. However, Smyth and John Robinson were convinced that they had to leave; in their view the Church of England was beyond hope of reform.

During 1607 and 1608, the Smyth congregation was harassed by the state and made the difficult decision to leave England for the free winds of Amsterdam, Holland. Upon their arrival they lived and worshiped in what had been the bakery of the East India Company and sought fellowship with the other English Separatist congregation in the city pastored by Francis Johnson. Differences soon began to appear between the two congregations. In a book Smyth published the year of his arrival in the Netherlands, *The Differences of the Churches of the Separation* (1608), he outlined areas of disagreement between his congregation and Johnson's. The most significant of these differences had to do with church leadership. The Johnson congregation had a single pastor who was responsible for preaching, discipline, and leading the congregation in the observance of the sacraments as well as serving as a teacher, who simply taught the Bible. Two ruling elders helped the pastor with the exercise of discipline. Smyth, however, believed that pastors, teachers, and elders were indistinguishable and that every congregation should have a plurality of these officers.

The net result of these differences was a rupture of fellowship between the two congregations as well as a split in the Smyth congregation. John Robinson and about 100 members could not agree with the direction Smyth was moving, and they separated from Smyth and relocated to Leiden. From Leiden, Robinson's congregation, who became known as the Pilgrims, eventually sailed to America on board the *Mayflower* and landed at Plymouth in southeastern Massachusetts in 1620. Robinson was to follow later, but he died in Holland in 1625. Following the split, Smyth's congregation numbered about fifty members, which was about a third of its original size.

In 1609, Smyth's thinking took another significant step as he came to accept believer's baptism. The issue of baptism was something of an embarrassment to the Separatists. According to their thinking, the Church of England was a false church. Yet all of them had been baptized as infants by this church. Was not the efficacy of their baptism in doubt, therefore? Most Separatists shrank from asking, let alone answering, this question. For many European Christians in the early seventeenth century, the baptism of believers seemed to lead to social and political disorder, as we have already noted.

Where others feared to tread, however, Smyth, ever the independent thinker, forged ahead. If, he reasoned, the Church of England is not a true church, then neither is her baptism a true baptism. Moreover, as he studied the Scriptures, he became convinced the New Testament knew only of believer's baptism and nothing of infant baptism. He outlined his new position in a treatise entitled *The Character of the Beast* (1609), which drew on a series of biblical texts like Acts 8:37 and Matthew 28:19. Baptism, Smyth argued, typifies the baptism with the Spirit and follows upon one's verbal confession of Christ; but infants cannot receive the baptism of the Spirit, nor can they confess Christ with their mouths. Nor are infants capable of repentance, which also must precede baptism. Smyth thus believed that he and his church were surrounded by a sea of apostasy. He recognized that he needed to be baptized, but in such a situation of total apostasy, he felt he had no one to whom he could turn for a proper baptism. He thus took the radical—and to his contemporaries, shocking—step of baptizing himself by pouring and then baptizing his congregation in the same manner.

In the controversy that followed the baptisms, Smyth was asked by his Separatist contemporaries how he could do such a thing; if self-baptism were permissible, then churches could be established of solitary men and women, which was ridiculous. Smyth's response was that he knew of no church that practiced baptism in accord with the New Testament. But, as Smyth's critics pointed out, he could have received believer's baptism from a Mennonite group in the Netherlands known as the Waterlanders. Smyth decided to approach the Waterlanders to investigate where they stood theologically.

By this point in time, Smyth had abandoned his earlier Calvinism and had adopted the views of the Dutch theologian Jacob Arminius, including the beliefs that election was conditioned on foreseen faith, saving grace could be resisted, and Christ died to save all men and women. Arminius's theological position was being heavily debated at the time in the Netherlands, and it is therefore understandable how Smyth came under the influence of this position. From the vantage point of his newly adopted Arminianism, the Waterlanders were orthodox, and Smyth came to regard his self-baptism as a premature and hasty step. Thus, together with forty-two other members of his congregation, he applied to join the Waterlander Mennonite church. This meant another baptism at the hands of the Waterlanders and consequently an admission on the part of the Smyth congregation that their baptism by Smyth was invalid. But some in Smyth's congregation refused to admit that their baptism was not valid. Led by Thomas Helwys, who came from landed gentry near Scrooby, Nottinghamshire, a handful of members refused to be absorbed into the Waterlander church. Instead they decided in 1612 to return to England. Smyth died the same year, and his congregation, eventually received into the Waterlander church, was ultimately assimilated into Dutch Mennonite culture.

The Helwys congregation, now based in Spitalfields, north London, retained the views they had adopted under Smyth's leadership and thus became known as General Baptists, so called because they believed Christ died to save all people (a general atonement). Helwys deserves to be remembered alongside Smyth as a Baptist pioneer. His treatise *A Short Declaration of the Mistery of Iniquity* (1612) contains a vigorous plea for religious liberty for all men and women: "Men's religion to God is between God and

---

Helwys's Inscription in *A Short Declaration of the Mistery of Iniquity*

Thomas Helwys penned the following inscription in the front of the copy of *A Short Declaration of the Mistery of Iniquity* that was sent to King James I. The inscription can be found in the copy of this book housed in the Bodleian Library, Oxford University. The following excerpt has been modernized.

"Hear, O king, and despise not the counsel of the poor, and let their complaints come before thee. The king is a mortal man and not God, therefore has no power over the immortal souls of his subjects, to make laws and ordinances for them, and to set spiritual lords over them. If the king has authority to make spiritual lords and laws, then he is an immortal God and not a mortal man. O king, be not seduced by deceivers to sin against God whom you ought to obey, nor against your poor subjects who ought and will obey you in all things with body, life, and goods, or else let their lives be taken from the earth. God save the king."

themselves. The king shall not answer for it. Neither may the king be judge between God and man. Let them be heretic, Turks, Jews, or whatsoever, it appertains not to the earthly power to punish them in the least measure." Helwys's book was the first of its kind in the English language. He addressed what he saw as the errors of not only the Roman Catholic Church and the Church of England but also the Puritans and the Separatists. For example, he accused the Separatist leader John Robinson of being "a malicious adversary of God's truth." Helwys was thrown into Newgate Prison almost as soon as the congregation returned to England; there he died before or in 1616. Helwys had sent a copy of *A Short Declaration* to King James I, which may have led to his arrest.

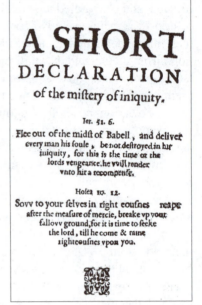

Helwys's book.

Helwys's small congregation, which must have consisted of no more than ten or so members when they first returned to England, survived their leader's imprisonment and death, eventually becoming the mother church of the General Baptist denomination. By 1626, they had established congregations in London, Coventry, Lincoln, Salisbury, and Tiverton, with a total of roughly 150 members. The General Baptists thus clearly emerged from the womb of Puritanism and the Separatist movement. Nevertheless, although the General Baptists were the first English-speaking Baptists, the Particular Baptists became the leading Baptist denomination in the centuries that followed.

Particular Baptist Origins

Notable Early Churches

The London-based congregation known to historians as the Jacob-Lathrop-Jessey Church or JLJ Church, so called because of the names of its first three pastors, lies at the fountainhead of the Particular Baptist movement. Henry Jacob and a group of like-minded believers in London established the congregation in 1616. To what extent Jacob and his church were influenced by Separatists like Francis Johnson and John Robinson remains an open question. Jacob met both of these men during his life, Johnson in 1599 and Robinson in 1610. What is clear, however, is that Jacob's congregation was determined not to cut itself off from all fellowship with Puritans in the Church of England. Unlike the Separatists, Jacob and his congregation believed true congregations existed within the Church of England; thus, it was not wrong to continue fellowshipping with them where this did not involve countenancing what Jacob's congregation regarded as definite error. It is not surprising that authorities in the Church of England harassed the congregation as a Separatist body, and Separatists in turn dubbed them "idolaters" since Separatists viewed the state church as a false church.

Due to this harassment and persecution, Jacob decided to leave England for Virginia in 1622, where he died two years later. His successor was John Lathrop. During Lathrop's pastorate at least two groups amicably withdrew from the Church to found Separatist congregations, one of which came to be pastored by Samuel Eaton. Eaton questioned the legitimacy of the baptism of infants by ministers in the Church of England, though it does not appear that he embraced believer's baptism as the only basis for membership in the Church. When William Laud, the Arminian archbishop of Canterbury, was seeking to rid England of Puritanism, Lathrop also decided to emigrate to the New World in 1634.

Henry Jessey became the new pastor of the JLJ Church in 1637. Jessey had become a Puritan while studying at Cambridge in the early 1620s. Ordained a priest in the Church of England in 1626, he grew increasingly uneasy with aspects of the liturgy and worship of the Established Church not directly supported by the Bible. In 1635 he came into contact with the Jacob-Lathrop Church, presumably began to worship with the congregation, and two years later was called to be the church's pastor. An irenic individual, Jessey continued to uphold the "Jacobite" tradition, that is, the policy established by Henry Jacob of fellowshipping with Puritans within the Church of England.

Henry Jessey (1603–1663)

A year or so after Jessey became the pastor of this church, the question of the validity of infant baptism arose. In a document drawn up at this time, the so-called "Kiffen Manuscript," we read that in 1638 "Mr. Thomas Wilson,

Mr. Pen, & H. Pen, & 3 more being convinced that baptism was not for infants, but professed believers joined with Mr. John Spilsbury the churches [*sic*] favour being desired therein." John Spilsbury was probably a cobbler by trade and may have been a member of the Jacob-Lathrop-Jessey Church at one point. His church is the first that can be definitely designated as Particular Baptist. The Particular Baptists were Calvinists noted for their belief that Christ died to save a particular elect people. Spilsbury wrote a number of small works that reveal his Calvinistic convictions. For example, in *God's Ordinance, the Saints' Privilege,* Spilsbury argued that "Christ hath not presented to his Father's justice a satisfaction for the sins of all men; but only for the sins of that do or shall believe in him; which are his elect only."

For many years Spilsbury's church met in an area of London called Wapping, which was on the north shore of the Thames River just east of the Tower of London. In the seventeenth century the district was a rough working-class community, largely populated by sailors or those engaged in maritime-related professions like mast making and ship repair. By 1670, around 300 regularly attended the services of this church. The Spilsbury congregation, which was probably little larger than a small house church when it began, maintained a good relationship with its mother church. There is evidence of joint gatherings for prayer, and members of the Spilsbury congregation continued to attend meetings at the Jacob-Lathrop-Jessey Church. Barrie R. White has observed that "there were no high walls of bitterness" between the mother church and groups that left, and "even the withdrawals are recorded as brotherly."

The Recovery of Baptism by Immersion

By May 1640, the Jacob-Lathrop-Jessey Church had grown to the point that it was too large to meet in one place. The decision was made to split the congregation in two, one half to continue under the pastoral leadership of Jessey and the other half under that of Praise-God Barebone, whose first name recalls the Puritan penchant for curious names. Around this time the question of baptism once again surfaced. A man named Richard Blunt, who had left the JLJ Church in 1633 with Samuel Eaton, began to fellowship with the church once again in 1640. Blunt soon aired the question of whether the baptism of believers by immersion was the only type of baptism to correspond to that practiced in New Testament times. The "Kiffen Manuscript" accordingly states that "Mr. Richard Blunt . . . being convinced of baptism that also it ought to be by dipping the body into the water, resembling burial and rising again . . . had sober conference about in the Church." The two texts that especially convinced Blunt the baptism of believers should be by immersion were Colossians 2:12 and Romans 6:4, both of which relate baptism to the believer's death, burial, and resurrection with Christ.

Blunt and those who were like-minded knew of no congregation in England that baptized believers by immersion and thus had no one close at hand to whom they could turn for instruction. Inquiries were made, and they discovered a group of believers in the Netherlands who baptized by immersion, a Mennonite body known as the Collegiants. Blunt, who spoke Dutch, went to Holland to discuss the issue with them and presumably to see a baptism firsthand. The "Kiffen Manuscript" tells us that upon his return Blunt baptized a certain "Mr. Blacklock that was a Teacher amongst them, & Mr. Blunt being Baptized, he & Mr. Blacklock Baptized the rest of their friends that were so minded"; forty-one were baptized in all. This is the first evidence of believers being baptized by immersion in England.

The Kiffen Manuscript

1633 Sundry of the Church whereof Mr. Jacob and Mr. John Lathorp [*sic*] had been Pastors, being dissatisfied with the Churches owning of English Parishes to be true Churches desired dismission & joined together among themselves, and Mr. Henry Parker, Mr. Thomas Shepard, Mr. Samuel Eaton, Mark Lukar, & others with whom joined Mr. William Kiffen.

1638 Mr. Thomas Wilson, Mr. Pen, & H. Pen, & 3 more being convinced that Baptism was not for Infants, but professed Believers joined with Mr. John Spilsbury the Churches favour being desired therein.

1640 3rd Month [i.e. May]: The Church became two by mutual consent just half being with Mr. P. Barebone, & the other half with Mr. H. Jessey Mr. Richard Blunt with him being convinced of Baptism that also it ought to be by dipping the Body into the Water, resembling Burial and rising again. 2 Col. 2.12 [*sic*]. Rom. 6.4. had sober conference about in the Church, & then with some of the forenamed who also were so convinced. And after Prayer & conference about their so enjoying it, none having then so so [*sic*] practised in England to professed Believers, & hearing that some in the Netherlands had so practised they agreed & sent over Mr. Richard Blunt (who understood Dutch)....

1641 They proceed on therein, viz., Those Persons that were persuaded Baptism should be by dipping the Body had met in two Companies, & did intend so to meet after this, all these agreed to proceed alike together.... Those two Companies did set apart one to Baptize the rest; So it was solemnly performed by them.

Mr Blunt Baptized Mr. Blacklock that was a Teacher amongst them, & Mr. Blunt being Baptized, he & Mr. Blacklock Baptized the rest of their friends that were so minded, & many being added to them they increased much.

The newly immersed Particular Baptists formed two churches pastored by Richard Blunt and Thomas Kilcop, respectively. Mark Lucar numbered among those baptized after Blunt's return from Holland; Lucar later played a significant role in the spread of Particular Baptist principles in America. Soon after Blunt's return Spilsbury and his congregation also adopted immersion as the proper mode of baptism. Until this point Spilsbury's congregation baptized believers by either sprinkling or pouring. Spilsbury later authored a treatise defending immersion as the biblical mode of baptism, though Stephen Wright has demonstrated that the General Baptist pastor Edward Barber was the first to publish a defense of immersion in his *A Small Treatise of Baptisme. Or, Dipping* (1641). Believer's baptism by immersion

The frontispiece of Daniel Featley, The Dippers dipt. Or, The Anabaptists duck'd and plunged Over Head and Eares *(London, 1645).*

proved controversial. Critics such as the Anglican cleric Daniel Featley accused Baptists of scurrilous practices such as stripping "stark naked, . . . men and women together, to their Jordans to be dipt."

The First London Confession of Faith

By the mid-1640s there were at least seven Particular Baptist congregations, all of them coming out of a Puritan background and all of them located in the metropolis of London. Due to their commitment to the baptism of believers, many in London confused them with the Anabaptists of the previous century. In order to dispel this confusion, refute other charges that had been leveled against them, and demonstrate their fundamental solidarity

The First London Confession of Faith (1644, modernized)

XXXIII

That Christ hath here on earth a spiritual Kingdom, which is the Church, which he hath purchased and redeemed to himself, as a peculiar inheritance: which Church, as it is visible to us, is a company of visible Saints, called & separated from the world, by the word and Spirit of God to the visible profession of the faith of the Gospel, being baptized into that faith, and joined to the Lord, and each other, by mutual agreement, in the practical enjoyment of the Ordinances, commanded by Christ their head and King.

XXXIX

That Baptism is an Ordinance of the new Testament, given by Christ, to be dispensed only upon persons professing faith, or that are Disciples, or taught, who upon a profession of faith, ought to be baptized.

XL

The way and manner of the dispensing of this Ordinance the Scripture holds out to be dipping or plunging the whole body under water: it being a sign, must answer the thing signified, which are these: first, the washing the whole soul in the blood of Christ: secondly, that interest the Saints have in the death, burial, and resurrection; thirdly, together with a confirmation of our faith, that as certainly as the body is buried under water, and riseth again, so certainly shall the bodies of the Saints be raised by the power of Christ, in the day of the resurrection, to reign with Christ.

XLVII

And although the particular Congregations be distinct and several Bodies, every one a compact and knit City in it self; yet are they all to walk by one and the same Rule, and by all means convenient to have the counsel and help one of another in all needful affairs of the Church, as members of one body in the common faith under Christ their only head.

with Calvinists throughout Western Europe, these Particular Baptists issued the First London Confession of Faith in 1644. The confession went through at least two printings in its first year of existence and was then reissued in a slightly amended second edition on November 30, 1646 (four days after the Presbyterian Westminster Confession of Faith was completed). Two subsequent editions appeared in the early 1650s. As the exemplary historical research of Barrie R. White has shown, this confession gave these early Calvinistic Baptists a clear and self-conscious sense of who they were, what they were seeking to achieve, and how they differed from other groups at this time.

Fifteen articles in the confession contain a substantial overview of the nature of the church and its life, an overview that is indebted to the ecclesiology of the Separatists in some respects. It is no exaggeration to say these articles set forth the basic channel in which Particular Baptist thought about the church would run well into the nineteenth century. Over against the Anglican and Presbyterian understandings of the parish church, Baptists maintained that a local church "is a company of visible saints, called & separated from the world, by the word and the Spirit of God, to the visible profession of the faith of the Gospel, being baptized into that faith, and joined to the Lord, and each other, by mutual agreement." In other words, the local church should consist only of those who have experienced conversion and who have borne visible witness to that experience by being baptized.

This vision of the church as a body of converted individuals who were subsequently baptized ran counter to a major aspect of the thinking of seventeenth-century Anglicans and Presbyterians. These two Christian communities conceived of the church as an established state entity, where the arm of the government maintained religious uniformity and infant baptism was all but required for citizenship. Baptists, on the other hand, were convinced that the church is ultimately a fellowship of those who have personally embraced the salvation freely offered in Christ, not an army of conscripted men and women who have no choice in the matter. This conviction is underscored by the phrase "being baptized into that faith" in the passage cited above from the First London Confession of Faith being placed after the words "profession of the faith of the Gospel." Only those who have knowingly professed faith should be baptized.

While this confessional document recognized the autonomy of each local congregation as a biblical given, it also highlighted that each congregation ultimately belongs to only one body and each shares the same head, the Lord Jesus Christ. As a result of this conviction, a number of associations of churches in geographic proximity were created in the 1640s and 1650s in regions such as the Midlands, the West Country, South Wales, and Ireland.

Associations especially facilitated church planting and were a sign of spiritual vitality. They also enabled the various Baptists around the British Isles to stay in touch with one another.

The First London Confession served the Particular Baptists well during the 1640s and 1650s when the rule of Parliament and then that of Oliver Cromwell, victorious in the British Civil Wars (1642–51) against King Charles I, afforded them an unprecedented degree of freedom to evangelize and plant new churches. By 1660, there were some 130 Particular Baptist congregations in England, Wales, and Ireland. General Baptist congregations, on the other hand, numbered around 115, with most of their strength concentrated in the south of England and the Midlands. An important evangelist responsible for some of this growth among the General Baptists was Thomas Lambe, a soap-boiler who pastored a congregation in London. Lambe was a General Baptist in that he held to general redemption, but he also repudiated "denying original sin, holding free will and falling away," views that aligned more with Particular Baptist sentiments. He well illustrates the argument of Stephen Wright that the division between General and Particular Baptists in this early period of Baptist history is not as clear-cut as some later historians of the Baptist movement have imagined. By the late 1650s a third group of Baptists, the Seventh Day Baptists, had also emerged. Never a large group, they were Calvinistic in theology but worshipped on Saturday rather than Sunday. Among their leading apologists was Edward Stennett, whose descendants played significant roles in the English Baptist community in the following century.

Baptist Origins in North America

Roger Williams and the First Baptist Church in America

Baptist growth in colonial America during the seventeenth century was not nearly as dramatic as what transpired in the British Isles during the same period of time. There were transatlantic links with the British Baptists, but by 1700 the American colonies had only twenty-four

Statue of Roger Williams (ca. 1603–1683) located in Geneva at the Reformation Wall.

Baptist churches. From then until the Great Awakening in the 1730s and 1740s, they all but ceased to grow. On the eve of this remarkable revival, Baptists in America were, as Winthrop S. Hudson has noted, "a small, undistinguished and little-noted religious group." Their meteoric rise to become eventually the largest religious body in the United States did not take place until after the American Revolution.

When the first Baptists emerged in New England, they found themselves ostracized by the Congregationalist hegemony. This is indeed ironic since in England the Baptists and the Congregationalists saw themselves as close cobelligerents against Anglican intolerance and persecution. For instance, the Baptist John Bunyan so highly regarded the Congregationalist John Owen that he modeled one of the captains in his allegory *The Holy War* on Owen. But early New England Baptists experienced no more toleration of their religious practice than their coreligionists received from the Anglican state church in the mother country. Massachusetts authorities strictly forbade Baptist gatherings for worship. When they persisted in gathering, Baptists (along with Quakers) suffered persecution. The stage was set for two critical events in American Baptist history.

The first involved a name famous in colonial New England, Roger Williams.

Born in London in either 1603 or 1604, Roger Williams became a Puritan during his studies for the Anglican ministry at Cambridge (BA, 1627). In 1630 he and his wife Mary Barnard, the daughter of a Puritan minister, sailed from Bristol, England, to Massachusetts, landing there on February 5, 1631. During the voyage Williams had time to conduct an intensive study of New Testament church polity, and he came to the conviction that the Puritans ought to separate entirely from the established church in England. As he argued over forty years later in a book written against the Quaker leader George Fox, God has delivered "the garden of his Church

The First Baptist Church in America, Providence, Rhode Island (est. 1638/39).

and saints" from "the howling desert of the whole world" that she might be "enclosed and separate."

When Williams arrived in New England, he was almost immediately invited to preach. But when he found that the church in Boston was what he called "an unseparated church," he said he could not lead worship there. He was convinced that the presence of the unregenerate in church meetings polluted their worship. In Williams's thinking the unregenerate had no more right to hear sermons than to receive the Lord's Supper. He was also deeply persuaded that the magistrate may not punish any breach of the first four of the Ten Commandments, namely, false worship, idolatry, blasphemy, and Sabbath breaking. He was certain every individual should be free to follow his own convictions in religious matters, for, in his words, "forced worship stinks in the nostrils of God."

Not surprisingly Williams clashed with Massachusetts authorities over these matters. In October 1635, the magistrates ordered him to be deported back to England. This decree of banishment was grounded on his aggressive and uncompromising hostility to the theocratic nature of the Massachusetts colony. His radical tenets, including complete separation of church and state and absolute voluntarism in matters of religion, and his refusal to have communion with any who gave countenance or support to the existing order, made his banishment seem necessary to the leaders of Massachusetts.

Roger Williams, Propositions Argued in *The Bloudy Tenent of Persecution* (1644)

First, that the blood of so many hundred thousand souls of Protestants and Papists, split in the wars of present and former ages, for their respective consciences, is not required nor accepted by Jesus Christ the Prince of Peace. . . .

Fourthly, the doctrine of persecution for cause of conscience is proved guilty of all the blood of the souls crying for vengeance under the altar.

Fifthly, all civil states with their officers of justice in their respective constitutions and administrations are proved essentially civil, and therefore not judges, governors, or defenders of the spiritual or Christian state and worship.

Sixthly, it is the will and command of God that (since the coming of his Son the Lord Jesus) a permission of the most paganish, Jewish, Turkish, or antichristian consciences and worships, be granted to all men in all nations and countries; and they are only to be fought against with that sword which is only (in soul matters) able to conquer, to wit, the sword of God's Spirit, the Word of God. . . .

Eighthly, God requireth not a uniformity of religion to be enacted and enforced in any civil state; which enforced uniformity (sooner or later) is the greatest occasion of civil war, ravishing of conscience, persecution of Christ Jesus in his servants, and of the hypocrisy and destruction of millions of souls.

Before the order could be carried out though, Williams, his wife, and some friends had fled south to the area that we now call Rhode Island. There he founded a settlement at Providence in the summer of 1636.

As the leader of the new colony he adopted the principle "God requireth not an uniformity of Religion" as the undergirding social infrastructure for the colony, thus guaranteeing religious liberty. On a trip back to London in 1644, in the middle of the British Civil Wars, Williams obtained a charter for the new colony, wherein complete religious liberty was guaranteed for all inhabitants. Also on this trip Williams published *The Bloudy Tenent of Persecution, for Cause of Conscience* (1644), his famous biblical argument for religious liberty or "soul freedom." On a later stay in London from 1651 to 1654, Williams became good friends with Oliver Cromwell, then ruling over England. Williams was delighted when he heard Cromwell once maintain in a public discussion "with much Christian zeal and affection . . . that he had rather that Mahumetanism [Islam] were permitted amongst us, than that one of God's children should be persecuted." Upon his return Williams served as president (governor) of the fledgling colony, and during his tenure in this capacity from 1654 to 1657, Jews and Quakers were admitted to the colony. Although Williams disagreed with the religious views of both groups, he sincerely believed they could all live together.

After arriving in Providence, Williams helped found a Baptist church in 1638 or 1639; that congregation is now called the First Baptist Church in America. Williams's conflict with the Massachusetts authorities while living in that colony did not involve the issue of baptism, and baptism is not mentioned in his opponents' charges against him. In 1638, though, some new settlers arrived in Rhode Island who had adopted antipedobaptist views in Massachusetts and been subjected to persecution. Williams may have influenced some of these religious dissenters while he was in Massachusetts, while some of them may have imbibed the views of English antipedobaptists before they left England.

Williams himself may have known something of the English Particular Baptists, whose origins we have already traced. John Winthrop, the Puritan governor of the Massachusetts Bay Colony, attributed Williams's adoption of Baptist principles—he called them Anabaptist views—to the influence of Katherine Scott, the youngest sister of Anne Hutchinson, who, like Williams, was driven out of the colony because of convictions at odds with the Puritan leadership of Massachusetts. Williams's thinking was also influenced by discussions about believer's baptism with Ezekiel Holliman. In the fall of 1638 or the spring of 1639—the date is disputed—Williams was baptized by Holliman and immediately proceeded to baptize Holliman and some ten other men and women. Thus was constituted the first Baptist church in America.

Williams remained with the little church only a few months. He became convinced that the ordinances had been lost in an apostasy that resulted from the fourth-century union of church and state when the Roman emperor Constantine befriended the church. At that point, he believed, "Christianity was eclipsed and the professors of it fell asleep." The rites and ministries of the church since that time were therefore mere "inventions of men," and they could not be validly restored without a special, divine commission. The latter would only come about when God raised up a new apostleship. Richard Scott, the husband of Katherine Scott, said of Williams at this time: "I walked with him in the Baptist way about three or four months, in which time he broke with the society and declared at large the grounds and reason for it—that their baptism could not be right because it was not administered by an apostle." This is indeed ironic. Williams was so radical at the time in his views regarding church and state, but he retained a belief in visible apostolic succession that was a central part of the platform of Anglicanism. He assumed the attitude of a "Seeker"—a common religious perspective in England prior to the rise of the Quakers. Williams was not satisfied that any group of Christians had all of the marks of the true Church. He outlived all of his contemporaries and died in 1683.

Williams's commitment to religious liberty has made him a revered figure among Baptists down through the years. In the eighteenth century Isaac Backus regarded him as playing an essential role in the creation of the Baptist cause. Sadly, in 1652, the church Williams founded split over Arminianism and the necessity of the "laying on of hands" for all believers after their baptism. The latter was considered the "sixth principle" taught in Hebrews 6—the other five being repentance, faith, baptism, resurrection of the dead, and final judgment. Advocates of the laying on of hands became known as Six-Principle Baptists. Around the same time the English General Baptists also experienced controversy over the imposition of hands. In the case of the Baptists of Providence, the Arminians and the Six-Principle Baptists won out. The adoption of these theological views, coupled with the lack of strong leadership among the Providence Baptists, prevented them from playing a significant role in the spread of Baptist ideas; New England Baptists outside of Rhode Island were Calvinistic. The Providence church would revert to Calvinism in the 1770s.

John Clarke and the Newport Baptists

The leading influence behind Baptist growth in New England during the seventeenth century proved to be the second Baptist congregation formed in the region, located in Newport, Rhode Island. The pastor was John Clarke, who had been trained as a physician at Leiden in Holland before arriving in Boston in the fall of 1637. Conflict with the authorities over religious matters soon followed his arrival, and Clarke relocated to Rhode Island, where he helped to found the church at Newport and then served as its minister for over thirty years. Historians debate the date of the church's founding. Though the present congregation maintains that it was founded in 1638, we probably could not consider it a Baptist church until 1644. That year a Particular Baptist from London named Mark Lucar joined the group, became a co-elder with Clarke, and persuaded the church to embrace immersion as the mode of believer's baptism. Lucar's involvement with this church, as well as letters Clarke wrote to English Particular Baptists, is an excellent reminder of the links between Baptists on both sides of the Atlantic. From 1644 onward the Newport Church was explicitly Baptist.

John Clarke (1609–1676)

The only Baptist ministry solidly active in New England by 1650 was that of John Clarke and his co-elders Mark Lucar and Obadiah Holmes. One individual who joined this church in 1652 was simply denominated as "Jack, a colored man," the earliest known African-American Baptist believer. The church lost a good number of members in a schism over the laying on of

---

John Clarke, Letter to Richard Bennett, December 25, 1658

    I am fully satisfied that there are two special designs which the Lord of Hosts hath very much on his heart to prosecute and to appear glorious in, in and about the days and times in which we live. The one is to bring in and set up that great and glorious kingdom of Christ. The other is to cast out and throw down the kingdom of Antichrist. And how well will it become the servants of the Lord to make it their business to wait upon him for wisdom and light whereby they may be directed to know their work, even that which doth most suit with the designs of their Lord, that so they may be at it, yea abounding therein, and that continually.

Original in the Archives of Southern Baptist Theological Seminary, Louisville, Kentucky.

hands in 1656. In 1671, about fifty others left due to Sabbatarian convictions and formed the first Seventh Day Baptist Church in America. The earliest recorded Native American Baptist, a man who gave his name as Japheth, belonged to this Seventh Day congregation in Newport.

In 1651, a Baptist by the name of William Witter was excommunicated by the Congregationalist church in Salem, Massachusetts, for being baptized as a believer and for saying that infant baptism was "sinful" and "a badge of the whore." At his trial Witter refused to repent of his views. Two years later he was taken before the county court again for saying "that they who stayed while a child was baptized do worship the devil." He was again ordered to make a public recantation. Again he refused. Further harassment did not take place, probably because of his advanced age.

Whipping of Obadiah Holmes.

That summer Witter asked John Clarke, Obadiah Holmes, and another member of the Newport Church, John Crandall, to visit him. Witter had joined the Newport Church though he lived in Massachusetts. A service was held in Witter's home on Sunday, July 20, 1651. Authorities were informed of the service, but nothing was done until the following Tuesday, when the Rhode Islanders were arrested and imprisoned. Eventually they were found guilty of holding a private meeting on the Lord's Day and undermining infant baptism. Holmes was sentenced to pay a fine of £30, while Clarke and Crandall had to pay £20 and £5 respectively. If they failed to pay, they were to be whipped. All three Baptists refused to pay the fines, but some of Clarke's friends posted bail for him, and Crandall was released after he changed his mind and paid his bail. They returned to Rhode Island. Holmes remained adamant that if his friends posted bail for him, he would be deeply offended. He languished in prison until September of the same year when it was decided that he would receive thirty lashes with a three-corded whip. He was accordingly whipped on the Boston Common. As Holmes later wrote in a letter to the English Baptists John Spilsbury and William Kiffen, he had "such a spiritual manifestation of God's presence" that it was as if he had been whipped "with roses."

One possible result of Holmes's public whipping was the subsequent embrace of antipedobaptist convictions by Henry Dunster, the first president of Harvard College. As Dunster affirmed at a private conference organized to convince him of the error of his ways, "All instituted Gospel Worship hath some express word of Scripture. But pedobaptism hath none." For Dunster the heart of the matter was that "only" visible believers were to be baptized, but infants were not visible believers. Dunster spoke his mind at the baptism

---

Henry Dunster on Infant Baptism

Dunster spoke his mind about pedobaptism during a baptismal service on July 30, 1654. He made five points. They were, according to the court records:

"1. That the subjects of Baptism were visible penitent believers, and they only by virtue of any rule, example, or any other light in the new testament.
2. That there was an action now to be done, which was not according to the institution of Christ.
3. That the exposition as it had been held forth was not the mind of Christ.
4. That the covenant of Abraham is not a ground for Baptism no not after the institution thereof.
5. That there were such corruptions stealing into the Church, which every faithful Christian ought to bear witness against."

From Jeremiah Chaplin, *Life of Henry Dunster: First President of Harvard* (Boston, 1872).

---

of an infant in the meetinghouse in Cambridge, Massachusetts, which led to his resignation as Harvard president in April 1655. But Dunster was not baptized as a believer, nor did he advocate his beliefs in print, thus diminishing the impact of his views. A second result of Holmes's whipping was that Rhode Island Baptists were careful not to venture into Massachusetts territory for many years. Baptist witness in Massachusetts was thus left without organization and leadership.

"Incendiaries . . . and . . . Infectors": Baptists Under the Cross in New England

Puritan fears about the Baptists were revealed in a piece of Massachusetts legislation passed in November 1644, which stated that because Baptists were "incendiaries of the commonwealths and the infectors of persons in main matters of religion," they were to be banished from the colony. To the Congregationalists, Baptists were not merely theological opponents but potential social and political subversives, threats to law and order, and liable to bring God's wrath down upon their communities. They were accordingly shunned in New England. Now some New England Baptists were ornery characters and all but brought persecution upon themselves! On one occasion when a baby was being baptized in Charlestown, just across the river from Boston, a Baptist who was in the congregation stomped up to the front of the meetinghouse, grabbed the baptismal basin, and dashed it to the floor. Not surprisingly, such publicly disruptive acts convinced Puritan authorities that the Baptists were revolutionary "incendiaries."

Apart from efforts of the two congregations in Rhode Island that have been discussed, any attempt at Baptist witness within Massachusetts or Connecticut was silenced or exiled. Baptists built a meetinghouse in the heart of Boston in 1679, for example, but it was boarded up when they tried to use it for worship. The length of time the New England Puritans were able to maintain their policy of intolerance is surprising. In 1669, thirteen Congregationalist ministers of England, including Thomas Goodwin, John Owen, and Philip Nye, wrote to their fellow Congregationalists in New England urging them to "trust God with his truths and ways so far, as to suspend all vigorous proceedings in corporal restraints and punishments, on persons that dissent" from them. But as late as 1681, Baptists in Massachusetts were still being attacked as "dangerous" and "arrogant."

A major reason for this persecution lasting so long lay in the key difference between Puritans and Baptists in America: New England Puritans were committed to the medieval model of a corporate Christian state while Baptists argued for a voluntaristic, individualistic social order. No matter how otherwise orthodox and Calvinistic the Baptists were in their theology, the Puritan order in New England could not help but regard them as heretical in their ideas of the relationship between church and state. As William McLoughlin put it: "What was ultimately at stake in this debate [between Puritans and Baptists] . . . was the breakdown of the corporate Christian state and the substitution for it of a state of free individuals relying on their own judgment to create the city of God." In the wooden meetinghouses on the outskirts of the transatlantic British world, a clash was being enacted between two worldviews: that of the medieval era and that of modernity.

For Further Study

Asher, Louis Franklin. *John Clarke (1609–1676): Pioneer in American Medicine, Democratic Ideals and Champion of Religious Liberty*. Pittsburgh, PA: Dorrance Publishing, 1997.

Gaustad, Edwin S. *Liberty of Conscience: Roger Williams in America*. Grand Rapids, MI: William B. Eerdmans, 1991.

Lee, Jason K. *The Theology of John Smyth: Puritan, Separatist, Baptist, Mennonite*. Macon, GA: Mercer University Press, 2003.

McLoughlin, William G. *Soul Liberty: The Baptists' Struggle in New England, 1630–1833*, chapters 1–2. Hanover/London: University Press of New England for Brown University Press, 1991.

White, B. R. *The English Separatist Tradition from the Marian Martyrs to the Pilgrim Fathers*. London: Oxford University Press, 1971.

_____. *The English Baptists of the Seventeenth Century*, rev. ed., chapters 1–2. London: The Baptist Historical Society, 1996.

Wolever, Terry, ed. *A Noble Company: Biographical Essays on Notable Particular-Regular Baptists in America*, vol. 1. Springfield, MO: Particular Baptist Press, 2006.

Wright, Stephen. *The Early English Baptists, 1603–1649*. Woodbridge, Suffolk: Boydell Press, 2006.

Yarnell, Malcolm, ed. *The Anabaptists and Contemporary Baptists: Restoring New Testament Christianity. Essays in Honor of Paige Patterson*. Nashville, TN: B&H, 2013.

Questions for Discussion

1. Who were the Anabaptists, and what did they believe? Why were they persecuted?

2. Outline the political and religious situation surrounding the origins of the Baptists.

3. Who were the two leading pioneers of the General Baptists? How did they contribute to the development of Baptist identity? Are their contributions still important today? Why or why not?

4. Sketch the development of the Jacob-Lathrop-Jessey Church.

5. What was the "Kiffen Manuscript"? Why are documents like this important for the study of Baptist history?

6. Identify three components of essential Baptist life in the First London Confession. Would you consider these essential to church life today? Why or why not?

7. What did Roger Williams contribute to the development of Baptist life in North America?

8. How was the first Baptist church formed in America?

9. Describe John Clarke's life and contributions to Baptists in America.

10. What were the differences between Baptists and the wider Puritan movement during the seventeenth century? Is it appropriate to describe Baptists as Puritans? Why or why not?

Chapter 2

LIVING UNDER THE CROSS

For British Baptists the halcyon days of growth and expansion in the 1640s and 1650s gave way to persecution, brutal at times, for three long decades, from 1660 to 1688. New England offered no respite from persecution, and the Baptist cause there remained small and struggling. However, the move of a Baptist congregation from Kittery, Maine, in 1696 to South Carolina held great promise for Baptist growth in the future. Unhappily, that promise was tarnished by Baptist involvement in the great social evil of the late seventeenth- and eighteenth-century Anglo-American world: chattel slavery.

English Baptist Piety

Despite the tumult and turbulence of civil wars in the British Isles during the 1640s and early 1650s, both the General and Particular Baptist causes prospered. By 1660 the British Isles had well over 200 Baptist churches. In many ways Abraham Cheare was a typical Baptist pastor of this era. Apart from a journey to London in the 1650s, Cheare appears to have spent the entirety of his life in the vicinity of Plymouth, where he was born and raised. Around 1648, Cheare says he was convinced "of his duty to the Lord, by evidence of scriptural light" and he "joined himself in an holy covenant, to walk in all the ordinances of the Lord blameless, to the best of his light and power, in fellowship with a poor and despised people." These "poor and despised people" were the Plymouth Particular Baptists. During the 1650s, Cheare became involved in the nationwide church planting of the Particular Baptists. For example, in January 1655 he helped with the organization of Particular Baptists in the neighboring county of Cornwall.

In May 1658, Cheare was present as the representative of the Plymouth Church at an important meeting of the churches in the West Country Association, a body that included congregations in the counties from Gloucestershire to Cornwall. At that meeting the Particular Baptists publicly rejected allying themselves with spokesmen for the "Fifth Monarchy" movement. These individuals believed the prophecies of Daniel 2 were going to be literally fulfilled in their lifetime and that Christ's millennial kingdom was shortly to be established. While one wing of the Fifth Monarchy movement was moderate, nonviolent, and included men like Henry Jessey, others had definite revolutionary tendencies and were convinced they should take an active, even violent, role in the fulfillment of the prophecies of Daniel 2. On this memorable occasion the Fifth Monarchy men failed to convince the representatives of the churches in the association, including Cheare, to espouse their ideals and goals publicly.

The Baptist Piety of Abraham Cheare

Oh! that all the Lord's people were so fully prepared, as a bride, to meet their blessed bridegroom; that we might all unfeignedly say with one accord, Even so, come Lord Jesus, come quickly.

Had we but truly noble spirits, how would these discoveries of glory ravish us, and our eye affect our heart? setting us with restless spirits, to be looking for, and hastening unto, that day of the Lord; this day of the manifest exalting Jesus, as King of saints, and King of nations? Nay, would it not fill our hearts with jealousy for his name, against all that standeth up in the earth, to oppose his kingdom glory, beginning at home in our own spirits? The zeal of the Lord's house would eat us up, and the love of it would crucify us more unto, and wean us from those interests of earth, and men, whereupon we have been apt to lean, and whereunto we have been deeply and dangerously engaged: causing us also to wait to be with Jesus, which is best of all; and in the mean time to pant, and thirst incessantly, for that holy Spirit of promise, that alone can present us with the ravishing glory of that expected day, and raise up our spirits to a sweet and suitable disposition, according to the will of God, to wait and act aright toward it.

Excerpted from Abraham Cheare, *Sighs for Sion* (London: Livewel Chapman, 1656), 17–18.

Cheare had a wide knowledge of the Scriptures which is reflected in *Sighs for Sion*, a tract published in 1656, with a second printing the following year. Written mostly by Cheare, but with the help of four other Baptist leaders, this tract essentially pled with the churches to which it was sent to overlook their differences of opinion regarding eschatology—the Fifth Monarchy Men come to mind—and to pray for the outpouring of the Holy Spirit the authors deemed vital if they were to see their churches quickened and strengthened. In many ways this tract is a fabulous window on Baptist piety in the middle of the seventeenth century. Reflecting their Puritan heritage, Particular and General Baptists were committed to a spirituality that centered on the Scriptures; emphasized preaching, prayer, and the ordinances of baptism and the Lord's Supper; and was lived out in the covenantal context of a gathered church of regenerated believers.

English Baptists and Persecution

When Oliver Cromwell died in 1658, some of the Puritan generals who fought alongside him during the British Civil Wars began to fear that anarchy was about to overtake the country. In a move that had profound implications down to the present day, they felt they had no choice but to restore the monarchy in the person of Charles II, the son of the previous monarch, Charles I, who had been executed in 1649. The generals asked Charles to ensure that religious liberty would continue as during the Cromwellian republic, and Charles guaranteed such freedom. Whether Charles was genuine in promising religious freedom is unclear, but those who came to power with him certainly had no intention of allowing the Puritans this liberty. Over the next few years Parliament passed a repressive body of legislation known as the Clarendon Code that had as its chief goal the destruction of the Puritan cause's power base. The rulers of England were determined that never again would the Puritans or their children exercise the sort of political power they had wielded

Oliver Cromwell (1599–1658)

during the 1640s and 1650s. Steeling their determination in this regard was a four-day violent rebellion in 1661, launched by Thomas Venner, a Fifth Monarchist, which was only put down after hand-to-hand street fighting in London. Baptist leaders in the capital, like William Kiffen, condemned the

Venner revolt but to no avail. In the wake of the revolt, about 400 Baptists were arrested.

The Clarendon Code, consisting of various acts over the next dozen years, forced the vast majority of Puritans out of the Church of England, including Presbyterians, a smattering of Independents or Congregationalists, and a few Baptists. These and others who had already left the state church (most Baptists fell into the latter category) now found themselves persecuted as second-class citizens. Between 1660 and 1688, the various Puritan communities—collectively known to history as Nonconformists or Dissenters—were persecuted fiercely. In the words of Gerald R. Cragg, "They were harried in their homes and in their meeting houses; they were arrested, tried and imprisoned. A few were transported [to the Caribbean in exile]; many died."

Abraham Cheare, obviously not sympathetic with the violent ideology of the Fifth-Monarchy men, was arrested not long after the Venner revolt for "encouraging religious assemblies" and imprisoned for three months in Exeter. He was imprisoned again in 1662 for holding "unlawful assemblies" and for refusing "to conform to the laws of the Established Church." His imprisonment in the Exeter jail lasted for three grueling years in which he suffered "under very hard circumstances, enduring many inhumanities from merciless jailers." In the meantime Cheare's congregation suffered bitterly at the hands of the Plymouth authorities in 1662 and 1663, with many congregants being imprisoned alongside Cheare. The mayor of Plymouth in these years was William Jennens, who was a zealot when it came to the suppression of nonconformity; Cheare and his fellow Baptists could expect no mercy under his regime.

To the north and east, another Baptist minister, John Bunyan, also experienced the judicial wrath of Charles II's regime. Bunyan is most famous for authoring his allegorical work *Pilgrim's Progress* (1678), which remains one of the best-selling books ever written in English. On November 12, 1660, authorities arrested Bunyan as he was about to preach in Lower Samsell, a hamlet near Harlington, Bedfordshire. Tried and convicted under the Elizabethan Conventicle Act of 1593, Bunyan spent most of the next twelve years

John Bunyan (1628–1688)

in prison. Bunyan's imprisonment proved to be the catalyst for developing his gifts as an author. Here he wrote his powerful apology for nonconformity, *I Will Pray with the Spirit* (1662), as well as a rebuttal of antinomianism, *Christian Behaviour* (1663), along with his classic *Grace Abounding to*

Elizabeth Bunyan Pleads for the Release of Her Husband John Bunyan (1660)

Justice Chester: My Lord, Bunyan is a pestilent fellow; there is not another such fellow in the country.

Judge Twisden (to Elizabeth): What! will your husband leave preaching? If he will do so, then send for him.

Elizabeth: My lord, he dares not leave preaching so long as he can speak.

Judge Twisden: See here! What should we talk any more about such a fellow! Must he do what he lists? He is a breaker of the peace.

Elizabeth: He desires to live peaceably and to follow his calling, that his family may be maintained. Moreover, my Lord, I have four small children that cannot help themselves, one of which is blind, and we have nothing to live upon but the charity of good people.

Judge Hale: Hast thou four children? Thou art but a young woman to have four children.

Elizabeth: I am but mother-in-law to them, having not been married to my husband yet full two years. Indeed I was with child when my husband was first apprehended; but being young and unaccustomed to such things, I being swayed [i.e. dismayed] at the news, fell into labour, and so continued for eight days, and then was delivered, but my child died.

Judge Hale: Alas! Poor woman!

Judge Twisden: You make poverty your cloak. I understand that your husband is maintained better by running up and down a-preaching than by following his calling.

Judge Hale: What is his calling?

A stander-by: A tinker, my lord.

Elizabeth: Yes, and because he is a tinker and a poor man, therefore he is despised and cannot have justice.

Judge Hale: I tell thee, woman, seeing it is so that they have taken what thy husband said for a conviction, thou must either apply thyself to the king, or sue out his pardon, or get a writ of error.

Justice Chester: My lord, he will preach and do what he lists.

Elizabeth: He preacheth nothing but the Word of God.

Judge Twisden: He preach the Word of God! He runneth up and down, and doeth harm.

Elizabeth: No, my lord, no! It is not so; God hath owned him, and done much good by him.

Judge Twisden (with an oath): His doctrine is the doctrine of the Devil.

Elizabeth: My lord, when the righteous Judge shall appear, it will be known that his doctrine is not the doctrine of the Devil.

Excerpted from *The Bible League Quarterly* 342 (July–September 1985): 345–46.

the Chief of Sinners (1666); the latter went through six editions in his life-time. One of the most powerful documents that arose out of these early years of persecution is a transcript of the attempt by Elizabeth Bunyan, whom Bunyan married after the death of his first wife, to secure his release. Her pleading with three local magistrates failed to convince them that her husband was simply an honest preacher seeking to be true to his calling as a gospel herald of his Lord and King, Jesus. As Bunyan later reflected on this time of suffering, he came to the conviction that "the church in the fire of persecution is like Esther in the perfuming chamber"—being made "fit for the presence of the king."

The final years of Charles II's reign in the 1680s witnessed an intensification of the persecution of Nonconformists. During this period nearly 4,000 London Dissenters were arrested or convicted for being present at what the state regarded as illegal religious meetings. A group of thuggish informers known as the Hilton gang terrorized London Dissenters, spying on their worship services, reporting them to the authorities, participating in their prosecution, and seizing their property if they could. There was also a significant increase in attacks on Dissenters in other parts of England. Meetinghouses in the West Country—at Lyme Regis, Dorset, and Taunton, Somerset—were physically attacked with pulpits and pews being destroyed by mobs loyal to the state church. Similar oppression occurred in Bedfordshire. The Bedford congregation of John Bunyan, for instance, appears to have held few meetings between August 1684 and December 1686 due to the harshness of persecution. In London the meetinghouse of Hercules Collins's congregation was attacked with the pulpit and pews being destroyed and windows smashed. In the summer of 1683, authorities cited Collins for failure to attend his local parish church. The following year he was imprisoned in Newgate Prison under provisions of the Five Mile Act (1665), which forbade Nonconformist preachers and pastors from living within "five miles of any city or town or borough." Newgate was the most notorious prison in seventeenth-century England. The cells were dark, damp, poorly ventilated, and frequently overcrowded with prisoners. In the heat of summer the stench of Newgate was appalling. The colder weather was equally difficult since the cells did not have fireplaces. In such conditions virulent outbreaks of typhus and other water-borne and air-borne diseases were frequent.

Not surprisingly, a number of those Dissenters imprisoned in Newgate during this time did not survive the ordeal. At least three Baptists who were with Collins in prison perished there: Francis Bampfield, a Seventh Day Baptist; Thomas Delaune, an Irish Baptist from Cork, where a Baptist congregation was established around 1651; and Zachariah Ralphson. After the deaths of Bampfield and Ralphson, Collins wrote a funeral sermon for them in which he expressed something of the horrors he saw in prison: men of "threescore, fourscore years of age"—Bampfield was close to seventy at the time of his arrest—"hurried to prison for nothing else but for worshipping their God."

William Kiffen and the Particular Baptists

Steadying the Baptist cause throughout these challenging times were a number of noteworthy leaders. One of them, William Kiffen, whose surname is often spelled as Kiffin, is rightly regarded as one of the founding fathers of the Particular Baptists. His remarkable life spanned almost the entirety of the seventeenth century, and he was the only man to sign both the First London Confession of Faith of 1644 and the Second London Confession of Faith of 1689. From humble beginnings Kiffen became one of the wealthiest men of his time; he was acquainted with kings and was a widely respected leader among all British Baptists.

William Kiffen (1616–1701)

Like most early Particular Baptist leaders, Kiffen did not have a formal theological education. He became skilled in theology and preaching as he first regularly listened to various preachers, then shared with others the way sermons impacted him, and finally preached for himself. By the fall of 1642, Kiffen was pastoring what became known as Devonshire Square Baptist Church, where he served till his death in 1701. Kiffen also played a prominent role in the expansion of Particular Baptists beyond London. Extant documents from places as far afield as Wales, Northumberland, Ireland, and the Midlands reveal Kiffen's involvement in planning the establishment of new churches and associations, then giving them advice and counsel, and generally providing stability to the Baptist cause during these early days of the movement. Something of his stature in this regard is evident in the fact that an anonymous publication from 1659 describes him as the "ordained Mufti of all Heretics and Sectaries."

During these years Kiffen was extensively engaged as a cloth merchant. A decision around 1645 to take a member of his church as a partner for a trading venture in Holland turned out to be the launching of an enormously successful business. In his own words: "It pleased God so to bless our endeavours, that, from scores of pounds, he brought it to many hundreds and thousands of pounds: giving me more of this world than ever I could have thought to have enjoyed." On a number of occasions, Kiffen used his position and wealth to intervene on behalf of fellow Dissenters. In 1664, he was able to rescue twelve General Baptists from Aylesbury, Buckinghamshire, who had been sentenced to death under an Elizabethan law for participation in an illegal conventicle. When Kiffen was informed of the plight of these individuals, he went directly to Charles II and obtained from him a reprieve for all of them. The following decade he used his influence at court to clear some New England Baptists from the false charge of murdering a Boston minister.

A quaint account of Kiffen's influential relationship with Charles II is found in a story related by the eighteenth-century Baptist historian Thomas Crosby. The king had supposedly asked Kiffen for a loan of £40,000. Kiffen was aware that if he gave the king such a loan, it would likely never be repaid. He thus offered to give the king a gift of £10,000, which the king gladly accepted. Afterward, according to Crosby, Kiffen jocosely remarked that he had saved himself £30,000. This story may well be an exaggerated recollection of an incident in the summer of 1670 when a financially burdened monarch approached the magistracy of London for a loan of £60,000. The response of the aldermen was halfhearted; they raised only a third of the needed loan. Seeing an opportunity to drive a wedge between the king and Parliament, London Dissenters organized the raising of the other two-thirds of the requested loan. Kiffen, who subscribed £3,600, was the largest contributor.

In the 1670s Kiffen became embroiled in a controversy with John Bunyan over the necessity of believer's baptism. Bunyan's *A Confession of My Faith, and A Reason of My Practice* (1672) and *Differences in Judgment About Water-Baptism, No Bar to Communion* (1673) rejected the standard Particular Baptist argument that believer's baptism must precede membership in the local church and the privileges of that membership, particularly participation in the Lord's Supper. While others responded in writing to Bunyan, Kiffen's *A Sober Discourse of Right to Church-Communion* (1681) represented the most noteworthy advocacy of the closed membership position in this controversy. Kiffen built his case on the regulative principle of worship (i.e., only what is explicitly commanded in Scripture is appropriate for the church's worship), various key Scripture texts, especially Matthew 28:19, examples from the patristic era, and logical reasoning. This controversy was revisited numerous times in Baptist history down to the early twentieth century, with the majority position normally reflecting that of Kiffen. Since the early 1900s, however, Baptists have embraced a wider variety of views on the relationship between baptism, communion, and church membership.

The period beginning in the mid-1680s proved difficult for Kiffen and his wife as a number of their children died. One of the sharpest blows, what Kiffen called "no small affliction," was the execution of two of his grandsons, William and Benjamin Hewling, for their involvement in the rebellion of the Duke of Monmouth, the illegitimate Protestant son of Charles II who sought to overthrow James II, Charles's Roman Catholic brother and heir. The rebellion was soon crushed at the Battle of Sedgemoor in Somerset in July 1685. The men were both executed in September after Kiffen unsuccessfully sought to obtain their freedom by offering £3,000 for their acquittal. A final letter by

Severall of ỹ Rebells hang'd upon a Tree

Contemporary drawing of the execution of the rebels after the Battle of Sedgemoor, July 6, 1685.

Benjamin Hewling's Letter to His Mother, Hannah Kiffen Hewling, Taunton, September 30, 1685

Honored Mother,

That news which I know you have a great while feared, and we expected, I must now acquaint you with, that notwithstanding the hopes you gave in your two last letters, warrants are come down for my execution, and within these few hours I expect it to be performed. Blessed be the Almighty God that gives comfort and support in such a day; how ought we to magnify his holy Name for all his mercies, that when we were running on in a course of sin, he should stop us in full career, and show us that Christ whom we had pierced, and out of his free grace enable us to look upon him with an eye of faith, believing him able to save to the utmost all such as come to him. . . . I bless God I am not ashamed of the cause for which I lay down my life; and as I have engaged in it, and fought for it, so now I am going to seal it with my blood. The Lord still carry on the same cause which hath been long on foot; and tho' we die in it and for it, I question not but in his own good time he will raise up other instruments more worthy to carry it on to the glory of his Name, and the advancement of his Church and people.

Benjamin Hewling revealed an unrepentant commitment to engage in revolution to further the Protestant cause, a component of Baptist life in this era that cannot be overlooked.

Other Baptists were also executed in the aftermath of Sedgemoor, including Sampson Clarke, minister of the Particular Baptist church in Lyme. Andrew Gifford, pastor of the Pithay Baptist Church in Bristol, actively supported the uprising by securing funds and ammunition for Monmouth's men. Happily for Gifford his links to the rebellion were not discovered until much later.

Thomas Grantham and General Baptist Theology

Seventeenth-century General Baptist beliefs are best captured in two confessional documents: The Standard Confession (1660), published on the verge of the restoration of the monarchy, and An Orthodox Creed (1678), printed at the height of the persecution. The Standard Confession was a response to the political and military confusion that reigned during the final days of the Cromwellian Commonwealth. The pastors who affirmed this confession in London, representing various Baptist congregations throughout England, made clear their intentions were peaceful and they simply wished to serve God in what they called "the good old Apostolical way." The Standard Confession remained the most popular summary of Arminian views among the Baptists and was later adopted by American Free Will Baptists in 1812.

The Standard Confession, Article 10

That all children dying in infancy, having not actually transgressed against the Law of God in their own persons, are only subject to the first death, which comes upon them by the sin of the first Adam, from whence they shall be all raised by the second Adam; and not that any one of them (dying in that estate) shall suffer for Adam's sin, eternal punishment in Hell (which is the second death) for of such belongs the Kingdom of Heaven, 1 Cor 15:22; Matt 19:14. Not daring to conclude with that uncharitable opinion of others, who though they plead much for the bringing of children into the visible Church here on earth by baptism, yet nevertheless by their doctrine that Christ died but for some, shut a great part of them out of the Kingdom of Heaven for ever.

Not all General Baptists were satisfied with the Standard Confession. In particular, some believed the section on the person of Christ was sufficiently vague that those who did not hold to a full-blooded Nicene Christology could affirm the document. An Orthodox Creed, a sophisticated confession drawn up by Thomas Monck, a messenger for the General Baptist churches in Buckinghamshire, sought to remedy this theological deficiency by devoting the first eight of its articles to a detailed explication of the Trinity and orthodox Christology. As Monck stated in a footnote to the confession's preface, "We are sure that the denying of baptism is a less evil, than to deny the divinity, or humanity of the Son of God." An Orthodox Creed also staked out a position between Arminianism and Calvinism. While the confession affirmed that "Christ died for all men," it also confessed that "those that are effectually called, according to God's eternal purpose, being justified by faith do receive such a measure of the holy unction, from the Holy Spirit, by which they shall certainly persevere unto eternal life." Despite the best efforts of the framers of An Orthodox Creed, heterodox views of Christ proved to be a perennial problem among General Baptists in the following decades.

Thomas Grantham was the foremost General Baptist leader during this period. He was a prolific author who wrote what can be described as the first systematic theological treatise by a Baptist, titled *Christianismus Primitivus: or, The Ancient Christian Religion* (1678). While Grantham's theology remained distinctively Arminian, as with Monck's An Orthodox Creed, Grantham disagreed with many of his Arminian contemporaries by affirming total depravity, a penal substitutionary view of the atonement, justification by faith alone, and the perseverance of the saints. Though many earlier Con-

Bunhill Fields, 38 City Road, London, the final resting place for about 120,000 bodies, most of them Nonconformists, including seventeenth-century Baptists William Kiffen and John Bunyan, and numerous eighteenth-century Baptists like John Gill and John Rippon.

tinental Arminians affirmed these doctrines, excluding perseverance, the English Arminians of the era typically rejected them for being too similar to Calvinism. As Matthew Pinson has ably demonstrated, Grantham's theological position cannot be neatly aligned with either consistent Calvinism or the mainstream Arminianism of his day.

Christianismus Primitivus not only contains a thorough elaboration of Grantham's doctrine of salvation but also provides in-depth discussions of other issues important to Baptists in this era. One of these issues was marriage, an area of significant debate during the Reformation, when Protestants denied that the celibate life was a superior form of spirituality. For Grantham, "marriage is a solemn and honourable ordinance of God," which God instituted for "the modest and orderly propagation of mankind." His calling marriage an "ordinance" is striking, for this was a word normally used by seventeenth-century Baptists to identify a means of grace. "Pollution of the marriage bed" was the only legitimate grounds for divorce. He pointed out that Christian men should not harden their hearts against their wives if the latter lose their beauty. As Grantham wisely stated: "He that putteth his wife out of his affection, dealeth no better than he that divorceth her. This want of love between husband and wife, is a grievous iniquity, a treasonable impiety, hateful in the sight of God." Grantham's comments here should be read in light of the fact that the nuclear family model, a social reality that predated the Reformation by at least a century, dominated England and other northern European nations. In such a familial context, if a husband spurned his wife, she did not have an extended household to which she could turn. Grantham also had in view the flagrant sexual immorality of Charles II, his court, and many of the English political leaders.

Grantham served the General Baptist cause as a pastor beginning in 1656. Ten years later he was appointed as a messenger, an office unique to the General Baptists analogous to what modern Christians refer to as a missionary. According to Grantham, consideration of what we now call the Great Commission in Matthew 28 and Mark 16 leads to the realization that "it is the will of God that the nations be taught, and that the Gospel should be preached to every creature." But how was this to be done unless someone gifted in preaching be set apart for this ministry? In Grantham's eyes such was the office of a messenger, whose calling was "to preach the gospel where it is not known; to plant churches where is none; to ordain elders in churches remote, and to assist in dispensing the holy mysteries." His faithful ministry in this office led to churches being planted in Lincolnshire, Warwickshire, and East Anglia. As Baptist historian C. B. Jewson once noted, "Grantham was a born organizer." His final years were spent in Norwich in Norfolk. Although he and John Connould, the Anglican vicar of Saint Stephen's, Norwich, carried on a lengthy debate on infant baptism by correspondence, Grantham obviously made a friend of Connould; when Grantham died, Connould conducted his burial service and approved his burial within the walls of the parish church. When Connould came to die a few years later, he requested that he be buried beside Grantham.

Religious Toleration

In 1688, James II's regime crumbled in the so-called Glorious Revolution in which William of Orange, James's Dutch son-in-law, seized the throne of England in a coup d'état, resulting in a new era for Dissenters. William III's authorization of the Act of Toleration in 1689, which guaranteed religious freedom for Trinitarian Protestant Dissenters, provided General and Particular Baptist leaders alike with the opportunity to issue calls for national assemblies of their respective communities. The General Baptists met first in May, when Grantham was asked to record the minutes of the meeting. The minutes—focused on discussions about such issues as marriage (marital unions outside of the General Baptist fold were strongly discouraged) and music (congregational hymn-singing was rejected as a "carnal formality")—reveal an introspective ethos that seriously hindered growth in the eighteenth century.

The Particular Baptist meeting occurred in the fall when representatives from more than 100 churches gathered. Among other decisions they adopted the Second London Confession of Faith, originally drawn up in 1677 by William Collins and Nehemiah Cox, co-pastors of the Petty France Church in London. This confession was drawn up to address such challenges as the emergence of the Quakers in the 1650s and their separation of Word and Spirit and also the theological defection of Thomas Collier, a key Particular Baptist leader in the West Country. Due to the persecution between 1660 and 1688, the Particular Baptists wanted to present a united front with fellow Dissenters—namely, the English Presbyterians and the Independents (Congregationalists)—against the vicious harassment they were experiencing.

The Second London Confession was based on the Westminster Confession of Faith and the Savoy Declaration (1658). The latter confession, which had been drawn up by John Owen and Thomas Goodwin, was a Congregationalist revision of the Westminster Confession. This new Baptist confession did not reproduce these confessions holus-bolus but made changes here and there, especially with regard to such obvious topics as baptism and church government. In time this confession became the most influential of all Baptist confessions of faith. The Second London Confession was essentially reproduced in the Philadelphia Confession of Faith (1742) in America, shaped the "Charleston tradition" among Baptists in the American South, influenced the Abstract of Principles (1858), drawn up by Basil Manly Jr. for the faculty of Southern Baptist Theological Seminary, and became a doctrinal reference point from the 1960s onward for Baptists committed to Calvinistic theology.

The Hymn-Singing Controversy

The unity experienced at the Particular Baptist assembly of 1689 proved short-lived due to a dispute over the singing of hymns in corporate worship gatherings. Michael Watts has maintained that the introduction of hymns into worship was "a major contribution" to the history of Christian devotion. Nevertheless, congregational hymn-singing provoked a bitter controversy among London Particular Baptists in the 1690s. As early as 1663, the Particular Baptist pastor Hanserd Knollys maintained that the singing of "spiritual songs and hymns" was "an ordinance of God's worship," although he held, on the basis of 1 Corinthians 14:15, that the only legitimate instance of such singing was when the Holy Spirit "dictated" the words and tune. The singing Knollys had in mind was

Hanserd Knollys (1599–1691)

apparently that performed by a solo voice and not congregational singing. Eight years later, the Welsh open-communion, open-membership Particular Baptist Vavasor Powell declared his conviction in a personal confession of faith that the "singing of psalms (particularly Scripture-psalms), hymns, and spiritual songs, is a continued gospel-ordinance, and duty; and to be performed by all, but especially in the Churches."

Other Particular Baptists, including those who formed the Baptist cause at Maze Pond in London, were convinced that this practice was an unscriptural innovation. The Maze Pond Church originated as a 1691 split from the Horselydown Baptist Church in Southwark, where Benjamin Keach, probably the most significant Baptist theologian of the late seventeenth century, was an ardent advocate of hymn-singing. Keach first introduced congregational hymns at Horselydown around 1673. In defending the practice, Keach built his case primarily on Scripture. He cited the angelic hosts in heaven singing praises to God and explicit commands in the New Testament that urged this practice on believers, including Ephesians 5:19, Colossians 3:16, and James 5:13.

Keach's main opponent was Isaac Marlow, a wealthy jeweler and a prolific pamphleteer. In the course of the hymn-singing controversy, Marlow wrote no fewer than eleven books that dealt with the issue. The heat generated by the controversy may be discerned to some degree by the terms that the two sides tossed at each other. Marlow tells us that he was labeled an "Enthusiast" (fanatic) and "Quaker"; the latter was a label close to being a swear word among Baptists in this era. But Marlow could give as good as he got. He viewed his opponents as "a coterie of book burning papists" who were seeking to undermine the Reformation, for, as far as he was concerned, they were endorsing a practice that had no scriptural warrant at all. These acerbic remarks by both sides in the debate indicate that the division over hymn-singing was no trivial matter. It rent the London Baptist community in two, and, in the words of Murdina MacDonald, "effectively destroyed the capacity of the Calvinistic Baptists as a whole to establish a national organization at this time." As MacDonald further notes, the extent of this division is well revealed by the fact that the community's two elder statesmen, Hanserd Knollys and William Kiffen, found themselves on opposing sides.

Defending the propriety of congregational hymn-singing naturally led to the production of various hymnals. One of the earliest such hymnals was the Seventh Day Baptist Joseph Stennett I's *Hymns in Commemoration of the Sufferings of Our Blessed Saviour Jesus Christ, Compos'd for the Celebration of His Holy Supper*. First published in 1697, it was twice enlarged in

---

"Thou Art All Love" (1697)
by Joseph Stennett I (1663–1713)

Thou art All Love, my dearest Lord,
Thou art All Lovely too:
Thy Love I at thy Table tast,
Thy Loveliness I view.

Thy Divine Beauty, vail'd with Flesh,
Thy Enemys despise;
Thy mangled Body they did disdain,
And turn from Thee their Eyes.

But thou more Lovely art to me
For all that thou hast born;
Each Cloud sets off thy Lustre more,
Thee all thy Scars adorn.

Thy Garments tincturd with thy Blood,
The best and noblest Dye,
Out-shine the Robes that Princes wear;
Thy Thorns their Gems out-vie.

That I may be All Love to Thee,
And Lovely like Thee too,
O cleanse me with thy Precious Blood,
And me thy Beauty shew.

My former Vows I now renew:
O Lord, as thou art Mine;
I freely give my Heart to Thee,
For ever I'll be Thine.

new editions that appeared in 1705 and 1709, with the number of hymns increasing from an original thirty-seven to eventually fifty.

In a poem of dedication that he placed before his hymns, Stennett specified the kindling of devotion to Christ as a central goal of his hymns:

> Happy! If these my Songs successful prove
> To make one Sinner look on Thee, and love;
> To make one Prodigal confess thy Charms,
> And fly for Pardon to thy dying Arms;
> To fan their pious Flame who Thee adore,
> And make the Souls that love Thee, love Thee more.

Stennett was also renowned as a preacher. A number of his published sermons dealt with political issues, such as one celebrating the English victory over the French at the Battle of Blenheim (1704), which especially pleased the monarch, Queen Anne, or one rejoicing in the union of England and Scotland (1707). It says much for the general respect in which he was held that an Anglican prelate once remarked that if Stennett were willing to relinquish his Baptist convictions and join the Established Church, no post within that church would be beyond his merit.

Pennepack Baptist Church (est. 1688).

Baptists in Pennsylvania

The oldest Baptist association in America was formed in the Quaker colony of Pennsylvania. Its roots go back to Thomas Dungan, whose family was among the first settlers in Newport, Rhode Island. As a Baptist minister Dungan moved to Cold Spring, Pennsylvania, a couple of miles west of where Tullytown is now located on the Delaware River, and established the first Baptist congregation in this colony in 1684. Although the church did not survive long after Dungan's death in 1688, he baptized Elias Keach, son of the famous London Baptist Benjamin Keach. Elias Keach had come to America posing as a Baptist minister, though he was not really a Christian. While preaching to the people who would form Pennepack Baptist Church, however, he came under conviction of sin and was converted by his own sermon!

After being baptized by Dungan, Keach pastored Pennepack Baptist Church but also ranged far and wide, preaching from Philadelphia down to Cohansey, New Jersey (now Bridgeton). Keach's absences from the congregation became a source of conflict within the church, which eventually led to Keach resigning in 1690. On the other hand, Keach's itinerant ministry led to the establishment of a number of churches in New Jersey and Delaware, which, together with Pennepack, formed the Philadelphia Association in 1707. This association became the pattern for numerous other Particular Baptist associations, including the Charleston Association that we will look at in the next chapter. In 1742, the Philadelphia Association adopted the Second London Confession of Faith as its confessional standard, though two chapters were added: chapters 23 and 31 on the necessity of congregational singing and the imposition of hands respectively, both of which can be traced back to personal convictions of Elias Keach.

First Baptist Church of Charleston, South Carolina

First Baptist Church of Charleston, South Carolina, is the mother church of much of the Baptist tradition in the American South. The congregation migrated to Charleston under the pastoral leadership of the Particular Baptist William Screven in 1696, relocating from Kittery, Maine, where the church had been constituted fourteen years earlier. At the time of this relocation, Screven was sixty-seven. Traditionally, the reason ascribed to such a remarkable move was persecution. But closer examination of the historical record reveals that the worst days of persecution in Massachusetts, which we noted in the previous chapter, were over. By the 1690s, Baptists in Boston were worshipping freely in a wooden meetinghouse in north Boston, at the corner of Salem and Stillman Streets. A more probable reason for the move was the violence of King William's War (1688–97), the first of six wars between Britain and France for hegemonic control of North America. Raids by the members of the Wabanaki Confederacy, Native American allies of the French, made it dangerous even to attend church meetings. Also much of the forest around Kittery was depleted, which created difficulties for members of the church whose livelihood involved supplying merchant vessels with masts.

The Kittery congregation found both General and Particular Baptists in Charleston when they arrived, who joined with the Maine congregation to form First Baptist Church. Within three years, they had acquired land at 61–63 Church Street, the site of the present sanctuary, from General Baptist William Elliott, who hailed from England. Over the next few years, the work prospered so that by 1708, of a population of 4,180 in and around Charleston, an estimated 10 percent were Baptist. First Baptist herself grew to about ninety members in this year. Other Christian groups maligned the Charleston Baptists as Anabaptists during Screven's pastoral tenure. Internally, the church experienced growing tensions between the Particular Baptists and the General Baptists, which a later pastor of the church, Basil Manly Sr., reckoned nearly destroyed the congregation in the 1740s. But an equally great challenge to this congregation proved to be their accommodation to the evils of slavery.

Charleston Baptists and Slavery

Great Britain's entry into the slave trade can be dated from 1562 when the Elizabethan adventurer Sir John Hawkins took a shipload of 300 West Africans and sold them to the Spanish in what is now the Dominican Republic. Elizabeth I, though, was not impressed with his actions; she called them "detestable," an attitude toward the slave trade that appears to have generally prevailed among the English into the first few decades of the seventeenth century. British involvement in the slave trade was primarily linked to their desire to encourage rapid economic development of their colonies in the New World. The key event that drew Britain into this pernicious trade was the introduction of sugar plantations to the West Indies. The growing and harvesting of sugar required prodigious numbers of workers, and Britain soon followed the example of the Spanish and Portuguese in manning their sugar plantations with armies of African slaves. In the final decades of the eighteenth century, the British engaged in transporting around 45,000 slaves a year from the West African coast to the Caribbean and the American South. Throughout their rapacious slave-trading history, the British were responsible for transporting some three million enslaved Africans to the New World, including port cities such as Charleston.

A letter written by a group of English Baptists to First Baptist Charleston in 1711 displays the way in which Baptists accommodated themselves to the slave trade and the institution of slavery. From 1696 to 1722, the colony of South Carolina legally required slave owners to castrate a slave who ran away for the fourth time. If the owner did not do so, he forfeited ownership of the slave to the first white informer. While few South Carolina slave owners actually carried out this hideous and cruel punishment, one did, a member of the Charleston church. Some of his co-religionists were appalled by what he had done, and they wrote to South Moulton Baptist Church in Devonshire, England, for advice on how to deal with the man. The response of the Devonshire Baptists, written on January 11, 1711, began by emphasizing that the action of the slave owner would have been "an abomination, savouring of injustice, cruelty, and unchristian behaviour" if he had castrated his slave "without the law of the magistrate, or in a spirit of revenge, . . . or if he aimeth by it at his slave's death." However, they felt that the man had not sinned, since such a punishment was regarded as legal in South Carolina: "this law was made by the magistrate, and so the more binding." The South Moulton Baptists believed that while man-made laws in themselves were not binding, when they were "agreeable to God's word, serve[d] for the common good, [stood] with good order, and hinder[ed] not the liberty of conscience," they should be obeyed. To these Baptists, the particular South Carolina law under consideration appeared to have been enacted with good ends in view. In their words, it sought "to prevent the vagrancy, theft, robbery, insurrections, and outrages of . . . [the] slaves" and in this way ultimately served "the common good" by preserving the social order.

Furthermore, they did not regard the law as a violation of God's Word. As far as the Devonshire Baptists were concerned, the South Carolina law

Buying of slaves.

appeared to reflect the distinction made in Leviticus 25:39–46 and Deuter-onomy 15:12–13, where Jewish slaves could only be held in captivity six years and then had to be released, while slaves from other ethnic groups could be owned in perpetuity. If "greater mercy was to be shown to the Jew than to the heathen," the letter suggested, was it not reasonable to suppose that penal laws for Jewish slaves were less severe than those for slaves of other nationalities? And was not the situation of African slaves, the Devon-shire Baptists argued, similar to that of non-Jewish slaves within Israel since the former were "a sort of rude, unpolished people, whose nature requireth a stricter hand over 'em." The letter finally suggested that if the slave had not been punished, then this would have encouraged him "in rebellion for the future," which might well have brought greater "hurt and damage of the commonwealth" of South Carolina.

The South Moulton Church went on to refer the matter to the Western Bap-tist Association, which supplied its answer at its annual meeting on Octo-ber 28, 1711. The representatives at this gathering supported the advice of the South Moulton Church. If it is lawful to purchase slaves, the churches represented at the association argued—and they deemed it was on the basis of Genesis 17:13, 23, and 27—then it is "lawful to keep them in order, and under government; and for self preservation, punish them to prevent far-ther mischief." The association tempered these remarks with a plea for the Charleston Baptists "to be merciful, and compassionate to all men, to slaves, and beast, as becomes those that profess the doctrine of a merciful Saviour."

This defense of British slavery and its attendant barbarities seriously skewed the Scriptures, as we shall see in chapter 4. Moreover, the South Moulton Church allowed British stereotypical images of Africans to shape their reading of Scripture. For at least the first two-thirds of the eighteenth century, British literature depicted Africans as, in the words of British his-torian James Walvin, "mendacious and cruel, lazy and untrustworthy." The South Moulton Baptists and those in Charleston seem to have imbibed this racist perspective, which viewed blacks, at best, as markedly inferior to whites, and, at worst, as mere things. This attitude bore especially bitter fruit in Baptist life in the American South.

For Further Study

Baker, Robert A., Paul J. Craven, and R. Marshall Blalock. *History of the First Baptist Church of Charleston, South Carolina 1682–2007*, 325th Anniversary Edition, chapters 1–3. Springfield, MO: Particular Baptist Press, 2007.

Davies, Hywel M. *Transatlantic Brethren: Rev. Samuel Jones (1735–1814) and His Friends. Baptists in Wales, Pennsylvania, and Beyond*, chapter 1. Bethlehem, PA: Lehigh University Press/London: Associated University Presses, 1995.

Essick, John Inscore. *Thomas Grantham: God's Messenger from Lincolnshire*. Macon, GA: Mercer University Press, 2013.

Gardner, Robert G. *Baptists of Early America: A Statistical History, 1639–1790*. Atlanta, GA: Georgia Baptist Historical Society, 1983.

Hanson Brian L., and Michael A. G. Haykin. *Waiting on the Spirit of Promise: The Life and Theology of Suffering of Abraham Cheare*. Monographs in Baptist History. Eugene, OR: Pickwick Publications, 2014.

Kreitzer, Larry J. *William Kiffen and His World*, 3 vols. Regent's Park College, Oxford: Centre for Baptist History and Heritage, 2010–13.

MacDonald, Murdina D. "London Calvinistic Baptists 1689–1727: Tensions Within a Dissenting Community Under Toleration." DPhil. Thesis, Regent's Park College, University of Oxford, 1982.

McLoughlin William G., and Winthrop D. Jordan. "Baptists Face the Barbarities of Slavery in 1710." *Journal of Southern History* 29 (1963): 495–501.

Pinson, J. Matthew. "The Diversity of Arminian Soteriology: Thomas Grantham, John Goodwin, and Jacobus Arminius." Paper presented at the American Society of Church History, Florida State University, Tallahassee, Florida (Spring 1998).

White, B. R. *The English Baptists of the Seventeenth Century*, rev. ed., chapter 3. London: The Baptist Historical Society, 1996.

Questions for Discussion

1. How can the life of Abraham Cheare serve as a model for Christian life today?

2. Outline the situation around the Venner revolt and the role Baptists played in the controversy.

3. Describe the sufferings of Baptists in the late seventeenth and early eighteenth centuries. Give two specific examples. Why is the study of persecution of believers in the past especially necessary for the modern church?

4. How did William Kiffen influence Baptist life and thought during the seventeenth century? What does his story tell you about the importance of leadership in the church?

5. Summarize the conflict between Bunyan and Kiffen. What side would you take in their disagreement? Why?

6. Compare and contrast the major Baptist confessions of faith that were written during the seventeenth century. Are confessions like these important for Baptists today? Why or why not?

7. What led to the end of Particular Baptist unity in the late 1680s? Describe the situation. What issues threaten Baptist unity today?

8. Describe the migration of the Baptist congregation from Kittery, Maine, to Charleston, South Carolina.

9. How did the Baptist understanding of slavery in Britain influence the Baptist position in America? How do you think these British Baptists reconciled their beliefs about slavery with Jesus' command to act toward others as you would like them to act toward you?

Chapter 3

THE AGE OF REASON AND REVIVAL

Historians often describe the eighteenth century as the Age of Reason, when some European intellectuals began to assert the epistemological primacy of human reason. This assertion impacted a number of Christian communities. Among the Baptists the English General Baptists were decimated as they abandoned key Christian verities such as the Trinity and the deity of Christ. But the Age of Reason was also a time when some Protestant denominations, especially in the English-speaking world, experienced not only renewal but also amazing growth. The English Particular Baptists, after a long season of decline, enjoyed a time of renewal; and in America revival was instrumental in creating an entire new body of Baptists, the Separate Baptists, as well as revitalizing sections of the older Baptist community.

Living and Worshipping

By the second decade of the eighteenth century, some 220 Particular Baptist congregations were scattered across England and Wales, with 110 General Baptist and 5 Seventh Day Baptist churches in England (Wales had neither General nor Seventh Day Baptists, though Dublin, Ireland, had a General Baptist church). A letter Joseph Pettit, pastor of the Cork Baptist Church, wrote in 1725 to the Boston Baptist minister Elisha Callendar, who had requested information about the Irish Baptists, indicates a small Baptist association of nine churches, with the three largest in Dublin, Cork, and Waterford. In the course of the eighteenth century, a good number of these Baptist causes either disappeared altogether or drifted off into various forms of heterodoxy. By mid-century close to a third of the Particular Baptist churches in England and Wales no longer existed, a good number of the General Baptists had either closed their doors or succumbed to Socinianism, that is, Unitarianism, and in Ireland only six Particular Baptist churches survived with one of those, the church at Legacory in County Armagh, in serious decline. Yet this story of decline can be easily exaggerated. Areas of spiritual vitality were evident, as found among many churches of the Western Association and in ministries like those of John Rootsey in Colchester; Alvery Jackson at Barnoldswick, Yorkshire; Andrew Gifford Jr. in London, and Edward Trivett in Worstead, Norfolk. And in the midst of the larger issues that fill much of this chapter, Christian men and women continued to live in Baptist communities and worship together week by week, year after year.

Andrew Gifford Jr. (1700–1784)

Eighteenth-century British Baptists were generally drawn from the lower classes of British society, being mostly farmers, artisans, tradesmen, cloth workers, and manual laborers. Of ninety-two men and women whose means of livelihood are identified on a 1735 list from Colchester Baptist Church, for example, thirty-eight were farmers, thirty-two were cloth workers, five were shoemakers, two were carpenters, two were thatchers, and one was a blacksmith—a Deborah Rudkin of Dedham. The Particular Baptist congregation in Liverpool had twenty-two members in 1741 with only one member who had any financial resources, namely, a certain Roger Fisher, a shipbuilder. When the Welsh Baptist Benjamin Francis was called to pastor the Baptist cause in Horsley,

Benjamin Francis (1734–1799)

Gloucestershire, in 1757, the church consisted of sixty-six members, few of whom were able to give any money toward his support. Francis described most of his flock as being "extremely indigent" and "poor, plain [people, who] . . . have not had the advantage of literature." To make ends meet, Francis had to rear pigs, grow his own fruit and vegetables, and run a school. At one point he decided to try his hand in business, the woolen trade, but he did not have a head for business and ended up losing a considerable amount of money. A good number of Francis's fellow pastors wrestled with similar financial difficulties and were bivocational as a result. John Dowding, one of two pastors in Bradford-on-Avon in the early 1720s, was a tanner; John Turner of Liverpool worked as an apothecary; John Rootsey, who pastored in Colchester from 1711 to 1738, was a miller; while John Yeomans, Burton Latimer's first pastor in the 1740s, was a carpenter.

Cote Baptist Church, Oxfordshire (est. 1703).

A shortage of finances meant that many congregations could not afford to put up their own buildings even though they were free to do so after the end of state persecution in 1689. The Particular Baptists in the village of Smarden, Kent, met for over fifty years in the farmhouse and buildings of the Gilham family before erecting a chapel in 1726. Likewise Soham Particular Baptist Church, founded in 1752, worshipped for the first thirty years of its existence in a thatched, wooden barn on Brook Dam Lane, not far from the site of the church's present building on Clay Street. These were not the only Baptist churches in this era to use farmhouses or barns for worship, so it is not surprising that critics of Baptists' worship described their faith as "the religion of barns." Many of the General Baptist congregations, accustomed as they were to worshipping in large farmhouses or barns during the era of persecution, decided to stay put in these familiar settings. The members of Horsham General Baptist Church, where the unorthodox Matthew Caffyn was pastor, met in farmhouses for the best part of sixty-five years before building a meetinghouse in either 1720 or 1721. And when they did build, it looked "to a casual glance [that it] . . . might very well be a detached private house," as one architect put it in 1914. The use of farms and barns in out of the way places worked to these churches' advantage in the seventeenth century in

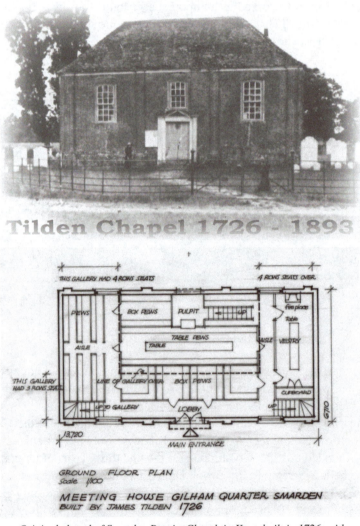

*Original chapel of Smarden Baptist Church in Kent, built in 1726, with
a diagram of its interior; the chapel could seat 300 worshippers.*

shielding them from persecution. In the freer days of the following century though, such locales fostered introspection and inhibited members' involvement in the larger world of Georgian society.

Baptist chapels from the eighteenth century were generally plain buildings from the outside. The interiors were usually oblong or nearly square in shape. Opposite the entrance in the middle of one wall (if oblong in shape, this was one of the long walls) was the pulpit in the middle of the other. Generally raised on a pedestal with access via a staircase, the pulpit was prominent and well within the sight and hearing of the entire congregation. Sometimes a sounding board was placed behind the pulpit to help project the preacher's voice throughout the building. This entire architectural arrangement bespoke an emphasis on the preached word in worship. The Baptist worshipper came primarily to the meetinghouse to hear the Scriptures expounded. These meetinghouses had a noticeable lack of adornment, with nothing to distract the attention of worshippers from the preaching of the Bible. The communion table was placed directly below the pulpit to indicate its subservience to the Scriptures. The congregation added a gallery if increased seating accommodations were needed. In keeping with the simplicity of the architectural design of these meetinghouses, the ceilings were flat and thus different in look from the vaulted or arched ceilings of Anglican churches.

Few eighteenth-century Baptist churches had indoor baptisteries, and the rite of baptism was celebrated in nearby streams, millponds, and rivers, where all and sundry could come and watch. The Baptists were thus provided with excellent opportunities to bear witness to their distinct convictions and commitment to Christ. For example, at the formation of a small Particular Baptist congregation in Redruth, Cornwall, in August 1802, four individuals were publicly baptized. According to an account written in the church records by the first pastor, F. H. Rowe, the day

> was one of those enchanting days when the sun clears the atmo-
> sphere of every cloud, not a leaf appeared to vibrate on the trees,
> or the smallest undulations be formed on the pool. We had selected
> a spot well suited for the purpose. It was the vale that lies between
> the bridge known by the name of "Blowing House Bridge" and
> the celebrated Carn Brea Hill. Owing to the excavations occa-
> sioned by the searching for ore, a large amphitheatre was formed.
> On this spot stood an immense concourse of people. The general
> impression was their number consisted of 15,000. No one but an
> eye-witness can conceive the pleasure derived from the sight of
> four believers in Christ taking up the easy yoke of their Master in
> the presence of so many.

Not surprisingly Andrew Fuller observed that public baptisms were often a vehicle for impressing upon many individuals "their first convictions of the reality of religion."

Andrew Gifford (1700–1784)
Baptizes Mrs. Deschamps

June 19, 1748. A wonderful appearance of providence at baptism. Mrs. Deschamps had been long disabled from walking alone by a rheumatic gout, but sometimes after the Lord was pleased to call her by his grace, she told the writer this: She was convinced that baptism by immersion was both her duty and privilege. He endeavoured to evade it and dissuade her from it as not absolutely necessary to salvation, but, not . . . satisfied with his arguments, she, after some time, solemnly demanded it of him as a minister of Jesus. Upon this the church was consulted, and after solemn searching the Lord it was agreed that if she persisted in the demand, it should be complied with. To this the pastor, A[ndrew] G[ifford], was forced to comply—with great reluctance, fear and trembling, lest it should be attended with any ill consequence. To this she said, "Don't you be afraid, I am persuaded God will prevent any scandal. . . ." Accordingly the ordinance was administered. Unable to walk, she was carried down into the water. She went out of the water well and rejoicing and triumphing in the Lord Jesus. Blessed be his name. . . . Sister Deschamps was so lame as to be carried down into the water. She went up out of it without the least help, rejoicing."

Excerpted from the Eagle Street Baptist Church *Minute Book*, cited
in A. T. Ward, *Kingsgate Chapel* (1912), 16–17.

However, the public nature of the rite also exposed Baptists to ridicule and censure. James Butterworth, who pastored at Bromsgrove near Birmingham from 1755 to 1794, stated at a baptismal service in 1774, "Baptism is a thing so universally despised, that few can submit to it, without apparent danger to their temporal interest; either from relations, friends, masters, or others with whom they have worldly connections." A couple of days following Andrew Fuller's baptism in the spring of 1770, he met a group of young men while he was riding through the fields near his home in Soham. "One of them," he later recorded, "called after me, in very abusive language, and cursed me for having been 'dipped.'" In 1778 Joseph Jenkins, who served as pastor of Baptist causes in Wrexham, Wales, and in London, refuted a series of unfounded charges against the Baptists, including assertions that they conducted baptisms in the nude, that they baptized "women apparelled in a *single* garment," and that they even immersed women in the final stages of pregnancy. This accusation that the Baptist practice of immersion involved immodesty had been common since the emergence of English Baptists in the mid-seventeenth century. Their first doctrinal standard, the First London Confession of Faith (1644), was issued in part to rebut the charge that the Baptists of that time were involved in "doing acts unseemly in the dispensing the ordinance of baptism, not to be named amongst Christians."

"For the Presenting of Children"
by Maria De Fleury (1753–94)

Father of Mercies, to thy feet
We come, in Jesus' name,
Pleading the promise of thy grace,
And merits of the Lamb.

To us and ours the word descends,
That brings salvation down;
All that the Lord our God shall call,
He will with glory crown.

Led by this hope, we venture near,
And bring our babes to thee:
O that they may, if so thy will,
Among that number be.

We would devote them to thy fear;
But, Lord, the work is thine:
O may thy Spirit fill their hearts,
With every grace divine.

Born from above, O may they prove
That thou art strong to save;
Then may they cheerful follow thee,
Down to the wat'ry grave.

Before the substance is possest,
The sign were but in vain;
We will baptize them with delight,
When they are born again.

Hymns for Believer's Baptism (London, 1786), 20–22.

Attentiveness to Scripture also shaped the Baptist experience of the time. Following in the train of the Puritans, eighteenth-century Baptists radically excised from their calendars all nonbiblical festivals—not only saints' feast days but also Christmas, Easter, and Pentecost—and instead focused on one day, the Sabbath, which they interpreted to be Sunday. Curiously they had one other red-letter day, November 5, which was the anniversary of both the discovery in 1605 of the Gunpowder Plot, when the Roman Catholic Guy Fawkes and a dozen co-conspirators had planned to blow up King James I and the House of Lords, and the landing of William III at Torbay in Devon in 1688 that led to toleration for Dissenters, including Baptists.

The Lord's Supper was usually celebrated once a month with a single cup. Most Baptists in this period viewed it as a time of rich fellowship both with their fellow

Great Gransden Baptist Church, Huntingdonshire (est. 1734/35).

believers and with Christ. Edward Trivett, pastor of the Particular Baptist Church at Worstead, Norfolk, wrote a number of hymns for the Lord's Supper. One of them included these lines: "There's flesh in bread and blood in wine/The banquet in the whole divine." These are not the words of one who held the Table to be simply a vehicle of remembrance; rather, it was a place of communion with Christ.

Anne Dutton evidenced a similar view in a tract she wrote on the Lord's Supper. Dutton was the wife of Benjamin Dutton, pastor of the Particular Baptist Church in Great Gransden, Huntingdonshire. She had an extensive ministry through various books and pamphlets, a number of which are known today only through one or two extant copies. Historian Michael Sciretti has described her as "a spiritual director." One of her correspondents, the greatest evangelist of the eighteenth century, George Whitefield, met her several times and observed, "Her conversation is as weighty as her letters." Dutton devoted the first section of her sixty-page *Thoughts on the Lord's Supper* (1748) to outlining its nature. "As our Lord is spiritually present in his own ordinance," she wrote, "so he therein and thereby doth actually communicate, or give himself, his body broken, and his blood shed, with all the benefits of his death, to the worthy receivers." For Dutton, Christ was indeed present at the celebration of his Supper and made it a means of grace for those who partook of it with faith. In fact, so highly did she prize this means of grace that she stated, with what other Baptists of her era might have described as some exaggeration, that the celebration of the Lord's Supper "admits" believers "into the nearest approach to his glorious Self [that is, of God], that we can make in an ordinance-way on the earth, on this side the presence of his glory in heaven."

John Gill

From the 1740s to the 1770s, John Gill was the leading Baptist theologian in the transatlantic British world. The English Baptist first became known for his exposition of the Song of Songs (1728), which regarded this portion of Scripture as an allegory of Christ and his church, a common perspective since the patristic era.

Gill's robust defense of Calvinism in the late 1730s, *The Cause of God and Truth* (1735–38), issued at a time when British Calvinism was a house in disarray, helped secure his reputation as one of the leading apologists of his day. The next decade saw the publication of Gill's critical commentary on the entire New Testament—his profoundly learned *Exposition of the New Testament*, published in three folio volumes between 1746 and 1748. Gill's companion to this commentary, his four-volume *Exposition of the Old*

Testament, appeared later (1763–66). These Bible commentaries came to occupy a central place in the libraries of Baptist ministers on both sides of the Atlantic. Also having a prominent place in those libraries was Gill's magnum opus, *The Body of Doctrinal and Practical Divinity*, issued in 1769–70, which represented the definitive codification of his theological perspective.

John Gill's Commentary on Song of Songs 4:12

A garden enclosed is my sister, my spouse: ... it is ... likely that the allusion is to a garden near Jerusalem, called the king's garden, ... which was shut up, and only for the king's use and pleasure, to which the church may be compared; for its being distinguished from the world's wide waste, by the sovereign grace of God; ... and for its pleasantness and fruitfulness, having pleasant and precious plants of great renown, or consisting of persons of different gifts and graces, in whose hearts these are not naturally, or do not grow there of themselves, but are sown or planted and raised up by the Spirit of God, for which the fallow ground of their hearts is thrown up; and that everything may be kept in good order, as in a garden, the plants are watered with the grace of God, the trees of righteousness are pruned by Christ's Father, the vinedresser, the fences are kept up, and the whole is watched over night and day; and here Christ, the owner of it, takes his delightful walks, and grants his presence with his people. And the church is like an "enclosed" garden; for distinction, being separated by the grace of God, in election, redemption, effectual calling, etc.; and for protection, being encompassed with the power of God, as a wall about it; and for secrecy, being so closely surrounded, that it is not to be seen nor known by the world; and indeed is not accessible to any but to believers in Christ.

Gill is frequently attacked as a hyper-Calvinist (or High Calvinist) whose opposition to the free offer of the gospel helped undermine Particular Baptist growth for much of his lifetime. The matter of Gill's hyper-Calvinism is a controverted issue not easily resolved, in part because scholars disagree on the best way to define hyper-Calvinism. However, Gill defended at least one hyper-Calvinist doctrine: eternal justification. He argued that just as God's determination to elect a people for salvation constitutes their election, so his purpose to declare them righteous in Christ is their actual justification. The pronouncement in time within the heart of a believer that he has been justified is simply a repetition of "that grand original sentence of it, conceived in the mind of God from all eternity." Gill's doctrine of eternal justification helped foster a climate of profound introspection. To come to Christ for salvation, one first had to determine if one was among the elect justified in eternity past. The net effect of this teaching—unintended by Gill—was to place the essence of conversion and faith not in believing the gospel but in believing that one was among the elect. Thus, Gill's theology did indeed hamper passionate evangelism and outreach. As Timothy George rightly comments: "We cannot quite exonerate Gill of all responsibility in the fostering of an atmosphere in which the forthright promulgation of the missionary mandate of the church was seen to be a threat to, rather than an extension of, the gospel of grace."

John Gill (1697–1771)

However, important facets to Gill's theology were vital for the revival that came to Particular Baptists at the close of the eighteenth century. His doctrine of the Trinity successfully resisted the growing tide of rationalism in the eighteenth century that led to what Philip Dixon has called a "fading of the trinitarian imagination." The trinitarianism of the ancient church had remained basically unchallenged until the rise of the Age of Reason in the seventeenth and eighteenth centuries. The confidence of this era in the "omnicompetence" of human reason led to the doctrine of the Trinity being dismissed as a philosophical and unbiblical construct of the post-Apostolic church, or its being rejected as utterly illogical. In its place some proposed a revived Arianism, which denied the full deity of Christ and his Holy Spirit. Others opted for Deism, which rejected the idea of special revelation, or advocated Socinianism, a version of unitarian belief that also denied substitutionary atonement.

This retooling of theological perspectives did not happen without significant conflict. For the Nonconformists, a major parting of ways came at the Salters' Hall Synod (1719), which met to determine the necessity of ministerial subscription to a trinitarian formula. The Congregationalists and the Particular Baptists, almost to a man, insisted on subscription to a trinitarian creed. The Presbyterians and the General Baptists, on the other hand, resisted subscription as the unnecessary imposition of a creed. The debate was resolved by an extremely small margin, four or five votes, by which it was decided that "no human compositions, or interpretations of the doctrine of the Trinity" should be required of ministers. By the 1750s the majority of English Presbyterians and General Baptists had abandoned trinitarian orthodoxy for Arianism or Socinianism. As Dan Taylor, a late eighteenth-century

General Baptist who sought to bring renewal to his denomination, put it: "They degraded Jesus Christ, and he degraded them."

John Rippon on John Gill's Orthodoxy

(Rippon was Gill's Pastoral Successor at Carter Lane Church in London)

The Doctor not only watched over his *people*, "with great affection, fidelity, and love"; but he watched his *pulpit* also. He would not, if he knew it, admit any one to preach for him, who was either cold-hearted to the doctrine of the Trinity; or who *denied* the divine filiation of the Son of God; or who *objected* to conclude his prayers with the usual *doxology* to Father, Son, and Holy Spirit, as three equal Persons in the one Jehovah. Sabellians, Arians, and Socinians, he considered as real enemies of the cross of Christ. They *dared* not ask him to preach, nor *could* he in conscience, permit them to officiate for him. He conceived that, by this uniformity of conduct, he adorned the pastoral office.

Thus, despite his hyper-Calvinist tendencies, Gill held fast to the trinitarian theology summarized in the creedal tradition of the patristic era during a season when heterodoxy was becoming increasingly common, enabling Particular Baptists to weather the intellectual storms of his day. His fidelity gave form and shape to the coals of orthodoxy upon which the fire of revival fell later in the century through men like Andrew Fuller, John Ryland Jr., Samuel Pearce, and William Carey.

Decline in the Midst of Revival

In a funeral sermon that Gill preached in 1750 for Samuel Wilson, pastor of Prescot Street Baptist Church, London, he lamented that "there are so few rising to fill the places of those that are removed; few that come forth with the same spirit, and are zealously attached to the truths of the everlasting gospel." A quarter of a century earlier, the Irish Baptist Joseph Pettit also lamented "the great decay of Christian piety" owing to "the withdrawment of the Spirit of God," and the fact that Baptist churches in Ireland were "infected with [this] common contagion." At mid-century, the London Baptist Benjamin Wallin stated in a sermon that he often felt he was living in a "melancholy day," a day of "present declensions" among Particular Baptist churches. Andrew Fuller, who played a key role in the revitalization of Baptists in the final decades of the century, summed up this situation in his own inimitable style when he declared: "If we had carried matters a little further, we should have been a very dunghill in society."

While these Baptists were lamenting decline, from the mid-1730s on, a power-ful movement of revival was occurring in the British Isles and America with such leaders as George Whitefield, one of the greatest evangelists of the eighteenth century; the Welsh preachers Howel Harris and Daniel Rowland; the New England divine Jonathan Edwards; and the Wesley brothers, John and Charles. Known as the eighteenth-century Evan-gelical Revival, or the First Great Awakening in America, the power of this movement was well depicted by Harris in a letter he wrote at the close of 1743 to Whitefield. Writing of the ministry of Rowland and another Welsh preacher by the name of Howel Davies, Harris told Whitefield,

George Whitefield (1714–1770)

> The outpouring of the Blessed Spirit is now so plentiful and com-mon, that I think it was our deliberate observation that not one sent by him opens his mouth without some remarkable showers. He comes either as a Spirit of wisdom to enlighten the soul, to teach and build up, and set out the works of light and darkness, or else a Spirit of tenderness and love, sweetly melting the souls like the dew, and watering the graces; or as the Spirit of hot burning zeal, setting their hearts in a flame, so that their eyes sparkle with fire, love, and joy; or also such a Spirit of uncommon power that the heavens seem to be rent, and hell to tremble.

As the revival moved powerfully throughout British society on both sides of the Atlantic, tens of thousands of men and women were shaken out of spiritual slumber and drawn to adore and to serve Christ.

Many Particular Baptists, however, had deep reservations about the revival. The Wesleys, of course, were Arminians and thus beyond the pale for these Baptists who prized their Calvinism. Furthermore, the Wesleys' view of Baptists was hardly conducive to good relations. In 1756, Charles Wesley spoke about the Baptists in his diary as follows: they are "a carnal . . . , con-tentious sect, always watching to steal away our children, and make them as dead as themselves." When his brother John visited Cork, he met a Mrs. Bentley, who had become convinced of believer's baptism and asked the

---

Anne Dutton, Letter to George Whitefield (ca. 1745)

Very dear and reverend sir,

Your last sweet letter was very savoury to my taste. It brought God to my soul. I feel much heart-union with you. I thank you for all the kind expressions of your increasing love. May the Lord reward you an hundred-fold in this world, and in that to come! Oh what a blessed instrument of much good, has the Lord made you to my poor soul! . . .

When the Lord winds up the love of his children to an high pitch, he delights to try it. And try us he will in our Isaacs, in that which is most near and dear to us. And if thus the Lord should try you, my dear brother, give him leave to do what he pleaseth. Call nothing your own, but God's great Self. Have no will but his; and then your will cannot be crossed. God called Abraham to offer up his son, his only son Isaac, whom he loved. He readily obeyed; and he was called "the friend of God." And the Lord grant you grace, to offer up all that he calls for, in a flame of love to him! And he will record your kindness, what a friend you was to him.

Methodist preacher to baptize her. Wesley responded in no uncertain terms that "what she called conviction was no other than the delusion of the devil." While the Wesleys were not favorably disposed to Particular Baptists, Whitefield was a Calvinist who had Baptist friends such as Andrew Gifford and Anne Dutton. Still, the fervency of his evangelism and his emotional pleading with the lost to embrace Christ prompted a number of Calvinistic Baptist critics to complain of what they termed his "Arminian accent."

Howel Harris (1714–1773)

Baptists were even more disturbed that the earliest leaders of the revival in the British Isles belonged to the Church of England. Their Baptist forebears in the seventeenth century, after all, had come out of the Church of England at great personal cost and suffering; they had suffered for their determination to establish what they considered to be true gospel churches, as we saw in chapter 2. The heritage that came down to the eighteenth-century Particular Baptists was thus intertwined with a great concern for proper New Testament church order. John Gill was adamant, for example, that the "Church of England has neither the form nor matter of a true church, nor is the Word of God purely preached in it." Similarly, William Herbert, a Welsh Baptist pastor and a friend of Howel Harris, was critical of the latter's decision to stay in the Church of England. In a letter he wrote to Harris early in 1737, a couple of years after the Evangelical Revival began in England and Wales, Herbert likened the Church of England to a pub "which is open to all comers," and to a "common field where every noisesome [harmful] beast may come." Surely Harris realized, Herbert continued, that the Scriptures—and he had in mind Song of Solomon 4:12—describe God's church as "a garden enclosed, a spring shut up, a fountain sealed," in other words, a body of believers "separate from the profane world." From Herbert's point of view, Harris's commitment to an apostate institution put a serious question mark on his entire ministry. A resolution passed by St. Mary's Baptist Church, Norwich, in 1754 reveals a similar attitude at work. The minute book for that year includes a note that "it is unlawful for any . . . to attend the meetings of the Methodists, or to join in any worship which is contrary to the doctrines and ordinances of our Lord Jesus." Many mid-eighteenth-century British Baptists were determined in their refusal to regard the Evangelical Revival as a genuine work of God, for from their perspective it simply did not issue in "true gospel churches."

American Baptists and the Great Awakening

George Whitefield made seven voyages across the Atlantic to America and preached in virtually every major town on the eastern seaboard of the North American colonies. As Harry Stout has noted, "So pervasive was Whitefield's impact in America that he can justly be styled America's first cultural hero. Before Whitefield, there was no unifying intercolonial person or event. . . . But by 1750 virtually every American loved and admired Whitefield and saw him as their champion." Unlike the majority of Baptists in the British Isles, numerous American Baptists openly supported Whitefield's ministry. In the South Carolina Low Country, Isaac Chanler, pastor of Ashley River Baptist Church, invited Whitefield to address overflowing crowds at his church in July 1740. In a sermon Chanler published that same year, he prayed, "May blessed Whitefield long live an extensive blessing to the Church of God!" Oliver Hart was not slow to speak about the great benefit he had received from listening to Whitefield's sermons, both in his native

Pennsylvania and in South Carolina where he pastored First Baptist Church of Charleston from 1750 to 1780. When Euhaw Baptist Church began worshipping in a new meetinghouse in March 1752, Whitefield was asked to give the first sermon in the building.

The Formation of the Charleston Association and Its Purpose (1751)

The settlement of Mr. [Oliver] Hart in Charleston is an important event in the annals of these churches [of South Carolina]. . . . Mr. Hart had seen, in the Philadelphia Association, the happy consequences of union and stated intercourse among churches maintaining the same faith and order. To accomplish similar purposes, a union of the four churches [in Charleston and vicinity] was contemplated and agreed on. Accordingly on the 21st of Oct. 1751 delegates from Ashley River and Welch Neck met those of Charleston in the said city. The messengers from Euhaw were prevented from attending. . . .

The object of the union was declared to be the promotion of the Redeemer's kingdom, by the maintenance of love and fellowship, and by mutual consultations for the peace and welfare of the churches. The independency of the churches was asserted, and the powers of the association restricted to those of a council of advice.

Excerpted from Wood Furman, *A History of the Charleston Association of Baptist Churches in the State of South-Carolina* (Charleston, 1811), 7–9.

In Pennsylvania, during his first trip to America in 1739, Whitefield developed a friendship with Jenkin Jones, a Welsh Baptist who was pastoring First Baptist Church in Philadelphia at the time and whom Whitefield considered to be "a spiritual man." Whitefield was deeply impressed with some of the members of his church, whom, he noted in his diary, "loved the Lord Jesus in sincerity." When Whitefield heard Jones preach the following year, he commented that he was the only minister in Philadelphia "who speaks feelingly and with authority." One of those converted under Whitefield's preaching was an African-American woman who began to worship with First Baptist Philadelphia. On one occasion, when Jones was away and another Welsh Baptist was preaching, "the Word came with such power to her heart," Whitefield recorded in his diary, "that at last she was obliged to cry out; and a great concern fell upon many in the congregation." Some of those in the meetinghouse, thinking her mad and "full of new wine," told her to be quiet, but she continued to utter aloud expressions of praise. When Whitefield talked to her, what she told him seemed "rational and solid, and I believe in that hour the Lord Jesus took a great possession of her soul." In fact, Whitefield was sure that when God called a significant number of African-Americans to faith in Christ, he would "highly favor them, to wipe off their reproach, and show that he is no respecter of persons, but that whosoever believeth in him shall be saved."

Yet not all American Baptists looked on the impact of Whitefield's ministry favorably. Ebenezer Kinnersley, a highly respected scientist and tutor at the College of Philadelphia, as well as a friend of Benjamin Franklin, was also a Baptist lay preacher and an assistant pastor with Jenkin Jones. According to an account in the *Philadelphia Gazette* of a July 1740 sermon Kinnersley preached at First Baptist Philadelphia, he was unsparing in his denunciation of Whitefield and those who imitated his affective style of preaching:

> What spirit such enthusiastic ravings proceed from, I shall not attempt to determine, but this I am sure of, that they proceed not from the Spirit of God; for our God is a God of order, and not of such confusion. . . . Such whining, roaring harangues, big with affected nonsense, have no other tendency, but to operate on the softer passions, and work them up to a warm pitch of enthusiasm.

In New England reaction among Baptists to Whitefield's itinerant ministry was similarly divided. For example, the refusal of Jeremiah Condy, pastor of the First Baptist Church of Boston, to support Whitefield led to a schism in his church in 1742 and the eventual formation of Second Baptist. Whitefield's ministry also became the impetus for the emergence of an entire generation of Baptist leaders, men like Isaac Backus and Shubal Stearns.

Isaac Backus and Baptist Growth

Isaac Backus was converted in the midst of the Great Awakening in 1741 when, in his words, "I was enabled by divine light to see the perfect righteousness of Christ and the freeness and riches of his grace, with such clearness, that my soul was drawn forth to trust Him for salvation." Four years later he joined a congregation in his hometown of Norwich that had

Isaac Backus (1724–1806)

come out of the Connecticut Congregationalist establishment, otherwise known as the Standing Order. This congregation, like hundreds of others in New England, called for a return to the original ideal of Congregationalism: the church is a congregation of visible saints or committed believers. Many of these Congregationalist Separatists went on to become Baptists. For instance, at Sturbridge, Massachusetts, sixty members of the Separate congregation underwent believer's baptism in June 1749, including all of the church's leadership. At least 130 new Baptist churches were formed by such disaffected Congregationalists, which helped transform the Baptists from an obscure sect in New England into a thriving popular religious movement. Backus is typical of those who made the transition.

In 1749, the year following Backus's ordination as a Separate preacher in Titicut parish, Massachusetts, Baptist minister Ebenezer Moulton came to the neighborhood. On this visit to Titicut, he baptized nine members of Backus's congregation while Backus was away. According to Backus, these things "made great shakings and contentions among the people and brought heavy trials upon my soul." His church was in turmoil for months. Finally, in 1751, Backus began reading a well-known defense of believer's baptism by the English Baptist Samuel Wilson. For five days or so, in July 1751, he studied this treatise, at the end of which he announced to his congregation that he no longer believed God commanded the baptism of infants. Later that summer Benjamin Pierce, a pastor from Rhode Island, immersed Backus. In 1756, Backus published his *A Short Description of the Difference Between the Bond-Woman and the Free*, a defense of believer's baptism that offered reasons for his change of mind. That same year he helped form the First Baptist Church in Middleborough, Massachusetts, accepting a call to be its first pastor.

When Backus became a Baptist pastor, Massachusetts and Connecticut had a total of twenty-nine Baptist churches. Virtually no new Baptist works had been formed in either colony between 1700 and 1730. However, over the fifty years following the Great Awakening of the 1740s, eighty-six new churches were started in Massachusetts alone. To take another example: by 1764 the middle colony of New York had only five Baptist churches. Twenty-six years later, the area had sixty-six Baptist churches with 4,149 members. In the half century following the revival of the 1740s, Baptists in America grew by an amazing 375 percent!

Backus played a role in establishing many of the new churches in New England. Between 1756 and 1767 alone, he traveled nearly 15,000 miles within the region. He visited the older Baptist churches, open-communion congregations, and new Separate Baptist groups that sought his help in the task of organizing as churches. Backus's efforts were augmented by the

Philadelphia Baptist Association, which sent key leaders to assist New Englanders and in so doing instilled in them a heightened sense of belonging to a movement that was broader than their own region. Under the leadership of the Philadelphia Baptists, the Baptists in New England formed the Warren Baptist Association in 1767. Although originally established to aid local churches, the association also become the political arm of the New England Baptists in their struggle with the established Congregationalist churches for complete religious freedom, a topic we will consider in more detail in chapter 4.

Shubal Stearns and the Sandy Creek Tradition

Another example of the spiritual impact of the Great Awakening and the ministry of George Whitefield may be seen in the life and ministry of Shubal Stearns. Born in Boston in 1706, Stearns moved with his family to Connecticut where he was converted through the ministry of Whitefield in 1745. After a time as a Separate preacher, Stearns came to Baptist convictions in 1751; together with his wife, five other couples, and their children,

The old Sandy Creek Baptist Church meetinghouse (built 1801).

he journeyed from New England to Virginia, convinced that God was leading him westward "to execute a great and extensive work." In Virginia, Stearns and his friends—most of whom were relatives—were joined by Stearns's brother-in-law Daniel Marshall and his wife Martha, Stearns's sister, who had spent a couple of years evangelizing Mohawk Indians. From Virginia this company of Separate Baptists moved again, this time 200 miles south and west, to Sandy Creek in Guilford County, North Carolina. There they established the first Separate Baptist church in North Carolina. Within a few years the congregation had grown to 590 members.

The Sandy Creek Church planted congregations throughout the Carolinas, Virginia, and Georgia, many of which originated as "arms" of the Sandy Creek Church before becoming autonomous sister churches. In 1758, the Sandy Creek Association was formed. Throughout the late 1750s and 1760s, both Stearns and Marshall, and a third preacher by the name of Philip Mulkey, itinerated widely. In 1762, Mulkey led a group of thirteen Separate Baptists to Broad River in South Carolina, north of present-day Columbia, where they established a church whose members soon increased to more than a hundred. From this church, eventually located at Fairforest, numerous churches were planted in surrounding areas of South Carolina and back into North Carolina. By the time Stearns died in late 1771, some forty-two churches and 125 ministers had come from the Sandy Creek church.

Baptists and other Dissenters were considered socially inferior to Anglicans in the southern colonies, who had codified a nominal establishment of the Church of England. Anglican friends and family often ostracized those who converted to Separate Baptist views. For example, Hannah Lee Corbin, a great aunt of Confederate General Robert E. Lee, was included among those who embraced Separate Baptist convictions in Virginia in the 1760s. Her newfound Baptist convictions scandalized her wealthy Episcopalian family. As she told her sister Alice Lee Shippen in a letter: "I am not surprised that you seem to have a mean opinion of the Baptist religion. I believe

Revival Among the Regular Baptists

Monday, August 26th, 1754

Six o'clock: Discoursed with Margaret and found her quite clear, with regard to the Lord's visiting her with his love last night. She had these words, "I have loved thee with an everlasting love," set home with so much light, and evidence, that she could not avoid taking comfort from them. . . . While I was conversing with Margaret there came in five young women; most of them under some awakenings. I asked Margaret if she could not now tell what God had done for her. "Oh yes sir," said she. "I could now speak for God if the world was to hear; for I now have felt his love and know that he hath loved me with an everlasting love; Oh! What a night had I last night! What a sweet night!" And then turning herself to one of the young women, "Oh Miss Betsy!" said she, "Jesus Christ is sweet, he is precious, had I known his sweetness . . . I would not have lived so long without him." And then turning herself to another, [she] said, "Oh, Oh! Miss Nancy, Christ is sweet! And since he hath had mercy on such a vile wretched sinner as me, I am sure none need ever to despair, Oh! Come Christ!" And thus she went on discoursing of Christ and his love for some time: the young women were all the same time much affected; those two whom she had in so particular a manner addressed herself could no longer contain but crying out, got up and went out of the house to vent their grief.

. . . Oh! May the mercies of this evening be writ for a memorial upon my very heart! I had such a sense of God's goodness, love, and mercy to me in every respect, that I had almost said, Lord it is enough; hold thy hand. And is all this possible! Is it really so! Lord, why me! Why me! Not unto us, not unto us O Lord, but unto thy name be all the praise!"

Excerpted from an entry in Oliver Hart's diary, found in the Oliver Hart Collection, Furman University.

that most people that are not of that profession are persuaded we are either enthusiasts or hypocrites. But, my dear sister, the followers of the Lamb have been ever esteemed so; that is our comfort. And we know in Whom we have believed." In a second letter to Alice, Hannah affirmed her convictions: "You express a fear . . . that I may have gone back after putting my hand to the plough, but my dear sister I hope so dreadful an evil will never happen to me. I hope I shall never live to see the day that I don't love God, for there can nothing I know befall me so horrible as to be left to myself."

Determining the theology of the Separate Baptists is far from easy. A good number of the Separate Baptist leaders believed in and preached a general atonement, including Abraham Marshall, Daniel Marshall's son. Yet John Taylor, a Separate Baptist pastor and church planter in Kentucky, was certain the Separates were Calvinistic. And when Daniel Marshall organized in 1772 what is now the oldest Baptist Church in Georgia, Kiokee Baptist Church—the Seventh Day Baptists founded the first Georgia Baptist congregation in 1759, but it ceased to exist not long afterward—its statement of faith was clearly Calvinistic. It declared the church's commitment to "the great doctrine of election, effectual calling, particular redemption, justification by the imputed righteousness of Christ alone, . . . the saints' absolute final perseverance in grace." Yet differences existed between this group of Baptists and the Calvinistic Baptists who were part of the northern Philadelphia Association or the Charleston Association in the South.

Preaching in the Sandy Creek tradition tended to be much more emotional and aimed at impacting the affections. Hearers in Separate Baptist preaching services commonly wept and screamed, trembled, and even were overcome to the point of physical collapse. As John Leland, a prominent Baptist leader from Massachusetts and Virginia, put it, God's work among the Separates was "very noisy." Elnathan Davis went to hear Shubal Stearns and mock him; not long after his arrival, he was seized with trembling and, seeking to leave the meeting, he found his strength fail completely, and he fell to the ground. When he came to, he was filled with "dread and anxiety, bordering on horror" at his spiritual state. All of this ultimately led to his conversion, and he eventually became a preacher himself. The Separate Baptists were also far more open to "leadings of the Holy Spirit" in the form of impressions, even visions, than other Calvinistic Baptists. In the words of the Virginia Baptist historian Robert Semple, "Stearns and most of the Separates had strong faith in the immediate teachings of the Spirit."

Of the various eighteenth-century evangelical groups, the Separates alone developed a unique leadership position that involved women serving as "eldresses." According to the colonial Baptist historian and preacher Morgan Edwards, these women baptized and taught fellow women. Some of them,

such as Daniel Marshall's wife Martha, even preached to mixed congregations of men and women. In the 1770s, Margaret Clay of Chesterfield County,
Virginia, was accused of unlicensed preaching and narrowly avoided a public whipping only when an unknown stranger paid her fine. By the following
century eldresses and women preachers had totally disappeared from Baptist
ranks. The Separates also had deaconesses to help with ministry to women
in their congregations. According to Edwards, nine Separate Baptist
Churches in Virginia had deaconesses during the 1770s. Edwards himself, a
pastor in good standing with the Philadelphia Baptist Association, reveals
the difference between these two groups of Baptists at this point: he was
totally opposed to women speaking, teaching, or even voting in the church.
However, Edwards's position was not shared by all within the Philadelphia
Association—not even within First Baptist in Philadelphia during the time
when Edwards pastored it. Joanna Anthony, a member of this congregation
during Edwards's pastorate, wrote in September 1764 "on behalf of the sisters" who insisted that women be allowed to vote as they had done in the
past. Edwards's restrictive views did not carry the day; the women were
allowed to vote, though not with their voices, only through a show of hands.

An early print of Brown University.

Theological Education

The Separates were more likely to oppose financially supporting their
pastors than Regular Baptists, that is, those Baptists in America who did

not emerge from Separate Congregationalism during the Great Awakening. When it came to formal theological education, Regular Baptists were decidedly tepid. In the eighteenth century the College in the English Colony of Rhode Island and Providence Plantations (the original name for Brown University) became the first Baptist college in America devoted to the education of ministers. The school was founded in 1764 through the joint efforts of Isaac Backus; Morgan Edwards; Samuel Stillman, the pastor of Boston's First Baptist Church; James Manning, pastor at the time of Warren Baptist Church, Rhode Island; and the Brown brothers—John, Nicholas, and Moses—prominent merchants and slave traders from Providence, Rhode Island, who eventually gave their name to the school. The college absorbed the Hopewell Academy, which had been founded in New Jersey in 1756 under the leadership of Isaac Eaton. Hopewell Academy trained a number of Baptist pastors, including Oliver Hart, Manning, and Stillman. Despite the founding of the college in Rhode Island, the concept of a learned ministry was still a foreign idea to American Baptists. When the school was founded, fewer than an estimated dozen Baptist ministers in the thirteen colonies could read the Greek New Testament.

The British scene was little better. The British Baptists had possessed an operational seminary since 1720—even though what became known as the Bristol Baptist Academy had financial provision since 1679. In the early 1770s, however, John Ryland Sr. estimated that only about 30 out of roughly 200 Particular Baptist ministers were able to read Greek. During the principalship of the Welsh Baptist Hugh Evans, who served the academy from

---

Hugh Evans and Caleb Evans on the Relationship of Spiritual Vitality and Theological Education

The truth is, whatever prejudices may be formed in the minds of some men against learning, it is certain that since the times of the Apostles, who had those miraculous helps which superseded every kind of learning, Divine Providence hath, in every age, put the greatest honour upon it. Consult the history of the Church, and you will uniformly find through every period of it, with *very few* exceptions, that those ministers who have been the most laborious and successful in their work, have been as eminent for sound learning as for substantial piety. Nor is it to be doubted but that whenever there is a revival of religion amongst us, men will be raised up, not only eminent for spiritual gifts, but who will endeavour zealously to improve those gifts, for the attainment of all that knowledge which, with the blessing of God, may render them able ministers of the New Testament.

Cited in Norman S. Moon, *Education for Ministry. Bristol Baptist College, 1679–1979* (Bristol: Bristol Baptist College, 1979), 130–31.

1758 till his death twenty-three years later, he and his son Caleb Evans founded the Bristol Education Society.

This society sought to provide the academy with a broader and more solid financial footing and to ensure that its students received a well-rounded liberal education. The eighteenth century was a time of great intellectual ferment, and significant advances had been made across a wide number of fronts in science, astronomy, medicine, and geography. The Evanses were forthright in their refusal to give their students an insular education and shield them from the intellectual challenges of the day.

Caleb Evans (1737–1791)

Some Baptists were openly hostile to the idea of formal theological education. They regarded any attempt to produce an educated ministry as fundamentally dishonoring to the Holy Spirit; from their perspective, education implied that the ministerial gifts of the Spirit were not sufficient for the task. For instance, the deacons of the Baptist Church in Westbury Leigh, Wiltshire, were deeply suspicious of Bristol Academy. It produced what they regarded as "men-made" ministers, and to seek a pastor from such a place was, in their view, "to go down to Egypt for help." When Samuel Davies, a Presbyterian minister from Virginia, sailed to Great Britain in September 1753 on a fund-raising expedition for the then-fledgling College of New Jersey (later to be renamed Princeton University), he made a point of meeting the leading Baptist divine John Gill on January 30, 1754. Gill was willing to lend his support to the new college, but he warned Davies not to expect much from the English Particular Baptists as a whole: "In general," he said, they "were unhappily ignorant of the importance of learning." Fifteen years later Daniel Turner, pastor of Abingdon Baptist Church, expressed a similar conviction when he observed that the Particular Baptists were "upon the decline." Why this decline? Turner gave two reasons: "Useful solid ministers are taken away"—so many "churches are destitute"—and "useful learning is rather discouraged amongst us." In the final two decades of the eighteenth century, however, the British Baptists would learn that theological education could be a friend to piety and spiritual vitality.

For Further Study

Brown, Raymond. *The English Baptists of the Eighteenth Century*, chapters 1–5. London: The Baptist Historical Society, 1986.

George, Timothy. "John Gill." in *Theologians of the Baptist Tradition*, edited by Timothy George and David Dockery, 11–33. Nashville, TN: B&H, 2001.

Hayden, Roger. *Continuity and Change: Evangelical Calvinism Among Eighteenth-Century Baptist Ministers Trained at Bristol Academy, 1690–1791*. Milton Under Wychwood, Chipping Norton, Oxfordshire: Nigel Lynn Publishing, 2006.

Kidd, Thomas S. *The Great Awakening: The Roots of Evangelical Christianity in Colonial America*, chapters 16 and 17. New Haven, CT: Yale University Press, 2007.

Lindman, Janet Moore. *Bodies of Belief: Baptist Community in Early America*. Philadelphia, PA: University of Pennsylvania Press, 2008.

Lumpkin, William L. *Baptist Foundations in the South: Tracing Through the Separates the Influence of the Great Awakening, 1754–1787*. Nashville, TN: Broadman, 1961.

Nettles, Tom. *The Baptists: Key People Involved in Forming a Baptist Identity*, vol. 1, chapters 4 and 7. Fearn, Ross-shire, Scotland: Mentor, 2005.

Ray, Thomas. *Daniel and Abraham Marshall: Pioneer Baptist Evangelists to the South*. Springfield, MO: Particular Baptist Press, 2006.

Sparks, John. *The Roots of Appalachian Christianity: The Life and Legacy of Elder Shubal Stearns*. Lexington, KY: The University Press of Kentucky, 2001.

Spyvee, Henry. *Colchester Baptist Church—the First 300 years, 1689–1989*. Colchester, England: Colchester Baptist Church, 1989.

Questions for Discussion

1. Delineate the piety and worship among English Baptists during this period. In what ways is contemporary Baptist worship similar? Are there areas of dissimilarity? Explain.

2. Describe the architecture of the typical Baptist chapel in England during this period. Is the physical context in which Baptists gather for worship important? How so?

3. How did John Gill help strengthen the Particular Baptist movement during the Age of Reason?

4. Should John Gill be considered a hyper-Calvinist? Why or why not?

5. In the final analysis, then, was Gill's theology a help or a hindrance to the Baptist cause?

6. Outline the General Baptist decline into Trinitarian heterodoxy during this period. What warning does the decline of the General Baptists have for us today?

7. Describe the typical English Baptist attitude toward the Evangelical Awakening prior to the 1770s. What accounted for this attitude?

8. Indicate the significance of George Whitefield, Isaac Backus, and Shubal Stearns among American Baptists during this period. Does the fact that an Anglican like Whitefield was used to revive and even advance the Baptist movement have anything to say about the relationship of Baptists to the larger Christian world?

9. What is the importance of the Sandy Creek church?

10. How did Baptists feel about theological education during this period? Do you think their attitude is biblical? Why is theological education important?

Chapter 4

RENEWAL AND ADVANCE

The closing decades of the eighteenth century were times of political revolution and religious revival for Baptists in the British Isles and America. Liberty, both religious and political, was never far from Baptist minds during this period. It was a time of spiritual renewal and significant growth for the Baptists as well, as they not only experienced expansion within the English-speaking world but also became pioneers in the modern missionary movement through men like George Liele in Jamaica and William Carey in India.

Baptists Seeking Freedom

In New England, Isaac Backus led the fight for religious freedom against the hegemony of the Congregationalist state church. Backus was convinced that "religion must at all times be a matter between God and individuals," for "true religion is a voluntary obedience unto God." Hence, he asked his Congregationalist opponents, "Since religion is ever a matter between God and individuals, how can any man become a member of a religious society without his own consent?" A state church cannot be a true church because it forces people to belong to it against their wills. Yet Backus was also convinced of Christianity's vital importance to society. Arguing from Jesus' statements about his disciples being the "salt of the earth" and the "light of the world" (Matt 5:13–14), Backus maintained that "religion is as necessary for the well-being of human society as salt is to preserve from putrefaction or as light is to direct our way." Civil government needed to have distinct limits in its authority over the churches so the latter might have the freedom to so preach the Scriptures that individuals would be genuinely converted and, once converted, become good citizens. In this interface of church and state, "civil rulers ought to be men fearing God, and hating covetousness, and to be terrors to evil doers, and a praise to them who do well; and as ministers ought to pray for rulers, and to teach the people to be subject to them; so there may be and ought to be a sweet harmony between them." There is little doubt that Backus saw Christianity as key to America's future. His goal, in Joe Coker's words, was "to stop government control over religion, but to still allow religion to have a continued influence over the government."

Final victory in the cause for which Backus struggled was not achieved within his lifetime. In 1818, twelve years after his death, the New England Baptists, led by John Leland, submitted a petition to the Connecticut legislature calling for religious freedom not only for all Protestants but for "infidels" also, echoing a phrase from Roger Williams. It was another fifteen years, however, before the last New England state, Massachusetts, finally disestablished the Congregational churches.

The struggle for religious liberty in Virginia in the closing decades of the eighteenth century was attended by more violence than there had ever been in New England. Here it was the Episcopal (Anglican) Church that resisted the Baptists.

The Dream of James Ireland

One night I dreamed I was taken prisoner by a man mounted on a red horse, who carried me over two mountains, there being a considerable distance between them. . . . I was then led into an old field, where several buildings were erected on our right, but in none of them was I to reside. I was conducted some distance into the field, and deposited in a little old open house, wherein I entered to remain a prisoner until by prayer and supplication, and other necessary methods, I was to be relieved and delivered therefrom.

. . . I journeyed again, and traveled through beautiful walks, gentle and delectable risings, rocky and cold valleys, sometimes in water and sometimes on land, until I came to a beautiful building above, called my Father's house; and then I awoke. But the impression it made upon my mind was a lasting one, nor could it be eradicated therefrom.

. . . It being then a persecuting time in our then colony of Virginia, and particularly so against the society with whom I soon after joined. I knew that the man on the red horse, spoken of in Revelation 6:4 denoted persecution, but in what character, I should suffer, I knew not then, though I had the woeful experience of it afterwards.

The Life of the Rev. James Ireland, ed. Keith Harper and C. Martin Jacumin
(Macon, GA: Mercer University Press, 2005), § 3:1.

A host of Virginia's Baptist preachers met with more than 160 physical attacks between 1760 and 1780. John Afferman was so cruelly beaten that he was unable to work; David Barrow was seized by twenty men, dunked in water, and nearly drowned; James Ireland was imprisoned and nearly blown up in a murder attempt; David Thomas was once attacked while preaching and physically dragged out of the meetinghouse while on another occasion an attempt was made to shoot him, but the gun was wrenched out of the assailant's hand by a bystander; John Waller was seized while leading a congregation in worship, his head smashed against the ground more than once, and finally he was horsewhipped with twenty lashes. Like these other Baptist preachers, Waller was, in the words of Jon Butler, "a feisty and resolute preacher." Before dying in 1802, he baptized more than 2,000 persons, participated in the ordination of twenty-seven preachers, and planted at least eighteen Baptist congregations all over Virginia.

Despite such mob violence, arrest, and derision, Virginia Baptists succeeded in their struggle for religious freedom. In part this had to do with their repeated argument that they were "loyal and quiet subjects," whose religious views were no threat to the state. They made this point time and again in petitioning campaigns they orchestrated. Their plight was also taken up by James Madison, the future fourth president of the United States, who was horrified when he heard of the imprisonment of "5 or 6 well meaning men" in 1774, one of whom may have been James Ireland, "for publishing their religious sentiments which in the main are very orthodox." Two years later Madison redrafted an article in Virginia's Declaration of Rights, which effectively guaranteed freedom of religion, though its "cool Enlightenment-style definition of religion," as Jon Butler puts it, was hardly to the taste of the Baptists of Virginia.

The Virginia Declaration of Rights, Article 16

That religion, or the duty which we owe to our Creator, and the manner of discharging it, can be directed only by reason and conviction, not by force or violence; and therefore all men are equally entitled to the free exercise of religion, according to the dictates of conscience; and that it is the mutual duty of all to practice Christian forbearance, love, and charity toward each other.

In both Virginia and New England, John Leland played a critical role in the fight for religious freedom. As a young man Leland was deeply influenced by Elhanan Winchester to embrace Christianity before the latter became a Universalist. Leland began his ministry in 1775 in Virginia. He saw firsthand the problems of a state church that sought to impose itself upon the consciences of men and women. As he came to argue, "Whenever men fly to the law or sword to protect their system of religion, and force it upon others, it is evident that they have something in their system that will not bear the light, and stand upon the basis of truth." He developed an unlikely friendship with Thomas Jefferson and also with James Madison. In 1784, Leland and other Baptists allied with Madison to defeat passage of a General Assessment bill that would have provided tax support to religion but allowed citizens to designate their taxes to the denomination of their choice. Patrick Henry and George Washington, as well as Episcopalians and most Presbyterians, supported the bill; Madison, Jefferson, and the Baptists opposed it.

When Jefferson, well known for his Deism, was elected president of the United States in 1801, numerous evangelicals were horrified. The New Divinity preacher Nathanael Emmons, for instance, preached a sermon on 2 Kings 17:21 implicitly comparing Jefferson to the wicked Jeroboam. Baptists in both America and Britain saw things differently. Baptists in Danbury, Connecticut, wrote to Jefferson, congratulating him on his election and telling him, "Our sentiments are uniformly on the side of religious liberty: that Religion is at all times and places a matter between God and individuals, that no man ought to suffer in name, person, or effects on account of his religious opinions, [and] that the legitimate power of civil government extends no further than to punish the man who works ill to his neighbor." Leland persuaded the women of his congregation in Cheshire, Massachusetts, to manufacture a mammoth cheese weighing 1,230 pounds as a token of their support for Jefferson. Leland then transported the cheese by wagon and sloop to Washington to present it to Jefferson on New Year's Day 1802. Leland preached all along the way and, at the invitation of Jefferson, preached before the House and the Senate on the verse, "Behold a greater than Solomon is here."

In England violent persecution of the Baptists technically ceased with the Act of Toleration. However, the Corporation and Test Acts, parts of the Clarendon Code that restricted political and military office to Anglicans, were still in force, and occasionally violence broke out against Baptists and other Dissenters. During Christmas 1792, for example, the Baptist meetinghouse in Guilsborough, near Northampton, was burned to the ground by incendiaries hostile to Baptists. A year and a half later, on May 18, 1794, James Hinton, pastor of New Road Baptist Church in Oxford, made a visit with a few companions to the nearby village of Woodstock to preach in a private home. A few minutes after Hinton began preaching, a mob of some 300–400 people appeared, many of them armed with bludgeons and stones. Storming the house, they violently attacked Hinton and his companions, who had to defend themselves from repeated blows to their heads. Not content with driving Hinton and his companions out of Woodstock, the mob pursued them, hurling insults and howling for blood. One of Hinton's companions, a Mr. Barnard, was knocked to the ground a dozen times in a row, the mob giving him time to rise on each occasion so as to have the brutal pleasure of knocking him down again. Deaf to his cries for mercy, the mob eventually dumped his bludgeoned body into a ditch and left him for dead. Hinton later discovered him and another of his companions, senseless and covered in blood.

In England the great Baptist champion of religious liberty was Robert Robinson, who was converted through the preaching of George Whitefield in the 1750s. After a short career as a Methodist preacher, Robinson went on to build a thriving work at St. Andrew's Street Baptist Church, Cambridge, where he became known as one of the finest preachers in England. Although he was roundly criticized for venturing into the realm of politics as a minister, Robinson used his Cambridge pulpit and the press to promote the view that a truly virtuous government protects an individual's security and liberty, guards the rights of individual conscience, and "renders justice cheap to the poor, easy to the illiterate,

Robert Robinson (1735–1790)

accessible to all." While the duty of Christians was to support a good government, to suppose that Christians were never to resist the tyranny of wicked rulers was a misreading of Scripture, particularly Romans 13. "Never was right of resistance more clearly ascertained," Robinson maintained in *A Political Catechism* (1782), and "passive obedience and non-resistance more fully exploded in any nation than in ours at the revolution [of 1688]."

Robinson's passion for liberty led him to build friendships with a variety of political and theological figures and authors like the Socinian Joseph Priestley. To what extent these friendships began to refashion Robinson's own theological convictions or whether it was a result of what the nineteenth-century hymnologist Samuel Duffield called Robinson's "intense and almost morbid devotion" to liberty, by the 1780s Robinson railed against the use of creeds. When an elderly minister in his congregation applied to the Particular Baptist Fund, which had been set up in London in the early eighteenth century to help prospective ministers as well as aged ones, he was told that unless he affirmed a statement of Christian orthodoxy that began with affirmation of the Trinity, he could expect no financial aid. Robinson was vehement in his denunciation of this requirement to affirm a creed, what he regarded as "a tyranny over men's consciences." He wrote to Mary Hays, who was one of his protégés and is today considered an early feminist author, that such a requirement was "absolute nonsense" and an "awful impiety!" In his church, he told Hays, "We all hold inviolably the perfection of Scripture without human additions." Of course, the Baptist leaders in London who managed the Particular Baptist Fund were thoroughly convinced that the doctrine of the Trinity was to be found in the Scriptures and, as such, was certainly not a "human addition." Moreover, they were of the same mind as Robinson's contemporary, Andrew Fuller, who argued that Robinson's interpretation of the right of private judgment was inconsistent with the practice of the early church: a "community must entirely renounce the name of a Christian church," Fuller maintained, if it cannot "withdraw from an individual whose principles they consider as false and injurious."

The American Revolution

The relationship between church and state came to a head during the American Revolution. When Robert MacGregor, pastor of Woolwich Baptist Church, Kent, reflected in 1772 on the relationship that existed between the Particular Baptists and the British government for much of that century, he declared with some measure of pride that his denomination had been consistently characterized by appreciative support for the government of the land. "We may glory in our loyalty," he stated, "for I never yet heard a single Baptist being concerned in any tumult, rebellion, or civil commotion, against the present royal family," that is the House of Hanover, the dynasty established by George I. Yet by the close of the American Revolution eleven years later, a dramatic shift had occurred in the political attitude of many Baptists toward their government. The London Baptist John Rippon, for instance, reopened correspondence with James Manning of Providence, Rhode Island, after the American Revolution came to a close in 1783, assuring Manning that all of the Baptist ministers in London save two "and most of our brethren in the country, were on the side of the Americans in the late dispute." A number of Baptist ministers in the British Isles were vocal in their support of America. Rees David, pastor of Saint Mary's Baptist Church in Norwich, preached a fiery sermon in the winter of 1781 against the British war effort, predicting, "God will call us to an account, and make us smart for every drop of innocent blood, which we have shed in this war." A year later David was still fulminating about the war "as cruel and unjust" as well as citing the British army's "converting places of worship into play-houses" and the "burning [of] public libraries and whole towns" as evidence of his assertion.

Excerpt from Joshua Toulmin, *The American War Lamented* (1776)

Unhappy nation! The treasure of which is employed, and whose inhabitants are sent to the field of battle, to support the impious glory of ambition. . . . [T]he pleasing intercourses of relative life are intercepted—the wife sits at home solitary and pensive, in anxious fears for the life of her beloved partner—the tender, aged parent, is full of thought and concern for an amiable son—friends are torn from friends . . . they, whom their country commands to arm for the battle, go forth to meet the arrows of death, or to breath out slaughter against their own race. . . . What promiscuous carnage! What mangled limbs! What hideous cries! Fields covered with ghastly corpses! Green pastures crimsoned with human gore!

The strongest critique of British policy in America, however, came from the pen of the Welsh Baptist Caleb Evans in his various responses to the Methodist leader John Wesley, who defended the British government in his widely read *A Calm Address to Our American Colonies* (1775). In his pamphlet debate with Wesley and then with his lieutenant John Fletcher, Evans essentially agreed with the Americans' argument that taxation without representation is nothing less than slavery. For Evans, whose political views had been profoundly shaped by his reading of the political philosopher John Locke, "the people, and the people only, are the source of power," a political perspective that was in some ways akin to his Congregationalism.

In America the only significant Baptist figure who opposed the revolution was the Welsh Baptist immigrant Morgan Edwards, who was kept under house arrest at his farm in Newark, Delaware, for most of the war. Some Baptist leaders, like John Gano (who, according to an oft-repeated myth, baptized George Washington by immersion at either Valley Forge or in the Potomac), David Jones, and Silas Mercer served as chaplains with the revolutionary forces. Other Baptist pastors used their position in society to advance the cause of the Revolution. In 1775, Oliver Hart traveled itinerantly in an effort to convince Loyalists of the Patriot cause. In March 1776, he was one of several ministers from the Charleston area who sent a resolution to the South Carolina Congress declaring their "hope yet to see hunted liberty sit Regent on the throne, and flourish more than ever." Not surprisingly, when the British took Charleston four years later, Hart had to flee the city with little more than the clothes on his back. Most of his personal possessions and papers fell into British hands, and the Baptist meetinghouse was commandeered to serve as a warehouse to store salt beef.

Regrettably, the American Revolution produced a deadening effect on spirituality. The reasons for this are at least three-fold. For a decade or so after the revolution, political issues rather than spiritual issues continued to dominate the minds of people. The absence of a significant number of husbands and fathers for lengthy periods of time during the fighting led to a breakdown of family piety. And the employment of French troops as allies of America in the war introduced into the United States levels of atheistic and deistic thinking unknown heretofore. As a result, spiritual decline marked many of the denominational bodies in the northern United States immediately

John Gano (1727–1804)

after 1783. Had Baptist growth in the northern states between 1770 and 1780, for example, been in keeping with the rate of growth from 1740 to 1770, Baptists would have numbered around 41,400. This would have been 56 percent more than their actual figure of 26,620. Clearly the war was not conducive to spiritual prosperity.

The Fight Against the Slave Trade

The slave trade was another great political and moral issue for Baptists in this era. In 1789, Isaac Backus made an extensive preaching trip to Virginia and North Carolina. He was there for five months with the aim of cementing relations between northern and southern Baptists. He must have noticed the differing regional attitudes toward slavery. Like many New England Baptists, Backus detested the institution. However, also like many of them, he felt no call to rebuke his slave-holding brethren or to attack the system. He genuinely hoped this wickedness would wither away under the providence of God. Generally speaking, the Baptists Backus met in the South, though they were interested in saving the souls of slaves, had no interest in discussing an end to slavery. For example, Backus attended a Baptist Association meeting in Virginia that discussed questions like the following: "What should be done when a man slave was owned by one master and his wife by another, and one was carried to such a distance as never to be likely to see the other in this world? Whether they must continue single or not?" Surely the institution of slavery was itself responsible for the moral dilemma posed by such questions.

Despite differing Baptist views on the subject, several other Christian communities in this period came to oppose slavery and the trade that supported it. Most Quaker communities on both sides of the Atlantic by 1760 or so were practicing church discipline against members who participated in the slave trade. In the next decade John Wesley and the British Methodists were also drawn firmly into the antislavery camp; Wesley henceforth abominated the slave trade as "that execrable sum of all villainies." From the 1780s onward, Anglican evangelicals such as John Newton and especially William Wilberforce became identified with opposition to the slave trade. During this same period a number of key English Baptists exhibited a growing revulsion at their nation's slave trading.

Not surprisingly, Robert Robinson spoke against slavery in a sermon preached in February 1788, arguing that after the apostolic era "Christians understood that the liberating of slaves was a part of Christianity, not indeed expressed in the direct words of a statute, but naturally and necessarily contained in the doctrines and precepts of it: in the precepts which equalized all, and in the first principle of all doctrines, the equal love of God to all mankind." A few months after Robinson's sermon in Cambridge, a meeting of church representatives of the Western Association expressed their "deepest abhorrence of the slave trade" and urged the pastors and "members of all our churches, to unite in promoting, to the utmost of our power, every scheme that is or may be proposed, to procure the abolition of a traffic so unjust, inhuman, and disgraceful." Four years later missions pioneer William Carey urged his fellow Baptists to give up using sugar, due to the fact that it had been produced by slave labor in the West Indies and so cleanse their "hands of blood."

Arguably one of the best sermons against the slave trade preached by an English Baptist during this era was Abraham Booth's *Commerce in the Human Species, and the Enslaving of Innocent Persons, Inimical to the Laws of Moses and the Gospel of Christ* (1792). Thomas Clarkson, a key abolitionist, considered it one of the most important documents in the early stages of the antislavery movement. The son of a Nottinghamshire farmer, Booth became a stocking weaver in his teens. He had no formal schooling and was compelled to teach himself to read and to write. His early Christian life was spent among the General Baptists, but by 1768 he had undergone a complete revolution in his soteriology and had become a Calvinist. *Commerce in the*

Human Species opened with the assertion that every human being is bound
"to adore our Almighty Maker, to confide in
the Lord Redeemer, and to exercise genuine benevolence toward all mankind."
Booth went on to emphasize that Christianity is intimately tied up with "the
exercise of moral justice, of benevolence, and of humanity," and on this
basis, and not that of promoting civil
and political liberty, he was prepared to take a public stand against
the slave trade.

After examining various Old Testament texts regarding slavery, Booth
asked why only white Europeans possessed the right to enslave black Africans. Surely it was not because the whites
were Christians and the blacks were pagans.
Christianity was "the religion of truth and

Abraham Booth (1734–1806)

Abraham Booth on the Slave Trade

The slave trade is . . . an effectual bar to the propagation of Christianity among
[the Africans]. . . . Zeal for the honor of Christ and love to our fellow-creatures ought
therefore to inspire us with ardent prayer that the horrid impediment may be removed and that Christ may be glorified among them. Nor ought we to pray merely
that God would abolish the infamous commerce in man on the shores of Africa,
but also for the gradual emancipation of oppressed Negroes in the West India islands, that the slavery of innocent persons may cease to exist and sink under the
detestation of all Europe. For what must the enslaved Africans in those islands think
of Christians, of Christianity, and of Christ under the tuition of their oppressors? . . .

Let your ardent and frequent prayers be accompanied with prudent, peaceable, and steady efforts in order to procure the total abolition of that criminal
traffic and of the cruel slavery consequent upon it. . . . As it is our design at this
time to make a collection for promoting the general design of that worthy society,
which has existed for some years in this metropolis, in order to effect the abolition
of the slave trade, I would earnestly exhort you to make a liberal contribution
for their assistance. The members of that benevolent society have done worthily.
They deserve the assistance and the thanks of every friend to moral justice and
to humanity. Let us therefore endeavor to strengthen their hands and to promote
the righteous cause in which they are united.

Excerpted from Abraham Booth, *Commerce in the Human Species* (1792).

of justice, of benevolence and of peace." The slave trade, on the other hand, was "unjust and cruel, barbarous and savage." Booth seemed to be hinting here at the racist basis of the British slave trade—blacks could be enslaved because they were deemed inferior to whites. But, Booth asserted, blacks are fully human and therefore have all "the rights of humanity" common to the human species. If slavery were legitimate, it would not at all be unlawful for blacks to raid London, Bristol, and Liverpool, the three main English ports that had grown rich from the traffic in human beings, and enslave free Britons. By thus imaginatively turning the tables, Booth wanted his hearers to put themselves in the shoes of the Africans and develop a heart of benevolence toward them. From Booth's perspective the slave trade was especially inimical to the ethical teaching of Christ because Christians were to love their enemies and do good to them that hate them (Luke 6:27). "If our sovereign Lord requires benevolence and active love to our enemies," surely, Booth reasoned,

COMMERCE IN THE HUMAN SPECIES, AND THE EN-
SLAVING OF INNOCENT PERSONS, INIMICAL TO THE
LAWS OF MOSES AND THE GOSPEL OF CHRIST.

A

S   E   R   M   O   N,

PREACHED IN

LITTLE PRESCOT STREET, GOODMAN's FIELDS,

JANUARY 29, 1792.

BY ABRAHAM BOOTH.

BEHOLD THE TEARS OF SUCH AS WERE OPPRESSED, AND THEY
HAD NO COMFORTER; AND ON THE SIDE OF THEIR OPPRES-
SORS THERE WAS POWER; BUT THEY HAD NO COMFORTER.
ECCLESIASTES. iv. I.

REMEMBER HEAVEN HAS AN AVENGING ROD;
TO SMITE THE POOR IS TREASON AGAINST GOD.   COWPER.

L O N D O N:

PRINTED BY L. WAYLAND; AND SOLD BY C. DILLY, POULTRY;
AND T. KNOTT, LOMBARD STREET.

M,DCC,XCII.

Title page of Abraham Booth's Commerce in the Human Species *(1792).*

he cannot require any less to those who are not our enemies, which would certainly include the Africans, who are unknown to the slave traders prior to their being enslaved.

Caleb Evans once said with regard to God's kingdom, "When we pray for the advancement of this kingdom, if we are not willing to do all we can to advance it, our prayers cannot be genuine, they are hypocritical." The prayers and "prudent, peaceable, and steady efforts" of the Baptists, along with those of other abolitionists, to effect the abolition of the slave trade finally bore fruit in 1807, when a motion to abolish British involvement in the slave trade passed in the House of Commons with an overwhelming 283 out of 299 members of Parliament voting to end the practice.

Three African-American Baptist Leaders

About two years before the outbreak of the American Revolution, a slave in Georgia by the name of George Liele was converted. Given his freedom shortly afterward, he was ordained in 1775 and went on to plant a work in Savannah, Georgia, which claims to be the oldest African-American Baptist church. With the defeat of the British cause, however, Liele and his family were in danger of being re-enslaved. Liele decided to relocate to Jamaica as an indentured servant, where he formed a small congregation in 1783. Liele was able to follow his calling as a preacher, and within seven years he saw around 500 conversions under his preaching, with 300 of those converts joining his church. Ten years later he had secured enough funds, about £400 from other Loyalists, to build the first Dissenting

"Am I not a man and a brother?" Created by Josiah Wedgwood (1730–95).

chapel on the island, Windward Road Chapel. By the time William Carey and his family set sail for India in 1793, Liele had been laboring as a missionary for a decade. He should, therefore, probably be considered the first Baptist missionary, though some historians of mission would demur, since a "missionary," by definition, is sent out by a church. Technically, Liele had not been sent out by a church. Nevertheless, by 1814, Liele's ministry had produced a rich harvest, some 8,000 Baptists in numerous chapels throughout the island.

Excerpt from George Liele, "The Covenant of the Anabaptist Church [of Jamaica]"

   I. We are of the Anabaptist persuasion, because we believe it agreeable to the Scriptures. Matt 3:1–3; 2 Cor 6:14–18. . . .

 III. We hold to be baptized in a river, or in a place where there is much water, in the name of the Father, and the Son, and the Holy Ghost. Matt 3:13, 16–17; Mark 16:15–16; Matt 28:19. . . .

  V. We hold to the ordinance of washing one another's feet. Jn 13:2–7. . . .

VII. We hold to pray over the sick, anointing them with oil in the name of the Lord. Jas 5:14–15.

Among those impacted by Leile's preaching in Georgia were Andrew Bryan and David George. After Leile left for Jamaica, Bryan, who had been baptized by Liele, assumed the leadership of the Georgia congregation. The church flourished under his powerful preaching; by 1802, the church had some 850 members. As for David George, his master left him and a number of other slaves to fend for themselves during the revolution, which prompted George and his family to flee to British-occupied Savannah, where he was given his freedom. When a British defeat seemed imminent in 1782, George and his family left the American South and joined the exodus of British loyalists to Nova Scotia.

George and his family spent ten years, from 1782 to 1792, in Shelburne, Nova Scotia, where he established a Particular Baptist Church. As knowledge of his preaching abilities spread throughout Nova Scotia and then New Brunswick, he began to receive invitations to preach farther and farther afield. In 1792, George, his family, and much of his congregation left the Canadian Maritimes to settle in West Africa. A company had been founded in England a few years earlier to establish a settlement in Sierra Leone, which would introduce European culture and Christianity to Africa and be a place where whites and blacks could live as equals. Similar to his experience in Nova Scotia, George played a vital role in the establishment of a Particular Baptist witness in this colony, which was called Freetown. Unhappily, the Sierra Leonean Baptists did not develop after George's death in 1810. In the final two decades of the twentieth century, his spiritual descendants numbered only about 825 in eleven congregations.

The French Revolution and the English Baptists

Bliss was it in that dawn to be alive,
But to be young was very heaven!

Thus did William Wordsworth—the English writer whose poetry is central to the canon of British Romanticism—describe the headiness of the early days of the French Revolution, which promised liberty but ended in bloodshed through tyranny and war. Wordsworth's naïve enthusiasm for what was happening in France was shared by a number of sectors of English society, including Baptists. For instance, Joseph Kinghorn, the pastor of Saint Mary's Baptist Church, Norwich, wrote to his father, David Kinghorn, in August 1789, the month after the storming of the Bastille: "I rejoice with all my heart at the destruction of that most infamous place the Bastille." Another Norwich Particular Baptist minister, Mark Wilks, began a sermon exactly a year later with the provocative statement, "Jesus Christ was a Revolutionist." He went on to inform his congregation that the French Revolution "is of God and that no power exists or can exist, by which it can be overthrown."

Robert Hall Jr., probably the most famous Baptist preacher in the early nineteenth century, was equally enthralled by what was taking place in France. In a famous tract that went through a number of pirated editions, *Christianity Consistent with a Love of Freedom* (1791), Hall stated, "Events have taken place of late, and revolutions have been effected, which, had they been foretold a very few years ago, would have been viewed as visionary and extravagant; and their influence is yet far from being spent. . . . The empire of darkness and of despotism has been smitten with a stroke which has sounded through the universe."

William Steadman on the Danger of Politics for Ministers

Politics is a subject, which, a few years ago, engrossed no small attention, and did no small injury both to ministers and people, by employing too much of their time and thoughts, as well as by exciting an improper party spirit. . . . I do not wish you to be wholly ignorant of the political state of your country, as you are a citizen as well as a preacher; but do not, I beseech you, let politics engross so much of your thoughts, or your conversation, as to cause the duties of the citizen to interfere with those of the preacher.

Excerpted from *The Christian Minister's Duty and Reward* (1807).

Such sentiments proved to be utterly naïve and uninformed. In 1793 and 1794 the Revolution descended into a vortex of unspeakable violence and totalitarian terror. During this period, known to history as the Reign of Terror, at least 300,000 were arrested with some 17,000 people being executed by the guillotine. Many others died in prison or were simply killed without the benefit of a trial. French revolutionary armies sought to spread the ideals of the Revolution to neighboring nations. What they exported though was unprecedented levels of destruction and warfare to the rest of Europe and so plunged the continent into a war that lasted until 1815. Not surprisingly, Baptists like Kinghorn and Hall became increasingly critical of what was taking place in France. By April 1798, Kinghorn was convinced that "all those notions of liberty which the

Robert Hall Jr. (1764–1831)

French Revolution very generally raised a few years ago are at an end, they [that is, the rulers of France] are the tyrants not the deliverers of men."

Hall's views likewise were transformed. In a sermon entitled *Modern Infidelity Considered, with Respect to Its Influence on Society* (1800), a work that made Hall a celebrity in England, he spoke of divine revelation having undergone "a total eclipse" in France, "while atheism, performing on a darkened theatre its strange and fearful tragedy, confounded the first elements of society, blended every age, rank, and sex in indiscriminate proscription and massacre, and convulsed all Europe to its centre." Hall was now convinced that at the root of the sanguinary violence of the Revolution—what he rightly described as "atrocities . . . committed with a wanton levity and brutal merriment"—lay in the skepticism and rationalism of *les philosophes*, men like Voltaire, Jean-Jacques Rousseau, and Denis Diderot. "Settle it therefore in your minds, as a maxim," he told his hearers, "that atheism"—he was referring to the rationalism of *les philosophes*—"is an inhuman, bloody, ferocious system . . . : its first object is to dethrone God, its next to destroy man." In another sermon preached two years later titled *Reflections on War* (1802), Hall expressed the opinion that the French Revolution was also in part God's judgment on the French nation for their brutal persecution in the previous century of the Huguenots, French believers who shared Hall's Calvinistic worldview.

Andrew Fuller and Fullerism

Just as John Gill had been the dominant theologian in many transatlantic Baptist communities during the middle decades of the eighteenth century, so Andrew Fuller was the leading Baptist thinker during the closing decades of the eighteenth century. Charles Haddon Spurgeon did not hesitate to describe Fuller as "the greatest theologian" of his century, and for a good portion of the nineteenth century, while American Baptist historian A. H. Newman noted that "his influence on American Baptists" was "incalculable." Fuller became the chief proponent of a theological trajectory that came

Andrew Fuller
(1754–1815)

to dominate British Particular Baptist life and strongly influenced Baptists in America.

Born and raised in East Anglia, a historic Puritan stronghold, Fuller sat under the ministry of John Eve at Soham, Cambridgeshire. According to

Soham Baptist Church, Cambridgeshire (est. 1752).

Fuller, Eve's theology was "tinged with false Calvinism," for he "had little or nothing to say to the unconverted." Nevertheless, in the late 1760s, Fuller began to experience strong conviction of sin, which resulted in his conversion in November 1769. He was baptized in April 1770 and joined the Soham church. Over the next few years, the church clearly saw that Fuller possessed definite ministerial gifts. Eve left the church in 1771 for another pastorate, and Fuller, who was self-taught when it came to theology and who had been preaching in the church for a couple of years, was formally inducted as pastor in the spring of 1775. The church consisted of forty-seven members and met for worship in a rented barn.

Fuller's pastorate at Soham, which lasted until 1782 when he moved to pastor the Baptist work in Kettering, Northamptonshire, was a decisive period for the shaping of his theological outlook. During these seven years Fuller began a lifelong study of the works of the New England theologian Jonathan Edwards, his chief theological mentor after the Scriptures. Also during this period he made the acquaintance of Robert Hall Sr., John Ryland Jr., and John Sutcliff, who later became his closest ministerial friends and colleagues. Finally, while pastoring at Soham, Fuller decisively rejected hyper-Calvinism and drew up a defense of his own theological position in

The Gospel Worthy of All Acceptation, though the first edition of this book was not published until 1785.

Due to the fact that John Eve's preaching was essentially the only homiletical model Fuller had ever known, he initially preached like Eve and failed to urge the unconverted to come to Christ. Increasingly though, he was dissatisfied with this approach to preaching and evangelism. He began to sense that his "preaching was anti-scriptural and defective in many respects." Robert Hall Sr., pastor of the Particular Baptist cause in Arnsby, Leicestershire, suggested that he read Jonathan Edwards's classic work on divine sovereignty and human responsibility, *A Careful and Strict Enquiry into the Modern Prevailing Notions of the Freedom of Will* (1754). The Arnsby pastor was convinced that this work would help clarify some of Fuller's thinking about the inability of sinful men and women to obey God.

Fuller also immersed himself in the works of John Bunyan and John Gill's *A Body of Doctrinal Divinity*. Fuller found much that was helpful in Gill's systematic work but was deeply troubled by the evident differences between Gill and Bunyan. Both were ardent Calvinists, but whereas Bunyan recommended "the free offer of salvation to sinners without distinction," Gill did not. Initially Fuller wrongly concluded that though Bunyan was "a great and good man," he was not as clear as Gill regarding the gospel. However, as Fuller studied the writings of other sixteenth- and seventeenth-century authors, in particular those of the Puritan theologian John Owen, he noted that they too "dealt . . . in free invitations to sinners to come to Christ and be saved." In other words, Fuller discerned that with regard to preaching there was a definite difference not only between Bunyan and Gill but more broadly between sixteenth- and seventeenth-century Calvinism and that of the early eighteenth century. This was the crucible in which *The Gospel Worthy of All Acceptation* was written.

A preliminary draft of the work was written by 1778, and what was roughly the final form of the treatise was completed by 1781. Two editions of the book were published in Fuller's lifetime. The first edition, published in Northampton in 1785, was subtitled *The Obligations of Men Fully to Credit, and Cordially to Approve, Whatever God Makes Known, Wherein Is Considered the Nature of Faith in Christ, and the Duty of Those Where the Gospel Comes in That Matter*. The second edition, which appeared in 1801, was more simply subtitled *The Duty of Sinners to Believe in Jesus Christ*, a subtitle that well expressed the overall theme of the book. The first and second editions had substantial differences, which Fuller freely admitted and which primarily related to the doctrine of particular redemption. The work's major theme, however, remained unaltered: "Faith in Christ is the duty of all men who hear, or have opportunity to hear, the gospel." This epoch-making book sought to be faithful to the central emphases of historic Calvinism while at the same time attempting to leave preachers with no alternative but to drive home to their hearers the universal obligations of repentance and faith.

The critical role played by Fuller in the controversy about the free offer of the gospel did not preclude his engaging in other vital areas of theological debate. Over a period of thirty years, he wrote definitive responses to Socinianism, Deism, Universalism, Antinomianism, and Sandemanianism (which promoted an intellectualist view of saving faith). He also penned the *Memoirs of the Rev. Samuel Pearce* (1800), which recounted the life of his close friend, Samuel Pearce of Birmingham, who died at age thirty-three. In some ways modeled after Jonathan Edwards's memoir of David Brainerd, it told of one whom Fuller regarded as a model of evangelical spirituality. Through the medium of Fuller's book, Pearce's extraordinary passion for Christ—which led to his being labeled the "seraphic Pearce" by contemporaries—had a powerful impact on his generation.

Gillites and Fullerites

Forty years ago [1820s] large bodies of our people were in a state of ferment and agitation, in consequence of some modifications of their old Calvinistic creed, as displayed in the writings of the late Andrew Fuller, of Kettering, England. This famous man maintained that the atonement of Christ was general in its nature, but particular in its application, in opposition to our old divines, who held that Christ died for the elect only. He also made a distinction between the natural and moral inability of men.

Dr. John Gill, of London, was, in his day, one of the most distinguished divines among the English Baptists, and as he was a noted advocate for the old system of a limited atonement, the terms "Gillites" and "Fullerites" were often applied to the parties in this discussion. Those who espoused the views of Mr. Fuller were denominated Arminians by the Gillite men, while they, in their turn, styled their opponents Hyper-Calvinists. Both parties claimed to be orthodox and evangelical, and differed but little on any other points except those which have been named. On election, the Trinity, etc., they all agreed.

In the age when this discussion arose among the American Baptists, as none of the modern subjects of agitation had been introduced into their churches, the speculative opinions thus briefly described, for a number of years were the occasion of unhappy debates and contentions in many locations.

Excerpted from David Benedict, *Fifty Years Among the Baptists* (New York: 1860).

Samuel Pearce's Sermon on the British Naval Victory over the French at the Battle of the Nile and the Repulse of a French Invasion Fleet off the Coast of Ireland (1798)

Should any one expect that I shall introduce the *destruction* of our foes, by the late victories gained off the coasts of Egypt and Ireland, as the object of pleasure and gratitude, he will be disappointed. The man who can take pleasure at the destruction of his fellow men, is a cannibal at heart; and for him New Zealand [where natives accepted cannibalism as a part of warfare] is a more fit habitation than civilized Europe . . . but to the heart of him who calls himself a disciple of the merciful Jesus, let such pleasure be an everlasting stranger. Since in that sacred volume, which I revere as the fair gift of heaven to man, I am taught, that "of one blood God hath made all nations" [Acts 17:26], it is impossible for me not to regard every man as my brother, and to consider, that national differences ought not to excite personal animosities.

But though we dare not rejoice at the misery of others, we ought to be thankful for the security we enjoy ourselves. It is well known that France has long meditated and threatened a descent upon our coasts, and an invasion of our country. Proposals to this purpose have been made in her assemblies, and she has actually attempted to ensure success to her designs against us, by her efforts to gain possession of Ireland, our sister kingdom. Had she succeeded in establishing her power there, where she might have victualled her fleets, and recruited her armies, England, in all probability, would have become an easy prey.

But God, the great guardian of our isle, has mercifully prevented the accomplishment of her first object. Ireland is not yet a department of France.

Excerpted from Samuel Pearce, *Motives to Gratitude* (1798).

The Baptist Missionary Society and William Carey

Fuller's *Gospel Worthy of All Acceptation* led directly to his wholehearted involvement in the formation in October 1792 of what came to be known as the Baptist Missionary Society (BMS) and the subsequent sending of the society's most famous missionary, William Carey, to India in 1793. Fuller served as the secretary of this society until his death in 1815. The work of the society consumed an enormous amount of Fuller's time as he regularly toured the country, representing the BMS and raising funds. On average he was away from home three months of the year. Between 1798 and 1813, moreover, he made five lengthy trips to Scotland for the mission as well as undertaking journeys to Wales and Ireland (1804). He also carried on an extensive correspondence on the mission's behalf. Fuller's commitment to the BMS was not only rooted in his missionary theology but also in his deep friendship with Carey. Fuller later compared the sending of Carey to India

to lowering him into a deep gold mine. Fuller and his close friends Sutcliff
and Ryland pledged themselves to "hold the ropes"
as long as Carey lived.

Arguably, the formation of the BMS, which
helped bring about the creation of a host of
like-minded missionary societies and thus
launched the modern missionary movement, was one of the most significant
events in Western Christianity since the
Reformation. That its first missionary,
Carey, an autodidact whose formal education ended by his early teens, went on
to become an inspiration for countless
others in the following century is remarkable. Carey's first seven years in India were
extremely difficult: he had no converts; he
was forced to take a position as the manager
of a new indigo factory in Mudnabatti, around
280 miles north of Calcutta; his wife Dorothy
experienced a total mental breakdown after

William Carey
(1761–1834)

the death of one of their sons, Peter, and was soon completely delusional.
During the early days of Dorothy's insanity, Carey wrote in his diary, "This
is indeed the valley of the shadow of death to me. . . . O what would I give
for a kind sympathetic friend such as I had in England to whom I might open
my heart." In June 1800, fellow missionary William Ward simply stated in
his diary: "Mrs. Carey is stark mad." Carey biographers have not been kind
to Dorothy: she has either been seen as something of a stumbling block in
the way of her husband's calling or generally ignored in the accounts of Carey's life. When she died in 1807, for example, all that was said of her in the
official publication of the BMS was, "Mrs. Carey, after having been ill about
a fortnight, died." Since the 1980s, historians have sought to see her life in
more sympathetic terms and view her as a tragic heroine, who unwittingly
gave her sanity, and ultimately her life, for Christ and his kingdom.

In 1800, Carey moved to Sermapore and linked up with two other missionaries who had been sent out by the BMS: Ward, a skilled printer who
became the best preacher at Serampore, and Joshua Marshman, the administrator and foreign secretary of the Serampore mission. In all of the extant
literature and manuscripts of these three men, no trace of mutual jealousy
or severe anger can be found. Henry Martyn, an evangelical Anglican and
missionary to Persia, said that never were "such men . . . so suited to
another and to their work."

Krishna Pal

Within a year of establishing the Serampore mission, Carey and his colleagues began to win converts to the faith. The first was Krishna Pal, a Hindu carpenter and longtime seeker after truth. Pal had heard the gospel already from one of the Moravian missionaries who labored in the vicinity of Serampore until 1792, but it made no lasting impression on his mind. On the morning of November 25, 1800, however, while he was washing in the River Hooghly, not far from the Serampore mission, he fell on the slippery bank and dislocated his shoulder.

The baptism of Krishna Pal in the Hooghly River.

Seeking medical help from the missionaries at Serampore, he also heard the gospel from them. A month or so later, Krishna Pal confessed that he believed "Christ gave his life up for the salvation of sinners" and that he had personally embraced this gospel truth. He subsequently broke caste by eating with the missionaries, and Ward commented, "The door of faith is open to the Gentiles; who shall shut it? The chain of the caste is broken, who shall mend it?" On Sunday, December 28, 1800, a few days after his profession of faith and in the presence of a huge crowd of Europeans, Hindus, and Muslims, Krishna Pal was baptized in the Hooghly River.

Pal was the first of hundreds who were converted through the witness of the Serampore mission over the next three decades. By 1821, more than 1,400 believers—half of them Indians—had been baptized; and Krishna Pal, who died the following year, had become one of the finest preachers of the mission. Carey once described an early sermon of this Indian brother as "fluent, perspicuous, and affectionate, in a very high degree." Pal became something of an international celebrity among Baptists in the English-speaking world, inspiring many to become foreign missionaries.

Krishna also wrote hymns to express his love, and that of his fellow Bengali believers, for Christ. One of them, translated into English, is still in use. Its first stanza runs thus:

> O thou, my soul, forget no more,
> The Friend who all thy misery bore;
> Let every idol be forgot,
> But, O my soul, forget him not.

In its cross-centeredness and emphasis on the cross's power to deliver from idolatry, this verse is quintessentially evangelical and well captures the heart of why Carey and his colleagues were in India. Heralding the gospel with its message of the crucified Christ, whose death alone delivered from sin and its consequences, was the main passion of Carey and his friends. The Serampore missionaries embraced a holistic mission strategy. In addition to their evangelistic labors, translation work, and printing interests, they were social reformers: they helped abolish such social ills as *sati* (the self-immolation of a widow on the funeral pyre of her husband) and the prostitution of children in the Hindu temples. They were also educational activists, founding Serampore College in 1818.

Baptist Revival

In 1794, two years after the formation of the BMS, John Rippon published a list of Calvinistic Baptist congregations and ministers in his *Baptist Annual Register*. Rippon estimated that there were at that time 326 churches in England and 56 in Wales, more than double the number that existed in 1750. He printed another list of churches four years later, according to which the numbers had grown to 361 churches in England and 84 in Wales. Reflecting on these numbers, Rippon wrote, "It is said, that more of our meeting houses have been enlarged, within the last five years, and built within the last fifteen, than had been built and enlarged for thirty years before." Rippon was not exaggerating. The Particular Baptists had enjoyed steady growth during the last four decades of the eighteenth century but in the final decade of the century saw a truly rapid influx of converts. At the heart of it was Fullerite theology and the passion for missions engendered by the BMS.

From a more personal angle, one can observe the revival that was taking place in the following extracts from the letters of Andrew Fuller. In 1810, Fuller noted in a letter to William Carey, "I preached a sermon to the youth last Lord's Day from 1 Thess 2:19. I think we must have had nearly one thousand. They came from all quarters. My heart's desire and prayer for them is that they may be saved." Fuller was still rejoicing when he wrote to Ryland that same year on December 28: "I hope the Lord is at work among our young people. Our Monday and Friday night meetings are much thronged." A couple of months later, he told Ryland, "The Friday evening discourses are now, and have been for nearly a year, much thronged, because they have been mostly addressed to persons under some concern about their salvation." What was happening in Fuller's church was also occurring in Baptist causes throughout the length and breadth of England and Wales.

As for the General Baptist churches, many of which were largely moribund by the late eighteenth century, a hope of renewal came through the ministry of Dan Taylor of Yorkshire. The preaching of George Whitefield, the Wesley brothers, and above all, William Grimshaw of Haworth, initially shaped Taylor's faith. By 1763, he had come to Baptist convictions. But when he sought to be baptized by a number of Particular Baptist pastors in West Yorkshire, they all refused because of his rejection of particular redemption. Eventually he found a General Baptist minister in Nottinghamshire who agreed to baptize him in the River Idle in February 1763. Taylor founded the first General Baptist church in Yorkshire at Birchcliffe that year and united himself and the church to the General Baptist denomination. As a denomination, however, the General Baptists firmly resisted Taylor's attempts to move them back toward a robust orthodoxy. So in 1770, together with a few other General Baptist pastors and churches, Taylor formed the New Connexion of General Baptists. Classical orthodox Christology, evangelical Arminianism, and a Methodist zeal for evangelism characterized this new body of Baptists. While the older General Baptists continued in the path of decline, the New Connexion thrived. When Taylor died in 1816, the number of churches in his denomination had grown to around seventy.

Across the Atlantic the Baptist churches were also experiencing significant growth in what has come to be called the Second Great Awakening. By 1790, there were roughly 68,000 Baptists in America. If we break these figures down state by state, we find that the six largest states for Baptist membership were Virginia, North Carolina, Massachusetts, South Carolina, New York, and Rhode Island. In 1750, the largest concentration of Baptists had been in Rhode Island. Clearly the heaviest concentration was shifting southward, for by 1790, 61 percent of Baptists were in the South. The Regular Baptists had twenty-nine associations and numbered some 57,436 members in 813 congregations. Ten years earlier, in 1780, the Separate Baptists had fifteen associations and numbered 9,881 members in 227 churches. By 1790, the Separate Baptists had declined to 4,022 members in eighty-one churches. The major reason for the decline was that almost half of the Separate Baptist congregations, comprising eleven of their associations, had become Regular Baptists. The great growth of the Regular Baptists thus owed much to the influx of the Separates. With regard to African-American Baptists, there were seven specifically African-American Baptist churches by 1790. The largest of these was the African Baptist Church in Savannah, Georgia, with 250 members, which George Liele founded. But most African-Americans were members of ethnically diverse churches.

Baptist Beginnings in Atlantic Canada

The late eighteenth century was also a period of revival for the fledgling Baptist cause in what became Atlantic Canada. In 1760, Ebenezer Moulton, who played a key role in Isaac Backus's coming to Baptistic convictions, arrived in Nova Scotia from Massachusetts. Moulton bears the distinction of having been the first Baptist minister to settle and serve in Canada as well as having planted the first indigenous Baptist church in Horton, Nova Scotia, in the Annapolis Valley in 1765. Now Wolfville Baptist Church, it is the oldest Baptist church in Canada. Faster-growing Baptist roots came from a more unlikely source, however. In the 1760s a number of Congregationalists found their way to Nova Scotia in pursuit of religious freedom, among them was Henry Alline, a boy of twelve when his family emigrated.

After experiencing great inner turmoil throughout his early years, Alline underwent a dramatic conversion in his mid-twenties and began to preach in 1776, just as war was breaking out over the rest of the British colonies in North America. As he itinerated throughout Nova Scotia, revival more often than not accompanied his preaching, and he came to be compared to George Whitefield, though Alline's theological sympathies were Arminian. Alline held to a grueling schedule, traveling on horseback and snowshoe through dense virgin forest or by boat to small settlements. Most of the fledgling congregations he left behind at his early death in 1784 were not committed to Baptist polity, but within a generation they embraced both Calvinism and Baptistic convictions. With only two Canadian churches bearing the name "Baptist" in 1795 (in Horton and Halifax), a veritable explosion in growth occurred over the next quarter century with more than 3,000 members in close to sixty churches by the year 1827.

For Further Study

Brewster, Paul. *Andrew Fuller: Model Pastor-Theologian*. Nashville: B&H Academic, 2010.

Brown, Raymond. *The English Baptists of the Eighteenth Century*, chapters 6–7. London: The Baptist Historical Society, 1986.

Butler, Jon. "James Ireland, John Leland, John 'Swearing Jack' Waller, and the Baptist Campaign for Religious Freedom in Revolutionary Virginia." Pages 169–84 in *Revolutionary Founders: Rebels, Radicals, and Reformers in the Making of the Nation*. Edited by Alfred F. Young, Gary B. Nash, and Ray Raphael. New York: Alfred A. Knopf, 2011.

Gardner, Robert G. "The Statistics of Early American Baptists: A Second Look," *Baptist History and Heritage* 24.4 (October 1989): 29–44.

Goodwin, Daniel C. *Into Deep Waters: Evangelical Spirituality and Maritime Calvinistic Baptist Ministers, 1790–1855*, chapters 1–4. Montreal, QC/Kingston, ON: McGill-Queen's University Press, 2010.

Haykin, Michael A. G. *Ardent Love to Jesus: English Baptists and the Experience of Revival in the Long Eighteenth Century*. Bryntirion, Bridgend, Wales: Bryntirion Press, 2013.

———. *The Armies of the Lamb: The Spirituality of Andrew Fuller*. Dundas, Ontario: Joshua Press, 2001.

Isaac, Rhys. *Transformation of Virginia, 1740–1790*. Chapel Hill: University of North Carolina Press, 1982.

McLoughlin, William G. *Isaac Backus and the American Pietistic Tradition*. Edited by Oscar Handlin. Boston: Little, Brown and Co., 1967.

Najar, Monica. *Evangelizing the South: A Social History of Church and State in Early America*. New York: Oxford University Press, 2007.

Neely, Alan. "Liele, George." Pages 400–401 in *Biographical Dictionary of Christian Missions*. Edited by Gerald H. Anderson. New York, NY: Macmillan, 1998.

Ragosta, John A. *Wellspring of Liberty: How Virginia's Religious Dissenters Helped Win the American Revolution and Secured Religious Liberty*. Oxford: Oxford University Press, 2010.

Smith, Karen. "The Liberty Not to Be a Christian: Robert Robinson (1735–1790) of Cambridge and Freedom of Conscience." Pages 151–70 in *Distinctively Baptist: Essays on Baptist History. A Festschrift in Honor of Walter B. Shurden*. Edited by Marc A. Jolley with John D. Pierce. Macon, GA: Mercer University Press, 2005.

Questions for Discussion

1 Summarize the contributions of Isaac Backus and John Leland toward the pursuit of religious liberty in America.

2 What role did Robert Robinson serve in the battle for religious liberty in England?

3. Compare and contrast the fight for religious liberty in America and England. What threatens religious liberty today? Should we be prepared to stand for religious liberty as our forebears did? Why or why not?

4. Elucidate the differing Baptist positions concerning the American Revolution. Should these Baptists have gotten involved in politics? Why or why not?

5. How did Baptists respond to the slave trade? What ethical issues are as significant for us today as slavery was for the eighteenth century?

6. Briefly outline the life and ministry of each of the following African-American Baptist leaders: George Liele, Andrew Bryan, and David George.

7. After Andrew Fuller's death, some historians regarded him and his teaching among the best things that ever happened to the Baptist cause. Would you agree or disagree? Why?

8. How was the Baptist Missionary Society formed? What did it accomplish? How has it influenced us today?

9. Describe William Carey's life and contributions. What issues does Dorothy Carey's experience raise for modern missionary couples?

10. What characterized the revival that came to transaltantic Baptist ranks in Britain, America, and Canada at the close of the eighteenth century?

Section Two

BAPTISTS IN THE

NINETEENTH CENTURY

Chapter 5

BAPTISTS AND THE WORLD BEFORE THEM

The nineteenth century was generous to Baptists in ways previous centuries were sparing. Opportunities to spread the gospel were no longer limited by governmental restriction or denominational suspicion—only by the imaginations and efforts of those willing to brave the new frontiers of the American and Canadian wilderness. Whereas previous generations of Baptists led the struggle for religious liberty, key leaders at the turn of the century suddenly found themselves able to plant churches in virtually any place they could establish a gathering. A desire to spread the gospel abroad and at home led to the formation of mission organizations and state conventions, the success of which depended on the skill and sacrifices of Baptist men and women alike. Their ability to overcome obstacles, including doctrinal controversies and societal sins, proved Baptist tenacity was more than a passing fad. In short, the transition from English sect to global movement became a reality after Baptists secured religious liberty for themselves and focused on sharing the gospel with others.

Outreach and Expansion

The numbers are telling. A decade before the nineteenth century began, Baptists in America numbered just under 70,000; by midcentury they had increased to more than 700,000. Only the Methodists, who passed one million members around the same time, matched this incredible rate of growth. Baptists surpassed Roman Catholics, Presbyterians, Congregationalists, and Episcopalians as the second largest religious body in America. Disestablishment leveled the evangelistic playing field, and Baptists welcomed the opportunity to add to their numbers without governmental interference, even though it meant opening the door for religious pluralism. The previous chapter discussed how Baptists made common cause with politicians such as James Madison and Thomas Jefferson in promoting religious liberty. In response to the Baptists of Danbury, Connecticut, Jefferson introduced his now famous phrase of "a wall of separation between church and state" to affirm his belief that religion needed to survive on its own merits apart from governmental support. Not only did this wall of separation allow Baptists to worship freely, but it also enabled Jefferson to practice his own deistic form of religion. Thus, the Baptist quest for religious liberty indirectly led to religious pluralism in America.

Thomas Jefferson's "Wall of Separation"

Believing with you that religion is a matter which lies solely between Man and his God, that he owes account to none other for his faith or his worship, that the legitimate powers of government reach actions only & not opinions, I contemplate with sovereign reverence that act of the whole American people which declared that their legislature should "make no law respecting an establishment of religion, or prohibiting the free exercise thereof," thus building a wall of separation between Church & State.

Excerpted from Thomas Jefferson, "Letter to the Danbury Baptist Association" (1802).

Gaining the freedom to worship removed an external obstacle for Baptists, but they still faced an internal impediment to growth. In contrast to Catholics, Methodists, and Presbyterians, Baptists did not baptize infants of Christian parents. Hence, membership in a Baptist church reflected more than christenings and confirmations. Ostensibly, every Baptist was a convert—one who had repented of his sins and trusted solely in the meritorious work of Christ for salvation—but conversion narratives of the early nineteenth century reveal that children rarely made professions of faith. Though they were instructed about God's commandments in the law and God's provision in Christ, typically they were not considered ready for conversion until their midteens or early twenties. When twelve-year-old Sarah Warren joined a Baptist church and related her conversion experience, the pastor and church members "expressed themselves much gratified at the relation of one so young." Baptists were virtually unanimous in affirming a personal, though not individualistic, faith. Publicly testifying before a congregation provided an additional form of assurance that one's conversion was genuine. Baptists often shared their stories of remaining under conviction of sin for years before experiencing saving faith. Such a struggle seemed to add credence to one's profession, as conversion was not understood as a mere decision one made but rather as a gift one received.

In addition to being numerically handicapped by adding only regenerate members to their churches, Baptists had the added difficulty of starting the century with minimal organizational structures beyond the local churches. While Baptist associations dotted the American landscape, state conventions and a national organization were in embryonic stages throughout the first two decades of the nineteenth century. Baptists had to act locally before they could go global with the gospel. Nevertheless, Baptist associations proved remarkably adept in aiding the nascent missionary enterprise. Though they possessed no authority over Baptist churches, associational meetings provided a forum for pastors and lay leaders alike to dream aloud regarding their responsibility to make Christ known. In 1801, for example, the Georgia and Hephzibah Baptist Associations encouraged their pastors to conduct itinerate preaching and provided specific direction on reaching frontier families with the gospel. Their planning was rewarded the following year with upward of 1,700 persons coming to faith in Christ. In nearby South Carolina, the Bethel Association reported that more than 2,000 people had been converted. Such results likely would not have materialized if local churches relied solely on their individual resources and Baptists were encouraged to find further venues of cooperation.

The reasons for Baptist success are not easy to establish, but a number of factors likely contributed. The turn of the century brought significant

Boundaries of the United States of America following the Louisiana Purchase.

changes for all Americans, including the Louisiana Purchase in 1803 and the War of 1812. The former event expanded the country's westward borders, adding more than 800,000 square miles to the American landscape. The expeditions of Meriwether Lewis (1774–1809) and William Clark (1770–1838) prompted expectations of developing territory all the way to the Pacific. Indeed, the population living west of the Alleghenies more than doubled by the second decade of the nineteenth century. The War of 1812 secured American independence, established trade routes, and bestowed a contagious sense of national identity. Baptists took full advantage of westward expansion and transatlantic trade as they planted churches in America and sent missionaries abroad.

American Baptists were also spurred to action by the activity of other Christian groups, especially the Methodists. The reality of denominational competition was admitted on all sides of the denominational divide, promoted through sermons, songs, and sayings. Itinerant evangelists sought new converts but also focused on those who had recently come to faith by way of preachers from different denominations. They not only wanted people to come to faith, but they also wanted people to practice the faith appropriately. Peter Cartwright rejoiced when Methodist itinerants reported a significant number of converts, but he lamented the fact that Baptist proselytizers nearly always followed. Congregational singing reinforced attitudes of denominational superiority, as depicted in the line of a frontier hymn: "The world, the devil and Tom Paine, have tried their force, but all in vain; they can't prevail, the reason is, the Lord defends the Methodists." Baptists responded with quaint observations of their own. One Baptist preacher quipped, "God made the world one-fourth land and three-fourths water, no doubt having baptism in view when he made it."

On a more serious note, Baptist preachers often held open debates with ministers from other denominations. Debates covered the proper subject (who) and mode (how) of baptism, along with differences in polity (church structure) and theology (notably predestination and perseverance). The nature of these open debates tempers the notion that denominational competition was unfriendly or unnecessary. Instead it marks the reality of the "democratization of Christianity," a phrase employed by historian Nathan Hatch to illustrate the manner in which Methodists and Baptists, as well as other groups, appealed to ordinary people in order to win their loyalty. Such appeals were necessary in a country where state-sponsored churches no longer existed, but this did not mean denominational leaders viewed their competitors as opponents or enemies. Baptists often opened their churches to other denominations as a courtesy on special occasions when their own buildings were too small. Some Baptists even pledged in their church covenants to allow "orderly ministers" of other denominations to preach in their pulpits.

Baptist polity played a key role in Baptists' nationwide expansion. Their emphasis on local church autonomy facilitated the founding of congregations without delay or interference from denominational superiors. Congregational polity and local church autonomy also contributed to the rise of Baptist churches among the African-American population. Though still enslaved, they experienced moments of freedom in Baptist churches by selecting their own pastors, voting on membership matters, and structuring their own worship services. Such freedom was limited since most African-American Baptist churches operated with the oversight of white church leaders. The First Colored Baptist Church of Savannah, Georgia, for example, was founded and led by slaves but remained accountable to white overseers. Slaves built the church but did not own the property, which belonged to Jonathan Bryan, the owner of slave-pastor Andrew Bryan. This church thrived nevertheless, consisting of 800 members by 1800.

First African Baptist Church of Savannah, Georgia (est. 1777);
formerly the First Colored Baptist Church of Savannah.

Most African-American Baptists complied with their white masters in matters of church organization, although a few challenged the standing order. In Harlem, New York, for example, a group of Ethiopian visitors were so offended upon being told they were required to sit in the balcony apart from white congregants that they left the service and formed their own church. The Abyssinian (meaning, Ethiopian) Baptist Church, formed in 1804, became the first independent African-American church in the North. In 1810 nearly forty independent black Baptist churches existed in major cities, including Boston, Philadelphia, and Detroit, with hundreds of integrated churches throughout the South and West. By the end of the nineteenth century, more African-Americans belonged to Baptist churches than to any other denomination.

Another way congregational polity and local church autonomy contributed to rapid Baptist expansion was by fast-tracking the ordination of ministers. Young men who sensed a call to preach could be ordained to the ministry prior to, or even without, obtaining a theological education. The method of affirming a person's call to preach was relatively simple. Leaders in the church sought out young men who demonstrated pastoral potential. They began serving as licentiates, or pastoral assistants, who shadowed the pastor and occasionally preached in his absence. The path to ordination involved meeting with a small group of pastors, a presbytery, who examined the doctrinal commitment and moral qualifications of a candidate for ministry. The local church confirmed or denied the person's sense of calling by congregational vote. This process enabled Baptists to stock their churches with pastors much faster than other denominations that required their candidates to undergo formal theological training, a process that often took years to complete.

Another factor contributing to Baptist expansion in America was the influence of a revivalistic culture, as leaders encouraged individual conversions in large group settings. Though theologians differ on the merits of revival versus revivalism (the former being essentially spontaneous, while the latter was planned in advance), evangelicals in the nineteenth century clearly added a revivalistic twist to their practice of evangelism. Preachers and listeners alike could get swept up in the excitement of the crowd and at times exhibit behavior that seemed more emotionally driven than spiritually based. The most famous example of this approach is the 1801 Cane Ridge Revival. Sparked by the fiery preaching of James McGready and fueled by the passion of Barton Stone, the revival attracted thousands of participants to Bourbon County, Kentucky. They arrived in covered wagons to hear a word from the Lord and share in the Lord's Supper. What they were accustomed to and what they encountered were two different things altogether. Instead of hearing learned sermons from educated Presbyterian pastors, the swelling crowds necessitated a large number of preachers, and the exhorters soon included Methodists and Baptists, males and females, at times preaching from tree stumps with little or no advance notice. Observers began to experience, apparently spontaneously, various spiritual "exercises" called "the jerks" (bodily agitations) or "the barks" (vocal animations). Bernard Weisberger aptly describes how the Cane Ridge Revival suited frontier residents: "The frontiersman . . . lived, worked and died hard. It was natural that he should convert hard; that he should cry aloud wrestling with his guilt; and that he should leap and twist and shout in rejoicing over his forgiveness."

Reflections on Camp Meeting "Exercises"

It was not unusual to have a large proportion of a congregation prostrate on the floor; and in some instances they have lost the use of their limbs. No distinct articulation could be heard from those immediately by: Screams, cries, groans, songs, shouts and hosannas, notes of grief and notes of joy, all heard at the same time, made a heavenly confusion, a sort of indescribable concert. Even the wicked and unenlightened were astonished and said, the Lord hath done great things for his people. . . . At first many of the preachers did not approve of this kind of work. They thought it extravagant. Others found it fire from heaven. It is not unworthy of notice that in those congregations where the preachers encouraged these exercises to much extent the work was more extensive and greater numbers were added.

Excerpted from Robert Semple, *A History of the Rise and Progress of Baptists in Virginia* (1810).

The revival continued for several days but had a longer-lasting impact on American evangelicalism, increasing the expectation of future revivals and highlighting the role of experience in conversion. Though originating in the South, frontier revivals spread throughout North America even to Upper Canada, with several hundred meetings annually reported a decade after the Cane Ridge revival. Some Baptists, including Henry Holcombe of Savannah, Georgia, were convinced the revivals signified that the millennial reign of Christ was near. But as the revivals passed and the millennium did not follow, many Baptists began looking wistfully to the past, comparing their uneventful state of existence to the exciting days of old. Other Baptists were more hesitant to embrace the revivals as a work of the Spirit, suggesting that fantastic outward displays were merely instances of emotional release. Even so, experience, not mere mental acquiescence, proved central to the Baptist understanding of conversion.

Canadian Baptist work proceeded at a much slower pace. Baptist missionary Asahel Morse described Upper Canada in the first decade of the nineteenth century as "a dismal region of moral darkness and the shadow of death" where most families possessed "no books, not even a Bible." Ontario, for example, had only fifteen churches and ten pastors in 1820, despite a quarter century of Baptist efforts in that area. By mid-century, Baptists in Upper and Lower Canada numbered just over 20,000; yet there was no theological college, denominational structure, organized church planting effort, or denominational newspaper. Methodists were far more influential during this period, capturing over 30 percent of Upper Canada's population by the first quarter of the nineteenth century.

Some of the same factors that spurred Baptist expansion in America limited it in Canada. The War of 1812 hindered Baptist migration into British-controlled Canada, as many preferred the separation of church and state in America. Baptist churches in Canada divided between their preferences for American or British customs. Canadian Baptists were also reluctant to embrace the associational principle, preferring to emphasize local church autonomy and guarding against any semblance of interdependence. Adding to their sense of isolation from one another was a controversy over open and closed communion. The majority of Canadian Baptists favored closed communion, but an influx of Scottish Baptist immigrants introduced an open communion perspective. While some historians have made more of this division than necessary, unity in missions and evangelism was muted, if not entirely prohibited, by differences over communion. Canadian Baptists were every bit as dedicated to planting churches as American Baptists but did not find their institutional strength until the latter half of the nineteenth century.

Farmer-Preachers and Foreign Missions

Preacher on horse back.

Historians have long pointed to the advantages frontier religion afforded the Baptist movement, in particular the work of "farmer-preachers." Since Baptists at the turn of the century had few educational opportunities and Baptist churches required little beyond a sense of divine call for their preachers to be ordained, the majority of their pastors were bi-vocational. Farming was the vocation most Baptist preachers used to sustain themselves, as it was the vocation of nearly 90 percent of the nation. Baptist farmer-preachers could plant churches virtually anywhere on the frontier, supporting themselves by taming the land and teaching the Bible. Unlike those whom Brooks Holifield has dubbed the "Gentlemen Theologians," city pastors who were more educated and sophisticated, Baptist farmer-preachers gained the respect of common rural Americans because they could take care of themselves while also taking care of their congregations. This ability to live off the land and not off the people fit well with the "rugged individualism" mentality of the Jacksonian era. As such, it was possible for a Baptist preacher to move with his entire congregation to a new frontier location, as William Screven did when relocating his church from Maine to South Carolina in 1696 (see chap. 2).

Baptist Itinerant Ministry on the American Frontier

Being obliged to ride in the night, on Friday night I got lost. The roads in this part of our country are none of them fenced, and are mostly through wood; I had to go in that night by roads, but little travelled—missed the way, got out of roads, at length into mere paths, and ultimately, lost the path—found myself alone in a dreary wilderness, unable to discover the point of compass; totally ignorant which way to direct my course, to find any road or habitation of men. I stopped and besought the Lord to lead me out—rose from my supplications and attempted to advance. In less perhaps, than two minutes, certainly in less than five, fell into the road which conducted me to the place that I calculated to reach that night, at which I arrived about 1 o'clock.

Excerpted from Luther Rice, *Journal* (September 12, 1819).

Technically the American frontier of the early nineteenth century refers to land west of the Alleghany Mountains, but practically speaking the frontier was any place where one had to plan days in advance to get produce from a market. Methodist preachers became famous as circuit riders, traveling throughout the frontier with little concern for distance or inclement weather. Methodist and Baptist church planters experienced remarkable challenges, especially in the Canadian landscape. John Winterbotham described one mission group as traversing parts of Canada "all the way from the Niagara River to Long Point, across swamps, over rivers and creeks, and through trackless woods, thus evincing their love for the souls of dying men." Baptist itinerants frequently got lost since roads were few and the ones that did exist often included intersections with no directional markers. They also braved the danger of possible attack from Native Americans, who were understandably protective of their land. Still, an itinerant preacher often found himself welcome in the homes of strangers who were eager to hear news from the outside world and tales of daring adventures along the way. The Baptist farmer-preacher could multiply his influence by simultaneously serving as many as four congregations, each meeting one Sunday a month, and between harvest and seedtime traveling by horseback to plant additional churches on the frontier.

Baptists on the frontier were not the only ones who had to sustain themselves while searching for converts. William Carey committed himself to doing the same nearly a decade before the nineteenth century began, working as a shoe mender, the manager of an indigo factory, and a language instructor for the British government at Fort William College. Moreover, he reduced the need for additional income by establishing a general fund for missionaries to draw from and by sharing a home with his missionary colleagues.

His meager lifestyle was also reflected in the early returns on his missionary efforts. During the time Baptists in Kentucky were reflecting on the great revival, Carey had just assumed responsibility for discipling his first convert in Serampore. In 1801, Carey published the first edition of the Bengali New Testament. Another eight years passed before he completed the Bengali Old Testament (1809). As discussed in chapter 4, Carey did not complete this work on his own as he belonged to the "Serampore Trio," which included Joshua Marshman and William Ward. Together they adopted a form of agreement, which detailed their own sense of mission, and together they endured difficulties, such as the destruction of their print shop by fire in 1812. Due to Carey's efforts and the remarkable perseverance of those on his team, portions of the Bible were made available in over forty languages before the first forty years of the nineteenth century had expired.

The Serampore Form of Agreement (1805)

1. To set an infinite value upon men's souls.
2. To acquaint ourselves with the snares which hold the minds of the people.
3. To abstain from whatever deepens India's prejudice against the gospel.
4. To watch for every chance of doing the people good.
5. To preach "Christ crucified" as the grand means of conversion.
6. To esteem and treat Indians always as our equals.
7. To guard and build up "the hosts that may be gathered."
8. To cultivate their spiritual gifts, ever pressing upon them their missionary obligation, since Indians only can win India for Christ.
9. To labor unceasingly in biblical translation.
10. To be instant in the nurture of personal religion.
11. To give ourselves without reserve to the Cause, "not counting even the clothes we wear our own."

Carey's commitment to self-sustenance mirrored that of frontier Baptists in America, but his dedication to cooperative mission efforts had a more pronounced impact on the denomination. His position on believer's baptism helped lead a husband and wife missionary team, Adoniram and Ann Judson, along with their missionary colleague Luther Rice, to abandon their belief in the validity of infant baptism. Their transition from Congregationalist to Baptist principles transformed their newly adopted denomination into a mission-sending organization of global proportions.

Ann Judson
(1789–1826)

Adoniram Judson
(1788–1850)

Adoniram Judson first met Ann Hasseltine while dining at her father's home in 1810 during a meeting of the American Board of Commissioners for Foreign Missions, the first organization in the United States dedicated to foreign missions. Adoniram was struck by Ann's beauty, but she did not respond immediately to his admiration. Eventually he won her over with his desire to share the gospel with people who had never heard it before. Ann decided to marry Adoniram not based on "attachment to an earthly object," she wrote, "but with a sense of obligation to God, and with a full conviction of [the marriage's] being a call in providence, and consequently, my duty."

Adoniram and Ann Judson set sail for India as Congregationalist missionaries on February 19, 1812, just two weeks after their wedding. In anticipation of meeting William Carey, Adoniram began studying his Greek New Testament in order to adduce proof that Baptists were incorrect in their insistence on believer's baptism. Ironically (or providentially according to the Judsons), Adoniram concluded instead that infant baptism was erroneous and believer's baptism was biblical. Adoniram adopted the Baptist position sooner than Ann, but her change of mind was no less deliberate. She had been entirely willing to sail across the world to share the gospel, but she was adamantly opposed to denying infant baptism even as her husband began to do so: "I have tried to have him give it up, and rest satisfied in his old sentiments, and frequently told him, that if he became a Baptist, I would not."

**Adoniram Judson Asks Permission to Propose
to Ann Hasseltine and Take Her Overseas**

I have now to ask, whether you can consent to part with your daughter early next spring, to see her no more in this world; whether you can consent to her departure, and her subjection to the hardships and sufferings of a missionary life; whether you can consent to her exposure to the dangers of the ocean; to the fatal influence of the southern climate of India; to every kind of want and distress; to degradation, insult, persecution, and perhaps a violent death. Can you consent to all this, for the sake of him who left his heavenly home, and died for her and for you; for the sake of perishing, immortal souls; for the sake of Zion, and the glory of God? Can you consent to all this, in hope of soon meeting your daughter in the world of glory, with the crown of righteousness, brightened with the acclamations of praise which shall redound to her Savior from heathens saved, through her means, from eternal woe and despair?

Excerpted from a letter from Adoniram Judson to John Hasseltine (1810).

Her change of mind came about through reading Scripture. Ann embraced believer's baptism, knowing that doing so involved great personal cost. An avid letter writer, she pleaded with a friend, "Can you, my dear Nancy, still love me, still desire to hear from me, when I tell you I have become a Baptist?" Her concern about people cutting ties with her and Adoniram was legitimate as the mission organization that funded their trip was a Congregationalist enterprise that adhered to infant baptism. In just over six months Ann Judson had left her family, her home, and her denomination without any guarantee of support while living in a strange country.

The Judsons were not left completely by themselves, however. They were well received by William Carey, baptized by his associate William Ward, and helped immensely by their missionary colleague Luther Rice, who returned to America to raise financial support for them from Baptist churches. Like the Judsons, he too had changed his view of infant baptism upon arriving in India, and each of the missionaries wrote letters of resignation to the Board of Commissioners. Unlike the Judsons, however, Rice never returned to the foreign mission field. This decision was not one of preference but necessity, as Rice soon discovered his effectiveness in marshaling Baptist support for missions. He had the advantage of being able to recount firsthand the need for missionaries in a foreign land, and he had the initiative to unite Baptists on a national level. Instead of appealing for support on a local level or merely stitching together interest from Baptist associations, Rice envisioned delegates from every state participating as a national body. The result was the General Missionary Convention of the Baptist Denomination in the United States of America for Foreign Missions.

Triennial Convention and Organizational Conflict

On May 18, 1814, the General Missionary Convention gathered for the first time at the First Baptist Church of Philadelphia. Richard Furman, a denominational statesman from South Carolina, was elected president of the convention, and Thomas Baldwin of Massachusetts was the first corresponding secretary. The confluence of leaders from the South and North working together for missions underscored the uniqueness of this gathering as the first national organization of Baptists in the United States. Thirty years later the convention mirrored the country's divide between the North and South when it split over the issue of slavery. Furman's proslavery arguments became an important part of the Southern Baptist rationale for leaving the convention.

The convention's delegates assembled every three years, leading to its shortened title of the "Triennial Convention." The choice of the term *convention* was significant as the original delegates differed sharply on the overall purpose of the organization. A convention implied that churches would participate through delegates who would decide on the best way to fund

First Baptist Church of Philadelphia, Pennsylvania (est. 1746).

multiple ministries, including international and home missions, as well as publishing and educational endeavors. The alternative, a triennial society, would be comprised of individuals who subscribed to and supported one specific cause—in this case, international missions. Either approach would have served the Judsons well.

This decision did not come easily, nor did it remain permanent. The 1814 meeting in Philadelphia was a Baptist version of the Constitutional Convention where extremely bright but opinionated men entered with a sense of omniscience but left with an agreement borne from compromise. Thirty-three delegates attended, half of which were from Philadelphia. At the heart of the discussion was the balance of power. William Staughton and Thomas Baldwin had in mind a societal approach, in part to protect the autonomy of local churches. If individuals could participate on their own recognizance, then churches need not fear losing their decision-making capacity, Staughton and Baldwin believed. Luther Rice and Richard Furman preferred a more centralized approach that would generate support in broader fashion. Building around churches instead of individuals promised wider interest through a shared identity, thereby increasing denominational loyalty. Francis Wayland, who later served as president of Brown University (1827–55), further illustrates the difficulty of choosing between these options as he initially supported the convention plan but later argued for the societal plan.

The initial agreement favored the societal model in terms of individuals participating, but the group incorporated the convention element of sponsoring multiple ministries through a general fund at the 1817 meeting, when home missions and theological education were added to the constitutional tasks of the Triennial Convention. The removal of these two ministries in 1826 and their subsequent placement under separate societies reveals the continued disagreement over which method of organization worked best for Baptists.

Triennial Convention delegates agreed to support the Judsons, sending them $1,000 as a first installment. Nevertheless, Adoniram and Ann had a difficult decade. They buried their firstborn son in 1816, the same year Adoniram began losing his eyesight due to extended periods of study. He regained his sight but lost his freedom in 1824 when the Burmese government imprisoned all white males under suspicion of being spies for the British. Though Ann regularly visited Adoniram, their time together was cut short when she died in July 1826, less than a year after his release. Their youngest daughter, Maria, died the following year. In the midst of imprisonment and death, Adoniram had at this time fewer than two dozen converts on account of his missionary efforts.

Luther Rice was still a missionary of sorts, though one approved by the convention to elicit support for missions as he traveled across America. His impact on Baptists was immediate. Within a year's time he garnered the support of more than 100 associations in connection with the Triennial

Convention. That same year, 1815, Rice met John Mason Peck, a pastor from New York who had an interest in missions but was uncertain about his ability to serve on the international field. Together, Rice and Peck determined to use the Triennial Convention to conduct missions on the American frontier. At the second meeting of the Triennial Convention (1817), John and Sarah "Sally" Peck were appointed as home missionaries to the Missouri Territory, along with James Welch. Their four-month journey to Saint Louis, which would have been trying for any individual or family, was all the more impressive as Sally was in her final trimester of pregnancy when they arrived.

From a financial standpoint the addition of home missions meant appropriating part of the convention's missionary funds for domestic purposes; from a practical standpoint it meant attention to missions was now split between Burma and Saint Louis. Although the Pecks proved themselves to be as dedicated to the mission field as Carey and the Judsons, the strain of adding additional ministries proved to be more than the convention, still in its infancy, could withstand. Support for home mission work was officially discontinued in 1820. Peck continued his missionary labors though, drawing support from local organizations until 1832, when he and Jonathan Going secured enough Baptist interest to form the American Baptist Home Mission Society (ABHMS). As a society its purpose was singular: "The great object of this Society shall be to promote the preaching of the gospel in North America." In less than ten years, the ABHMS appointed nearly 100 missionaries and established more than 500 new churches. The Triennial Convention

The Need for Ministerial Education

Is not this apparent to persons of common discernment; and are not the defects in language and knowledge, lamented by their friends, while they become the matter of scoff and derision to their enemies? Do not even children, who have obtained a tolerable portion of regular education, see these defects in them; and when they have made a little advance in knowledge and experience, do they not begin to discover them themselves, and feel embarrassed, especially when they have to speak before an enlightened audience? . . . When entrance into the ministry is made so easy that any person with warm passions, apparent piety, and little fluency of speech, can easily get into the ministerial character and work just as he is . . . the consequences of these sentiments and their influence in practice is that in a very large portion of our churches our ministers have but little of the improvement which is to be obtained by rational means.

Excerpted from Richard Furman, John Roberts, and Joseph Cook,
To the Different Associations of the State Baptist Convention of South Carolina, 1820.

also decided to focus on one ministry at a time, once members came to terms with the failure of its first educational endeavor, Columbian College.

Columbian College and the Great Reversal

As previously mentioned, Baptists were well aware of their educational deficiencies. At the turn of the century, a standard ministerial education consisted of time spent under the watchful care of a senior minister who opened his home to study with one or two pastoral prospects. Many farmer-preachers studied as they worked, committing Scripture to memory with Bibles attached to their plows. Knowledge of Hebrew and Greek was rare among frontier preachers, though some such as William Calmes Buck taught themselves. (He was baptized at the age of eighteen and began preaching that same year, but he did not learn Hebrew and Greek until after turning fifty.) Educational pursuits were more than personal ambitions; they became means of evangelism as well. The ability to engage in polemical theology with educated pastors of other denominations was needed all the more as public debates became more popular, taking on an aura of theological entertainment. The religious free market beckoned Baptists to enhance their intellectual reputation by founding and supporting their own schools. However, their intentions often outpaced their experience, leading to a combination of success and failure.

As recounted in chapter 3, Baptist hopes for an educated ministry emerged in 1764 with the founding of the College of Rhode Island, now Brown University. It had strong support from the Philadelphia Association, was capably led by James Manning, and was financially sound due to a generous gift from the family of Nicholas Brown. Columbian College, begun by the Triennial Convention, became deficient in all three areas despite initial signs of success. Rice's vision for a national Baptist college was translated into action almost as quickly as the thought crossed his mind. As he began raising money for missions, he determined that an educated ministry was essential if missionaries were to be successful. At

Dr. William Staughton
(1770–1829)

the 1817 Triennial Convention, Rice led delegates to adopt a plan for the school, ostensibly as a separate enterprise from the ongoing mission work at home and abroad. Nearly fifty acres of land were purchased in Washington, DC, and by 1820 the first building was completed. William Staughton was a natural choice for principal, having been educated in England and having already founded a theological institute in Philadelphia.

Nevertheless, the demise of Columbian College was in the making by the fourth meeting of the Triennial Convention (1823). A nationwide financial crisis hindered Rice's ability to raise funds for both missions and education. Rice also lost the trust of board members when he failed to report his financial activities to the convention, due, in his words, to his "incessant labors" on their behalf. Though he was eventually exonerated of financial wrongdoing, the accumulation of debt and distrust opened the door for key leaders to leave the college. Staughton departed in order to assume the presidency of Georgetown College, though he died before serving in that capacity.

The Triennial Convention's decision to discontinue educational endeavors was dubbed the "Great Reversal" after delegates voted in 1826 to return to a society method wherein they exclusively supported overseas missions. Rice continued raising funds for Columbian College independently of the convention, but it took an act of Congress to save the school with a grant of $25,000 provided in 1832. Baptists later succeeded in other educational endeavors, but the school begun by Luther Rice was not part of their future. By 1904, Columbian College had become George Washington University and was formally discontinued as a Baptist institution.

The General Union and Communion Controversies

Baptists in Great Britain faced similar difficulties when they attempted to unite local interests with larger cooperative purposes. The formation of the General Union in 1813 (renamed the Baptist Union in 1832) was the brainchild of Joseph Ivimey, whose 1811 essay "Union Essential to Prosperity" provided a foundation for Baptist cooperation. Though Particular Baptists in England were historically reluctant to support organizational efforts that might challenge the independence of the local church, notable Baptist leaders such as John Rippon and James Hinton offered their support. The first meeting of the General Union took place at Ivimey's church in London, where the sixty delegates in attendance agreed that the organization should exist for "the promotion of the cause of Christ in general; and the interests of the denomination in particular; with a primary view to the encouragement and support of the Baptist Mission." Like the aims of the Triennial Convention, the goals of the General Union were almost too broad to be realistic. In addition to promoting Sunday schools, itinerant preaching, and fund-raising for church buildings, the annual meetings were designed to address "whatever relates to the real interests of the denomination at home and abroad."

The union's ambitions exceeded the interests of Particular Baptists, and support waned for the first fifty years of its existence. In addition to the independent spirit of Particular Baptists and broadly defined focus of the General union, theological issues hindered immediate connectionalism. Though Ivimey promoted the General Union as a way to unite Baptists, he was opposed to open communion, which at the time was being promoted by Robert Hall Jr. In a treatise entitled *On Terms of Communion with a Particular View to the Case of Baptists and Paedobaptists* (1816), Hall argued that a Christian in good standing with his or her church should not be barred from sharing in the Lord's Supper with other Baptists, even if the person had been baptized as an infant. He contended that baptism and the Lord's Supper were not so inherently connected as to demand a perfect understanding of the former before participating in the latter and that the only scriptural reason for barring a Christian from communion was a moral lapse unaccompanied by genuine repentance. Though Hall held to believer's baptism, he contended that believers holding other views should be admitted to the Lord's Supper.

Defending Open Communion

The right of rejecting those whom Christ has received; of refusing the communion of eminently holy men, on account of unessential differences of opinion, is not the avowed tenant of any sect or community in Christendom, with the exception of the majority of the Baptists, who, while they are at variance with the whole world on a point of such magnitude, are loud in accusing their brethren of singularity. If we have presumed to resist the current of opinion, it is on a subject of no practical moment; it respects an obscure and neglected corner of theology; while their singularity is replete with most alarming consequences, destroys at once the unity of the church, and pronounces a sentence of excommunication on the whole Christian world.

Excerpted from Robert Hall Jr., *On Terms of Communion* (1816).

Hall's detractors took issue with his assertion that believer's baptism and communion were not closely related, nor did they concur with his belief that unity in the church was damaged by Baptists who held to their convictions. Joseph Kinghorn published a response to Hall titled *Baptism a Term of Communion at the Lord's Supper* (1820). Kinghorn acknowledged his admiration and respect for Hall, noting that he would "readily bow to him with the greatest deference" given his influence among Baptists in England. However, Kinghorn would not defer to him in the matter of who should be admitted to the Lord's Table. If infant baptism prevented a person from joining a Baptist church, then the same person should not be allowed to take communion in a Baptist setting where membership ties were being strengthened.

Particular Baptists did not readily embrace the practice of open communion. In 1829, the Suffolk and Norfolk Strict Association was formed, consisting of area churches that stood opposed not only to open communion but also to innovative evangelistic techniques, which they associated with Fullerism (see chap. 4). In 1841, the Strict Communion Society was formed in London, another sign that some Baptists were concerned about losing their distinctive Baptist beliefs in the name of unity. Yet a change of opinion was underway. Though fewer than 10 percent of the Particular Baptist churches practiced open communion in 1824, by 1857 even Kinghorn's former church removed baptism as a prerequisite to communion and before the end of the century closed communionists were squarely on the defensive.

Periodicals and Publicity

Baptist controversies, as well as the stories of missionaries like the Careys and the Judsons, were made public through the advent of religious periodicals. Letters written by missionaries reached a large audience when published through Baptist periodicals and played a significant role in raising money for missions. In keeping with revivalism's emphasis on experiential religion, such letters enabled Baptists at home to feel the need of missions abroad. Baptists in England began publishing *The Baptist Annual Register* in 1790, with Baptists in America not far behind with the *Massachusetts Baptist Missionary Magazine* in 1803. The Triennial Convention incorporated the latter as its own periodical in 1817,

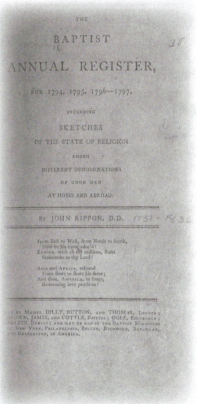

The Baptist Annual Register *(est. 1790).*

dispensing with its local title and renaming it the *American Baptist Magazine*. Luther Rice purchased *The Columbian Star*, a weekly periodical emanating from Washington, DC, later picked up by Jesse Mercer and rebranded as *The Christian Index*. Mercer donated *The Christian Index* to the Georgia Baptist Convention, and it is still in publication to this day.

Religious newspapers connected Baptists in an early version of the information highway. In addition to missionary letters, Baptist periodicals published sermons, doctrinal instruction, financial appeals, and news of revivals. Editors were thus able to set the tone for conversation among Baptists. However, they soon discovered that readers of their periodicals had their own opinions as they received letters to the editor seeking to supplement or correct what had appeared in print. Baptists found that they were able to shape public opinion and even governmental policy through the print medium. For example, Andrew Fuller used the *Baptist Magazine* to generate a petition for Parliament, which garnered more than 50,000 signatures, calling for protection of Baptist missionary interests.

Connectionalism and State Conventions

As Baptists connected through missions and media, they also reinforced their ties locally. Itinerant societies continued to develop, and participants often reported great success. English Particular Baptists formed The Society for the Encouragement and Support of Itinerant Preaching (1797) for Londoners, and a Northern Itinerant Society was formed in 1809 to reach areas

Women's "Mites" for Foreign Missions

We have no doubt, our sisters feel with us, that it is our duty on these occasions, particularly to bear on our hearts the ministers of the gospel; especially our Missionary brethren. When we consider how much wisdom, prudence, faith, patience and grace they need, to qualify them for the office; how much they need the supports and comforts of religion in their own souls, in order to render them faithful to the souls of others; and how necessary the influences of the Holy Spirit, to accompany their labors, we must feel culpable if we are not engaged in "holding up their hands." . . . Should every Christian in the United States contribute the inconsiderable sum of 25 cents per year to this purpose [of Bible translation in India], some thousands of dollars would be annually devoted to aid a work of the greatest magnitude in which it is possible for mortals to be engaged. And whoever bestows a mite to that object, will no doubt be instrumental of conveying a blessing to the latest posterity.

Excerpted from Mary Webb, "Address," Boston Female Society (1813).

around Lincolnshire. Baptists in America and Canada developed their own itinerant ministries, led by Isaac Backus in New England and continuing with the founding of the Massachusetts Bay Missionary Society in 1802. The lines between domestic and international missions blurred as work that began in New England, New York, and Pennsylvania expanded into Upper Canada, Nova Scotia, and New Brunswick by 1804.

Cooperation extended beyond the Baptist camp as societal participants included members of other denominations. The Boston Female Society for Missionary Purposes was open to both Baptist and Congregationalist women who pledged their "mites" (so named after the widow's offering in Mark 12:42 KJV) to support missionaries. Not only was this the first women's missionary society formed in America; it demonstrated that physical limitations did not preclude one from having a global impact. Mary Webb had been paralyzed since age five but served as secretary-treasurer of the BFMS for half a century. From her home, sitting in her wheelchair, Webb wrote thousands of letters raising awareness and financial support for missions. She noted that members of the society were not trying to render themselves important but useful, alluding to the concern of some that these women had overstepped their proper boundaries. "We have no wish to go out of our province," she wrote, "nor do we undertake to become teachers in Israel." Instead, she and her colaborers felt obligated to share the gospel they had received with those who had not yet heard the good news. Men on the mission field were deeply indebted to her and other females who sacrificially gave their time, resources, and leadership skills.

Baptists also crossed denominational lines through their support of the American Board of Commissioners for Foreign Missions before they began to support the Judsons. Moreover, Baptists joined believers of other denominations to support the American Bible Society (ABS), formed in 1816 with the purpose of publishing and distributing Bibles throughout the world. Baptists were also a sizable constituency in the American Tract Society (ATS), formed in 1825. The impact of these multidenominational efforts was phenomenal. The ABS and the ATS printed more religious literature in the middle of the nineteenth century than all other American publishing companies combined.

State conventions provided yet another means of Baptist connectionalism. The first Baptist state convention was formed in South Carolina (1821), followed by Georgia (1822), Virginia (1823), Alabama (1823), and North Carolina (1830). The idea of state conventions was a natural outgrowth of associational work, but the prospects for success were not immediately apparent. Distance between churches hindered attempts at cooperation, and interest in state conventions easily waned apart from the prodding of leading pastors in each state. The potential of a state convention was seldom recognized until it became operational. Richard Furman's role in the formation of the State Convention of Baptists in South Carolina illustrates this point well.

The Charleston Association made the first proposal for a South Carolina state convention in 1819, but two years passed before the convention assembled, and even then a mere nine delegates attended. Furman had previously served as president of the Triennial Convention and was president of the Charleston Association. His experience at the national and local levels provided him with a platform for exerting his influence regionally. Consequently, Furman was invited to serve on two committees, one that was appointed to prepare a constitution and another to deliver an address explaining the purpose of a state convention to churches and associations throughout the state. When detractors raised the perennial concerns of losing

Richard Furman
(1755–1825)

local church autonomy, Furman reassured them that the convention was not designed, nor did it desire, to assert authority over churches. When objections were raised about the potential mismanagement of funds under a convention system, Furman reassured his constituents that their gifts would be directed appropriately through a constitutional provision. Most importantly, he succeeded in securing the twin emphases of missions and education as central to the purpose of the state convention, while including subsidiary emphases such as promoting Sunday schools, providing ministerial support, and disseminating information to the churches. By incorporating education and missions together, Furman enabled his state convention to do what associations were not capable of doing on their own and what the Triennial Convention was no longer willing to do. His organizational plan of connecting local churches to associations and state conventions without sacrificing their autonomy provided a template for Baptist cooperation on the state and national levels. These connections enabled Baptists to embrace national, and ultimately global, purposes.

Cooperation Among African-American Baptists

The ability to organize for cooperative purposes was not the sole property of affluent or majority Baptists. African-American Baptists were also aware that their discipleship involved taking the gospel beyond their communities. Chapter 4 discussed the life of George Leile, who relocated to Jamaica ten years before William Carey set sail from England, becoming the first Baptist foreign missionary. In large part due to Leile's missionary successes, the British Baptist Missionary Society sent twenty-five missionaries to Jamaica between 1814 and 1831. The Jamaica Baptist Association was formed in 1814 and reported more than 7,000 Baptists in the nation by 1829. Leile became the first of many African-American Baptists who served as foreign missionaries.

Lott Carey was another former slave whose impact on the Baptist movement defied the obstacles he had to overcome. He worked for the tobacco industry in Richmond, Virginia, and purchased his freedom with money he earned by selling leftover bits of tobacco he gathered from the warehouse floor. In 1807, he converted to Christianity upon hearing a sermon on John 3:16, and his heart was immediately set on reaching Africans and African-Americans with the gospel. A white Baptist deacon, William Crane, taught him to read, and Carey later became an assistant pastor for black members of the First Baptist Church of Richmond. Deacon Crane also sponsored the Richmond African Baptist Missionary Society, founded in 1815 and led by Carey and another former slave, Collin Teague.

Lott Carey
(1780–1820)

A movement to repatriate former slaves to their native countries in order to alleviate racial tension coalesced in 1816 with the formation of the American Colonization Society. Carey believed that moving to Africa presented an unparalleled opportunity to spread the gospel where there was little Christian impact. He was also aware that white missionaries did not typically survive the tropical African climate as many died from disease. Carey and Teague left America for Africa on January 16, 1821, and settled in the newly founded country of Liberia, so named in honor of the liberty its citizens possessed.

Carey founded the First Baptist Church of Monrovia and throughout his life-time continued to establish churches, build schools, provide administrative leadership, and even practice medicine. His legacy was later honored with the formation of the Lott Carey Foreign Mission Convention (1897) and the Lott Carey Mission School (1908).

In addition to participating in mission societies, African-American Baptists began forming associations, beginning with the Providence Baptist Association in 1834 and the Association of Regular Baptist Churches of Color in Ohio in 1836. By this time African-Americans had found their collective voice in protesting the evils of slavery, which understandably provoked their associations to promote social reform alongside the cause of missions. Denominational organization among white Baptists, however, was hampered by significant tension in subsequent years as questions relating to slavery and missions ended much of the official cooperation between northern and southern Baptists.

For Further Study

Anderson, Courtney. *To the Golden Shore: The Life of Adoniram Judson*. Reprint ed. Valley Forge: Judson, 1987.

Benedict, David. *Fifty Years Among the Baptists*. New York: Sheldon and Company, 1860.

Boles, John. *The Great Revival: 1787–1805*. Lexington, KY: University Press of Kentucky, 1972.

Conkin, Paul K. *Cane Ridge: America's Pentecost*. Madison, WI: University of Wisconsin Press, 1990.

Duesing, Jason G., ed. *Adoniram Judson: A Bicentennial Appreciation of the Pioneer American Missionary*. Nashville: B&H Academic, 2012.

Halbrooks, G. Thomas. "Francis Wayland and 'The Great Reversal.'" *Foundations* 20.4 (July–September, 1977): 196–214.

Hatch, Nathan. *The Democratization of American Christianity*. New Haven: Yale University Press, 1991.

Holifield, E. Brooks. *The Gentlemen Theologians: American Theology in Southern Culture, 1795–1860*. Durham: Duke University Press, 1978.

Rogers, James. *Richard Furman: Life and Legacy*. Macon, GA: Mercer University Press, 2001.

Shannon, David T., Sr., with Julia Frazier White and Deborah Van Broekhoven. *George Liele's Life and Legacy: An Unsung Hero*. Macon, GA: Mercer University Press, 2013.

Questions for Discussion

1. Why did disestablishment necessitate an increase in evangelistic efforts among Baptists? How did the implementation of religious liberty open the door for religious pluralism? In what ways do you find religious liberty helping or hindering Baptists to spread and practice their faith today?

2. What factors contributed to numerical growth among American Baptists during this period? Do you find the debates between Baptists and other denominations appealing or appalling as it relates to "denominational competition"?

3. Describe the lives and contributions of Adoniram and Ann Judson. Have you ever changed your mind on a theological issue that changed the course of your life? If so, explain.

4. How did local Baptist churches relate to one another prior to the Triennial Convention? In what areas can Baptist churches cooperate together today without losing their local church autonomy?

5. How did the decision to include home missions and education affect the outcome of the Triennial Convention? In what ways does this period in Baptist history underscore the experimental phase of Baptist cooperation?

6. Discuss the level of pastoral training and educational opportunities of Baptists in the early nineteenth century. In what ways did Baptists like Richard Furman express a sense of shame in this regard?

7. Describe cooperative efforts in Britain during the early nineteenth century. What factors hindered the early progress of the General Union?

8. What issues were at stake between British Baptists and their understanding of communion? Do you find Robert Hall's or Joseph Kinghorn's arguments more persuasive in this matter? Explain.

9. What factors contributed to Baptist connectionalism during this period? Discuss the obstacles overcome and accomplishments made with relation to cooperative efforts among African-American Baptists.

Chapter 6

PROGRESS AND SETBACKS

The second quarter of the nineteenth century proved to be as transformative as the first for Baptists but with mixed results. Baptists' three "great societies" included the Triennial Convention (1814), the Baptist General Tract Society (1824), and the American Baptist Home Mission Society (1832). More than a dozen state conventions were formed between 1821 and 1850, including in upper northeast states such as Vermont and Maine (1824) and in the west in California during the year it was granted statehood (1850).

Educational opportunities increased greatly with the formation of regional institutions of higher learning, including the schools that came to be known as Union University (1823), Furman University (1826), Georgetown College (1829), Mercer University (1833), Wake Forest University (1834), Samford University (1841), and Baylor University (1845), to name just a few. Connectivity and communication increased through the rise of dozens of Baptist periodicals. By 1836, Baptists in Maine were reading *Zion's Advocate* and *The Eastern Baptist*; J. H. Purkitt of Boston was editor of *The Sabbath School Treasury*; Richmond residents had access to *The Religious Herald*; New York Baptists laid claim to *The Baptist Review* and *The Mother's Journal*; and stories of mission work throughout the country and the world circulated in *The American Baptist* and *The Triennial Register*.

In spite of their growth and attendant opportunities, Baptists experienced conflict over theological and practical matters. New confessions of faith demonstrated the need for Baptist subgroups to distinguish themselves from other Baptists. The rise of Primitive or "Old School" Baptists revealed division over the methodology of missions; the teaching of Alexander Campbell and William Miller led to the formation of new denominations; and the question of what to do about American slavery split Baptists into Northern and

141

Southern conventions long before Fort Sumter was fired upon. But these divisions did not destroy the Baptist movement. Baptists continued to experience growth in North America and Great Britain, and the seeds of future growth were being planted throughout Canada, Ireland, Scotland, Australia, and South Africa.

A Baptist Historian Reflects on the Past Generation

When I look back I can hardly realize the changes which have taken place in our denomination, in my day, in the means of intelligence and benevolence. It seems almost incredible that a society which so lately was so slow to engage in any new enterprise, and was so jealous of any collegiate training for its ministers, should at this early period have so many colleges and kindred institutions spread over the land; that such a flood of periodicals of different kinds should so soon be added to the old magazine; that so much should have been done by this people in the home and foreign missions departments, in the Bible cause, in the publication of Baptist literature, in Sunday Schools and Bible classes, and in kindred labors of various kinds; and all since I first began to collect the scanty and scattered materials for their history.

Excerpted from David Benedict, *Fifty Years Among the Baptists* (1860).

Theological Identity

One key to understanding controversies among Baptists is realizing that institutional advancements nearly always involved theological changes. The phrase "methods may change but the message never does" is partially true, but it fails to recognize that methodology of any sort is based on a theological perspective. When David Benedict wrote *Fifty Years Among the Baptists* (1860), he candidly described how the rapid spread of the Baptist movement affected Baptist identity. One of the most notable changes related to the priesthood of all believers, the doctrine that every Christian is gifted by God and given a responsibility to serve others. Benedict noted that the rise of mission and benevolent institutions in Baptist life inadvertently promoted the notion that one could pass off his or her responsibility to serve by sending money to a society where those who were trained to do the work were expected, even employed, to do so. A similar phenomenon occurred with the advent of revival preachers. Though pastors once led their churches in seasons of revival, they were increasingly expected to call for revival preachers who specialized in spurring periods of excitement and growth.

Increased mobility affected ministerial longevity. Referring to them as "migratory shepherds," Benedict commented on the tendency of Baptist ministers in the mid-nineteenth century to leave their churches after a few years of service in search of congregations more amenable to their preferences. Baptists living in larger cities rarely used the words "brother" and "sister" to refer to fellow church members as was once common practice, a sign to Benedict that a new emphasis on social standing reduced the importance of ecclesiological ties. Associational gatherings and convention meetings were affected by the growth of Baptists institutions. Benedict noted that ministers who once devoted their energy to spreading the gospel began taking their stand on methodological issues, such that "there were men always ready to introduce resolutions in favor of their *anti-isms* of various kinds."

There was no "one size fits all" theological system for Baptists in the nineteenth century. Two confessions of faith, the New Hampshire Confession, published in 1833, and the Free Will Baptist Confession of 1834, illustrate this principle well. Prior to adopting these confessions, most Baptists in America relied on the Philadelphia Confession of Faith (1742), whose Calvinistic overtones were noted in chapter 2. Thus, it was not surprising that Baptists who embraced an Arminian perspective on predestination and perseverance chose to subscribe to a different statement of faith.

*David Benedict
(1779–1874)*

The Free Will Baptists, who traced their origin to Benjamin Randall in 1780, were so named because they believed the decision to receive or reject Christ as Savior rested ultimately with the individual and did not stem from God's eternal decrees. Consequently, their confession of faith, "Treatise on the Faith and Practice of Free Will Baptists," stated, "The power to believe is the gift of God, but believing is an act of the creature, which is required as a condition of pardon, and without which the sinner cannot obtain salvation." The exercise of free will necessary for entrance into the faith also made it possible to exit from the faith. The confession stated that although "there are strong grounds to hope that the truly regenerate will persevere unto the end and be saved . . . their future obedience and final salvation are neither determined nor certain, since through infirmity and manifold temptations they are in danger of falling."

The possibility of apostasy was never widely accepted in Baptist life, but Free Will Baptists often pushed the theological envelope. They practiced open communion, promoted women to leadership positions, and were among the first to protest slavery. Therefore, even those who were not in full agreement with the Calvinistic theology of the Philadelphia Confession could not necessarily find fellowship among the Free Will Baptists. An alternative route became available through the adoption of the New Hampshire Confession of 1833. Though published a year before the Free Will Confession, its contents contained a clear rejection of apostasy, noting "that such only are real believers as endure to the end."

The New Hampshire Confession's statement on election and its omission of sections on providence and the divine decrees allowed Calvinists and non-Calvinists alike to embrace the confession. Imputation of Adam's guilt to his posterity was not mentioned, with the confession noting instead that humans choose to sin in accordance with Adam and Eve's rebellion. The confession defined election as "the eternal purpose of God, according to which he graciously regenerates, sanctifies and saves sinners," worded in such a way that a non-Calvinist could agree. Although the confession noted that election is "perfectly consistent with the free agency of man," it intentionally avoided the words "free will" since many Baptists did not subscribe to human freedom in the same sense as Free Will Baptists. More notably the confession stipulated, "The blessings of salvation are made free to all by the gospel," and said nothing about limited atonement, a doctrine that was conspicuously present in the Philadelphia Confession.

These changes were not denials of Calvinism but modifications that muted points of Calvinistic theology in an attempt to express the beliefs of an ever-broadening Baptist constituency. The New Hampshire Confession was partly a reaction to Free Will teaching and partly an update of Baptist beliefs. When delegates of the New Hampshire Baptist Convention appointed a committee to draw up a confession, their stated desire was to produce a work "as may be thought agreeable and consistent with the views of all churches in this state." Even though the New Hampshire Confession became the most popular confession of faith among Baptists in the nineteenth century, it could not possibly capture the views of all Baptist churches in that or any other state. Diversity was already integral to the Baptist movement and divisions stemming from that diversity occurred to an extent previously unimagined.

Antimission Controversies

One major Baptist controversy during the nineteenth century began with the appearance of the antimission movement. When Baptists debated the structure of the Triennial Convention, theirs was a debate of how, not whether, to conduct missions. The convention's framers did not anticipate that a sizable portion of Baptists would soon challenge the idea of missions regardless of the funding structure adopted. Opposition to missions became so prominent that thirty years after the formation of the Triennial Convention, 1,600 churches in America belonged to antimission movements, identifying themselves either as Primitive Baptists or as Old School Baptists. Their detractors called them Hardshell Baptists or Anti-Effort Baptists, but regardless of the designation, their numbers illustrate that they were successful in converting others to their point of view. Baptists in England experienced similar divisions with the rise of Strict Baptists, who rejected the duty faith teaching of Andrew Fuller and consequently dismissed the Baptist Union's attempt to unite English Baptists for missions. Canadian Baptists also experienced this division, albeit on a smaller scale, with the rise of the Covenanted Baptist Church in 1820.

The movement was largely reactionary as leaders argued against the new methods of mission promoters, particularly the steady stream of requests to help fund missionaries. Baptists had not employed traveling agents prior to their interest in organized missions, and a systematic form of giving through local churches would not be in place until the early twentieth century. When Baptists began sending agents to frontier churches to solicit financial support, opposition mounted from preachers who had built their own churches without financial backing and preached the gospel free of charge.

John Taylor attacked the missionary enterprise by questioning the motives and methods of fundraisers. The disdain he felt for two Congregationalist agents who suggested that he could improve his own financial situation by promoting missions contributed to Taylor's dislike of the lead fundraiser in Baptist life, Luther Rice. Taylor was convinced Rice was in the ministry for money, and Taylor never lacked a current illustration to make his point. In his 1819 treatise *Thoughts on Missions*, Taylor compared Rice's pleas for money to those of Johann Tetzel, the prominent seller of indulgences on the eve of the Reformation. Like Tetzel's nemesis Martin Luther, Taylor was determined to drive the "Judas-like money grabber" out of Baptist life.

Taylor's references to Rice as the "New England Rat" and "Yankee" reveal an additional impetus of his disdain, namely sectional prejudice. Taylor struck a chord in Kentucky and tapped into the concerns of Baptists in the central and southern Appalachian Mountains who feared that mission societies were "aristocracies" bent on violating the independent nature of Baptist churches. Although leaders of the mission societies stressed the inviolable nature of local church autonomy, their organizational structure included presidents, board members, and conventions, which made decisions outside the authority of any single congregation. Primitive and Old School Baptist views were strongest where localism was dominant.

Antimission Baptists also believed the theological underpinnings of the mission movement were suspect. Missionary Baptists embraced Fuller's evangelical Calvinism, whereas Primitive Baptists reverted to hyper-Calvinism. In general, both groups held that God elected people to salvation apart from any consideration of good works or foreseen faith, but they were divided on whether, and to what degree, God employed the work of missionary organizations to accomplish his plan of salvation.

Among the most extreme antimission Baptists was Daniel Parker, whose views on predestination bore no resemblance to historic Calvinism yet mobilized antimission Baptists against the efforts of mission-friendly Baptists. In his 1826 work *Views on the Two Seeds*, Parker cited Genesis 3:15 as the text that explained why some people come to faith and others do not, noting that God placed enmity between the offspring of the serpent and the woman. Cain and Abel were prime illustrations that people were born with either the serpent's seed or the seed of Christ, each having their destinies more or less genetically determined. Ishmael and Isaac, along with Esau and Jacob, served as further confirmation of the continuing line of "tares and wheat." Parker's unique doctrine came to be known as Two-Seed-in-the-Spirit Predestinarianism, the implications of which diminished evangelism and encouraged isolationism. With virtually no hope of converting the nonelect, adherents of the Two-Seed-in-the-Spirit theory directed their energies toward exposing the beliefs of Catholics and Protestant non-Baptists as false gospels and their gatherings as false churches. Despite their aberrant theology,

---

The Two Seeds

Fifty or sixty years ago, was there any application made to the Baptists, by any of these daughters of the old mother Rome, for communion? I think not. At that time the Baptists were looked down at with contempt, while the foot of persecution was on their neck. Was not the enmity of the serpent's seed plainly seen and felt then? But since liberty of conscience has been protected by our civil law, truth has had full liberty to defend her cause, Satan and his kingdom has begun to tremble. His last stratagem is to deceive, by appearing as an angel of light, and his ministers as ministers of righteousness, and by his cunning art in coming as nigh the truth as his nature can admit, have drawn off a number of the precious children of God, both preachers and laity, who have taken up their abode in the synagogue of Satan, while others stand amazed in wonder at the enmity and war between the two seeds.

Excerpted from Daniel Parker, *Views on the Two Seeds* (1826).

Two-Seed-in-the-Spirit Predestinarian Baptists established churches throughout Arkansas, Kentucky, Mississippi, Tennessee, and Texas by 1850, though never more than 500 congregations.

Though leading figures of the missionary movement claimed to be Calvinists, leaders of the antimission movement questioned whether they genuinely believed in God's sovereignty since they promoted "means," or methods, designed to bring sinners into the family of God. Primitive Baptists railed against Sunday schools, evangelistic tracts, mission agencies, revival gatherings, and ministerial education. Missionary Baptists stopped short of claiming that God needed their organized efforts to bring the elect to faith, but their constant pleas for financial support and ongoing plans for outreach convinced antimission Baptists that their Calvinistic doctrines and innovative methods were hopelessly at odds with their own.

Associations split apart and then reorganized on antimission platforms, beginning in 1828 with the Canoochee Association in Georgia and extending to the Apple Creek Association of Illinois in 1830. In 1832, Maryland Old School Baptists issued a statement outlining their differences with mission-friendly Baptists. Known as the "Black Rock Address," the document opened with a statement declaring "a new era in the history of the Baptists" when believers like themselves were faulted for "refusing to go beyond the word of God." They then listed examples of mission-friendly Baptists adopting methods not found in the Bible and asked which of the two, antimission or mission-friendly Baptists, had departed from the old ways.

Excerpt from the Black Rock Address (1832)

There is, brethren, one radical difference between us and those who advocate these various institutions which we have noticed to which we wish to call your attention. It is this: they declare the gospel to be a system of means; these means it appears they believe to be of human contrivance; and they act accordingly. But we believe the gospel dispensation to embrace a system of faith and obedience, and we would act according to our belief. We believe, for instance, that the seasons of declension, of darkness, of persecutions, &c., to which the church of Christ is at times subject, are designed by the wise Disposer of all events; not for calling forth the inventive geniuses of men to remove the difficulties, but for trying the faith of God's people in his wisdom, power and faithfulness to sustain his church. On him, therefore, would we repose our trust, and wait his hour of deliverance, rather than rely upon an arm of flesh.

The Black Rock Address cited tract societies as an example of mission advocates championing their methods solely because they reached people who were otherwise unlikely to read the entire Bible. From the antimission perspective, tract societies wrongly abbreviated the Bible to the essential message of salvation, thus encouraging people to find eternal life without stumbling over lengthy books like Leviticus or obscure books like Obadiah. Sunday schools also came under scrutiny. Even though Missionary Baptists claimed thousands of conversions through an additional study session outside the time of congregational worship, Old School Baptists said Sunday schools did little more than teach Bible facts to people who were not truly converted, thus making them hypocrites. Bible societies were criticized for continually appealing for funds to support their efforts rather than using publishing companies already in existence and saving money. Once again, the charge of greed was levied.

Regarding missions, the Black Rock Address attempted to clear up misrepresentations of antimission Baptists. They were not, as some had charged, unaware of the Great Commission text in Matthew 28:18–20, nor were they under the impression that the charge applied only to the apostles in the first century. They affirmed the need for financial support of missions, provided the principles of doing so were not "a subversion of the order marked out in the New Testament." This reference to order represents a key idea in the antimission argument, namely that the Bible not only contained a command to spread the gospel but also provided the methodology as well. The central complaint against mission societies was that they were not churches and as such were formed under different rules of membership and guided by different principles. The fact that a person could join a mission society by paying an annual fee practically invited unregenerate persons to participate and perhaps even lead. Missions, from an antimission perspective, should be conducted solely through the local church in order to safeguard the gospel message.

The final two areas of concern were ministerial education and protracted meetings. The rapid formation of Baptist colleges demonstrated an eagerness on the part of Baptist ministers to acquire intellectual capacity for preaching well, but it also reflected a desire for social respectability. Primitive and Old School Baptists mocked the efforts of those living in cosmopolitan areas to fit in with the upper class. Moreover, they charged that Missionary Baptists wrongly equated matters of revelation with human sciences—one could not learn the ministry in the same way one could learn mathematics. The call to ministry was, from their vantage point, a command to begin preaching rather than a hiatus to prepare polished sermons. Protracted meetings, or scheduled times for evangelistic services in hope of bringing a revival, were criticized for presuming that the Holy Spirit was obliged to move in the hearts of people simply because a church decided to meet for evangelistic purposes. The lack of doctrinal preaching and the employment of altar calls at the end of sermons suggested that Missionary Baptists relied too heavily on human instrumentality to elicit professions of faith.

The Black Rock Address helped draw a line of demarcation between Missionary and antimissionary Baptists. This division was solidified through publication of Primitive Baptist periodicals like Gilbert Beebe's *Signs of the Times*, which waged war with "Arminianism the mother and her whole brood of institutions," and Joshua Lawrence's *The Primitive Baptist*, which called antimission Baptists to "come ye out from among them" and be separate. A handful of Primitive Baptist associations declared that baptisms performed by missionary-friendly churches were invalid. The divisions were so deep that attempts at reconciliation consistently failed to change minds on either side.

Each group determined its own standards of success. Missionary Baptists cited their ever-growing number of converts, missionaries, and institutions as evidence of God's favor. Old School Baptists peaked in membership by midcentury and then declined as Americans embraced progress over primitivism. Still, antimission Baptists claimed to be God's faithful remnant, citing numerous biblical texts that portrayed the people of God as the minority in a world where false religion abounded.

Campbellites and Millerites

The division between Primitive and Missionary Baptists was an internecine affair in Baptist life, in which two groups advanced rival claims to be the legitimate heirs to the Baptist story. Other Baptist battles spawned new movements rather than divisions within the Baptist family. The formation of the Disciples of Christ and the Seventh-day Adventists are examples of two groups rejecting their denominational heritage in search of a better version of the New Testament church.

Alexander Campbell, founder of the Disciples of Christ, was born in Ireland

Alexander Campbell (1788–1866)

and raised as a Presbyterian, but he left his country and denomination when he immigrated to America in 1809. His father, Thomas, likewise withdrew from the Presbyterians, and together they founded the Brush Run Church in western Pennsylvania. Rereading the Bible apart from denominational ties, they concluded that believer's baptism by immersion was the biblical model for disciples and in 1815, as a symbol of unity, began to cooperate with the Redstone Baptist Association.

Differences between Alexander Campbell and the Baptists

Your opinions on some other points are, I think, dangerous, unless you are mis-understood, such as casting off the Old Testament, exploding experimental reli-gion for its common acceptation, denying the existence of gifts in the present day commonly believed to exist among all spiritual Christians, such as preaching & etc. Some of your opinions, though true, are pushed to extremes, such as those upon the use of creeds, confessions, & etc. Your views of ministerial support, directed against abuses on that head, would be useful, but leveled against all support to ministers (unless by way of alms) is so palpably contrary to scripture and common sense, that I persuade myself that there must be some misunderstanding. In short your views are generally so contrary to those of the Baptists in general, that if a party was to go fully into the practice of your principles I should say a new sect had sprung up, radically different from the Baptists, as they now are.

Excerpted from a letter from Robert Semple to Alexander Campbell (1825).

Campbell's conversion to Baptist views was something of a mixed bless-ing for Baptists. On one hand, he proved himself one of their most capa-ble debaters against Catholics, Presbyterians, and Methodists. Yet the same tenacity that helped him succeed in debates contributed to his leaving the Baptists seventeen years later on a quest for a more biblical form of Christi-anity that relied less heavily on confessions of faith. Like Taylor and Parker, Alexander Campbell opposed mission societies on the basis that they were unscriptural innovations. Unlike Taylor and Parker, however, Campbell rejected Calvinistic theology because he believed it represented a move beyond the Bible's simple message to creedal positions that divided rather than united Christians.

Campbell's rejection of creedal Christianity was part of a larger Resto-rationist movement already set in motion by Barton Stone. Restorationists were convinced denominational divisions could be overcome by a common sense reading of the New Testament, one that was not influenced by doctri-nal positions passed on from denominational founders. For Campbell, this interpretive approach led to the rejection of doctrines like limited atonement and practices like calling ministers "Reverend." Put simply, whatever could not be deduced from a simple reading of the Bible should not be embraced by followers of Christ. When Campbell's Brush Run Church joined the Redstone Baptist Association, they did not affirm the association's confession of faith; and when he left the Baptist movement, he shed the denominational name altogether.

Campbell's departure cost Baptists thousands of church members in Kentucky, Ohio, Pennsylvania, Virginia, and Tennessee as many resonated with his desire for a clearer, less convoluted, Christian faith. He also acquired thousands of followers through the publication of his two periodicals, *The Christian Baptist* (1823–30) and *The Millennial Harbinger* (1830–66). However, his attempt at biblical simplicity did not result in denominational unity, as Campbell replaced traditional Baptist beliefs with a competing theological system of his own. He equated bare mental assent with genuine faith; he taught that salvation was incomplete without believer's baptism, thus giving the strong impression that being immersed in water made the work of Christ effectual; and he dismissed the Old Testament as having no practical value in the Christian life. In 1832 his movement merged with Barton Stone's Christian Church, and their followers became known as the Disciples of Christ. This new denomination experienced remarkable growth, becoming the largest indigenous American religious body in the nineteenth century. Baptists distanced themselves from Campbell and his teaching. However, his "no creed but the Bible" mantra entered the vocabulary of many Baptists, which raised significant challenges to Baptist confessions for years to come.

The year following the formation of the Disciples of Christ, William Miller was licensed to preach by a Baptist church in Low Hampton, New York. Miller was a self-educated farmer who, as Mark Noll rightly notes, "exemplified extraordinary religious creativity in the boisterous climate of the early United States." Unlike Campbell, who advocated a simple reading of Scripture, Miller focused on minute details of prophetic literature in an attempt to discover the timing of Christ's return. During the 1820s and 1830s, evangelicals were shifting in their understanding of the millennial reign of Christ, with many coming to believe that he would return to earth first and then begin his thousand-year reign. Many evangelicals from earlier generations believed the millennium would occur as the church succeeded in its mission with Christ returning afterward. Miller advocated the premillennial view and, after being licensed as a Baptist preacher, announced that he knew the year in which Christ would return—1843—basing his prediction on the book of Daniel. He interpreted "days" in Daniel's prophetic passages as "years" and used the Jewish calendar to mark Christ's second advent at precisely 2,300 years from Artaxerxes's decree to rebuild Jerusalem. Audiences were intrigued by his precision, and his message received widespread attention through Joshua Himes's paper, *The Midnight Cry*. Thousands became convinced of Miller's prediction when a financial panic struck the nation in 1837, bringing about a major recession. People on the edge of economic catastrophe believed it to be a warning that the end was near.

Of course, the date passed without Christ's second advent, leading Miller to recalculate the date to October 22, 1844. When his second prediction proved false, many "Millerites" left organized religion altogether. Baptists, already wary of his interpretive daring, disassociated themselves from him and his followers in 1845. However, the movement gained new momentum under the leadership of Ellen White, who fostered Adventist hope further by focusing on Sabbath observance and dietary reforms as a means of hastening Christ's return. White's movement came to be known as Seventh-day Adventists.

Newspaper headline denoting
"The End of the World."

Northern and Southern Baptists

The formation of the Southern Baptist Convention (SBC) in 1845 foreshadowed the differences between the North and South sixteen years before the American Civil War began. The morality of slavery was the central issue that led to the formation of the SBC, although Southern Baptists at the time emphasized missions as the main factor precipitating their decision to form an alternate body to the Triennial Convention. Indeed, their constitution did not mention slavery, highlighting instead the singular task of "directing the energies of the whole denomination in one sacred effort, for the propagation of the Gospel." Despite attempts at contextualization, Leon McBeth correctly referred to the central role of slavery in the SBC's founding as a "blunt historical fact."

British Baptists Oppose Slavery

Dear Brethren:

We, the members of the Board of Baptist Ministers in and near London, desire affectionately and with much earnestness, to commend ourselves to your candid and Christian attention. . . . We understand that the number of slaves in the United States is considerably above two million, while the system under which they are held is said to be characterized by some features peculiarly revolting and oppressive. But it is not our purpose to enter into details; we wish rather to fix your attention on the system as a whole—its unchristian character, its degrading tendency, the misery it generates, the injustice, the cruelty and wretchedness it involves. Is it not an awful breach of the Divine law, a manifest infraction of that social compact which is always and everywhere binding? And if it be so, are you not, as Christians, and especially as Christian ministers, bound to protest against it, and to seek, by all legitimate means, its speedy and entire destruction? You have a high and holy part, dear brethren, to act; and future generations will bless your name, and the God whom you serve will approve your conduct, if you are prompt and diligent in its performance.

Excerpted from a letter from the Board of Baptist Ministers in London to Baptists in America (1833).

As mentioned in chapter 2, Baptists in the American South accepted slavery as a way of life and largely dealt with issues related to master-slave relations on a case-by-case basis. In this instance, however, an entire denomination was created in defense of the "peculiar institution." Students of Baptist history do well to ask why this sinful perspective made sense to Southern Baptists two centuries ago. What was it about the world they lived in, the values they inherited, and the Bible they read that gave them the impression that the Christian faith was compatible with American slavery?

To enter that world it should be noted that neither Baptists nor Christians were the first or the only religious groups to embrace slavery. It had been practiced in the ancient world before its arrival in the New World, was enforced by Romans as well as Muslims, and included multiple ethnicities before Africans were singled out in discriminatory fashion. Moreover, the abolition of the slave trade was of particular concern to Christians even when it pitted them against members of their own faith. From the Middle Ages, when popes issued decrees against the practice of slavery, to the late modern period, when Parliament outlawed the Atlantic slave trade, opposition to slavery was frequent and firm. The defense of slavery largely came from those with vested economic interests, which naturally included residents of the American South, dependent as they were at the turn of the nineteenth century upon an agrarian economy. Northerners who protested slavery were on the right side of history, but on the whole they did not promote abolition until it was in their economic interest to do so.

In addition to citing the long history of slavery and the economic advantage it afforded, Baptists in the South regarded it as legitimate because they read about it in the Bible. Both the Old and New Testaments provided instructions regarding the treatment of slaves, and neither Testament contained a single verse that directly prohibited slavery. Passages such as Exodus 20:17 and Leviticus 25:44–46 could not easily be dismissed as belonging to the Jews only since these references were echoed in Paul's instruction to the churches in Ephesians 6:5 and Colossians 3:22. Richard Furman, in his 1822 address to the South Carolina legislature, spoke for many Baptists in the South in this regard: "Had the holding of slaves been a moral evil, it cannot be supposed that the inspired Apostles, who feared not the faces of men, and were ready to lay down their lives in the cause of their God, would have tolerated it for a moment in the Christian church."

Along with this primary argument that Scripture regulated slavery without ever prohibiting it, Southerners offered other biblical arguments that were weaker exegetically. Borrowing from rabbinical and early church interpretations, some Baptists who favored slavery argued that it originated relatively early in world history, claiming that Noah's curse on Canaan and his descendants (Gen 9:25) foretold the subjugation of the African people. Many even believed the mark of Cain (Gen 4:15) referred to his skin pigmentation, illustrating that people of color were socially inferior by divine design. Neither of these

An American slave auction.

arguments can be defended with any seriousness today, but they were painfully effective at the time in justifying an inherited social order.

Baptist Protectors and Defenders

After the Civil War a commonsense reading of slavery passages prevailed. Baptists and other Christians recognized the difference between the existence of slavery in biblical times and the extermination of slavery in their own time. Put simply, God had indeed provided regulations for a practice he was actually against. Prior to the Civil War, however, Southerners who read the Bible to their advantage demanded chapter and verse prohibition of slavery. Hence, if abolitionists were going to convince slave-owning Baptists of the error of their ways, they needed direct scriptural support for their position. This was no simple task as abolitionists' key biblical texts either related only tangentially to slavery or did not produce the desired result. Jesus' admonition to treat others as one would wish to be treated (Matt 7:12) could be applied in any number of ways apart from a slave owner reconsidering how he might feel if the tables were turned. Moreover, Jesus' announcement that he had come to set the captives free (Luke 4:18) evidently had a spiritual fulfillment since Roman slavery continued well into the fourth century. The apostle Paul suggested that Philemon give Onesimus his freedom (Phlm 12–16) but did not require him to do so, and he elsewhere asserted that slaves should learn to lean on Christ rather than long for their freedom (1 Cor 7:20–22).

Those who pressed the case primarily using reason rather than biblical revelation risked being identified with Quakers, Episcopalians, and Unitarians, who agreed that slavery was inhumane but had abandoned orthodox doctrine in other areas. Guilt by association carried significant weight and made Baptists hesitant to side with theologically aberrant groups. Moreover, slave revolts led by Denmark Vessey in South Carolina and Nat Turner in Virginia, occurring in 1822 and 1831 respectively, further galvanized Southerners against a completely free society.

The lack of biblical commands to end slavery and the fears roused by slave revolts did not diminish the rhetoric or the spirit of antislavery activists. David Barrow, a Free Will Baptist in Kentucky, formed an association of churches committed to abolition. He argued against slavery from multiple angles as suggested by the title of his treatise, *Involuntary, Unmerited, Perpetual, Absolute, Hereditary Slavery Examined on the Principles of Nature, Reason, Justice, Policy and Scripture*. In 1840, Baptists in New York formed the American Baptist Anti-Slavery Convention, and their colleagues in Boston formed the American Baptist Free Mission Society. Additional support for abolition (or agitation, from a Southern perspective) came from Baptists across the Atlantic who helped eliminate slavery from the British West Indies in 1833 and called on their American counterparts to do the same in their country. Members of the Baptist Union wrote a letter to the leaders of the Triennial Convention, urging them to stop slavery. British Baptists Francis Cox and James Hoby crossed the Atlantic in 1834 to make personal efforts at persuasion, but to no avail. In response to such efforts, Southern Baptists recalled that northern and British Baptists had once participated in the very institution they now sought to demolish.

Richard Furman's *Treatise on Slavery* (1822) was a revealing Baptist work. Believing as he did that Scripture permitted slavery, Furman made additional arguments concerning the well-being of blacks. He noted that slaves in America experienced a higher standard of living than they likely would have in their native homelands. Their lives were by no means easy, but their life expectancy increased significantly with their placement in a more civilized country. They were also under masters with legal obligation to provide for their needs whether young or old, healthy or sick. Additionally, Furman argued that the impact of Christianity on slaves surpassed both their physical status and their temporal state. Unlike some Southerners, he believed blacks were on equal ground with whites in terms of having an eternal soul and facing a day of judgment whereupon they would give an account of their lives: "Their religious interests claim a regard from their masters of the most serious nature, and it is indispensable. Nor can the community at large, in a right estimate of their duty and happiness, be indifferent on this subject." Masters therefore had a dual obligation to care for the body and soul of their slaves. Still, Furman wrote as a man tied to his time. He envisioned a day when blacks might enjoy the full liberties of free people, yet he could not envision a time in which slavery as an institution, regardless of ethnicity, would not exist.

A modern reprint of Domestic Slavery Considered as a Scriptural Institution (image courtesy of Mercer University Press).

Although one can rightly take issue with Furman's arguments, the spread of Christianity among slaves was remarkable. The gospel message of the First Great Awakening brought a type of freedom to slaves that political arguments of the Revolutionary War did not: equal standing with others before God and semiequal footing with whites in the church. Slaves were invited to believe in Jesus, but they were directed to sit in the balcony of the church in order to respect societal segregation. Prior to the 1830s, when slavery became more of a political issue, Baptists licensed black ministers to preach, some of whom spoke to white congregations. Biracial worship was not the only way enslaved Christians found a modicum of freedom. Slaves often participated in church discipline, and they found that the practice of removing sinful persons from church membership added a layer of protection against unbearable, violent masters.

The debate over slavery was placed in the public eye when Richard Fuller (not to be confused with Richard Furman) and Francis Wayland debated the institution's merits in a series of letters published in 1844 and 1845 for the *Christian Reflector*, a Boston-based Baptist newspaper. Those letters and an additional letter by Wayland were later bound as a single volume entitled *Domestic Slavery Considered as a Scriptural Institution* (1845). Their correspondence reveals how each struggled to address a problem they had inherited from history. Both were educated men, Fuller having studied at Harvard and Wayland serving as president of Brown University; both were deeply invested in missions through their work in the Triennial Convention. However, Fuller was convinced slavery was a biblically sanctioned institution whereas Wayland considered it a moral evil. Their letters stood out to readers as a courteous disagreement that generated more light than heat. On a personal level, they agreed to disagree and demonstrated how to discuss the

---

Francis Wayland and Richard Fuller Debate Slavery

It is needless to assure you that I have read your letters in reply to mine on Domestic Slavery, with profound attention and unfeigned admiration. To the acuteness of one profession and the learning of another, in both of which you have attained the highest distinction, you have here added a fervor of eloquence and a richness of illustration peculiarly your own. Never before, I presume, has the defense of slavery on Christian principles been so ably conducted. Never before, I think, has anything been written so admirably calculated to make a favorable impression on those who hold the opposite opinions. . . . The warm spirit of philanthropy which pervades every part of your argument must melt away every prejudice by which it could be resisted. . . . While, however, I say this, and I say it from my heart, I do not perceive that you have overthrown a single position which I have attempted to establish.

Francis Wayland, in response to Richard Fuller, excerpted from *Domestic Slavery Considered as a Scriptural Institution* (1845).

issue without demonizing one's opponent. Fuller later carried this balancing act to his pastorate in Baltimore where he guided his congregation through the Civil War, even as sons of members fought for both the Confederate and Union armies. Wayland's attitude was such that he attracted Southern ministers to attend Brown University.

Formation of the Southern Baptist Convention

Baptists were not the only religious group struggling with the slavery question. New School Presbyterians separated over slavery in 1837, and the Methodists split in 1844. The breaking point for Baptists in the Southern states came through correspondence with the Triennial Convention and the American Baptist Home Mission Society (ABHMS). Both organizations attempted to avoid the slavery question by claiming neutrality in the matter, but their efforts to do so did not last long. During the early 1840s, home and foreign mission advocates discussed rising concerns about slavery, but neither the Triennial Convention nor the ABHMS spoke for or against it. Since the Triennial Convention and ABHMS were formed before slavery became a political issue, their constitutions did not address it. But history caught up to them, and Baptists in Georgia and Alabama forced them to take a side in the debate.

In 1844, Georgia Baptists nominated a slave owner for appointment as a home missionary through the ABHMS. Apart from the slavery question, James Reeve, their nominee, was qualified to serve and came with the financial backing of Georgia Baptists to secure his appointment. The fact that he owned slaves and intended to continue doing so if appointed made him a test case of sorts. The strategy of Georgia Baptists was simple enough: if the ABHMS refused to appoint Reeve, then the society's claim of being neutral on slavery would be exposed as false. If the ABHMS did appoint Reeve as a missionary, abolitionists would conclude that the society was no longer neutral but rather in favor of slavery.

Georgia Baptists had seemingly forced the ABHMS to take a position on slavery, but the board deftly responded by refusing to receive the application. In other words, they neither appointed nor rejected him. However, they replied to Georgia Baptists, citing them—though not formally accusing them—of starting a controversy on a matter that had already been decided as a nonissue. Nevertheless, the board members of the ABHMS were narrowly divided, voting seven to five against taking action on Reeve's application. For their part, Georgia Baptists were convinced that the failure to appoint Reeve revealed there was little future for slave owners in the ABHMS.

Alabama Baptists employed a similar strategy with the Triennial Convention, but instead of nominating a slave owner for appointment to foreign missions, they sent a letter demanding the board members of the Triennial Convention directly address the matter. As a state convention, Baptists in Alabama claimed their right to participate in decisions regarding missionary appointments. Neutrality was not an option, they said, since slaveholders were legitimate participants in the convention. As a practical matter, they determined to withhold funds from the Triennial Convention until the board produced a satisfactory statement on slavery.

The response by board members was both tailored and terse. The members stated that since the founding of the Triennial Convention neither slave owners nor those who did not own slaves had received any special privileges. Moreover, to their knowledge, no slave owner had ever applied to become a missionary. In essence, then, the question put forth by Alabama Baptists was merely hypothetical, and the board took offense at being placed in the position to answer for the entire Triennial Convention. But rather than allow the question to remain unanswered, as the ABHMS had done, the board determined to be as forthright as possible: "If, however, any one should offer himself as a missionary, having slaves, and should insist on retaining them as his property, we could not appoint them. One thing is certain, we can never be a party to any arrangement which would imply approbation of slavery." The board had thus deemed slavery in America immoral.

Despite moderating attempts to placate Baptists in the South, a new missionary organization open to slave owners was formed on May 8, 1845, in Augusta, Georgia. A total of 293 delegates assembled, 273 of whom were from Georgia, South Carolina, and Virginia. The number of churches and church members represented was substantial. At its inception, the Southern Baptist Convention, as the organization was to be called, had 4,126 cooperating churches with 351,951 members. The choice of William Bullein Johnson as the first

Image of founding of Southern Baptist Convention meeting.

president of the SBC was something of a symbolic victory for the South, given the fact that he was president of the Triennial Convention from 1841 to 1844. He had stepped down a year earlier and was replaced, not coincidentally, by Francis Wayland. Johnson's experience in drafting constitutions for the Triennial Convention and the state convention of South Carolina had prepared him for the moment when, a week prior to the Augusta meeting, he pulled from his pocket a proposed constitution for the SBC. The document revealed Johnson's preference for a convention plan, which combined foreign and home missions, as well as "other important objects connected with the Redeemer's kingdom." The SBC would therefore differ from the Triennial Convention not only in its acceptance of slavery but also in its method of funding ministries. Fears that a North-South split would hinder mission work among

William Bullein Johnson
(1782–1862)

Baptists were ultimately unrealized, as the SBC became the largest Baptist denomination in America during the century that followed.

Numerical results notwithstanding, the acceptance of American slavery as a scripturally ordained institution periodically led Southern Baptists to distance themselves from their history. In his "Address to the Public," Johnson framed the division between Northern and Southern Baptists as being strictly related to missions. They did not differ on matters of faith, he noted, nor did they consider one another unchristian. He noted they had worked together for many years until the board of the Triennial Convention changed the rules of participation in the middle of the game, thus prohibiting slave-owning Baptists from becoming missionaries. Slavery, according to Johnson, was not the fundamental issue. Rather, Southerners had been "forbidden" from "speaking unto the Gentiles." The formation of a new mission organization was necessary in order for slavery advocates to obey the Great Commission.

The Civil War and the Civil Rights Movement both passed before Southern Baptists formally attempted to put their past behind them. Meeting in Atlanta, Georgia, in 1995, messengers to the Southern Baptist Convention adopted a "Resolution on Racial Reconciliation on the 150th Anniversary of the Southern Baptist Convention." The resolution stated that Eve was the "mother of all living," contradicting the idea that God favored one ethnic group over another. It also admitted that the founding of the SBC stemmed in part from racial prejudice against blacks, a sin Southern Baptists declared "profoundly distorts our understanding of Christian morality."

For Further Study

Benedict, David. *Fifty Years Among the Baptists*. New York: Sheldon and Company, 1860.

Briggs, John H. Y. *The English Baptists of the 19th Century*, chapter 3. London: The Baptist Historical Society, 1994.

Chute, Anthony. *A Piety Above the Common Standard: Jesse Mercer and the Defense of Evangelistic Calvinism*. Macon, GA: Mercer University Press, 2004.

Crowley, John G. *Primitive Baptists of the Wiregrass South: 1815 to the Present*. Gainesville, FL: University Press of Florida, 1988.

Gardner, Robert G. *A Decade of Debate and Division: Georgia Baptists and the Formation of the Southern Baptist Convention*. Macon, GA: Mercer University Press, 1995.

Mathis, James R. *The Making of the Primitive Baptists: A Cultural and Intellectual History of the Anti-Mission Movement, 1800–1840*. New York: Routledge, 2004.

McKivigan, John R., and Mitchell Snay, eds. *Religion and the Antebellum Debate over Slavery*. Athens, GA: University of Georgia Press, 1998.

Noll, Mark A. *A History of Christianity in the United States and Canada*, chapters 7–11. Grand Rapids, MI: Eerdmans, 1992.

Oliver, Robert W. *History of the English Calvinistic Baptists 1771–1892: From John Gill to C. H. Spurgeon*, chapters 9–14. Carlisle, PA: Banner of Truth, 2006.

Snay, Mitchell. *Gospel of Disunion: Religion and Separatism in the Antebellum South*. Chapel Hill, NC: University of North Carolina Press, 1997.

Wayland, Francis, and Richard Fuller. *Domestic Slavery Considered as a Scriptural Institution*, new ed. Edited by Nathan A. Finn and Keith Harper. Macon, GA: Mercer University Press, 2008.

Questions for Discussion

1. Describe David Benedict's understanding of the theological transformation of Baptists in the early nineteenth century. How would you assess the phrase "methods may change but the message never does"?

2. Explain the establishment of the Free Will Baptists. What were their key doctrinal distinctives? How did the New Hampshire Confession reflect interaction with Free Will Baptist teachings?

3. What was the antimission movement? Who were the key figures, and what were their major concerns? Suppose the antimission movement became the dominant strand of Baptist thinking—what areas of contemporary Baptist life would be affected or no longer exist?

4. Evaluate how Missionary Baptists and Old School Baptists determined their level of success. What is problematic with each approach? Can you provide an alternative to understanding how a church or denomination might measure its success?

5. What motivated Alexander Campbell to begin a new movement after leaving the Baptists? In what way was the formation of the Disciples of Christ an ironic twist on his concerns? Explain how the phrase "no creed but the Bible" can be helpful and/or harmful to Christians today.

6. Who were the Seventh-day Adventists? How were they established? What were their core convictions? What distinguishes them from Seventh Day Baptists?

7. How did Southern Baptists and other Southern evangelicals justify slavery during this period? How would you respond to a person who dismisses Christianity because of its involvement in buying and selling people as slaves?

8. How did Baptist abolitionists respond to the practice of slavery among Christians? How and when did Southern Baptists formally put their history with slavery behind them?

9. Evaluate William B. Johnson's rationale for the formation of the Southern Baptist Convention. Was it possible for Southerners to conduct missions apart from the question of slavery? What ramifications do you believe exist today because of American involvement in slavery?

Chapter 7

EXPANSION AND ADAPTATION

Though controversy was prominent among nineteenth-century Baptists, it was not their defining mark. Even in the midst of controversy, Baptists were able to plant churches, establish institutions, and form connections that had a lasting impact. The missionary work of Johann Gerhard Oncken brought about a level of church planting throughout continental Europe that was refreshingly reminiscent of apostolic times. The persecution he experienced from government officials was reminiscent of an earlier time for Baptists, as he and his colleagues had to contend for the right to worship. Baptists in America, though divided between North and South, managed to double their missionary efforts. While a renewed emphasis on Baptist localism hindered cooperative efforts and a Civil War threatened to undo the fabric of the nation, Baptists found that their institutions could withstand tumultuous times. In addition, African-American Baptists received their freedom and capitalized on the opportunity to establish their own churches. Although Southern Baptists found themselves on the losing side of the war, they looked to the future by educating pastors and laity through a newly formed seminary and Sunday School Board.

Baptist Missions in Europe

Johann Oncken had such an impact on Baptists in Europe that he has been called the "Father of Continental Baptists" and a "one-man mission society, theological seminary and literature distribution center." At the time of his birth in 1800, there were no Baptist churches on the continent; by the turn of the century, just sixteen years after his death, there were nearly a quarter million Baptists. Either Oncken or someone he trained was involved in beginning Baptist work in Germany, Sweden, Denmark, Austria, Hungary, and Romania. He also influenced work in Russia, Switzerland, the Balkans, and South Africa.

Oncken never knew his father because the elder Oncken was exiled from the family's homeland of Germany for political reasons. But he found a father figure in a merchant to whom he was apprenticed at age thirteen. He left Germany for Scotland, and as part of his apprenticeship traveled throughout Europe for nearly a decade. This experience enabled him to become multilingual and prepared him for his future career as a traveling missionary. In 1820, while living in London, Oncken gave his life to Christ and developed an immediate desire to share his faith with others. He began missionary work through the Continental Society for the Diffusion of Religious Knowledge over the Continent of Europe and later partici-

Johann Gerhard Oncken
(1800–1884)

pated in the Edinburgh Bible Society. Both organizations specialized in Bible and tract distribution. He personally took Bibles and tracts to ships and near the end of his life estimated that he had sent two million Bibles throughout Europe. In 1828 he founded the Oncken Verlag, a publishing house that later became one of Germany's most recognizable religious presses.

When Oncken became convinced that Scripture commanded believer's baptism by immersion, he found himself in a position similar to that of John Smyth two centuries earlier: there was no other Baptist around who could baptize him. Robert Haldane corresponded with Oncken advising him to do exactly as Smyth had done, but Oncken rejected the idea of self-baptism. Through a series of events, Oncken made contact with Barna Sears, professor of biblical theology at Hamilton Literary and Theological Institute in New York. Sears traveled to Hamburg and baptized Oncken and six others in the Elbe River at midnight, due to fear of persecution by government authorities. Interestingly, Sears wrote to his wife that "several more are asking for baptism, but we think it prudent to defer it a little." It is not clear whether they were refused baptism in order to keep a low profile or to receive additional instruction in Baptist principles. Oncken was also ordained by Sears as pastor of the church in Hamburg, which has since become the oldest surviving Baptist church in Germany.

Gerhard Oncken's Baptism and Call to Gospel Ministry

Dear Brother Oncken:

This is to testify to all whom it may concern, that, at the request of the Baptist church in this place, after being fully satisfied of your personal piety, of the correctness of your views of Christian doctrine, of your possessing those ministerial qualifications specified in Scripture, & of your being called both by the Spirit and Providence of God to the work of the ministry, I have by prayer and the imposition of hands solemnly set you apart to that responsible office; and in the name of the church in which I hold an official standing as a regular ordained minister, pronounce you scripturally invested with all the powers which belong to a pastor of the flock of Christ and to a minister of the gospel. May the Lord grant that you may have a higher testimony than man can give, that you be recognized by him as a good minister of Jesus Christ; and may it be your exalted privilege to win, through grace, many souls to his love; and to build up, in true knowledge, faith, and every Christian virtue, the church, redeemed by his precious blood. I also commend you to the confidence of the Christian public, as a minister of the gospel, and to the affectionate regards of all who love our Lord Jesus Christ.

Excerpt from a letter from Barna Sears to Gerhard Oncken (April 23, 1834).

When Oncken began his ministry, Germany's state-sponsored Lutheranism had fallen into a quagmire of spiritual decline. His message of living faith resulting in lively service helped revive the pietistic impulse that had awakened German churches in years past. He began receiving financial support from the Triennial Convention and later, after its 1845 split, from the northern American Baptist Missionary Union. With a thrifty lifestyle and an indefatigable desire to enlist others in the mission movement, he proved himself worthy of the support. His own church provided funds for more than twenty new church buildings throughout Europe, even though the Hamburg congregation continued to meet in a converted warehouse. Oncken's key idea was *Jeder Baptist ein Missionar* ("every Baptist a missionary"). On one occasion someone asked him how many Baptist missionaries resided in Germany, and he replied, "Seven thousand," the total number of German Baptists.

Julius Köbner and Gottfried Wilhelm Lehmann, who embraced believer's baptism under Oncken's influence, became two of his most important co-laborers. Known as the *Kleeblatt*, or "cloverleaf," the three men coordinated their efforts in training pastors and planting churches throughout continental Europe. Their church-planting strategy relied heavily on lay preachers who supported themselves with secular employment. But they did mission work themselves too. Köbner and Oncken baptized converts on a mission trip to Copenhagen, leading to the first Baptist church in Denmark. Köbner later became pastor of that church and compiled a hymnbook, the first for Danish Baptists. Lehmann became pastor of the first Baptist church in Berlin and formed the first regional Baptist association in Prussia.

German Christians baptized.

Yet there were obstacles to overcome. Religious liberty was limited in Europe, and the *Kleeblatt* experienced seizure of their personal property and arrest on multiple occasions. Hamburg city officials even forced members of Oncken's church to baptize their infant children. When night-time baptisms led to rumors about secret meetings, Oncken boldly decided to baptize people during the day. The high visibility of such baptisms led to further persecution but did little to deter Oncken. His tenacity was evident in an exchange he had with the Hamburg police chief, who warned, "As long as I can lift this little finger, you will feel the force of it." Oncken's response was trenchant: "I see a greater arm, and that is the arm of God. So long as that arm moves, you will never silence me."

Temporary relief from persecution came in 1842 when Baptists helped townspeople after a devastating fire nearly destroyed Hamburg. Their kindness endeared them to fellow Hamburg residents. More lasting protection came with the revolution of 1848, when the newly elected Parliament drafted a constitution that established religious toleration. Köbner attempted to promote full-fledged religious liberty in his 1848 treatise, *Manifesto of Free Primitive Christianity of the German People*. Referencing Roger Williams and Thomas Helwys, the treatise argued for the right to worship according to one's conscience, not only for Baptists but also for people of other faiths or no faith at all. German citizens, who were accustomed to a state-church alliance, were infuriated at Köbner's call for religious liberty. Unlike Karl Marx's *Communist Manifesto*, published that same year, Köbner's *Manifesto* on religious liberty had a limited shelf life.

German Baptists Advocating Religious Liberty

We do not receive this precious freedom only today from some benevolent state power; we have for the past fifteen years considered it our inalienable right and continuously enjoyed it even at the expense of our earthly possessions and freedom. But we maintain not only our religious liberty, we demand it for every human being who inhabits the soil of the fatherland, we demand it equally for all, be they Christians, Jews, Mohammadans, or whatever. We consider it not only a totally unchristian sin to lay the iron fist of coercion upon any human with regard to his/her way of worshipping God, we also believe that the advantage of each religious party demands a totally equal right of all.

Julius Köbner, *To the Community: Selected Writings* (1927). Cited in Erich Geldbach, "Julius Köbner's Contribution to Baptist Identity," in *Baptist Identities: International Studies from the Seventeenth to the Twentieth Centuries* (Paternoster, 2006).

A Baptist document that stood the test of time was the confession of faith produced by Oncken and Köbner in 1837. With some modifications by Lehmann in 1845, it was adopted in 1849 by the Union of Baptist Churches in Germany and Denmark and is still in use today. The Confession of Faith and Constitution of the Churches of Baptized Christians Commonly Called Baptists describes standard elements of Baptist belief. Scripture is described as "the only true divine revelation," God is portrayed using orthodox trinitarian language, and election is defined in Calvinistic terms. Conversion is described as the work of the Holy Spirit in conjunction with the Word of God, producing faith and repentance. Baptism by immersion should be administered only to one who has "recognized the frightfulness of sin and damnability of his whole being" and "sets all his hope solely on the death and resurrection of Jesus Christ his Savior," according to the confession. The Lord's Supper is portrayed as both a memorial and spiritual meal that makes the Son of God "appear to their souls anew in his bloody beauty" and serves as a divine pledge that one's sins have been forgiven.

**Confession of Faith and Constitution of the
Churches of Baptized Christians
Commonly Called Baptists, Article X (1847)**

Through baptism we are taken up into the church of Christ on earth, and the Lord has ordained this as a means of grace for us. In accordance with the commands of Jesus and his apostles, as also the example of apostolic times, and in order to bring all the ordinances of the New Testament into operation, it is the duty of every believer converted to God not to stand alone for himself, but to unite himself with other disciples of the Lord as a member of a body, and as the living stones of a house of God, in order mutually to edify one another, to comfort and help each other on the way of salvation, in order to continue in the apostle's doctrine, in fellowship, in the breaking of bread and prayer. Such a union of the true disciples of Christ, regulated according to the word of God, is a Christian church. The unchangeable rule and plumb-line of the church remains the New Testament.

Unlike the dominant Lutheran Church, these Baptists recognized no ecclesiastical authority above the local church. Every member had a vote in the affairs of the church, and leaders were "obligated to carry into effect the conclusions of the church." Preachers, according to the confession, were accountable to the congregation for their manner of teaching and way of life: "In respect to the evangelical purity of their teachings they stand under the oversight of the united church, which in case a preacher departs from the doctrines of the gospel as they are conceived in this Confession of faith, and persists in his departure notwithstanding all warnings, can remove the same from his office." The introduction of congregationalism set European Baptists apart from the standing order of state-sponsored churches. Not only did laypersons have input in the direction of the church; leaders were put on notice that holding office was not a right but a privilege.

The visionary leadership of Oncken and his team, combined with increased religious liberty throughout Europe and a confessional union of churches, made for healthy church plants. Oncken baptized Fredrik Nillson in 1847, who in turn formed a Baptist church in Sweden. Later Swedish Baptists founded the Baptist Union of Sweden. Baptist work in Norway commenced under the leadership of Fredrik Rymer, who founded the first Norwegian Baptist church in 1860. Leaders of the Dutch Baptist Union, which was formed in 1881, received training in Hamburg from Oncken and Köbner. The first Baptist church in Zurich began in 1849 after Oncken conducted a preaching tour and sent Freidrich Maier to unite converts into Baptist churches. Baptist work in France began with the preaching of Swiss evangelist Henri Pyt in 1819, which led to the formation of a church the following year. In 1832, the Triennial Convention enlisted Casimir Rostan as a missionary in Paris, and by 1849 the first Baptist association in France was in place. Oncken continued his missionary labors as late as 1870, traveling through Russia, Turkey, Romania, Transylvania, Hungary, and Austria, preaching the gospel and planting churches. Baptist work throughout Eastern Europe developed more slowly, but initial efforts in the nineteenth century proved foundational to establishing a Baptist presence during the twentieth century.

Landmarkism

During the same period European Baptists were benefitting from the work of the *Kleeblatt*, Baptists in America were becoming familiar with the "Great Triumvirate" of James Robinson Graves, James Madison Pendleton, and Amos Cooper Dayton. The American trio was every bit as passionate as their European counterparts, but there was a key difference. Whereas Oncken affirmed "every Baptist a missionary," Graves declared "every church a Baptist church." Despite the fact that Graves considered Oncken a fellow "Landmarker," there was little similarity between the two in their understandings of the church. In short, Graves introduced a theological innovation that came to be known as Landmarkism.

J. R. Graves
(1820–93)

The name for the Landmark movement was drawn from two passages in the Old Testament, Job 24:2 and Proverbs 22:28, both of which warn against removing "landmarks," or property markers. Originally a call to respect boundaries between landowners, these passages were invoked to call for guarding Baptist doctrine against the encroachment of non-Baptist teaching. The fundamental idea of Landmarkism was that Baptist churches were the only true churches. Christians belonging to other denominations may comprise a religious society of sorts, but they lack the biblical marks of a church, Landmarkism taught. Landmarkers also believed an unbroken line of Baptist churches stretched back to the apostles. This view affected preaching, baptism, communion, and missions. In terms of geographical impact,

Landmarkism was strongest in Tennessee, Kentucky, Alabama, Arkansas, Mississippi, Texas, and Louisiana, with pockets of influence in southern Illinois, southern Missouri, northern Florida, South Carolina, Georgia, California, and Oregon.

Landmarkism began with a simple question: "Is a baptism valid if it is performed by a pedobaptist?" The question had been asked before, but the affirmative response provided in 1848 by John Lightfoot Waller, editor of *The Western Baptist Review*, a Kentucky Baptist periodical, raised the ire of J. R. Graves. According to Graves, who was editor of his own paper, *The Tennessee Baptist*, baptisms were only valid if performed by someone who had been immersed as a believer. Graves asserted that excluding from church membership people who were not properly immersed was "the unbroken practice of the Baptist Church, from deep antiquity." This unbroken practice, he believed, reached all the way to the first century when the Baptist movement began.

Graves defined the church as a local, visible entity, rejecting the idea of a universal church that extends through space and time. By denying the universal, or invisible, component of the church, Graves expected all churches to follow the specific design appropriated by Christ himself. No true church deviated from the Baptist model, Graves said. A corollary of this conclusion was that the kingdom of God is the aggregate of Baptist churches. To enter the kingdom, one had to become a Baptist.

In making his case for an unbroken succession of Baptist churches, Graves cited George Herbert Orchard's 1838 treatise, *A Concise History of Baptists from the Time of Christ Their Founder to the 18th Century*. Orchard advocated Baptist successionism, arguing that Baptist churches existed continuously from the first century in fulfillment of Jesus' promise in Matthew 16:18 to build, protect, and perpetuate his church. For Orchard, a key piece of evidence that Jesus intended to found Baptist churches was the fact that John the Baptist immersed him in the Jordan River. One difficulty in sustaining the historical argument for unbroken succession was that the term *Baptist* was notably absent throughout much of church history. Yet Orchard traced Baptist succession through eighteen centuries by focusing on dissenting movements such as the Cathari, Albigensians, Novatianists, and Waldensians, among others. Though not Baptist in name, Orchard claimed, they were Baptist in principle. In reality, the tie that bound them together was their dissension from the Catholic Church, and Orchard assumed his conclusion rather than proving it. Nonetheless, Graves republished Orchard's book in 1855. To account for the missing denominational label throughout church history, he added the word *foreign* to the original title: *A Concise History of Foreign Baptists from the Time of Christ Their Founder to the 18th Century*.

Despite the weakness of Graves's arguments, Landmarkism gained significant traction as it provided Baptists with confidence that they, out of the ever-growing number of denominations, were doctrinally correct and always had been. Landmarkism also isolated Baptists from other groups. When the Landmark movement officially commenced in 1851 at a meeting in Cotton Grove, Tennessee, five questions were presented to attendees regarding the nature of Baptist relationships to non-Baptist movements. With the exception of the fourth, each query was answered in the negative, thereby severing relational ties to Christians of other denominations. Landmarkism claimed that the activities of a church—preaching, baptizing, and communion—were reserved for Baptists only. Hence, non-Baptists were no longer allowed to preach in Landmark churches; baptisms that were performed by non-Baptists were considered "alien immersions"; and the Lord's Supper was "closed Communion," reserved for members of Baptist churches. While most nineteenth-century Baptists only recognized Baptist baptisms and had restricted the Lord's Supper to Baptist church members, the nuance provided by the Landmark movement was that there was no such thing as a non-Baptist church. Denying communion to a Presbyterian or Methodist, for example, was no different than refusing communion to a person who belonged to nothing more than a book club.

J. M. Pendleton and A. C. Dayton contributed significant writings to Landmark theology. Pendleton was a pastor in Bowling Green, Kentucky, when he met Graves during a series of revival meetings. Graves was the scheduled speaker but nearly declined the opportunity when he discovered that he and Pendleton held different views regarding alien immersion. Pendleton convinced Graves to stay and preach, and Graves convinced Pendleton of his position on baptism. Interestingly, the articles Pendleton wrote on behalf of the Landmark movement centered on the question of pulpit exchange, the topic that nearly wrecked their relationship. Pendleton's *An Old Landmark Re-set*, published by Graves in 1854, gave the movement its

*J. M. Pendleton
(1811–1891)*

name (citing the passages previously mentioned) and started a controversy among Baptists that made Landmarkism nearly impossible to ignore.

The Cotton Grove Resolutions (1851)

1st Can Baptists, consistently with their principles or the Scriptures, recognize those societies not organized according to the pattern of the Jerusalem Church, but possessing different *governments*, different *officers*, a different class of *members*, different *ordinances, doctrines*, and *practices*, as churches of Christ?

2nd Ought they to be called gospel churches, or churches in a religious sense?

3rd Can we consistently recognize the ministers of such irregular and unscriptural bodies as gospel ministers?

4th Is it not virtually recognizing them as official ministers to invite them into our pulpits, or *by any other acts that would or could* be construed into such a recognition?

5th Can we consistently address as *brethren* those professing Christianity who not only have not the doctrines of Christ and walk not according to his commandments, but are arrayed in direct and bitter opposition to them?

Pendleton asserted, and Graves agreed, that pulpit exchange was unacceptable between Baptists and ministers of other denominations:

> Where there is no baptism, there are no visible churches. There is no baptism among Pedo-baptists, therefore, there are no visible churches. Where there are no visible churches, there is no gospel authority to preach. There are no visible churches among Pedo-baptists. Therefore, there is no authority to preach. It follows, then, that Baptists ought not to recognize Pedo-baptist preachers as gospel ministers.

Pendleton also published *Church Manual Designed for the Use of Baptist Churches* (1867). A less polemical work than *An Old Landmark Re-set*, the *Church Manual* nevertheless described the organization of the church with considerable Landmark flavor, influencing pastors well into the twentieth century to embrace closed communion, reject alien immersion, and promote Baptist successionism. Leon McBeth observed that "through this manual, generations of Southern Baptist pastors have absorbed Landmarkism without knowing it."

A. C. Dayton's literary contribution to Landmark teaching was more subtle, coming in the form of a novel. Dayton was a Presbyterian who practiced dentistry before becoming a Baptist and accepting a pastorate. His interest in writing led him to contribute nearly a thousand articles to twenty different periodicals and propelled him to serve as corresponding secretary of the short-lived Bible Board of the Southern Baptist Convention. His best-known work, *Theodosia Ernest, or Heroine of the Faith*, first appeared serially in Graves's *Tennessee Baptist* from 1856 to 1857 and was later published as a two-volume work totaling nearly a thousand pages. It describes the journey of a young Presbyterian girl whose earnest love for God (hence the title) compels her to search for the true church. She ultimately finds rest for her soul among Baptists but not without difficulty, as her relationship with a man not yet convinced of Baptist views threatens to

A. C. Dayton remembered by Georgia Baptists.

divide her loyalty. Along the way she encounters objections from educated non-Baptist ministers who attempt to persuade her to return to the Presbyterian fold. Undeterred, Theodosia overcomes their arguments with her knowledge of Hebrew and Greek, as well as church history, all from the Landmark perspective, and eventually convinces the man who had captured her heart. They later marry and begin a life of spreading Landmark views. While today's reader might find Dayton's style a bit over the top, nineteenth-century Baptists were entertained, and the fact that the lead character was an intelligent Baptist female was not lost on the largely female audience. Interestingly, Dayton's wife, Lucianda, remained a Presbyterian until five months before his death in 1865.

Baptist isolationism was but one casualty of the Landmark movement. It also severed ties between certain Baptists and nearly put an end to the nascent Foreign Mission Board of the Southern Baptist Convention. A personal dispute between Graves and Robert Boyte Crawford Howell led to a confrontation at the 1859 meeting of the SBC. Howell had long been a titanic figure in Baptist life, at various times serving as president of the Foreign Mission Board, the Bible Board, and the Sunday School Board. In addition, he was president of the SBC from 1851 to 1859 and pastor of the influential First Baptist Church of Nashville, Tennessee, where Graves held his membership. Both Howell and Graves understood the power of publishing to influence Baptists, and when Graves proposed establishing the Southern Baptist Sunday School Union, Howell gave his support to the burgeoning Southern Baptist Publication Society. Graves subsequently pilloried Howell

The Conversion of Theodosia Ernest
to Baptist Principles

Theodosia retired to her chamber, where she spent a few moments in prayer to God for the guidance of the Holy Spirit, and then took her Testament and read how they were baptized of John *in the river of Jordan*. . . . She compared these statements with [the baptism] she had seen at the river, and did not need any *Lexicons* to satisfy her that John's baptism . . . was immersion. Why else did they go into the water? Why else was it done in the river? Ministers don't go into the river to sprinkle their subjects now-a-days. There was no reason for doing it then. "Must I unite with this obscure sect and be immersed? Must I break away from the communion that I love so dearly—from all my friends and relatives?" . . . The very thought was terrible. She threw herself on her bed and wept aloud. Her crying brought her mother to her side. She kneeled beside the bed . . . and bade her to banish this distressing subject from her thoughts. It was not worthwhile, she said, for a young girl like her to set up her own opinions. . . . As for herself, if her pastor, Mr. Johnson said any thing was in the Bible, she always *took it for granted it was there*. . . . "But mother," sobbed the weeping girl, "I must answer to *God*, and not to Pastor Johnson. Much as I love him, I trust and love my Saviour better; and if my pastor says *one* thing, and Jesus Christ *another* . . . I have no choice; *I must obey my Saviour*."

Excerpted from *Theodosia Ernest* (1857).

in the *Tennessee Baptist* whereupon members of First Baptist Nashville cited Graves for "grossly immoral and unchristian conduct" and dismissed him from their membership. In retaliation, Graves started his own church, which he claimed was the "true First Baptist Church."

During the 1859 meeting of the SBC, Graves brought his Landmark views and disdain for Howell together when he called for abolishing the Foreign Mission Board. The local church, Graves argued, was the only entity Scripture authorized to examine, appoint, and direct the work of missionaries. An entire day was given to debate the topic, and though feelings were exceptionally strong on both sides, the SBC voted to retain the Foreign Mission Board. An additional blow to Graves's agenda occurred when Howell was reelected to the convention's presidency. To his credit, Howell immediately resigned in order to prevent further conflict with the Landmarkers. Had Graves been successful in controlling the publications of the SBC and abolishing the mission board, Landmarkism might well have become a defining trait of the Southern Baptist Convention. Instead, the onset of the Civil War hindered Landmark progress, relegating it to regional influence.

Baptists and the American Civil War

The split between Northern and Southern Baptists was but a prelude to the larger division among the American people. The issue of slavery was ultimately settled on the battlefields of the American Civil War (1861–65). By and large, responses to the war by Northern and Southern Baptists were predictable. The Charleston Baptist Association passed a resolution one month before South Carolina's secession from the Union, expressing confidence in the scriptural legitimacy of slavery and backing secession: "In resisting the encroachments of the enemies of our domestic institution, and opposing the 'perverse disputings of men of corrupt minds, and destitute of this truth,' our duty to God coincides with our duty to our country." A week after the Confederate Congress declared that a state of war existed with the United States (May 6, 1861), Southern Baptists convened in Savannah, Georgia, and declared themselves on the side of the Confederacy and its leaders, pledging, "With them are our hearts and our hearty cooperation." Northern Baptists expressed support for the Union with equal resolve. Free Will Baptists supported the Union without exception since they had long opposed slavery.

William Jones, Civil War chaplain and author of Christ in the Camp.

Baptists in border states like Maryland and Kentucky endured the added difficulty of attending churches where some members supported the Union and others the Confederacy. Pastors struggled to address their divided congregations, causing some to leave their pastorates in search of churches with members of like mind regarding the war. At times Baptists in the South also disagreed about the war. In South Carolina, Baptist leaders like James Boyce and John Broadus owned slaves but opposed secession. Once the war was underway, however, they served as chaplains for the Confederacy, motivated by a sense of duty to their country and their concern for soldiers. Boyce and Broadus encouraged pastors in training to preach to the troops and provide them with Bibles and Christian books. Boyce viewed the war as a time when ministers of the gospel were especially needed: "The field of labor is increased. The threatening circumstances of war have occasioned this.

Multitudes are away from home in immediate peril of life. These require the faithful warnings of such as would wean them from their temptations of the camp, and teach them the way to that home to which alone perhaps shall they ever go." Baptist chaplains were in short supply though, since the denomination generally opposed governmental support of religious services. Baptist associations attempted to fill the gap by raising support for chaplains while editors of Baptist newspapers published pleadings for volunteers to perform chaplaincy tasks.

Baptists on both sides of the battle lines secured Bibles and Christian books for their respective armies, though the task proved more difficult for Baptists in the South, who relied on Northern publishing agencies, particularly the American Baptist Publication Society. One of the most popular works for soldiers was "A Mother's Parting Words to Her Soldier Boy." Written from the perspective of a Confederate mother, the tract began with a justification of the war (liberties lost due to Northern encroachment). The fictional mother then apologized for not addressing matters of religion while her son lived at home and expressed hope that he would dedicate himself to Jesus while serving in the military.

A Civil War Era Gospel Tract

You must, my dear boy, be a Christian or suffer sad and irreparable defeat. You may, without faith in Christ, storm citadels, win battles, achieve the independence of your beloved country, and gain imperishable renown; but you cannot secure the kingdom of heaven. . . . It is not reasonable to suppose that God will accept the services rendered to Caesar for those due to himself; or that patriotism should be a substitute for piety. The heroic, but ungodly soldier, may fill a grave honored by a nation's tears and marked by a towering monument; but his soul, alas! must perish. I would have you, my son, not only to be a Christian, but to honor that sacred name. Make the Bible your constant companion—prayer your delightful employment—and the glory of Christ the end of all your deeds. . . . Keep aloof from all the vices which corrupt and degrade the army. I need not warn you against profanity, that common but ill-bred sin, which you have been taught to detest; but I would especially guard you against drunkenness, that most insidious, prevalent and degrading vice. . . . I am sure, my child, you will not be a worse soldier for being a good Christian. Piety will not make you effeminate or cowardly. Some of the bravest soldiers in the world have been humble Christians.

Excerpt from "A Mother's Parting Words to Her Soldier Boy" (1861).

The impact of Baptist chaplains and colporteurs (book distributors) was mixed. A popular book written by Baptist J. William Jones, entitled *Christ in the Camp: Religion in Lee's Army* (1887), described individual conversions and group revivals that took place among the troops. Generals Robert E. Lee and "Stonewall" Jackson were presented as model Christians; stories were told of soldiers who repented of their previously godless lifestyles after hearing sermons or reading tracts. Especially poignant were stories of deathbed conversions. George Rable's work, *God's Almost Chosen Peoples* (2010), presents a different perspective. Lee and Jackson's public faith notwithstanding, Rable notes that numerous officers were distinctly irreligious and promoted vice rather than virtue. Attendance at religious services was strikingly low during the first two years of the war while consumption of alcohol, gambling, and sexual immorality trended upward. Moreover, despite the impact of "A Mother's Parting Words," soldiers often avoided practicing their faith openly lest they appear effeminate before their comrades. Still, reports of revival should not be entirely dismissed. Since soldiers experienced extended times of boredom between moments of fighting, a preacher visiting the troops could break up the monotony as easily as a bottle of alcohol.

Letters to family and minutes from church meetings provide insight into the effects of war on soldiers and citizens alike. Soldiers longed for a return to normalcy back home, and church meetings became strangely silent regarding the war. Southerners began to question whether God was against them. John Leadley Dagg, whose résumé included several pastorates, a college presidency, and the first systematic theology written by a Southern Baptist, vocalized the South's thinking about the war. Still taking for granted that American slavery was justified, Dagg concluded that Southerners had not treated their slaves biblically, in particular by failing to evangelize them and by separating slaves from their spouses and families. The shift from certainty to self-examination became even more prominent among Southerners after the war, leading them to adopt what has been called the religion of the "lost cause." The war was lost and slaves were free, but the South took a lesson from the war, namely, to distance itself from the

John L. Dagg (1794–1884)

Northern way of life, which Southerners characterized as immoral, secular, and theologically suspect.

Accepting this characterization of the North, Southern Baptists rebuffed suggestions by the American Baptist Home Mission Society (ABHMS) that they should reunite with Northern Baptists. The ABHMS proposals appeared to be genuine—"If the Government is to be one, why should not the Baptist denomination be one?"—but reunion was complicated. In 1864, the ABHMS secured authorization from the War Department to take over abandoned Baptist churches in the South "in which a loyal minister of said church does not now officiate." This authorization provided considerable opportunity for Northern Baptists to acquire property, which they claimed was done for purposes of preservation. Southern Baptists viewed the seizure of churches as unnecessarily aggressive and, worse, unbaptistic. Opponents of reunion also noted that the two bodies had different structures—convention versus society again—and that the SBC had grown so large that few buildings would be able to house a combined meeting of Northern and Southern Baptists. Attempts to reunite Northern and Southern Baptists continued through 1877, but none overrode an 1866 resolution declaring the SBC to be a "permanent institution."

Baptists in the War's Aftermath

Following the Civil War, former slaves began leaving the Southern Baptist Convention by the hundreds of thousands. Nearly half a million African-Americans separated from biracial congregations to begin their own churches. White Baptists, Northern and Southern, attempted to help, since black Baptists were growing faster than their supply of leaders. The ABHMS established a Freedman's Institute to provide doctrinal and leadership instruction for African-American pastors and deacons. Colleges were also established by the ABHMS, including Shaw University in North Carolina, Morehouse College in Georgia, and Bishop College in Texas. African-American Baptist colleges proved to be one of the few initiatives in which Baptists in the South and North could cooperate.

Some Southerners donated their church buildings to African-American congregations or provided financial assistance to help them build new churches. Equality, however, was not to be found. In 1866 the Charleston Association heard a report from its "Committee on the Colored People" (an unfortunate use of language that was used regularly among whites in the North and South), appointed to formulate an appropriate response to "one of the greatest social changes which the history of the world presents." The committee concluded that African-American Baptists should have their own churches and Sunday schools and that they might appreciate help from white pastors who could instruct them in ordination of pastors and admission of members. In short, segregation replaced slavery in post-Civil War America. In spite of such obstacles, African-American Baptists were quick to develop regional associations and managed to achieve national unity by the end of the century with the formation of the National Baptist Convention in 1895 (see chap. 9).

Following the Union's victory, many wondered whether Southern Baptists could regroup and continue the movement they had begun. Northern Baptists suffered little in terms of institutional stability as they retained control of the American Baptist Missionary Union (ABMU), the ABHMS, and the American Baptist Publication Society (ABPS). The ABMU suffered no financial loss with the departure of Southern Baptists and throughout the remainder of the nineteenth century made great progress in its attempt to "diffuse the knowledge of the religion of Jesus Christ, by means of missions, throughout the world." Between 1846 and 1900, the number of ABMU missionaries increased from 99 to 474, and

Henrietta Shuck
(1817–1844)

the number of supporting churches increased from 82 to 928. The ABMU's most effective work occurred in Burma, South India, China, Japan, Africa, and the Philippines. As previously mentioned, the ABHMS gained a foothold in the South through the acquisition of Baptist church buildings and the Freedman's Institute. By 1869, nearly a third of ABHMS missionaries were located in southern states. Mission work also expanded into the western portion of the United States, where the ABHMS provided grants and loans for the construction of church buildings. By the end of the nineteenth century, the ABHMS employed more than 1,100 missionaries. The ABPS continued as before the war, with Northern and Southern Baptists using its resources to supply their members with religious literature.

The outlook for Southern Baptists was less promising. The mission agencies formed at the founding of the SBC mirrored those of Northern Baptists, including a Foreign Mission Board (FMB) and a Domestic Mission

Board (DMB). Prior to the war Southern Baptists conducted foreign mission work in China through the work of J. Lewis Shuck, originally appointed by the Triennial Convention. He and his wife, Henrietta, founded the first Baptist church in Hong Kong in 1843. Henrietta's death the following year led Lewis to return to the United States, where he received a commission by the newly formed SBC. He planted churches in Canton, Shanghai, and Shantung but returned to America in 1851 after his second wife died. Upon his return Shuck began working with Chinese Christians in California under the auspices of the DMB, establishing the first Chinese Baptist church in America, located in Sacramento. Work in China continued through various SBC missionaries, including Samuel Clopton and Rosewell H. Graves. The SBC also began mission work in Africa prior to the war, with the appointment of John Day in 1846 and development of Baptist work in Liberia by Lott Carey and Colin Teague. Despite multiple missionary deaths early on, mainly due to disease, growth of the missions enterprise was constant. Even Northern Baptists recognized the success of Southern Baptists in missions by transferring their Liberian ministry to the SBC in 1856.

The war, however, diverted attention from the foreign mission field and nearly destroyed the work of home missions. Raising funds for missions became difficult as many field agents focused their energies in other areas, often becoming chaplains and colporteurs. Delivering funds also proved difficult as Northern armies blocked Southern traffic to the north and abroad. Some missionaries managed to continue their work through salary advances they received before blockades were in place. Others became dependent on the gifts of missionary societies from other denominations. Southern Baptists even discovered ways to ship cotton to England and sell it at an inflated price, using the proceeds to support their missionaries in China and Africa. These were temporary measures, however, and by war's end it became clear that unless visionary Baptist leaders emerged, the SBC was in trouble. The work among Chinese Christians in California was suspended; missions to Native Americans came to an end; and two attempts at publishing, the Bible Board in Nashville and the Southern Baptist Publication Society in Charleston, both failed entirely. The first Baptist seminary in the South, Greenville's The Southern Baptist Theological Seminary, also closed during the war. However, capable leaders sustained the school, and it played a defining role in Southern Baptist life.

Southern Seminary and the Sunday School Board

After nearly three decades of discussion about the need for a Baptist seminary in the South, The Southern Baptist Theological Seminary was founded in 1859 on the campus of Furman University. Among the Northern Baptist seminaries already in existence were Hamilton (later Colgate) Theological Seminary (1820), Newton Theological Institute (1826), and Rochester Theological Seminary (1850), but their stances against slavery made them unappealing options for Southern ministerial students. With the SBC refusing to invest in a theological institution, advocates of a new seminary called an Education Convention, which met in Augusta, Georgia, in 1856. The convention could not agree on the seminary's location and did not know whether it would succeed. The choice to move forward using the resources of Furman University the following year was largely the result of James Petigru Boyce's leadership. Boyce, as a professor of theology at Furman, convinced delegates that South Carolinians alone could raise $100,000, a quarter of which would be guaranteed through Furman's endowment. Raising funds proved to be a constant difficulty for the seminary.

Confessional Fidelity and Theological Education

It is, therefore, gentlemen, in perfect consistency with the position of Baptists, as well as of Bible Christians, that the test of doctrine I have suggested to you, should be adopted. It is based upon principles and practices sanctioned by the authority of Scripture, and by the usage of our people. In so doing, you will be acting simply in accordance with propriety and righteousness. You will infringe the rights of no man, and you will secure the rights of those who have established here an instrumentality for the production of a sound Ministry. It is no hardship to those who teach here, to be called upon to sign the declaration of their principles, for there are fields of usefulness open everywhere to every man, and none need accept your call who cannot conscientiously sign your formulary. And while all this is true, you will receive by this an assurance . . . that the Ministry that go forth have here learned to distinguish truth from error . . . and that the same precious truths of the Bible which were so dear to the hearts of its founders, and which I trust are equally dear to yours, will be prorogated in our Churches.

Excerpt from James P. Boyce, "Three Changes in Theological Institutions" (1856).

Boyce brought a novel vision to the school. On the same day his proposal was adopted, he delivered a message titled "Three Changes in Theological Institutions," which explained how the new seminary would be different from other theological schools. First, students would be able to attend the seminary without having previously completed collegiate or classical studies. Boyce encouraged use of the English Bible, thereby allowing students without proficiency in Hebrew or Greek to study in the same class as students whose linguistic skills were more refined. Second, gifted students would be able to pursue advanced studies in order to advance Baptist

scholarship. Boyce noted that budding professors relied too heavily on ideas
from theologically suspect institutions. He believed
an emphasis on training young, pious scholars
would curb this trend. Third, professors at the
seminary would teach in accordance with a
confession of faith. Boyce recognized that
many Baptists were averse to using creeds,
noting the lingering influence of Alexander Campbell. However, Boyce dismissed
the "no creed but the Bible" mantra by
reminding his constituents that "peculiar
obligations rest . . . upon those to whom
are entrusted the education of the rising
Ministry." In order to safeguard the seminary from incipient or outright liberalism,
and to keep the school accountable to Southern
Baptists, Boyce pressed for a confession of faith
that all professors would be required to sign without reservation.

James P. Boyce
(1827–1888)

Boyce became the founding president of Southern Seminary, assisted by
two faculty members, John Broadus and Basil Manly Jr. Broadus graduated
from the University of Virginia and received his first teaching post there as
professor of Latin and Greek. Upon his arrival at Southern, Broadus implemented a version of the University of Virginia's elective system, which gave
students freedom to take classes in various departments. This arrangement
permitted students with little collegiate background to take courses alongside advanced students while at the same time giving advanced students
opportunities to improve their own expertise. Manly had the difficult task
of writing a confession of faith that was comprehensive but not controversial. At the time the SBC had no confession of faith from which he could
draw, so Manly drew from a trio of confessions: the Westminster Confession
of Faith (used by Presbyterians), the Second London Confession, and the
New Hampshire Confession. The resulting document was the Abstract of
Principles, adopted by the seminary in 1858. Every professor employed by
Southern Seminary, from its founding to the present, has been required to
sign a statement pledging to teach "in accordance with, and not contrary to"
the Abstract of Principles.

The abstract contains twenty articles representing the consensus of Southern Baptist churches on matters such as Scripture, God, election, regeneration, justification, sanctification, the church, the Lord's Day, and liberty of
conscience. The section on providence states: "God from eternity, decrees

or permits all things that come to pass, and perpetually upholds, directs and governs all creatures and all events; yet so as not in any wise to be the author or approver of sin nor to destroy the free will and responsibility of intelligent creatures." Manly's original proposal used slightly different language, omitting the word "permits," which prompted a discussion about the extent to which humans were responsible for their own actions. The final version, as quoted above, could not have been more prophetic about the seminary's future in light of the onset of Civil War just two years later. Boyce, Broadus, and Manly, along with a fourth faculty member, William Williams, found themselves for the next decade and a half relying on the providence of God while also working as though the seminary's survival depended on them.

Due to the Civil War, Southern Seminary officially suspended operations in 1862. Unlike many other colleges that closed around the same time, however, it reopened and regained momentum. On paper the seminary had little to work with as only seven students matriculated for the first session. The four faculty members served as chaplains or pastors and remained bivocational for several years after the seminary reopened. Boyce loaned $3,000 to his colleagues in order to supplement their salaries while he raised funds. The seminary's endowment disappeared during Reconstruction since investments made prior to the war were tied to Confederate state bonds. Creditors hounded Boyce, seeking personal reimbursement for the stock Boyce once held in various defunct corporations. Southerners, who had prospered from slave labor, now lived on the edge of economic collapse.

And yet the seminary survived. Boyce raised funds from individuals, Manly began a fund to provide for the neediest students, and Broadus taught a course on preaching using the highest standards of scholarship even though he had but one student (a blind man) enrolled. Their personal commitment to the seminary was demonstrated by their refusal to take other positions that would have made their lives far more comfortable. Leading corporations, churches, and universities made offers to Boyce and Broadus in particular, including the South Carolina Railroad, First Baptist Church of Richmond, and the University of Chicago. Their refusal to leave the seminary helped secure its future, as did their willingness to humbly receive donations from Northern Baptists. A decision in 1872 to move the seminary from Greenville to Louisville, Kentucky, was based on the need to relocate to an area less devastated by the war and more capable of providing financial support, but even this did not end the harrowing times of near default. Ultimately the seminary survived long enough to become the SBC's flagship seminary. One key to its success was a prayer meeting held in Boyce's South Carolina home shortly before the school reopened. With the question of the seminary's future on the line, Broadus reportedly said, "Suppose we quietly agree that the seminary may die, but we'll die first."

Such dedication spilled over into other ventures as well. Southern Baptists spent nearly half a century attempting to establish a successful publishing agency but failed on multiple occasions. The tide began to turn in 1863 when Manly pressed for the adoption of a Sunday School Board, contending that "the Sunday School is the nursery of the Church, the camp of instruction for her young soldiers, the great missionary to the future." Manly became president of the board, and Broadus was elected as corresponding sec-

Norton Hall at Southern Seminary.

retary. Together they produced reading material designed to communicate Christian truths to children and youth. Their most famous series, *Kind Words for the Sunday School Children*, contained pictures, Bible verses, and short Bible stories. It was widely read until its discontinuation in 1929.

The publication venture as a whole stalled, however, due to its inability to compete with northern publishers. Hope for a sustained publishing operation nearly disappeared when the Sunday School Board merged with J. R. Graves's Sunday School Union in 1868 and was all but forgotten when the SBC transferred its print ministries to the Home Mission Board. However, under the leadership of Isaac Taylor Tichenor and James Marion Frost, Southern Baptists were able to establish a permanent publication agency. In 1891, the SBC voted to approve formation of the Baptist Sunday School Board (BSSB), to be located in Nashville, Tennessee, which would assume the responsibility, as Frost put it, of being "a unifying element in our denominational life and enterprises." Broadus reportedly wept when the convention voted to adopt the BSSB. In recognition of his and Manly's earlier contributions to educating Baptist laity, the print agency of the BSSB was called Broadman Press.

For Further Study

Briggs, John H. Y., ed. *A Dictionary of European Baptist Life and Thought*. Milton Keynes, UK: Paternoster, 2009.

Cooke, John Hunt. *Johann Gerhard Oncken: His Life and Work*. London: S. W. Partridge and Co., 1908.

Estep, William R. *Whole Gospel Whole World: The Foreign Mission Board of the Southern Baptist Convention 1845–1995*. Nashville, TN: Broadman, 1994.

Fitts, Leroy. *A History of Black Baptists*, chapter 2. Nashville, TN: Broadman, 1985.

Patterson, James. *James Robinson Graves: Staking the Boundaries of Baptist Identity*. Nashville, TN: B&H Academic, 2012.

Pierard, Richard V. "Germany and Baptist Expansion in Nineteenth-Century Europe." Pages 189–208 in *The Gospel in the World: International Baptist Studies*. Edited by D. W. Bebbington. Carlisle, Cumbria, UK: Paternoster, 2002.

Rable, George. *God's Almost Chosen Peoples: A Religious History of the American Civil War*. Chapel Hill, NC: University of North Carolina Press, 2010.

Tull, James. *High-Church Baptists in the South: The Origin, Nature and Influence of Landmarkism*. Macon, GA: Mercer University Press, 2000.

Wills, Gregory A. *Southern Baptist Theological Seminary, 1859–2009*. New York: Oxford University Press, 2009.

Questions for Discussion

1. Describe Johann Oncken's contributions to European Baptists. Do you agree or disagree with his key idea of "every Baptist a missionary"? In what way might this phrase apply to you or the people in your church?

2. Who else was involved in Oncken's ministry in Europe? How did they contribute to growth of Baptists during this time? What difficulties did they face?

3. Who were the key leaders of the Landmark movement in America? What were the core ecclesiological convictions of Landmark Baptists? What impact did these teachings have on Baptists as a whole?

4. From which key texts did Landmark Baptists draw their name? Is this an accurate understanding or application of those texts? Do you know of other Christian movements that derive their name from specific texts in the Bible?

5. What was the Graves-Howell Controversy of 1859, and what were its effects on Southern Baptist life? What factors contributed to this controversy's becoming public? What impact did Howell's stepping down have on the controversy? Can you think of ways Christians engaged in public controversies today ought to conduct themselves?

6. How did Baptists respond to the American Civil War? Provide at least three examples.

7. Describe Baptist life in America following the Civil War. What adjustments did white Baptists need to make? What adjustments did African-American Baptists need to make?

8. How did the Civil War affect Baptist missionary efforts at home and abroad? How did other minority groups suffer as a result of the war?

9. Discuss the formation of the Southern Baptist Theological Seminary and the Sunday School Board. Who were the key figures in the early years of these ministries? Does the sacrifice of such people as those mentioned here move you to pray more and give more to kingdom causes? Explain.

Chapter 8

TRANSITIONS AND TRENDS

The nineteenth century was a time of transition, and its closing decades reveal as much in Baptist life. Women received more opportunities to serve in leadership roles, and immigrants who flooded into America benefitted from ministries directed especially toward their needs. Other aspects of Baptist life, like the practice of church discipline, began fading into the background near the turn of the century. Baptist church manuals written between 1850 and 1900 attempted to instill a pattern of church life that would stand the test of time; however, they came to reflect an ideal from the past rather than a practice of the present. Perhaps the most notable transitions related to theological institutions. New schools were built, new directions were taken, and new challenges were faced. Baptist leaders living at the end of the century, like Charles Spurgeon and John Clifford, confronted this era of transition by adopting differing views on tradition and progress.

Visibility for Women and Immigrants

Women have nearly always outnumbered men as members of Baptist churches, but the paucity of female office holders, such as pastors or deacons, can obscure the impact women have had in initiating, organizing, and supporting Baptist causes. Baptists differ on whether it is biblical or discriminatory to exclude women from the offices of pastor, elder and deacon. In either case, prior to the twentieth century few women aspired to the pastorate, and few claimed to be victims of discrimination. Women often viewed their responsibilities as belonging to a separate sphere than those of men. In fact, seating in many Baptist churches was segregated according to gender well into the nineteenth century, a practice that changed not in the name of equality but in order to seat families together. Many Baptist churches had both deacons and deaconesses, recognizing that certain ministries to women were best performed by other women, in particular preparing them for baptism and visiting them when they were sick. However, deaconesses were not normally ordained in the nineteenth century, nor did they serve the Lord's Supper.

Women attended church in greater numbers than men, and they proved themselves to be more than passive hearers of their preachers' sermons. Abigail Harris, a New Jersey Baptist, listened with considerable discernment to her pastor, writing to a friend that he "made a good discourse from 1 John 5 and 10." She added, however, that he rambled a bit and that she disagreed with his statement that faith was "as manifest to every real Christian as the book which he held in his hand was to the eye of the spectator." She concluded, "I could not agree with him, for I believe that there is many a child of God that has not that visible witness given to them." Many women not only took notes during sermons, but some also distributed copies to members of their family. Women often wrote letters counseling their friends with passages from Scripture and offering encouragement.

Women impacted Baptist life in numerous ways: as authors of hymns and fictional literature, as guardians of the home and child-care workers in Sunday schools, as philanthropists for voluntary societies, and as leaders in higher education for women. Special gatherings, many of which were designed to encourage spiritual growth for women, were common in the eighteenth and nineteenth centuries. Between 1837 and 1852, for example, women at Prospect Place New Connexion Chapel in Bradford, Yorkshire, provided mutual spiritual benefit during their "experience meetings."

Maria Saffery, "The Good Shepherd" (1834)

There is a little lonely fold,
Whose flock one Shepherd keeps,
Through summer's heat and winter's cold,
With eye that never sleeps.

By evil beast, or burning sky,
Or damp of midnight air,
Not one in all that flock shall die,
Beneath that Shepherd's care.

For if, unheeding and beguiled,
In danger's path they roam,
His pity follows through the wild,
And guards them safely home.

O gentle Shepherd, still behold,
Thy helpless charge in me,
And take a wanderer to Thy fold,
That trembling turns to Thee.

Some women conveyed their Christian experiences through poetry, much of which was set to music and made into hymns sung by men and women alike. Annie Sherwood Hawks published her first poem at age fourteen, and by the end of her life she had written more than 400 hymns. Her most famous hymn, "I Need Thee Every Hour," reportedly came to mind as she went about the daily routine of caring for her family and home. Having her thoughts on the Lord while her hands were at work reflects the typical expectations of a nineteenth-century Christian woman. Hawks gave the poem to her pastor, Robert Lowry, who in turn set it to music and provided its refrain: "I need Thee, O I need Thee/ Every hour I need Thee/ O bless me now, my Savior/ I come to Thee." After her husband died, Hawks testified that the song even comforted her: "I did not understand why this hymn had touched the throbbing heart of humanity. It was not until long after, when the shadow fell over my way, the shadow of a great loss, that I understood something of the comforting power in the words which I had been permitted to give out to others in my hour of sweet serenity and peace." Maria Grace Saffery, whose husband and son were both English Baptist pastors, was another accomplished hymn writer. Her poem "The Good Shepherd," published in multiple denominational hymnals, highlights the affectionate care of the Lord for his people.

Baptist women made their mark in and outside the home. The Women's American Baptist Home Mission Society, formed in 1877, adopted the phrase "Christ in every home" as its motto. The society's founding president, Rumah Avilla Crouse, considered it a high calling to serve as a wife and mother. African-American women, such as Sophia Packard and Harriet Giles, established the Atlanta Baptist Female Seminary in 1881, later known as Spelman College. The school illustrated the noteworthy gender, ethnic,

Women at Spelman College (est. 1881).

and economic diversity among Baptists of the late nineteenth century: it was founded by women in a church where the pastor was a former slave and was funded in part by oil tycoon John D. Rockefeller Jr.

A few Baptist women sought and received ordination to the ministry during the nineteenth century, beginning with M. A. Brennan, who was ordained by the Bellevernon Free Will Baptist Church of Pennsylvania in 1876. Even though Free Will Baptists were open to women's ordination, their churches ordained only two other women prior to the turn of the century. Lura Maines was called as pastor of two Free Will Baptist churches in Michigan, and Louisa Fenner ministered to Free Will Baptist churches in Rhode Island and Connecticut. Two women from the Northern Baptist Convention, May C. Jones and Frances E. Townsley, were ordained in 1882 and 1885 respectively. Jones's ordination was controversial but ultimately successful. When opponents of the action walked out of the ordination meeting, it opened the door for her supporters to move forward. She served as interim pastor of Seattle's First Baptist Church (1882) and then as pastor of six other Baptist churches throughout the area that became Washington State in 1889. Frances Townsley preached regularly throughout New England before becoming pastor of Fairfield Baptist Church, Nebraska. Since she was not an ordained minister, the church regularly sent for male pastors to preside over the Lord's Supper and officiate at weddings. The inefficiency of this process led the church to pursue ordination for Townsley, who initially resisted in order to avoid controversy. Criticisms notwithstanding, she consented after fourteen Baptist churches participated in her examination and unanimously recommended her for ordination. Seventh Day Baptists were also open to women serving in leadership, as demonstrated by the ordination of Experience Fitz Randolph Burdick, who pastored several churches in New York from 1885 to 1890.

Though nineteenth-century Baptist women made their greatest contributions to the church behind the scenes, their most notable visibility came through their participation in mission societies. Women who served on the mission field usually accompanied their husbands, as the appointment of single women was rare. In addition to believing that Scripture differentiated between men's and women's roles in the church, Baptists wanted to prevent the gospel itself from becoming confused with Western concepts of social equality. Women who served alongside their husbands were often referenced in missionary magazines as "& wife," using the husband's name alone, according to the custom of the times. That women were not entirely overshadowed by men is demonstrated by the 1872 publication of Arabella Wilson's *Lives of the Three Mrs. Judsons*. Wilson's goal in memorializing Ann Hasseltine, Sarah Hall Boardman, and Emily Chubbuck—the successive wives of Adoniram Judson—was to provide spiritual biographies of women who exemplified "Christian heroism and fortitude" in service to their "Heavenly Master." By providing full biographies of each woman, Wilson went beyond the standard practice of promoting female piety through Christian fiction.

The need for female missionaries became evident as Baptists entered Asian countries where gender roles were deeply embedded. The Triennial Convention appointed its first single female missionaries to Burma in 1832. Harriet Baker became the first single woman appointed as a missionary by the Southern Baptist Convention when she was sent to Canton in 1849. Nearly twenty-five years elapsed before the SBC appointed its next two single, female missionaries in 1872, Lula Whilden and Edmonia Moon. Sometimes single missionaries alleviated their own obstacles by getting married while on the mission field. The group known as "The Serving Seven," a Canadian missionary team that included two married couples and three single persons, exemplifies this trend as the latter three each married missionaries after arriving in Burma.

In addition to their service on the mission field, women took the lead in organizing societies that raised funds to support missionaries. Such societies often functioned as auxiliary organizations of existing mission agencies. Hannah Maria Norris proved to be one of the most effective organizers among Canadian Baptist women, forming thirty-two societies throughout the Maritime Provinces in the span of only three months. She later became a missionary to Burma, and the societies she founded contributed to the formation of the Woman's Baptist Mission Union in Moncton (1884). The Woman's Baptist Foreign Missionary Society of the East, headquartered in Boston, and the Woman's Baptist Missionary Society of the West, headquartered in Chicago, were both formed in 1871 by women connected to the American Baptist Missionary Union. Women's home mission societies were also formed in Boston and Chicago, with the stated purpose of promoting "Christianization of homes by means of missions and mission schools, with special reference to the freed peoples, the Indians, and immigrant heathen populations." Such target groups underscored the concern that many women felt for the poor and marginalized.

The Woman's Missionary Union (WMU), formed in 1888, involved two women whose names became associated with Christmas and Easter offerings for international and North American missions, respectively. Its beginnings can be traced to a missionary prayer meeting in 1867 arranged by Ann Graves, whose son was a medical missionary serving in China. When Dr. Roswell Graves reported to his mother the success he had in teaching Bible stories to Chinese women, who in turn shared the stories with their families at home, she responded by calling the meeting. The following year Graves organized a meeting for women who were accompanying their

husbands to the Southern Baptist Convention
in Baltimore. Graves read to the women
letters from her son, inspiring them to
continue seeking ways to assist in the
mission work. That led to additional
gatherings coinciding with SBC
annual meetings. Additional support for women's societies came
from Henry Allan Tupper, secretary of the Foreign Mission Board
(FMB), who led Southern Baptists
to organize Central Committees
in each state to establish mission
societies. The culmination of these
efforts was the formation of a national
committee, the WMU. As an auxiliary
to the SBC, the WMU appointed its own
leaders and determined its own strategies
while working through the established
mission network of Southern Baptists.

Charlotte "Lottie" Moon
(1840–1912)

The two women whose names became associated with SBC missions offerings were instrumental in the early success of the WMU. Charlotte Diggs
"Lottie" Moon was a gifted linguist who set
aside her intention to become a teacher after
she responded to a missionary sermon,
telling her pastor, "I have long known
that God wanted me in China." Moon
served in Tengchow and Pingtu for
nearly four decades, drawing her
last breath on Christmas Eve 1912.
Her dedication to serving the Lord
in a strange land was demonstrated
by her willingness to adopt Chinese
customs and by her refusal to accept
well-deserved furloughs until her
post could be filled in her absence.
Moon's suggestion in 1888 for a week
of prayer followed by a mission offering
during the Christmas season was heartily
embraced by the WMU and became an
annual event. Annie Armstrong, corresponding

Annie Armstrong
(1850–1938)

secretary of the WMU, recommended the Christmas offering be named in Moon's honor.

Armstrong proved to be an exceptional organizer for the WMU, framing its constitution and nearly tripling its local affiliates in her two decades of service. She was particularly helpful in curbing women's interest in the Gospel Mission movement, an approach to missions with Landmark tendencies that called for local churches to withdraw support from denominational entities and support their own missionaries. The movement's chief propagator, Tarleton Perry Crawford, even influenced Moon to criticize the FMB, but Armstrong remained fully committed to the WMU's role as an auxiliary to the SBC. She took the unprecedented step of publicly rebuking state WMU leaders who sympathized with Crawford. Both Moon and Armstrong were instrumental in raising awareness of and finances for Baptist missionary work. Despite persistent criticism regarding their roles and challenges in relating to denominational boards, both women insisted on continuing their work in cooperation with the SBC.

Immigrants became the focus of various missionary efforts toward the latter half of the nineteenth century. Twenty million immigrants arrived in the United States between 1880 and 1890. Baptists were concerned about the changing cultural and religious landscape but also sensed an opportunity to evangelize. J. Lewis Shuck was successful in reaching the Chinese population in California, partly due to his previous mission work in China. Baptists reached immigrants of other nationalities thanks to leaders who shared their ethnicities. Swedish Baptists who were forced out of their country due to religious persecution found security in the Midwest. Wiberga and Gustaf Palmquist founded the first Swedish Baptist church in America at Rock Island, Illinois, in 1852, and John Alexis Edgren founded the Swedish Baptist Seminary of Chicago in 1881. By the end of the century, more than 20,000 Swedish-American Baptists were worshipping in their own language in more than 300 churches. German Baptists took root in Canada and the United States, largely through the work of August Rauschenbusch and Conrad Fleischman but also with the help of the General Missionary Society of German Baptists and the ABHMS. German Baptists formed their own denomination in 1851 and created their own school, with courses taught in their own language, at Rochester Theological Seminary in 1858. The ABHMS also promoted evangelistic work among the Hispanic population of Texas, the Polish population of Michigan, French Canadians in New England, and Italians in New York.

Baptists proved innovative in their evangelistic methods, evidenced by the introduction of the chapel train car in 1891. The idea for using a railroad car as an evangelistic tool—complete with pulpit, pews, stained glass, and an organ—originated with the American Baptist Publication Society in conjunction with a number of Baptist railroad executives, including Colgate Hoyt and John D. Rockefeller Jr. *Evangel*, the first of seven chapel cars, began its inaugural trip in Cincinnati, Ohio, with Boston Smith as its host evangelist. Smith conducted services and distributed Bibles and Sunday school literature at each stop through Minnesota, North Dakota, Missouri, and Montana. For the next fifty years the chapel car ministry provided evangelists and missionaries with opportunities to share the gospel throughout the United States.

A Baptist chapel car.

Church Manuals and Church Discipline

Less visible than other changes in the late nineteenth century but no less significant was the disappearance of practices that had formed and shaped Baptist identity during centuries prior. Such elements that faded with time included ordering churches strictly according to Scripture, employing pastoral visitation as a means of soul care, and practicing church discipline on a regular basis. These transitions were a striking departure from the procedures outlined in dozens of church manuals and treatises on polity written by Baptists during the nineteenth century. Such manuals and treatises were rooted in the Bible and attempted to outline the New Testament pattern of church organization.

Church manuals specialized in describing the Baptist rationale for church structure, offices, membership, worship, and discipline. Among the most popular manuals were William Crowell's *The Church Member's Manual* (1845), J. Newton Brown's *The Baptist Church Manual* (1853), Edward Hiscox's *The Baptist Church Directory* (1859), and J. M. Pendleton's *Church Manual* (1867). While manuals focused on multiple issues, treatises usually dealt with singular topics, such as W. B. Johnson's *The Gospel Developed* (1846), Joseph Baker's *Church Discipline* (1847), J. L. Reynolds's *Church Polity, or the Kingdom of Christ* (1849), P. H. Mell's *Corrective Church Discipline* (1860), Eleazar Savage's *Manual of Church Discipline* (1863), and William Williams's *Apostolical Church Polity* (1874). J. L. Dagg supplemented his *A Manual of Theology* (1857) with *A Manual of Church Order* (1858). Church covenants were the most important statements regarding behavioral expectations for Baptist church members. They were brief declarations, normally one page in length, which focused on core Christian beliefs and shared Baptist values. Those who wished to join a Baptist church in the nineteenth century subscribed to the covenant of that local church, whereupon their private lives became public property.

Polity was of utmost importance to nineteenth-century Baptists. Even so, they differed on many issues, including whether churches should have elders in addition to pastors and deacons or whether the pastoral office was synonymous with that of an elder. A transition was clearly underway as W. B. Johnson advocated for a plurality of elders in the local church, whereas Pendleton, writing some two decades later, believed a single pastor would suffice with the aid of deacons. Pastors were often referred to as "Elder" with their name following during the first half of the nineteenth century, but by the twentieth century the term "Reverend" had come into vogue.

The role of the pastor was understood primarily in terms of preaching and providing oversight to the church, though often pastors were expected to conduct pastoral visitation as well. Hiscox noted in his *Church Directory* that the minister must first of all be a teacher, referring to his work behind the pulpit, but is "peculiarly . . . the pastor" when he visits the flock: "He must know his people in their homes; must know their joys and sorrows as they themselves will relate them. They must know him, as they cannot know him in pulpit supply. Both he and they miss boundless good if this is not done. These visits must be brief and religious. They should not degenerate into social chit-chat, or even into religious gossip." The fact that pastors were not as keen on this advice toward the end of the nineteenth century is evidenced by Hiscox's words to the up-and-coming generation: "Young ministers may find it hard work, and dread it as a drudgery; but they will come to feel differently when for a few times they have been able to comfort the sorrowing, relieve the burdened, and know the luxury of doing good to those in trouble." Authors of manuals and treatises cited examples of pastoral visitation in an attempt to encourage the practice. Reminiscing about the life of P. H. Mell, pastor of churches in Georgia and president of the SBC for nearly fifteen years, his son wrote: "Very much of his power as a preacher lay in the way he had of getting close to his people. His custom was to visit all of them and so anxious were they not to miss the expected pleasure that he made engagements ahead often as far as three months."

Church manuals and treatises also informed church members of their duties within the body. One of the chief expectations was attendance at all meetings, including worship and business. Crowell echoed what virtually every church covenant stipulated:

> Church members are bound to attend all the meetings of the church, when in their power, to feel a deep interest in its welfare, to seek its peace and prosperity by devoting their abilities of every

kind to its service. This they virtually pledged themselves to do, in becoming members. They have no right to scatter their attendance on different meetings, to the neglect of those in the church.

The idea that members were under obligation to submit their lives to the congregation was consistent with the Baptist understanding that the church "has no right to alter the terms or conditions of membership, but must conform strictly to those prescribed by the Law-giver; much less can the will of the pastor be allowed to change these conditions . . . still less can the desire or judgment of the candidate himself modify the divinely prescribed conditions."

The terms of membership, according to Hiscox's *Manual*, included a regenerate heart, agreement with a confession of faith, the reception of baptism, and a lifestyle evidencing Christian belief. If a person failed to meet any one of these terms, he or she

THE

BAPTIST CHURCH DIRECTORY.

A GUIDE TO THE

DOCTRINES AND DISCIPLINE,

OFFICERS AND ORDINANCES,

PRINCIPLES AND PRACTICES,

OF

BAPTIST CHURCHES.

EMBRACING A CONCISE VIEW OF THE QUESTIONS OF

BAPTISM AND COMMUNION.

BY

EDWARD T. HISCOX, D.D.,

PASTOR OF STANTON STREET BAPTIST CHURCH, NEW YORK.

NEW YORK:
SHELDON & COMPANY.
MACON, GEO.:
GEORGIA BAPTIST BIBLE AND COLPORTEUR SOCIETY,
SAMUEL BOYKIN, DEPOSITORY AGENT.

Image of the front page of Hiscox's
The Baptist Church Directory.

would be refused membership. Hiscox was critical of Baptists who allowed unregenerate persons to take part in the life of the church instead of insisting on being born again as the first requirement for membership. The profession of faith was a testimony given by the candidate for membership in front of the congregation as a way of personally vouching for his or her change of life. Hiscox described the public sharing of one's spiritual experience as "the old Baptist way, from time immemorial," while realizing it was falling out of favor. "This custom," he wrote, "must be heroically maintained." Some churches offered members an opportunity to question candidates after they gave their testimonies, and most Baptist churches required a unanimous vote for a person to be granted membership.

Baptism was the symbolic expression of one's profession of faith, and Baptist churches required it. Gregory Wills relates the story of a woman who was refused membership in a Baptist church in 1856 because she believed her infant baptism was sufficient and should be accepted by members of the church. The pastor, Basil Manly Jr., based his refusal to admit her on the virtual unanimity of Baptist churches in his day: "Why should she set up her judgment against that of the whole body of churches of the only people under heaven who are striving to keep the ordinance of baptism as Christ delivered it?" This was not a Landmark position but rather a basic premise that Baptists shared regarding entry into the church.

The final requirement for obtaining membership in a Baptist church, a lifestyle evidencing Christian belief, was also a requirement for maintaining membership. A mere profession, even if theologically sound, did not suffice if a person's lifestyle was sinful and reckless. Hiscox's observation in this regard was both representative and blunt: "An external Christian life must corroborate the profession of an internal Christian faith, . . . And if there cannot be a good degree of conformity between the professed and the practical, persons had better remain out of the Church than to enter it." Those who joined the church and subsequently fell into sin were subject to a process of church discipline, a topic mentioned in virtually every church manual of the time. Baptists leaned heavily on core passages about discipline: Matthew 18:15–17; 1 Corinthians 5; 2 Thessalonians 3:6; and Titus 3:10. Church manuals provided step-by-step instructions on how to exercise discipline in a biblical, loving manner. Typically, Baptists distinguished between private and public offenses and responded to each category of sin differently. Ideally private offenses were addressed in private, with the offender repenting of his offense and making restitution to the offended person outside the purview of the church body. In cases where a public sin was committed or a private offense could not be resolved, church members were expected to address the issue among "two or three witnesses." If an offender still did not repent, the case was brought before the church body, usually during a monthly conference meeting.

Historians have used the phrase "moral court" in referring to this stage of Baptist church discipline. The entire congregation was expected to participate in determining the merits of a case and the outcome for the accused. In order to keep the church's reputation pure in the community, testimony against church members was allowed by those with no church affiliation; and, unlike civil court procedures in the Southern states, slaves could testify against whites. Some accusations were deemed superfluous, and sometimes a person was acquitted of the charges. If evidence convinced the church that the accused was guilty, the accused could admit to the charges and express heartfelt sorrow, in which case the church would normally offer an admonition to avoid similar sins in the future, followed by a public extension of the church's forgiveness.

Church Discipline in Baptist Churches

Just as soon as these and other gross crimes are proved upon one that is "called a brother," he should be withdrawn from.

1. For the sake of public morals and the reputation of the Church, she should testify unmistakably. This course would meet with approbation more heartily from no one than from the offender himself if he is a Christian; for to such the honor of the Master and the reputation of His Church are dearer than his own good name, or even than life itself. . . .

2. For the good of the offender himself. If he is not a Christian, he should not be a member of the Church; if he is a Christian, excommunication will not harm him. Corrective discipline, even in its highest censures, is an act of kindness to the offender, and designed not to injure but to reform. Such was the effect of the discipline inflicted upon the incestuous man at Corinth. While undisturbed by his brethren and permitted to go on in sin with impunity, he seemed not to be aware of the enormity of his crime; but after expulsion he is brought to reflection and penitence.

Excerpted from P. H. Mell, *Corrective Church Discipline* (1860).

Those who were found guilty in spite of their professed innocence, as well as those who admitted their guilt but rejected the church's authority over them, were excommunicated, or excluded from the life of the church. Baptists did not believe that excommunication affected one's eternal destiny, but there were more immediate ramifications. A person excluded from the church was no longer referred to as "Brother" or "Sister," could not receive the Lord's Supper or help select the church's officers, and could not participate in church conference meetings. Having been dismissed from one Baptist church, unrepentant offenders could not simply join another Baptist church, as membership covenants required that transfers arrive "in good standing" with their former congregation. One goal in every case was restoration of the offender, which occurred once repentance was expressed by the offender and evident to the church body.

While church manuals provided instruction on how to conduct disciplinary meetings, they did not address specific cases. In general, sins such as sexual immorality, drunkenness, theft, Sabbath-breaking, absenteeism, and heresy led to discipline. In cases involving special circumstances, churches sometimes asked for advice during associational meetings or through Baptist periodicals as a means of gathering the opinions of leaders whose years of experience and detachment from the situation aided in resolving the matter biblically. Queries ranged from the curious to the more consequential, with questions being raised about the meaning of the unpardonable sin and whether a man could serve as a deacon if his wife had left the faith.

Several noticeable shifts occurred in the latter half of the nineteenth century, signaling the demise of church discipline as a regular practice. Dancing, considered by antebellum Baptists a "worldly amusement," no longer received automatic censure and even put Baptists on the defensive as they tried not to alienate their younger members. Many Baptists stressed "formative" discipline over "corrective" discipline. Attention was given to enlisting members in church activities with the hope that they would find less time for and have less interest in mingling with the world. By the end of the nineteenth century, Baptists turned their attention toward evangelism and away from discipline. Larger churches enabled members to live their lives in anonymity, and questions of morality in an ever-changing culture were easier left unanswered. Gregory Wills's summary observation reveals much about the change in Baptist practice: "No one publicly advocated the demise of discipline. No Baptist leader arose to call for an end to congregational censures. No theologians argued that discipline was unsound in principle or practice. No 'freedom party' arose to quash the tyranny of the redeemed. It simply faded away, as if Baptists had grown weary of holding one another accountable."

Baptists and Temperance

The fading of church discipline did not mean Baptists stopped registering their disapproval of sin. In many cases that responsibility fell to benevolent societies. An example of this was the temperance movement. Prior to the nineteenth century, Baptists took no offense at moderate or medicinal uses of alcohol. Pastors were served after-dinner drinks when staying as guests in people's homes, and some packed an extra flask for the return trip. Prominent English Baptists, such as Matthew Vassar and John Jones, participated in the industrial production of beer. Baptist legend even credited one of its own rough-and-tumble preachers, Elijah Craig, with inventing Kentucky bourbon. In 1886, however, the Southern Baptist Convention began adopting resolutions against alcohol, declaring it to be "opposed to the best interests of society and government and the progress of our holy religion."

The beginning of the temperance crusade by Lyman Beecher in the 1820s and its acceleration following the formation of the Women's Christian Temperance Union (WCTU) in 1874, helped shift Baptists from approving of moderate drinking toward advocating total abstinence. Jesse Mercer, a leading Baptist pastor in Georgia, illustrates this shift well. Mercer drank brandy for

A temperance poster showing the dangers of alcohol abuse.

medicinal purposes and also stated that he did not believe casual drinking to be a sin. Not only did he change his mind and habits after learning that others were citing his example as an excuse to drink to excess, but he also formed a temperance society and published a temperance paper. Baptists in England underwent a similar transformation coinciding with the founding of the Baptist Total Abstinence Association in 1874. Canadians began their crusade that same year with Letitia Youmans founding a branch of the WCTU in Ontario.

A major reason for the change in attitude regarding alcohol consumption was the personal harm and domestic abuse that resulted from liquor becoming more accessible. Women, who were seen as protectors of the family unit, gave particular impetus to the temperance movement. While most historians associate Frances Willard with the success of the temperance movement on a national level, hundreds of other women were responsible for mobilizing their churches and towns to embrace abstinence. When W. A. Borum, a Baptist pastor in Mississippi, attempted to suppress the sale of alcohol by using the pulpit and the newspapers, he found no traction. Then one Sunday evening he reportedly stated that "the way to put whiskey out of Greenville [is] to get the women of the community to sign a resolution to the effect that they [will] exert themselves to prevent the men of their families from signing another petition of a saloon keeper for a license to sell liquor." His subsequent call for a "Deborah to take the lead" went unheeded until the following day when a young lady came to his study and said that God had laid it on her heart to take up the task. Within a week many of Greenville's women had signed the resolution, and it was noted, "The men were not so aroused at first, but they soon heard from home."

Southern Baptist Convention Resolution Against Beverage Alcohol

Resolved, That we, the members of the Southern Baptist Convention, reassert our truceless and uncompromising hostility to the manufacture, sale, importation and transportation, of alcoholic beverages in any and all their forms. We regard the policy of issuing government licenses for the purpose of carrying on the liquor traffic as a sin against God and a dishonor to our people. We furthermore announce it as our conviction that we should by all legitimate means oppose the liquor traffic in municipality, county, state, and nation.

Furthermore, we announce it as the sense of this body that no person should be retained in the fellowship of a Baptist church who engages in the manufacture or sale of alcoholic liquors, either at wholesale or retail, who invests his money in the manufacture or sale of alcoholic liquors, or who rents his property to be used for distilleries, wholesale liquor houses, or saloons. Nor do we believe that any church should retain in its fellowship any member who drinks intoxicating liquors as a beverage, or visits saloons or drinking places for the purpose of such indulgence.

Excerpted from the *Annual of the Southern Baptist Convention* (1896).

As attitudes toward alcohol changed, Baptist commentaries on the Bible did too. John Gill's eighteenth-century explanation of Titus 1:7, which states that a pastor should not be "given to wine" (KJV), stipulated that while drunkenness was not permitted, "it is lawful for persons in such an office to drink wine, and sometimes absolutely necessary." Hezekiah Harvey wrote of the same verse in 1890: "If not absolutely prohibitory of wine, [the text] certainly requires temperance in the use of it." By the time prohibition became federal law, some Baptist commentators were claiming that positive references to wine in the Bible either referred to diluted forms of alcohol or unfermented grape juice. The latter option, though not impossible, was improbable since grape juice did not become an acceptable substitute for communion in Baptist circles until James Welch, a Methodist layman and temperance sympathizer, perfected the pasteurization process in 1869, thus enabling grape juice to be mass produced. Notably, Primitive Baptists continued to make their own communion wine well into the twentieth century.

Theological Institutions and Changes in Theology

The temperance movement was one of the few occasions in Baptist history where theological conservatives and liberals worked toward the same goal. The divide became more apparent in the area of theological education. Baptist institutions of higher learning were founded with hopes of training pastors who would "earnestly contend for the faith which was delivered unto the saints" (Jude 3 KJV), but often they drifted into theological liberalism, forcing constituents to either reclaim their original vision or concede that a new era had arrived.

McMaster University in Ontario, Canada, was a case in point. As we saw in chapter 4, Baptists arrived in Ontario just prior to the nineteenth century, but it took nearly eighty years for them to establish a successful school for training pastors. A Scottish-Canadian pastor, Robert Alexander Fyfe, led the way in the establishment of Canada Literary Institute, McMaster's predecessor institution, located in Woodstock. Fyfe studied at the Hamilton Literary and Theological Institution in New York before assuming the pastorate at Toronto's March Street Baptist Church (later Bond Street Baptist Church and today Jarvis Street Baptist Church). He and seven other pastors called for a

Robert Alexander Fyfe (1816–1878)

convention to discuss starting a school for pastors, and four years later, in 1860, the Canadian Literary Institute opened with seventy-nine students and five teachers. The school's motto, generated by Fyfe, was *Sit Lux*, or "Let there be light."

Fyfe's commitment to training pastors was indefatigable. His teaching load consisted of six hours of instruction per day for five days a week; his service to the church included preaching on Sundays and leading Sunday school classes; and his summer travels were spent raising money for the school. He took only two vacations during his seventeen-year tenure as principal of the institute, leading some to conclude that his death in 1878 resulted from overwork. The institute's move from Woodstock to Toronto occurred through the influence and leadership of William McMaster, an Irish immigrant and Baptist layman who had become one of the wealthiest men in Toronto. McMaster made his fortune in the wholesale industry but later involved himself in banking, where he helped found the Canadian Bank of Commerce in 1867. His interest in relocating the institute stemmed from his desire to have a Baptist presence in the heart of one of Ontario's most influential cities. In 1881, the Toronto Baptist College opened, in large part due to McMaster's gift of over $100,000. The school was renamed McMaster University after a million-dollar gift was given from McMaster's estate.

Canadian Baptists had longed for a college that would train pastors in godliness as well as academics. In an earlier attempt to establish such a school in Montreal, Benjamin Davies, a Welsh Baptist scholar who served as the school's principal, declared, "Much as we desire a *learned* ministry, we desire a *pious* ministry more. . . . It is our solemn conviction that no literary attainments, no powers of rhetoric, can give fitness for the work, if the heart be not engaged in it." In the same vein the founding deed of Toronto Baptist College set forth an evangelical statement of faith. Those associated with the school were required to affirm "the divine inspiration of the Scriptures . . . and their absolute supremacy and sufficiency in matters of faith and practice"; "the election and effectual calling of all God's people, [and] the atoning efficacy of the death of Christ"; "the necessity and efficacy of the influence of the Spirit in regeneration and sanctification"; and "the everlasting happiness of the righteous and the everlasting misery of the wicked." Personal piety was encouraged through the "McMaster Hymn," a song written by Daniel Arthur McGregor as he lay on his deathbed just one year after becoming principal at Toronto Baptist College.

In spite of its founders' intentions and the safeguards their successors put in place, McMaster's reputation for gospel preservation was called into question when it hired William Newton Clarke in 1880 and accusations of heresy were leveled against several professors by T. T. Shields in the twentieth century. Details of these events can be found in chapter 10, but the foundation for them was laid in the mid-nineteenth century as modernization began encroaching into nearly every area of life. The democratic and industrial revolutions combined with scientific and intellectual revolutions to challenge the old boundaries of thought. Though Charles Darwin's *Origin of Species* (1859) is often cited as the most significant book to challenge traditional Christian orthodoxy, higher biblical criticism had been pouring out of European universities for at least a century prior to its publication, calling Scripture into question on philosophical and ethical grounds. Higher criticism opened another door for doubt to find its way into the pulpit and pew through the halls of academia. While Baptists were aware that schools like Harvard and Yale had departed from the vision of their founders, many were caught unaware when theological progressives emerged in their midst, as occurred at Southern Baptist Theological Seminary when it became the first American school to dismiss a teacher for promoting liberal theology.

D. A. McGregor, "Jesus, Wondrous Saviour" (1889)

Jesus, wondrous Saviour!
Christ, of kings the King!
Angels fall before Thee
Prostrate, worshipping.
Fairest they confess Thee
In the Heavens above,
We would sing Thee fairest
Here in hymns of love.

Fairer far than sunlight
Unto eyes that wait
Amid fear and darkness
Till the morning break;
Fairer than the day-dawn,
Hills and dates among,
When its tide of glory
Wakes the tide of song.

Life is death if severed
From Thy throbbing heart.
Death with life abundant
At Thy touch would start.
Worlds and men and angels
All consist in Thee;
Yet Thou camest to us
In humility.

Jesus! all perfections
Rise and end in Thee;
Brightness of God's glory
Thou, eternally.
Favour'd beyond measure
They Thy face who see;
May we, gracious Saviour,
Share this ecstasy.

Crawford H. Toy was dubbed "modernism's first martyr" when his career at Southern Seminary abruptly came to an end. Toy was a graduate of Southern and would have become a missionary to Japan were it not for a shortage of funds. He also likely would have become the husband of Lottie Moon were it not for his evolving views on the inspiration of Scripture. Moon's decision to rebuff his romantic overtures was based on her fore-sight of their theological incompati-bility; administrators at Southern Seminary were not as prescient. When he was hired to teach Old Testament interpretation and oriental languages in 1869, he professed to be in full agreement with the seminary's Abstract of Principles, even delivering an inaugural address in

*Crawford H. Toy
(1836–1919)*

which he claimed the Bible was "in every iota of its substance absolutely and infallibly true." However, his academic training at the University of Berlin and growing interest in German philosophical theology soon led him to differentiate between the truth of spiritual matters and the fallibility of historical assertions. As a result, he denied the Genesis creation account in favor of Darwinian evolution, rejected Mosaic authorship of the Pentateuch in favor of the Documentary Hypothesis, and reinterpreted messianic predictions in the Old Testament from a rationalistic perspective. James Boyce and John Broadus, Toy's colleagues at Southern, attempted to convince him to change his views and even shifted his teaching responsibilities to prevent him from teaching in areas where his thoughts on inspiration would have an impact. Toy carried his views into every class, however, and his popularity among students increased his visibility among the Southern Baptist constituency. Pressure was brought on the seminary to force Toy's resignation, which he submitted in 1879 under the impression that it would be rejected. He knew his beliefs were out of step with the seminary but was convinced, as were many progressive theologians, that he was helping the church transition from an outdated orthodoxy to an accommodating theology more suited to the modern age. To Toy's surprise, his resignation was accepted by all but two of the seminary's eighteen trustees. Southern Seminary had rendered its verdict, on behalf of the denomination, that fidelity to the past was the seminary's direction for the future.

In spite of his disappointment at the trustees' decision, Toy found employment at Harvard, where his continued drift leftward raised no hackles at all. Broadus was likely more distraught than Toy, as revealed in a letter to his wife: "We have lost our jewel of learning, our beloved and noble brother, the

---

Positive Statement of the Doctrine of Inspiration

This may be briefly comprehended in three points:

1. The Bible is truly the Word of God, having both infallible truth and divine authority in all that it affirms or enjoins.

2. The Bible is truly the production of men. It is marked by all the evidences of human authorship as clearly and certainly as any other book that was written by men.

3. This twofold authorship extends to every part of Scripture, and to the language as well as to the general ideas expressed.

Or it may be summed up in one single statement: The whole Bible is truly God's Word written by men.

Excerpted from Basil Manly Jr., *The Bible Doctrine of Inspiration Explained and Vindicated* (1888).

pride of the Seminary. God bless our Seminary, God bless Toy and God help us, sadly but steadfastly to do our providential duty." Broadus's mourning over Toy's departure from the seminary was later multiplied when Toy left the faith altogether. To prevent future challenges to biblical authority, Southern Seminary elected Basil Manly Jr., author of the Abstract of Principles, as Toy's replacement only two days after his resignation. In 1888, Manly published *The Bible Doctrine of Inspiration Explained and Vindicated*.

Not all Baptists who embraced progressive thought went as far as Toy. Many were more circumspect in their teaching and their conclusions. Alvah Hovey, professor and later president at Newton Theological Seminary, and Calvin Goodspeed, professor of systematic theology and apologetics at McMaster, were known as careful, irenic scholars who responded to modernism with minimal adaptation of their theology. Other theologians, like Ezekiel Gilman Robinson, professor and president of Rochester Seminary, and Augustus Hopkins Strong, professor and later president of Rochester, were mediating theologians who held to orthodox beliefs in general but took new directions in areas of special interest to them. Robinson emphasized experience over doctrine and embraced a form of evolution. Strong also emphasized experience over doctrine at times, embraced a form of evolution, and viewed some higher biblical criticism positively. Both blazed new paths for Baptists and taught in institutions somewhat open to progressive thought, though neither could be described as a full-fledged theological liberal.

In general Baptist theologians of the nineteenth century continued to hold common theological convictions but began to differ in their methodological approaches. For example, John L. Dagg's *Manual of Theology* (1857) and Strong's *Systematic Theology* (1886; revised in eight editions through 1909), which were both frequently required in Baptist colleges and seminaries, drew similar conclusions pertaining to the truthfulness of Scripture, the unity of the Godhead, the fall of humanity, the freeness of salvation, the uniqueness of the church, and the reality of eternity. Their differing approaches to ascertaining theological truth, however, were apparent. Dagg's *Manual of Theology* lacked appeals to any authority outside of Scripture, whereas Strong's *Systematic Theology* drew from philosophical and natural theology in conjunction with the biblical text. Dagg essentially reproduced what Baptists had believed in the past whereas Strong attempted to make a statement about what Baptists should believe in the future. Neither methodological approach lasted long beyond the nineteenth century, but both men rightly gained a place among the most influential theologians of their time.

Southern Seminary experienced another crisis leading to a resignation when its president, William Whitsitt, published an article claiming that English Baptists did not baptize by immersion until 1641 and that American

Baptists followed no earlier than 1644. Whitsitt was not the first person to propose this theory, but his subsequent book, *A Question in Baptist History*, raised eyebrows among Landmark Baptists, who strongly believed the denomination had its beginnings in the first century. Whitsitt's publications, based on documented evidence, exposed the impossibility of their claims. Although history was on Whitsitt's side, Texas pastor and Southern Seminary trustee Benajah Harvey Carroll was against him, and he proved to be the stronger of the two. Whitsitt was especially vulnerable to opponents because of his shifting views on Baptist ecclesiology. Though he was president of the seminary, he privately advocated abandoning the practices of immersion and closed communion. These views placed him in opposition to the Abstract of Principles. Under increasing pressure Whitsitt resigned the presidency in 1898. His views on Baptist origins, however, were vindicated the following century.

Charles Spurgeon on Orthodox Christology

To talk of improving upon our perfect Saviour is to insult him. He is God's propitiation: what would you want more? . . . There is but one Saviour, and that one Saviour is the same forever. His doctrine is the same in every age and is not yea and nay. . . . What a strange result we should obtain in the general assembly of heaven if some were saved by the gospel of the first century, and others by the gospel of the second, and others by the gospel of the seventeenth, and others by the gospel of the nineteenth century! . . . We should need a different song of praise for the clients of these various periods, and the mingled chorus would be rather to the glory of man's culture than to the praise of the one Lord. No such mottled heaven, and no such discordant song, shall ever be produced. . . . To eternal glory there is but one way; to walk therein we must hold fast to one truth, and be quickened by one life. We stand fast by the unaltered, unalterable, eternal name of Jesus Christ our Lord.

Excerpted from Charles H. Spurgeon, "Holding Fast the Faith" (1888).

Theological modernism was not merely a topic of academic debates. The legendary "Down Grade Controversy" demonstrates that tension regarding modernism existed at the grassroots and denominational levels, involving as it did two titans of English Baptist life, Charles Spurgeon and John Clifford.

Spurgeon was pastor of London's Metropolitan Tabernacle, the largest Baptist church in the world. He was such a celebrity that he often had to ask members of his church not to attend the Sunday evening services in order that visitors might find a seat. His sermons eventually filled over sixty-four volumes, totaling over twenty million words. He was a wordsmith whose statements ranged from the seemingly harsh ("There is enough dust on some of your Bibles to write *damnation* with your fingers") to the stirringly gentle ("The heaviest end of the cross lies ever on [Christ's] shoulders. If He bids us carry a burden, He carries it also"). Spurgeon was immensely active outside the pulpit—founding a college, writing more than 150 books, and starting dozens of ministries to care for London's poor. Spurgeon was indebted to the English Puritans, whom he considered to be, in John Bunyan's words, "valiant for truth."

It was no wonder, then, that when Spurgeon encountered modernistic theology, he attempted to rebut it in order to defend the gospel and protect his flock. In his newspaper, *The Sword and the Trowel*, Spurgeon declared of modernism, "A new religion has been initiated, which is no more Christianity than chalk is cheese." He alleged that the new theology led to decreased church attendance, deviant doctrine, and openness to worldly amusements. Spurgeon fully expected that once he sounded the trumpet, Baptist leaders would follow him to the battle, but he was mistaken. The Baptist Union, meeting in 1887, effectively ignored the alarm.

Charles Haddon Spurgeon
(1834–1892)

Spurgeon gained their attention, and the attention of the evangelical world, when he resigned from the Baptist Union that same year. When leaders of the Baptist Union, including Clifford, approached Spurgeon to ask that he return, Spurgeon declined on the basis of the Union's refusal to curb theological deviance within its ranks. His proposal that the Baptist Union adopt a confession of faith, which would disqualify those holding liberal theological views, was declined; and, in a remarkable turn of events, the Baptist Union voted to censure Spurgeon for his actions. Clifford spoke for many moderates when he queried, "Is it too late to ask Mr. Spurgeon to pause and consider whether this is the best work to which the Baptists of Great Britain and Ireland can be put?" Clifford believed union among Baptists was necessary for expanding their influence and reforming society; Spurgeon believed union without agreement on doctrinal boundaries was unwise and ungodly.

When the Baptist Union formally adopted a confession, it passed overwhelmingly: 2,000 members voting to approve with only seven declining. Yet Spurgeon was convinced the vote simply revealed how broadly the confession could be interpreted. Thus, he never rejoined the Union. Whether the "Down Grade Controversy" led to Spurgeon's untimely death in 1892 is debatable, but a passing of the guard seems to have taken place as Clifford went on to become the first president of the Baptist World Alliance, the premier global organization for Baptist ecumenism (see chap. 9). By the end of the nineteenth century, denominational cooperation among British Baptists trumped doctrinal conviction. The Baptist Union had rendered its verdict on Spurgeon and his theology, concluding that it was a relic of the past.

For Further Study

Deweese, Charles W. *Baptist Church Covenants*. Nashville, TN: Broadman, 1990.

George, Timothy, and David Dockery, eds. *Theologians of the Baptist Tradition*. Nashville, TN: B&H Academic, 2001.

Harper, Keith, ed. *Rescue the Perishing: Selected Correspondence of Annie W. Armstrong*. Macon, GA: Mercer University Press, 2004.

————, ed. *Send the Light: Lottie Moon's Letters and Other Writings*. Macon, GA: Mercer University Press, 2002.

Morden, Peter. *Communion with Christ and His People: The Spirituality of C. H. Spurgeon (1834–1892)*. Oxford: Regent's Park College Press, 2010.

Nettles, Tom J. *Living by Revealed Truth: The Life and Pastoral Theology of Charles Haddon Spurgeon*. Fearne, Ross-Shire, UK: Christian Focus Publications, 2013.

Williams, Michael, and Walter Shurden, eds. *Turning Points in Baptist History: A Festschrift in Honor of Harry Leon McBeth*. Macon, Georgia: Mercer University Press, 2008.

Wills, Gregory A. *Democratic Religion: Freedom, Authority, and Church Discipline in the Baptist South, 1785–1900*. New York: Oxford University Press, 1997.

Questions for Discussion

1. In what ways were women involved in Baptist life during this period? How would you assess the following: "Prior to the twentieth century, few women aspired to the pastorate, and few claimed to be victims of discrimination." Does this claim diminish their roles in the church in any way?

2. How were Baptists involved with immigrants toward the end of the nineteenth century? Do you know of any Baptist ministries designed to assist immigrants today? If so, which ones?

3. Baptists introduced the chapel train car as a means of sharing the gospel throughout the rural United States. Can you think of any other innovative techniques Baptists have used in the past that have more or less become obsolete?

4. What was the purpose of church manuals? What information do they reveal to us about transitions in Baptist life since the nineteenth century?

5. Describe the process of church discipline in nineteenth-century Baptist churches. What were the steps and possible outcomes? Why did it decline? Do you think a renewed emphasis on church discipline would help or hurt churches today? Explain your answer.

6. Describe the relationship between Baptists and the temperance movement. How did the changing attitudes toward alcohol affect Baptist interpretation of the Bible? Can you think of other areas in Baptist life where similar interpretive shifts have occurred? If so, explain.

7. Describe the establishment and development of McMaster University. In what way did its founders attempt to combine learning and piety? Were they ultimately successful in keeping this approach? Why or why not?

8. Who was Crawford Toy, and why was he controversial among Southern Baptists? Which do you believe is more important, a teacher who is popular with students or a teacher who is faithful to the vision of the institution?

9. Describe the life and contributions of Charles H. Spurgeon. What was his role in the Down Grade Controversy, and how did it affect British Baptist life? What limits would you place on denominational cooperation and doctrinal conviction in a similar situation?

Section Three

BAPTISTS IN THE TWENTIETH
AND TWENTY-FIRST CENTURIES

Chapter 9

THE EARLY TWENTIETH CENTURY

The early twentieth century offered both promise and peril to Baptists. Denominational optimism was at an all-time high. Baptists the world over came together for the first time to form a global network to give witness to Baptist distinctives and emphases. Baptists were long past their days as a persecuted sect in the English-speaking world and were becoming one of the largest global movements among Protestant Christians. Ministry practices were modernized in many churches, adapted to meet the needs of a more urban, educated, and technological era. New clergy roles were developed, and women provided greater public leadership in churches and denominations than in previous centuries. The First World War dampened much of the optimism, especially among European Baptists, who suffered many devastating setbacks because of the conflict. Yet despite the horrors of war and its aftermath, new Baptist bodies were formed, and many older Baptist groups experienced significant numeric growth and organizational modernization.

The Baptist World Alliance

At the turn of the twentieth century, Baptists had been engaged in foreign missions for well over a century. Their missionary labors had borne significant numerical fruit. Though Baptists remained concentrated in North America and the British Isles, during the nineteenth century the movement had taken root in Continental Europe, Asia, Africa, and South America. By 1904, there were almost 6.2 million Baptists in the world, approximately 5.5 million of whom were located in the United States and Canada. Just a half century earlier, there had been about 1.2 million Baptists in the world, with around 80 percent living in North America.

As Baptists recognized the increasingly global nature of their movement, a growing chorus began to call for a worldwide meeting of Baptists. The desire to promote fellowship among Baptists in different parts of the world was not new. British Baptist leaders such as Thomas Grantham in the seventeenth century and John Rippon in the eighteenth century had expressed hope that world Baptists would periodically meet together for the good of the wider movement. By the late nineteenth century, European and Russian Baptists were seeking closer fellowship with British Baptists, while the latter and their American counterparts were expanding missionary efforts into new lands such as Chile, Argentina, Cuba, South Africa, Malawi, and Zambia. New conventions and associations were being formed with every passing decade. The time was ripe for a world Baptist organization.

Some Southern Baptists began advocating for a "Pan-Baptist Conference" in the late nineteenth century. Kentuckians J. N. Prestridge and A. T. Robertson took up the cause when they called for a "World Baptist Congress" similar to the annual Baptist congresses that had been held in America since the 1880s. Robertson hoped "the Baptists of the world would send some of [their] mission and education leaders for a conference on Baptist world problems." In response, the Baptist Union of Great Britain invited world Baptists to attend a gathering in London in July 1905. At the meeting, 3,250 delegates representing Baptists in twenty-three countries formed the Baptist World Alliance (BWA). Alexander Maclaren, the famed Scottish preacher and pastor of

Alexander Maclaren (1826–1910)

Union Chapel in Manchester, presided over the meeting, which opened with delegates reciting the Apostles' Creed. London pastor John Clifford was elected to serve as the first president of the BWA, while Baptist Union secretary J. H. Shakespeare was tapped to serve as the first general secretary. In 1928, English Baptist J H. Rushbrooke became the first full-time secretary of the BWA.

World Baptists Recite the Apostles' Creed

I should like the first act of this Congress to be the audible and unanimous acknowledgment of our Faith. So I have suggested that, given your consent, it would be an impressive and a right thing, and would clear away a good many misunderstandings and stop the mouth of a good deal of slander—if we here and now, in the face of the world, not as a piece of coercion of discipline, but as a simple acknowledgment of where we stand and what we believe, would rise to our feet and, following the lead of your President, would repeat the Apostles' Creed. Will You?

Excerpted from Alexander Maclaren, "In the Name of Christ . . . by the Power of the Spirit" (1905).

The BWA was not a global association or convention but rather functioned as a voluntary organization to promote fellowship among different Baptist groups and to advocate Baptist principles, especially religious liberty. The BWA periodically convened Baptist World Congresses before deciding in the mid-twentieth century to meet every five years. In its early years the organization was led by some of the most well-known Baptists in the world, including Americans E. Y. Mullins (1923–28) and George W. Truett (1934–39), Canadian John MacNeil (1928–34), and Britain's James H. Rushbrooke (1939–47). The latter served as BWA president after stepping down as general secretary. Though not all Baptist groups participated in the BWA, it would be fair to say the organization represented the convictions and priorities of a majority of the world's Baptists until theological controversies began increasingly dividing Baptists during the final third of the twentieth century.

Ministry in the New Century

An increasing emphasis on professionalization among Baptist ministers emerged during the early twentieth century. In the English-speaking world, a growing number of Baptist pastors embraced the title "reverend," a term previously associated with Catholicism and other more hierarchical traditions. Many churches, especially in cities and towns, desired that their pastors have at least a college education. A growing number of urban churches preferred at least some seminary education. Several new Baptist colleges were started around the turn of the century in North America and Britain, many of them in rural areas. In Britain, Baptists debated whether there should be a college education requirement for pastors. In the end they adopted a process of distinguishing between probationary ministers and accredited ministers, based on factors such as education, ministry experience, and scores on an examination prepared by the Baptist Union—though, of course, churches remained free to call whomever they pleased to serve as their pastors. Among Baptists in the American South, the earlier practice of an "annual call" for ministers gradually fell into disfavor as churches entered into semipermanent relationships with their pastors.

Professionalization also influenced the ministries of many local churches. Larger congregations began to employ associate pastors to assist with pastoral care and preaching responsibilities. Some churches also began to employ additional ministry staff, especially paid choir directors and Christian education directors. Though preaching remained the central facet of Baptist worship, church music was becoming increasingly elaborate as many urban churches formed choirs and installed organs. Congregational singing was also evolving. The revivals of the previous century influenced evangelical hymnody, and Baptist denominations in America and England published hymnals that included both the older hymns of Isaac Watts and Charles Wesley and newer songs written by Philip Bliss, Ira Sankey, Fanny Crosby, and Southern Baptist B. B. McKinney. In addition to choir directors, larger churches frequently compensated instrumentalists, especially pianists and organists. Many colleges and seminaries established programs in church music to accommodate this growing ministry emphasis.

"Wherever He Leads, I'll Go"
by B. B. McKinney © 1936

"Take up thy cross and follow Me,"
  I heard my Master say;
"I gave My life to ransom thee,

  Surrender your all today."

Chorus:
Wherever He leads I'll go,
  Wherever He leads I'll go,
I'll follow my Christ who loves me so,
  Wherever He leads I'll go.

He drew me closer to His side,
  I sought His will to know,

And in that will I now abide,
  Wherever He leads I'll go.

It may be thro' the shadows dim,
  Or o'er the stormy sea,
I take my cross and follow Him,
  Wherever He leadeth me.

My heart, my life, my all I bring
  To Christ who loves me so;
He is my Master, Lord, and King,
  Wherever He leads I'll go.

Christian education directors typically coordinated Sunday school and outreach, which were often paired together, especially in North America. Many Baptists adopted a Sunday school strategy that focused on teaching the whole Bible to students over the course of a prescribed period, normally seven years. Arthur Flake of the Southern Baptist Sunday School Board published an important book titled *Building a Standard Sunday School* (1922). Flake emphasized age-graded classes to facilitate using Sunday school for evangelism. He wrote, "The supreme business of Christianity is to win the Lost to Christ. This is what churches are for . . . . surely then the Sunday school must relate itself to the winning of the lost to Christ as an ultimate objective." "Flake's Formula," as this approach came to be known, significantly influenced Southern Baptists and, through them, numerous other groups. As with music ministry, colleges and seminaries increasingly offered training in Christian education. By the mid-twentieth century, many churches were ordaining choir and education directors, often using the more clerical titles "minister of music" and "minister of education."

Many Baptist churches, especially in urban centers, upgraded their buildings around the turn of the new century. Urban churches increasingly abandoned the simple wood or brick structures of previous generations in favor of neo-Gothic sanctuaries with high steeples. Some urban Baptist churches with particularly gifted preachers adopted the "temple church" model, constructing enormous sanctuaries with padded pews and wrap-around balconies. Charles Spurgeon's Metropolitan Tabernacle was the prototype for this approach; many similar churches were named the Metropolitan Tabernacle in honor of Spurgeon's congregation. Among the locations of temple or tabernacle-style churches were America, Australia, New Zealand, and Northern Ireland.

A Baptist "Prosperity Gospel"

I say that you ought to get rich, and it is our duty to get rich. How many of my pious brethren say to me, "Do you, a Christian minister, spend your time going up and down the country advising young people to get rich, to get money?" "Yes, of course I do." They say, "Isn't that awful! Why don't you preach the gospel instead of preaching about man's making money?" "Because to make money honestly is to preach the gospel." That is the reason.

Excerpted from Russell Conwell, "Acres of Diamonds."

Prominent temple churches in the United States included the Tremont Temple in Boston, Tabernacle Baptist Church in Atlanta, and especially Russell Conwell's Baptist Temple in Philadelphia. Conwell was among the most prominent Baptist pastors in America during the late nineteenth and early twentieth centuries. He is also noteworthy for founding Temple University in Philadelphia and delivering his lecture "Acres of Diamonds" at least 6,000 times to audiences all over the world. The lecture argued that it is God's will for faithful Christians to enjoy material wealth, making Conwell a forerunner of the so-called prosperity gospel of the late-twentieth century. In 1969, the former Conwell School of Theology, previously affiliated with Temple, merged with Gordon Divinity School near Boston. The latter was named for Conwell's contemporary Adoniram Judson Gordon, a fellow Baptist, close friend of D. L. Moody's, and a noteworthy proponent of international missions and premillennial eschatology. The new evangelical school was called Gordon-Conwell Theological Seminary.

Some city churches in North America adopted the "institutional church" model, wherein the church became a community center dedicated to reaching the urban masses. Institutional churches offered education classes for adults and after-school programs for young people, constructed gymnasiums for community use, and operated clothing closets and soup kitchens for the poor. Judson Memorial Church in New York City was the most influential Baptist institutional church. The congregation was named for Adoniram Judson and was led for many years by his son, Edward Judson. The younger Judson argued, "I should be recreant to my duty if I did not declare that the large remoteness of those who represent Christ and His Church from any intimate or frequent contact with those whom they profess to serve

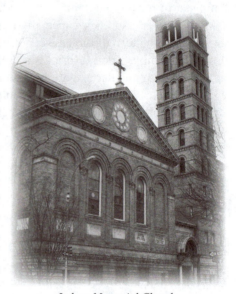

Judson Memorial Church, New York City (est. 1890).

is one of the most grotesque incongruities—one of the most absolutely indefensible inconsistencies of our modern Christianity." John D. Rockefeller, a Northern Baptist layman, philanthropist, and one of the wealthiest men in America, financed the Judson Memorial edifice. Rockefeller gave money to numerous Baptist institutions, including the University of Chicago, Southern Baptist Theological Seminary, and Spelman College in Atlanta. The rise of institutional churches coincided with an emphasis on the Social Gospel, which stressed social uplift and ministries to the poor and needy (see chap. 10). This emphasis reached its apex during the early decades of the twentieth century. Conservative Baptist pastors such as Amzi C. Dixon of Brooklyn and Len Broughton of Atlanta emphasized evangelistic preaching and traditional outreach more than progressives such as Judson, though conservatives also emphasized ministries to the poor and needy.

Baptist churches of all sizes increasingly adopted a committee structure to facilitate ministry. This was especially true in North America, where many churches formed finance committees to oversee their budgets. The idea of an annual budget was relatively new as many churches transitioned from a pledge system to encouraging members to tithe regularly, a practice facilitated through the use of weekly offering envelopes. Many larger churches had youth or music committees that provided oversight to those ministries. Early in the century deacons remained focused on the temporal needs of the congregation, complementing the clergy, who focused on spiritual needs. By midcentury, however, deacons were increasingly taking on a managerial role, often functioning like an advisory board to the pastor. In times of ministerial turnover, deacons provided leadership continuity. In many churches the deacons functioned as the congregation's chief committee. Women's auxiliaries such as the Woman's Missionary Union also functioned like committees.

World War I

World War I, originally called the Great War, engulfed Europe from August 1914 until November 1918. The war was fought between the Central Powers and the Allied Powers. The Central Powers included Germany, Austria-Hungary, Bulgaria, and the Ottoman Empire. The Allies originally included the British Empire, France, and Russia. In 1917, the United States entered the war on the side of the Allies after three years of neutrality, and President Woodrow Wilson promised that victory would "make the world safe for democracy." More than 70 million combatants were involved in the war, with more than 9 million combat fatalities. Baptists responded to World War I in a variety of ways. As a general rule, Baptist groups sided with their respective nations in the conflict. Millions of Baptists fought in the conflict on both sides, and thousands of Baptist clergy served as military chaplains.

In Britain the Baptist Union supported the war and was tasked by the government with recruiting Baptist chaplains for the military. Some clergy refused to serve in the chaplaincy but accepted short-term preaching assignments through the YMCA. In the early years of the war, key leaders as diverse as John Clifford and F. B. Meyer provided vocal support to the British government and recruited Baptists to serve in the military. Clifford, who was introduced in chapter 8, was probably the leading progressive in the Baptist Union, while Meyer was a theological conservative and noteworthy promoter of holiness views. In the latter years of the war, a growing number of British Baptists became conscientious objectors, particularly after Parliament passed a conscription act in 1916. Meyer was appalled at the treatment of conscientious objectors in France who were sentenced to death for failure to follow orders. His pamphlet on the topic, *The Majesty of Conscience* (1917), included material from the atheist philosopher Bertrand Russell. Clifford argued against compulsory military service as a violation of liberty of conscience. The war greatly strained relations between British and German Baptists, which had historically been close-knit due to the role Scottish Baptists played in convincing German Baptist pioneer Johann Gerhard Oncken of Baptist views (see chap. 7).

John Clifford
(1836–1923)

Though most Baptists in America did not embrace pacifism, like most Americans they adopted an isolationist posture that was opposed to involving the nation in foreign wars. By 1917, though, many Baptists became convinced that America's entry into the war was regrettably necessary to defend freedom and democracy. Southern Baptists passed a resolution in 1917, pledging their

George W. Truett preaches "Baptists and Religious Liberty"
from the steps of the US Capitol Building.

The Baptist Witness to Religious Liberty

Baptists have one consistent record concerning liberty throughout all their long and eventful history. They have never been a party to oppression of conscience. They have forever been the unwavering champions of liberty, both religious and civil. Their contention now, is, and has been, and, please God, must ever be, that it is the natural and fundamental and indefeasible right of every human being to worship God or not, according to the dictates of his conscience, and, as long as he does not infringe upon the rights of others, he is to be held accountable alone to God for all religious beliefs and practices. . . . It is the consistent and insistent contention of our Baptist people, always and everywhere, that religion must be forever voluntary and uncoerced, and that it is not the prerogative of any power, whether civil or ecclesiastical, to compel men to conform to any religious creed or form of worship, or to pay taxes for the support of a religious organization to which they do not believe. God wants free worshipers and no other kind.

Excerpted from George W. Truett, "Baptists and Religious Liberty" (1920).

support to President Wilson and the war effort, though they also affirmed the peaceable vision of the Sermon on the Mount and longed for the cessation of all war. Southern Baptist pastor George Truett was one of twenty ministers (and the only Baptist) whom President Wilson invited to spend six months with the YMCA preaching to American troops in Europe in 1917–18. Truett, pastor of First Baptist Church of Dallas, Texas, was perhaps the leading Southern Baptist pastor of this era. In addition to serving as president of both the SBC and the BWA, Truett was a strong promoter of Baptist principles, especially religious liberty. His 1920 address "Baptists and Religious Liberty," delivered from the steps of the United States Capitol, is considered a classic statement of the Baptist commitment to full religious liberty. Truett argued, "A denomination is molded by its ruling principles, just as a nation is thus molded and just as individual life is thus molded. Our fundamental essential principles have made our Baptist people, of all ages and countries, to be the unyielding protagonists of religious liberty, not only for themselves, but for everybody else as well."

Seventh Day Baptists in America participated in the War-Time Commission of the Federal Council of Churches and formed a Wartime Reconstruction Board to minister to the spiritual needs of returning soldiers. Even many modernists such as Northern Baptist pastor and professor Harry Emerson Fosdick supported American entry into the war, embracing President Wilson's almost millennial vision of the war as a righteous effort to bring political and religious freedom to the world. For some Baptists in America, supporting the war came at a great cost. In an effort to show their patriotism, many German-speaking Baptist churches began worshipping in the English language during the war; some even severed ties with the historically German denomination, the North American Baptist Conference.

Relatively few Baptists in America became conscientious objectors during World War I, Social Gospel advocate Walter Rauschenbusch being a notable exception. It was more common for Baptists to return from combat and gravitate toward pacifist views. That was what happened with Fosdick, perhaps the most noteworthy Baptist pacifist. The famous pastor was haunted by the scenes of violence he witnessed as a chaplain while serving in the trenches of France. In 1933, Fosdick preached a famous sermon titled "The Unknown Soldier" wherein he asked, "Can you imagine anything madder than this, that all the nations should pick out their best, use their scientific skill to make certain that they are the best, and then in one mighty holocaust offer ten million of them on the battlefields of one war?"

Modern Baptist Denominationalism

The early decades of the twentieth century witnessed an emphasis on denominational centralization and expansion among many Christian groups in the English-speaking world. The time seemed ripe for growth. In America the culture had largely reflected the mores of evangelical Protestantism since at least the latter part of the Second Great Awakening. Though pitched battles between fundamentalists and modernists were on the horizon, the lines were not yet clearly drawn, and most Protestants affirmed broadly

A Baptist Memorial to Religious Liberty

Let this memorial proclaim the indebtedness in the capital of the republic where the once despised dogma has become the foundation of the civic structure. Men of all religious beliefs stand equal before the law. They are not to be punished by reason of their creeds or forms of worship so long as they respect the public peace and the equal rights of others. No one is exposed to civil disability either as a witness in our courts or with respect to qualification for any public office by reasons of his religious faith. Nor are the people to be taxed and public moneys to be used for the support of any sort of religion. . . . The effort to dominate the conscience of men by the use of civil power has always been destructive of civil liberty itself. If there are any who would pervert our institutions to make them servants of religious dogma, they should be regarded as enemies of both religion and the State, as the success of their endeavors would undermine both.

Excerpted from Charles Evans Hughes's address at the laying of the cornerstone for the
National Baptist Memorial to Roger Williams in Washington, DC (1922).

evangelical sentiments. A generically Protestant civil religion coupled with growing local church involvement led to an optimistic outlook on the part of numerous denominations. Baptists were enthusiastic participants in this trend.

The Northern Baptist Convention

Baptists in the North had long avoided any sort of ecclesiastical centralization, mostly because of their historic commitment to societal cooperation. While this organizational structure perpetuated the earliest form of intra-denominational cooperation among American Baptists, by the end of the nineteenth century various Baptist societies in the North felt the burden of overlapping responsibilities and competing fund-raising efforts. As early as the 1890s, some began calling for greater unity among the societies, and several tangible steps were taken to draw the societies closer together in planning and fund-raising. The formation of the Baptist World Alliance was a major catalyst in bringing about a consolidated denominational structure in the North. In the wake of the BWA's inaugural meeting, the heads of the various northern societies invited Baptists in the North to a consultative meeting in Washington, DC, in May 1907.

The Washington meeting led to a subsequent gathering in Oklahoma City, where the Northern Baptist Convention (NBC) was constituted in 1908. The convention's first president was Charles Evans Hughes, known as "Charles the Baptist," a layman and Sunday school teacher from New York who later served as chief justice of the Supreme Court of the United States from 1930 to 1941. The name of the new denomination conceded the regional divisions among Baptists in America; prior to this time Baptists in the North had consistently claimed their societies were national rather than regional ministries. The new NBC approved a governing board that represented the interests of all Northern Baptists between annual meetings. The various societies were brought under the board's oversight, an action that evidenced a transition from societal cooperation to the convention method of cooperation among Baptists in the North (see chap. 5).

Prior to the formation of the NBC, Northern Baptists had already been dialoging with the Free Baptist General Conference, a Free Will Baptist group that traced its roots to Benjamin Randall's movement in the late eighteenth century (see chap. 6). By the turn of the twentieth century, Northern Baptists had tempered their Calvinism and increasingly downplayed their historic commitment to close communion. This opened the door for a merger with the historically Arminian and open communion Free Baptists. In 1911, the Free Baptists were absorbed by the NBC; the majority of Free Will Baptists in the North were now part of the main body of Baptists in that region. The

NBC-Free Baptist merger reflected the increasing popularity of downplaying doctrinal particulars and the growing emphasis on ecumenism among Baptists in the North. During the 1930s the NBC entered into similar merger talks with the Disciples of Christ, though no union ever came of those discussions.

The NBC became a charter member of the Federal Council of Churches (FCC), which was also formed in 1908. The FCC was comprised of most of the major Protestant denominations and was dedicated to promoting unity. Northern Baptists subsequently participated in several ecumenical initiatives, including the World Conference on Faith and Order and the Universal Christian Council for Life and Work, both of which were formed in the years following the Edinburgh Missionary Conference of 1910. Northern Baptists also joined in calling for an international ecumenical group in the mid-1930s, though the World Council of Churches (WCC) was not formed until 1948 because of World War II. As with the FCC, the NBC was a charter member of the WCC.

Helen Barrett Montgomery of Rochester, New York, emerged as a key leader within the Northern Baptist Convention during these years. Montgomery was a tireless activist who championed public education reform and advocated for women's rights. She collaborated with the famous Susan B. Anthony in the latter. Montgomery was also a leading missions promoter, serving as president of the Woman's American Baptist Mission Society from 1914 to 1924. In 1924, she became the first woman to publish a translation of the New Testament from the original Greek when the American Baptist Publication Society published her *Centenary Translation of the New Testament*. She also wrote a groundbreaking book titled *The Bible and Missions* (1920), arguing, "The Bible is the great Missionary charter of the church." Perhaps most important for the Baptist story, Montgomery was elected president of the Northern Baptist Convention in 1921. She was the first woman to serve as the head of a major American denomination.

Following World War I, American Protestants were optimistic about their prospects for expanding God's kingdom on earth. Many denominations affiliated with the Federal Council of Churches embraced an initiative called the Interchurch World Movement (IWM), which attempted to raise money in support of evangelism, education, and social improvement. Participating denominations pooled their financial resources and coordinated their work to eliminate overlap among foreign missionaries. The NBC participated in the IWM, naming its fund-raising initiative the New World Movement. Northern Baptists pledged $100 million, which was to be collected between 1919 and 1924. A Board of Promotion was appointed to solicit pledges from each congregation, following the model the United States government had used in selling Liberty Bonds during World War I.

The New World Movement proved to be a disaster. Within a year of the campaign's launch, the NBC distanced its fund-raising efforts from the IWM because of grassroots complaints about the wider movement. The New World Movement overlapped with the early years of the Fundamentalist-Modernist Controversy, and a growing number of conservative churches expressed concern about ecumenical entanglements. Tensions only increased when the IWM sided with steel workers in a nationwide strike in 1919, a move that angered Northern Baptists who were suspicious of organized labor. While the ecumenism and labor advocacy of the early New World Movement concerned many conservative Northern Baptists, progressives were disheartened when the New World Movement severed ties with the IWM. Enthusiasm waned, and by the campaign's conclusion only $45 million had been collected. Though a significant sum, the convention's agencies had planned for a much larger amount. In the ensuing years overall gifts to the NBC's various ministries plummeted, likely due to both the fallout of the New World Movement and growing theological tensions. By the start of World War II, the NBC had cut its overseas missions force almost in half and had begun losing churches because of the Fundamentalist-Modernist Controversy.

The Southern Baptist Convention

Southern Baptists began expanding their denominational ministries during the latter half of the nineteenth century. This trend continued into the first decades of the twentieth century. Two important new educational institutions were formed prior to the end of World War I. Southwestern Baptist Theological Seminary (SWBTS) was founded in Waco, Texas, in 1908. In the early years of the new century, Texas Baptists desired a seminary for at least two reasons. First, many were concerned the distance to Southern Baptist Theological Seminary in Louisville, Kentucky, hindered Baptists in the Southwest from securing a seminary education. Second, many Texas Baptists were sympathetic to Landmark doctrine, which caused them to be suspicious of Southern Seminary in the years following the Whitsitt Controversy (see chap. 8).

B. H. Carroll's Parting Words to His Successor, L. R. Scarborough

Lee, keep the Seminary lashed to the cross. If heresy ever comes in the teaching, take it to the faculty. If they will not hear you and take prompt action, take it to the trustees of the Seminary. If they will not hear you, take it to the Convention that appoints the Board of Trustees, and if they will not hear you, take it to the great common people of our churches. You will not fail to get a hearing then.

B. H. Carroll, the pastor of Waco's First Baptist Church, was the chief personality behind the new seminary. Carroll was a respected preacher and author of numerous books, his most famous work being the thirteen-volume commentary series *Interpretation of the English Bible*, published between 1913 and 1917. Carroll had previously served as a trustee at Southern Seminary during the Whitsitt Controversy (see chap. 8). SWBTS was preceded by a seminary department at Baylor University, organized in 1905 and led by Carroll. Due to governance tensions, in 1908 the seminary separated from the university and reconstituted as the autonomous Southwestern Baptist Theological Seminary. Two years later Carroll relocated the fledgling school to Fort Worth. Upon his death in 1914, Carroll's protégé, Lee R. Scarborough, became the seminary's sec-

Benajah Harvey Carroll (1843–1914)

ond president and served until 1945. Scarborough was one of the leading evangelists in the SBC and author of the influential book *With Christ After the Lost* (1919). In 1925, ownership of SWBTS passed from the Baptist General Convention of Texas to the Southern Baptist Convention.

In 1917, the Southern Baptist Convention founded the Baptist Bible Institute in New Orleans. This marked the first time an institution was established by a direct act of the SBC. The first president was B. H. DeMent, a former faculty member at Southern Seminary. The Baptist Bible Institute specialized in educating prospective missionaries who desired to serve in Latin American fields. Because of the school's location, it also trained students to serve churches in predominantly Roman Catholic contexts. Though the Baptist Bible Institute began as a Bible college, in 1946 the SBC gave the school permission to revise its charter and become New Orleans Baptist Theological Seminary (NOBTS). The school's president at the time was Duke McCall, a leader who personified the managerial emphasis that came to predominate Southern Baptist institutions in the post-World War II era.

Southern Baptists founded a number of other denominational ministries during these years. The Layman's Missionary Movement (1907), intended as a male counterpart to the Woman's Missionary Union, helped mobilize

Baptist men to support foreign missions. The ministry became the Baptist Brotherhood of the South (1926) and eventually the Brotherhood Commission (1950). The Social Service Commission (1914) addressed perceived social ills, particularly alcohol consumption and gambling. The ministry later expanded and became the Christian Life Commission (1953). The Education Commission (1915) helped raise money for the seminaries and state Baptist colleges. The Relief and Annuity Board (1918) coordinated retirement plans and insurance for ministers. This ministry found its impetus in 1916 when a group of Nashville pastors convinced the Sunday School Board to set aside $100,000 for ministerial relief.

Southern Baptists Form an Executive Committee

Recognizing, however, that there is a strong sentiment in favor of greater unity in the general direction of the Convention's affairs, and believing that some improvement in the methods of conducting the work would be attained by the creation of a standing committee of the Convention to act for the body between its sessions in ways hereinafter set forth, we recommend that an executive committee of seven, representing the different parts of the territory of the Convention, be elected annually by the Convention as are its standing committees.

Excerpted from the *Annual of the Southern Baptist Convention* (1917).

The Executive Committee (EC) was the most important new agency formed by the SBC during these years. Though the convention had tasked a number of committees with studying denominational efficiency as far back as 1898, in 1914 Georgia pastor John White proposed the SBC create a Commission on Efficiency to study the convention's structure and strategy. The Commission on Efficiency paved the way for the Executive Committee, which was established in 1917 to represent the interests of the SBC between annual meetings. The formation of the EC marked the beginning of the Southern Baptist Convention's transformation into a modern denomination. Although the convention only technically existed for one week a year, when messengers assembled for the annual meeting, the SBC now had a body to transact business on its behalf year-round in the Executive Committee. Early on some Southern Baptists expressed concern that the EC represented an unhealthy step toward denominational centralization. Despite these apprehensions, by 1927 the Executive Committee had expanded enough to hire a full-time secretary, Austin Crouch. The EC became the most important tool in promoting a programmatic approach to Southern Baptist identity and cooperation in the years following World War II.

Southern Baptist women were also expanding their programs, particularly through the Woman's Missionary Union. In 1906, under the leadership of president Fannie Heck of Raleigh, North Carolina, the WMU founded the Woman's Missionary Union Training School in Louisville, Kentucky. The training school prepared single women to serve as missionaries through the Foreign Mission Board. Additionally, Heck was instrumental in forming the Royal Ambassadors (1908) and Girl's Auxiliary (1909) as education ministries to teach Southern Baptist children about foreign missions. These ministries complemented the Sunbeam Band (1886), which focused on preschoolers, and the Acteens (1912), which focused on teenage girls. The WMU continued to raise money for Southern Baptist missions work through two annual offerings: the Christmas offering

Fannie Exile Scudder Heck (1862–1915)

for foreign missions, begun in 1888 and named for Lottie Moon in 1918, and the Easter offering for home missions, begun in 1895 and named for Annie Armstrong in 1934.

Though the SBC was a founding member of the Baptist World Alliance, for a variety of reasons, it never became involved in the Federal Council of Churches. First, because of their regional identity, most Southern Baptists remained relatively isolated from other denominations, especially those outside the South and Southwest. Many Southern Baptists were also concerned about the theological latitude latent within the ecumenical movement. Finally, many Southern Baptists remained influenced by Landmarkism, which rejected the idea that Baptists are Protestants, thus raising doubts about the merits of interdenominational cooperation. For example, many Southern Baptist military chaplains resented being classified as Protestants during World War I and World War II. Even non-Landmark Southern Baptists opposed denominational union because it seemed to entail a downplaying of Baptist principles.

Like other denominations the SBC launched a major fund-raising initiative in the years following the First World War. The Seventy-Five Million Campaign was a coordinated effort to raise $75 million for denominational ministries between 1919 and 1924. A campaign commission, led by Scarborough, provided oversight. Campaign directors were selected for every state convention, association, and many churches. Most Southern Baptists enthusiastically embraced the Seventy-Five Million Campaign, and more than $92 million was pledged during the first year. The 1920 SBC annual meeting was proclaimed a "Victory Convention," and Baptist-related mission boards, colleges, seminaries, hospitals, and orphanages secured bank loans and undertook capital improvements based on the expectation of a financial windfall.

As with the Northern Baptists, the windfall never came. In 1920, economic recession crippled the South when crop prices plummeted. Agricultural revenue was cut in half from wartime highs a couple of years earlier. This was devastating for Southern Baptists because approximately 90 percent of the almost 26,000 churches were located in rural areas and small towns. Many Southern Baptists reneged on their pledges because of reduced income, relocation, or (unfounded) concerns that some of the money would support ecumenical endeavors. Fundamentalists who opposed the campaign perpetuated such rumors. By the end of the Seventy-Five Million Campaign in 1924, Southern Baptists had collected only $58.5 million. Denominational ministries were mired in debt and struggling to regain sound financial footing. Adding insult to injury, the Home Mission Board discovered in 1928 that its treasurer had embezzled more than $900,000. Though the HMB recovered more than $600,000, the episode undermined confidence in the emerging denominational structures. In 1929, the New York Stock Exchange crashed, and the ensuing Great Depression further crippled the southern economy. Most denominational ministries struggled financially until the nation's unprecedented prosperity in the aftermath of World War II.

Though the Seventy-Five Million Campaign was a failure, it did contribute to the creation of a new financial structure that arguably represented the apex of the convention approach to cooperation. For the first time Southern Baptists had united in a common cause, and some 9,000 churches that had never before supported denominational causes gave money to the campaign. At the 1925 Memphis convention, a Committee on Future Program proposed a "Co-Operative Program of the Southern Baptist Convention," later shortened to Cooperative Program (CP). The chairman of the Committee on Future Program was M. E. Dodd, pastor of First Baptist Church in Shreveport, Louisiana. Dodd was an author, educator, and influential leader among Southern Baptists. He was elected president of the Southern Baptist Convention (1934–35) and served as a member of the executive committee of the Baptist World Alliance.

The Cooperative Program was a unified denominational budget. By 1929, after minor adjustments, the CP assumed a structure that continued into the early twenty-first century. Every SBC church was encouraged to designate a percentage of its budget to forward to its state convention. Some of that

money was designated to help fund state ministries, and some of it was forwarded to the EC. The exact percentage to be forwarded and kept by each
state convention was determined by messengers to that convention's annual
meeting. The EC then distributed its CP receipts to the mission boards,
seminaries, and other convention-wide ministries. As with the states, the
CP allocations were voted upon by messengers to the SBC annual meeting.
The convention's original recommendation was for CP dollars to be evenly
distributed between state conventions and the EC after the states deducted
"shared expenses" used for CP promotion and administration. In practice
though, states normally kept most of the money. The CP ended interagency
fundraising competition and tied together the budgets of state conventions
and national ministries. In order to preserve the autonomy of local churches
and state conventions, participation in the CP was voluntary. This alleviated
concerns about denominational centralization.

By midcentury, the Cooperative Program had helped set the SBC and state
conventions on sounder financial footing. The Lottie Moon Christmas Offering and the Annie Armstrong Easter Offering augmented the income of the
two mission boards. As more and more churches embraced the CP, "cooperation" was increasingly equated with supporting the CP and other denominational programs and emphases. This programmatic emphasis gradually
became a key facet of Southern Baptist identity. The Executive Committee
proved crucial in promoting the emerging programmatic identity among
Southern Baptists.

African-American Baptists

Prior to the late nineteenth century, African-American Baptists did not
have a national denominational structure. Instead they cooperated through
local associations, mission societies, and in some cases state conventions.
Between 1880 and 1893, three regional conventions were formed: the Baptist Missionary Convention in Alabama, the American National Baptist Convention in Saint Louis, and the National Baptist Education Convention in
Washington, DC. Though all three bodies had aspirations to become national
denominations, by the mid-1890s their competition gave way to cooperation. In 1895, the three conventions merged into a national denomination
called the National Baptist Convention (NBC). The three earlier ministries
became boards of the new body. Like the Southern Baptist Convention, the
NBC embraced the convention method of cooperation.

E. C. Morris was elected the first president of the NBC and served in that
role for twenty-seven consecutive years. Morris, who was born into a slave
family in Georgia, was a shoemaker before becoming an ordained Baptist
minister in his mid-twenties. In 1879, he became the pastor of Centennial

Baptist Church in Helena, Arkansas, and served the church until his death in 1922. He was also a co-founder of Arkansas Baptist College, a leader in the Arkansas Baptist State Convention, which he served as president for thirty-five years, and the editor of a denominational periodical, the *Baptist Vanguard*. Beyond African-American Baptist life, Morris held leadership roles in the Baptist World Alliance and the Federal Council of Churches. He was active in Republican politics, serving on several occasions as a delegate to the Republican National Convention. Regarding the formation of the NBC, Morris claimed, "Until thrown into separate organization, such as this, it was not known what part those of our race in Baptist churches were bearing in the mighty conquest against the kingdom of darkness and in the upbuilding of the Master's kingdom on earth."

The NBC experienced two schisms during its first two decades of existence. The first split occurred in 1897 when the Lott Carey Baptist Foreign Mission Convention was formed. The architects of the new group were concerned about the National Baptist Convention's unwillingness to cooperate with white Baptists, especially the northern societies, in mission work on the African continent. They also opposed the decision to relocate the NBC's Foreign Mission Board from Montgomery, Alabama, to Louisville, Kentucky. As a result of these tensions, a group withdrew from the NBC and formed the Lott Carey Convention, named for the well-known missionary to Liberia (see chap. 7). Because the new organization was technically a mission society rather than a new general convention, it represented a rejection of the convention method of cooperation in favor of the societal method. Despite the separation the NBC and the Lott Carey Convention continued to cooperate in certain foreign mission endeavors.

The second schism was mostly the result of leadership tension between NBC President E. C. Morris and R. H. Boyd, head of the denomination's Home Mission Board. Shortly after the merger that formed the NBC, the convention established the National Baptist Publishing Board (NBPB) as a new ministry under the oversight of the Home Mission Board. The impetus for the new publishing ministry was the perception that both the American Baptist Publication Society and Baptist Sunday School Board (SBC) published material written for a Caucasian readership. By virtue of his position at the Home Mission Board, Boyd was in charge of the Publishing Board. Within a few years the latter was occupying most of his energy. In 1905, the NBC ordered the oversight of the NBPB to be shifted away from that of the Home Mission Board. Boyd defied the directive and continued to lead both ministries. Morris became convinced Boyd exercised too much influence over the NBPB and, through the board, the wider NBC. Morris was also concerned that the board's charter was too ambiguous in terms of ownership and control.

When Morris attempted to separate the NBPB from the Home Mission Board, Boyd responded with a lawsuit. The court sided with Boyd because he had purchased property and undertaken capital improvements for the NBPB with his own money, and he retained the NBPB's deeds and copyrights in his own name. Boyd and his allies separated from the NBC and formed a new denomination, which they named the National Baptist Convention of America, Inc. In response to the schism, the NBC restructured to prevent individual boards from operating independent of denominational oversight. The NBC also incorporated to ensure that the denomination retained ownership and oversight of all of its boards and other ministries. In 1918,

Richard Henry Boyd (1843–1922)

a peace committee that included representatives from both groups as well as the Southern Baptist Convention attempted to bring about reconciliation, but to no avail. Even after the schisms the older NBC remained the largest African-American Baptist denomination in the United States.

Smaller Baptist Bodies in North America

Many of the smaller Baptist bodies in North America formed or expanded their ministries in the early decades of the twentieth century. The largest of these groups included the various types of Free Will Baptists. Among the Free Will Baptists in the North, around 250 churches refused to participate in the merger with the Northern Baptist Convention in 1911. Five years later some of these congregations formed the Cooperative General Association of Free Will Baptists. The southern Free Will Baptists formed a General Conference in 1921. The two movements began dialoguing about a merger, and in 1935 they came together to organize the National Association of Free Will Baptists (NAFWB). The new denomination established a headquarters in Nashville, Tennessee. In 1942, they opened the Free Will Baptist Bible College (now Welch College) in Nashville.

Seventh Day Baptists and even some Primitive Baptists also participated in the move toward denominationalism. In 1919, the Seventh Day Baptist

General Conference rejected the societal method in favor of the convention method by creating a general board to provide oversight to its ministries. In 1929, the group dedicated a new denominational headquarters in Plainfield, New Jersey. In the 1890s a group of Primitive Baptists in Georgia abandoned the historic Primitive Baptist hesitancy toward instrumental music, paid clergy, and Sunday schools. In 1910, the Primitive Baptists in Georgia split, with the so-called Progressive

Cades Cove Primitive Baptist Church, Great Smoky Mountains, North Carolina (est. 1827).

Primitive Baptists embracing practices the wider movement dismissed as extrabiblical innovations. Primitives of all stripes continued to cooperate primarily through local associations. The one exception was African-American Primitive Baptists, who had some methodological affinity with the Progressive Primitive Baptists. In 1907 they formed a general convention called the National Primitive Baptist Convention.

Many smaller Baptist groups were comprised of recent immigrants to America. By the early decades of the twentieth century, some of these groups had grown enough to form denominations, though in most cases they maintained fraternal ties to the Northern Baptist Convention. Some groups were larger. Swedish Baptists formed their own General Conference in 1879 and continued to show steady growth during the first half of the twentieth century. By midcentury most Swedish congregations were worshipping in English due to assimilation into the broader American culture. During the first half of the twentieth century, the Swedish Baptist General Conference used Northern Baptist Sunday school material and conducted mission work through the Northern Baptist boards. However, in 1944 the group formed its own Board of Foreign Missions, partly in reaction to progressive theological trends in the NBC. In 1945, "Swedish" was dropped, and the denomination became the Baptist General Conference of America (BGC). In 1947, the BGC's junior college expanded its programs and became Bethel College and Seminary.

German Baptists had been organized since the mid-nineteenth century, though they too cooperated closely with Northern Baptists. For much of the nineteenth century, German immigrants were a focus of the American Baptist Home Mission Society, and Rochester Theological Seminary included a German Department. Karl August Rauschenbusch, who was the leading German Baptist pastor in America and the father of the famous Social Gospel thinker Walter Rauschenbusch, led the German Department. In 1934, the General Conference of German Baptist Churches in North America dropped "German" from its name and formed a General Council to oversee denominational ministries. In 1946, it incorporated as the North American Baptist Conference (NABC). Three years later the German Department separated from Rochester Seminary and was relocated to Sioux Falls, South Dakota, where it was named North American Baptist Seminary.

In the Southwest, Baptists engaged in home mission work among Hispanic immigrants, mostly from Mexico. In 1910, the Mexican Baptist Convention was formed at a meeting hosted by the First Mexican Baptist Church of San Antonio. The new group had close ties to the Baptist General Convention of Texas. By the 1920s the Mexican Baptists had established a women's auxiliary modeled after the SBC's Woman's Missionary Union, had established local associations, and were publishing a periodical titled *El Bautista Mexicana*. Further denominational expansion came in the 1940s. During that decade Mexican Baptists restructured their convention, employed their first full-time executive secretary, and launched a number of new evangelism and discipleship initiatives. Under the leadership of missionary Paul Siebenmann, a Bible college called the Mexican Baptist Bible Institute opened in San Antonio in 1947. The school is now known as Baptist University of the Americas. A Hispanic Baptist Convention of New Mexico was formed in 1923, though it was much smaller than its counterpart in Texas.

Canadian Baptists also moved toward a more centralized denominational structure. At the end of the century's first decade, Canadian Baptists were divided into three regional conventions. The Baptist Convention of Ontario and Quebec, located in Canada's central provinces, is the oldest of these conventions, dating to 1888. In the Atlantic provinces on Canada's eastern coast, the Arminian Free Baptists merged with the historically Calvinistic Regular Baptists to form the Convention of Atlantic Baptist Churches in 1905/1906. In 1907, Baptists in the western provinces formed the Baptist Convention of Western Canada, which was renamed the Baptist Union of Western Canada two years later. In 1944, these three regional conventions joined in a national body called the Baptist Federation of Canada. A few dozen German-speaking congregations in Canada related to the North American Baptist Conference. German Baptists in Canada organized at least two associations in the early years of the twentieth century.

European Baptists

The largest Baptist denomination in Europe at the turn of the twentieth century was the Baptist Union of Great Britain. The Baptist Union significantly expanded its denominational ministries under the leadership of John

Howard Shakespeare, who served as general secretary from 1898 to 1924. He proved to be a gifted administrator and was respected by Baptists the world over for his leadership skills, as evidenced in his service as the first general secretary of the Baptist World Alliance. During his tenure as general secretary of the Baptist Union, Shakespeare was the architect of two significant fund drives. The Twentieth Century Fund (1899–1902) raised more than £250,000, primarily for new church starts, annuity, and a new denominational headquarters. The Sustentation Fund (1902–14) raised £250,000 to supplement pastoral salaries. In 1903, the Baptist Church House opened in London, providing the Baptist Union with a headquarters in the capital city.

Shakespeare led the Baptist Union in a major denominational restructuring in 1916. England and Wales were divided into ten districts, each of which was served by a general superintendent. The general superintendent provided pastoral care to clergy and helped connect ministerial candidates with prospective churches. The restructuring made the Baptist Union considerably more connectional than Baptist denominations in North America and placed the general superintendent in a bishop-like role. Shakespeare was critical of the strict independence that had often characterized Baptists. He not only led the Baptist Union in a more connectional direction, but he also advocated ecumenism more

John Howard Shakespeare (1857–1928)

than any other Baptist leader of his day. He argued for the merger of British Baptists with other nonconformists into a proposed United Free Church of England, which he hoped would be a prelude to an eventual reunion of all English Protestants with the Church of England. The Baptist Union did not embrace Shakespeare's vision for church union, but along with the Northern Baptist Convention it remained among the most ecumenically minded Baptist groups.

A number of smaller European Baptist denominations were formed during this period. The Irish Baptist Union, which like its Scottish counterpart remained independent of the Baptist Union of England and Wales, was formed in 1895. In 1924, the Irish Baptist Union formed its own foreign mission society. In Central Europe, Czech Baptists formed the Unity of Brethren in 1919. The group's name indicated affinity with the fifteenth-century Bohemian reform movement of the same name that stemmed from the ministry of John Hus. In Poland, Slavic Baptists formed the Union of Slavic Baptists in 1922. The denomination grew rapidly in its first two decades of existence. In Switzerland, German-speaking Baptists formed the Union of Baptist Churches. This group was initially an association within the German Baptist Union, though in 1948 it became an independent denomination. Other European Baptists might have organized into denominations during this period had the continent not been decimated by World War I and World War II.

For Further Study

Brackney, William H. *Baptists in North America: An Historical Perspective*, chapters 4 and 5. Oxford, UK, and Malden, MA: Blackwell, 2006.

Brand, Chad, and David Hankins. *One Sacred Effort: The Cooperative Program of Southern Baptists*, chapter 5. Nashville, TN: B&H, 2006.

Dekar, Paul R. *For the Healing of the Nations: Baptist Peacemakers*. Macon, GA: Smyth & Helwys, 1993.

Durso, Keith. E. *Thy Will Be Done: A Biography of George W. Truett*. Macon, GA: Mercer University Press, 2009.

Fitts, Leroy. *A History of Black Baptists*, chapter 2. Nashville, TN: Broadman, 1985.

Pierard, Richard V., ed. *Baptists Together for Christ 1905–2005: A Hundred-Year History of the Baptist World Alliance*. Falls Church, VA: BWA, 2005.

Randall, Ian M. *The English Baptists of the Twentieth Century, A History of the English Baptists*, vol. 4, chapters 2 and 3. Didcot, Oxford, UK: The Baptist Historical Society, 2005.

Shepherd, Peter. *The Making of a Modern Denomination: John Howard Shakespeare and the English Baptists 1898–1924*. Carlisle, Cumbria, UK: Paternoster, 2001.

Wardin, Albert W., ed. *Baptists Around the World*. Nashville, TN: B&H, 1995.

Questions for Discussion

1. Describe the formation and purpose of the Baptist World Alliance. Using the Internet, find out how many Baptist organizations participate in the Baptist World Alliance today. What issues has the Baptist World Alliance addressed in recent years?

2. How did professionalization affect Baptist churches during this period? Which of these emphases would you consider still effective for churches today? Which emphases would you consider outdated for ministry today?

3. How did various Baptists respond to World War I? How might you respond to Baptists who were conscientious objectors or pacifists if a similar conflict took place today? Do you think churches should have specific roles during wartime? Why or why not?

4. Describe the formation and early history of the Northern Baptist Convention. How did the societal method offer challenges to their understanding of cooperation? How did Northern Baptist involvement with the New World Movement affect their future?

5. Before reading this section, were you aware of Helen Barrett Montgomery and her accomplishments? In what ways does her involvement among Northern Baptists highlight the diversity of the global Baptist movement?

6. In what ways can the Seventy-Five Million Campaign among Southern Baptists be considered both a failure and a success?

7. Describe the formation and purpose of the Southern Baptist Cooperative Program. Does your church currently participate in the Cooperative Program? Using the Internet, research the current giving levels of Southern Baptists to the Cooperative Program and outline the distribution of funds to various Southern Baptist agencies.

8. What is the National Baptist Convention? How was it formed? What unique challenges did National Baptists encounter in light of their cooperative efforts?

9. Describe the life and contributions of John Howard Shakespeare. Are you familiar with anyone who serves Baptists in similar fashion today? If so, who?

Chapter 10

TENSION AND EXPANSION

During the first third of the twentieth century, Baptist denominations, especially in North America, were rocked by controversies. Ongoing theological conflicts in many Baptist denominations between modernists and fundamentalists led to acrimonious debates, political intrigue, and eventually schisms. Southern Baptists were absorbed into additional controversies due to Landmarkism, which remained prevalent in parts of the Southwest. Some Landmark Baptists formed new movements to compete with the SBC. As the denominational controversies were subsiding, much of the world became engulfed in World War II, which, like World War I, significantly affected Baptists. The end of the war coincided with the rise of global communism, which led to dramatic changes among European Baptists in particular.

Among Baptists in North America, denominational conflict and global wars did little to curtail numeric growth and institutional expansion. Both Northern Baptists and Southern Baptists abandoned their prior comity (territorial) agreements by midcentury and emerged as national denominations. Southern Baptists even began to extend into Canada, especially in the Pacific Northwest, while Canadian Baptists also formed new denominations. Baptists in each of these groups and others expanded their institutions, increasing their denominational footprint during the heady days of growth in the postwar era.

Denominational Controversies

Fundamentalist-Modernist Controversies

Following the American Civil War, Darwinian evolution and the historical-critical method of biblical interpretation increasingly influenced

Protestant theology. Many Protestants embraced an optimistic view of human nature and redefined traditional doctrines such as original sin, the atonement, the exclusivity of Christ, and the inspiration of Scripture. Some Baptists imbibed of the new views, leading to controversy. In Britain the new theology was a source of contention during the Downgrade Controversy of the late 1880s. C. H. Toy's resignation from the faculty of Southern Baptist Theological Seminary in 1879, discussed in chapter 8, marked the earliest similar controversy among Baptists in America. During the early decades of the twentieth century, North American Baptists experienced ongoing conflict between theological progressives, often called "modernists" or "liberals," and conservatives, often called "fundamentalists."

Modernist ideas first took hold in colleges and seminaries. In the North modernist ideas were propagated at Baptist schools such as Newton Seminary, Rochester Seminary, Crozer Seminary, Colgate University, Brown University, and especially the University of Chicago. Many influential Northern Baptist scholars identified with progressive views, including William Rainey Harper, Shailer Mathews, and G. B. Foster of Chicago; W. H. P. Faunce of Brown University; Henry Clay Vedder of Crozer; and William Newton Clarke of Colgate. Clarke authored *Outline of Christian Theology* (1894), the first systematic theology written from a modernist perspective. He denied biblical inerrancy, dismissed the Genesis account of humanity's fall into sin, affirmed evolution, and rejected substitutionary atonement. Presidents Alvah Hovey of Newton and A. H. Strong of Rochester each wrote systematic theologies that were more conservative, but these leaders tolerated modernist ideas and allowed them to be openly advocated in their respective seminaries.

Few Southern Baptist theologians were openly modernist, perhaps reflecting the generally conservative sentiments of the wider denomination. Nevertheless, several Baptist schools in the South employed modernist faculty members. When professors at Baylor University and Mercer University were accused of advocating evolution, several either resigned or were terminated. Southern Seminary professors C. S. Gardner and W. O. Carver were influenced by modernism while remaining largely evangelical in their piety and emphases. President Richard Vann of Meredith College openly rejected the verbal inspiration of Scripture. Perhaps the most widely known modernists in the SBC were the Poteat family. William Louis Poteat, an evolutionary biologist, was president of Wake Forest College. His brother, Edwin McNeill Poteat Sr., served as president of Furman University and pastored both Southern and Northern Baptist churches. The latter's son, Edwin McNeill Poteat Jr., pastored Southern Baptist churches, wrote *Jesus and the Liberal*

Mind (1934), and from 1944 served as president of Colgate-Rochester Theological Seminary.

Around the turn of the twentieth century, many pastors and scholars advanced a Christian critique of laissez-faire capitalism, which they interpreted as the root of numerous social ills. They also embraced a combination of Darwinism and postmillennialism, believing God would usher in his kingdom as systemic injustice was conquered through human progress. This "Social Gospel" arose within a particular cultural context that included increased industrialization, urbanization, and immigration; many immigrants were Catholics who moved into ethnic enclaves in large cities. This milieu contributed to widespread economic inequality between the urban poor, agricultural laborers, and mill and mine workers on the one hand and the great entrepreneurs, bankers, and industrial leaders of the age on the other. The context gave rise to excessively long work hours, high crime rates, gang violence, urban slums, and oppressive mill towns.

The Social Gospel

We have seen that in the prophetic religion of the Old Testament and in the aims of Jesus Christ the reconstruction of the whole of human life in accordance with the will of God and under the motive power of religion was the ruling purpose. Primitive Christianity, while under the fresh impulse of Jesus, was filled with social forces. In its later history the reconstructive capacities of Christianity were paralyzed by alien influences, but through the evolution of the Christian spirit in the Church it has now arrived at a stage in its development where it is fit and free for its largest social mission. . . . Thus the will of God revealed in Christ and in the highest manifestations of the religions spirit, the call of human duty, and the motives of self-protection, alike summon Christian men singly and collectively to put their hands to the plough and not to look back till public morality shall be at least as much Christianized as private morality now is.

Excerpted from Walter Rauschenbusch, *Christianity and the Social Crisis* (1908).

Like modernism, the Social Gospel was an ecumenical movement, including such luminaries as Congregationalist pastors Washington Gladden and Charles Sheldon and Episcopal economist Richard Ely. Walter Rauschenbusch, whose father Karl August Rauschenbusch was a pioneering German Baptist pastor in America, emerged as the leading Social Gospel advocate among American Baptists. Walter began his career as pastor of a German Baptist congregation in the slums of Hell's Kitchen, New York City. In 1892, Rauschenbusch formed the Brotherhood of the Kingdom, a coalition of Northern Baptist ministers committed to promoting social justice in urban settings. In 1897, he followed in his father's footsteps and became a church history professor at Rochester Theological Seminary, where he authored two seminal books: *Christianity and the Social Crisis* (1908) and *Theology for the Social Gospel* (1917). Rauschenbusch was also a pacifist who opposed American intervention in World War I. He spoke of his Baptist convictions in a famous series of essays published in 1905: "I am a Baptist, then, because in our church life we have a minimum of emphasis on ritual and creed, and a maximum of emphasis on spiritual experience, and the more I study the history of religion, the more I see how great and fruitful such a position is."

Walter Rauschenbusch (1861–1918)

The Social Gospel impacted North American Baptists to varying degrees. Northern Baptist theologian Shailer Mathews of the University of Chicago published his own treatise advocating the Social Gospel in 1909. Many civil rights activists, most famously Martin Luther King Jr., were influenced by the movement. Most Southern Baptists rejected the more radical political tenets of the Social Gospel, though some progressives were favorable toward them, including John White of Second Baptist Church in Atlanta and C. S. Gardner of Southern Seminary. In Canada, Rochester graduates D. R. Sharpe, A. A. Shaw, J. A. Huntley, and H. R. McGill championed the Social Gospel. Tommy Douglas, a Baptist minister influenced by the Social Gospel, became a leader of the New Democratic Party and was the architect of Canada's universal healthcare program.

Fundamentalism originated as an interdenominational movement within evangelical Protestantism that dissented from progressive theology within the mainline churches. Fundamentalists championed traditional evangelical emphases, but they were also influenced by several late-nineteenth-century trends, including the mass revivalism popularized by Charles Finney and especially D. L. Moody; various understandings of holiness; the technical definition of inerrancy articulated at Princeton Theological Seminary under A. A. Hodge, Charles Hodge, and B. B. Warfield; and premillennialism, increasingly of the dispensational variety. As modernism infiltrated

Protestantism, fundamentalists were those conservative evangelicals who actively resisted, often to the point of schism.

Controversies over modernism periodically erupted among Baptists. In the Northern Baptist Convention conservatives responded to the liberalism of the University of Chicago's Divinity School by founding Northern Baptist Theological Seminary in 1913. Fundamentalists caucused before the 1920 Buffalo convention. The leaders of this group included William Bell Riley of Minneapolis and John Roach Straton and J. C. Massee of New York. The fundamentalist caucus assumed the name Fundamentalist Federation after *Watchman-Examiner* editor Curtis Lee Laws argued in a 1920 article that fundamentalists were conservatives willing to do "battle royal" for the fundamentals of Christianity. It was popular at the time

William Bell Riley
(1861–1947)

to refer to basic evangelical doctrines as the fundamentals of the faith, as evidenced by the five-volume series *The Fundamentals* (1910–15), financed by Lyman and Milton Stewart and edited by A. C. Dixon and R. A. Torrey.

Controversy continued throughout the decade. In 1921, an investigative committee formed in Buffalo the previous year exonerated the denomination's schools of modernism. At the Indianapolis convention in 1922, fundamentalists proposed the NBC adopt the New Hampshire Confession. The proposal was defeated by an almost two-to-one margin after Cornelius Woelfkin of New York offered a counterproposal that the convention affirm the New Testament as a sufficient guide for faith and practice. In 1924, an investigation judged NBC missionaries sufficiently orthodox, much to the chagrin of fundamentalists. That same year the NBC declared itself inclusive of a variety of theological opinions. Ongoing fundamentalist criticisms of the American Baptist Publication Society during the 1920s were rebuffed. Though not directly related to Northern Baptists, the Scopes Trial of 1925 dealt a crushing blow to fundamentalism's public image as journalists such as H. L. Mencken lampooned the incident.

A key moment in the controversy was Union Theological Seminary professor Harry Emerson Fosdick's 1922 sermon "Shall the Fundamentalists

Win?"—preached at the First Presbyterian Church of New York, where Fosdick was filling the pulpit. His provocative
address proved instrumental in the fundamentalist-modernist controversy among
both Northern Baptists and Northern
Presbyterians. Fundamentalists such
as Baptist John Roach Stratton and
Presbyterian Clarence McCartney
responded to Fosdick with sermons of their own. Northern Presbyterians opened an investigation
into Fosdick's theology, a futile
effort since he was a Baptist.
Northern Presbyterian fundamentalists, led by Princeton Seminary
professor J. Gresham Machen, eventually left their denomination during
the 1930s. For his part Fosdick became
pastor of New York's Park Avenue Baptist
Church in 1926. In 1931, that congregation
changed its name to Riverside Church and
moved into a massive new Gothic building,

*Harry Emerson Fosdick
(1878–1969)*

paid for in part by John D. Rockefeller Jr. Fosdick remained arguably the
best-known preacher in America until his retirement in 1946.

Harry Emerson Fosdick Criticizes Fundamentalism

Two groups exist in the Christian churches and the question raised by the Fundamentalists is—Shall one of them drive the other out? Will that get us anywhere? Multitudes of young men and women at this season of the year are graduating from our schools of learning, thousands of them Christians who may make us older ones ashamed by the sincerity of their devotion to God's will on earth. They are not thinking in ancient terms that leave ideas of progress out. They cannot think in those terms. There could be no greater tragedy than that the Fundamentalists should shut the door of the Christian fellowship against such.

I do not believe for one moment that the Fundamentalists are going to succeed.

Excerpted from Harry Emerson Fosdick, "Shall the Fundamentalists Win?"

Northern Baptist fundamentalists responded to these setbacks in numerous ways. They founded the Baptist Bible Union (BBU) in 1923, a group that included Baptist fundamentalists from outside the NBC. They also established Eastern Baptist Theological Seminary in Philadelphia in 1925. During the next decade fundamentalists began to disagree over the best strategy to counter progressive trends within the NBC. Some "denominational fundamentalists," led by Massee and Riley, remained within the convention and worked through independent ministries that competed with official NBC schools and boards. A Conservative Baptist Foreign Mission Society drew the support of fundamentalist churches. Denominational fundamentalists also agitated against the NBC's ongoing involvement in the ecumenical movement.

Separatist fundamentalists completely severed ties with the NBC. They took this action based on their interpretation of 2 Corinthians 6:17: "Wherefore come out from among them, and be ye separate, saith the Lord, and touch not the unclean thing; and I will receive you" (KJV). Some became independent Baptists, refusing to participate in any denomination. Others left the NBC and formed new groups. In 1932, one faction formed the General Association of Regular Baptist Churches (GARBC). The GARBC adopted an amended version of the New Hampshire Confession that affirmed premillennialism. They established Grand Rapids Baptist Bible College in Grand Rapids, Michigan, and Baptist Bible College in Johnson City, New York. In 1953, the GARBC took control of Cedarville College in Cedarville, Ohio. Over time many denominational fundamentalists also gave up on the convention. When the NBC refused to cooperate with the Conservative Baptist Foreign Mission Board, Riley and others formed the Conservative Baptist Association in 1947. Conservative Baptists founded Denver Seminary in Denver, Colorado, and Western Theological Seminary in Portland, Oregon. Whether separatists or denominationalists, Franklin Goodchild spoke for all Northern Baptist fundamentalists when he argued, "Fundamentalists stand where loyal Baptists have always stood. We believe that the Bible is God's Word, that it was written by men divinely inspired, and that it has supreme authority in all matters of faith and conduct."

Canadian Baptists experienced a controversy that focused on the theology department at McMaster University, then in Toronto. Modernist views had been taught at McMaster since the 1880s, when William Newton Clarke served on the faculty. Clarke taught G. B. Cross and I. G. Mathews, two younger scholars who joined the McMaster faculty before moving on to Northern Baptist seminaries. Though Cross was the more liberal of the two professors, Mathews proved to be the more controversial. Mathews was tried for heresy in 1910 for his view that the Old Testament offered a more primitive revelation than the New Testament. Though Mathews was acquitted, in 1919 he found himself at the center of another controversy over an anonymous editorial in *The Canadian Baptist* advocating a modernist understanding of biblical inspiration and authority. Mathews denied he authored the provocative editorial but resigned that same year to teach at Crozer Seminary.

The leading critic of liberalism at McMaster was T. T. Shields, pastor of Jarvis Street Baptist Church in Toronto, then the largest Baptist church in Canada. He also served as editor of *The Gospel Witness*, a leading fundamentalist periodical in Canada, and held leadership roles in several pan-fundamentalist organizations. In 1919, Shields, who was a trustee at McMaster, agitated for a rightward turn at the school following Mathews's resignation. Tensions escalated to such a degree that Shields was removed from the trustee board and established Toronto Baptist Seminary and Bible College at Jarvis Street Church in 1927. In response, the Baptist Convention of Ontario and Quebec disfellowshipped Jarvis Street Church

Thomas Todhunter Shields (1873–1955)

and twelve other congregations in 1927. Shields retaliated by founding the Union of Regular Baptist Churches of Ontario and Quebec, a denomination that split just four years later in 1931 over concerns about Shields's control of the group.

Shields played a central role in the purchase of Des Moines University in Iowa by the Baptist Bible Union in 1927. He became acting president and had high hopes for the school, writing, "Christ must be put first, the end of all education must be to know Him better. If we study languages, mathematics, literature, history, or any of the sciences, it must be with a view to obtaining a better knowledge of Christ." Despite his noble aspirations, within two years the university was battling insolvency, and the press blamed Shields. He publicly broke ties with his handpicked presidential successor and was accused of having an affair with the school's secretary, who was also an employee of the Baptist Bible Union (he was eventually exonerated of the latter charge). Students revolted against the administration, and the school shut down in 1929. The debacle helped bring about the end of the BBU, which dissolved in 1930. Following the collapse of Des Moines University,

Shields became less involved in the wider fundamentalist movement, focusing instead on conservative dissent in Canada.

Southern Baptists were spared a convention-wide fundamentalist-modernist controversy in part because there were relatively few modernists to whom fundamentalists could react. However, this does not mean the SBC was untouched by the controversy. The leading fundamentalist among Southern Baptists was J. Frank Norris, pastor of First Baptist Church of Fort Worth, Texas, from 1909 to 1952. Norris, known as the "Texas Cyclone," was an outspoken critic of modernism, communism, and Roman Catholicism, and he was a staunch proponent of premillennial theology and the prohibition of beverage alcohol. Norris was also famous for announcing in advance sensational and provocative sermon titles that were crafted to attract as many attendees as possible to his worship services.

Norris is known for two famous legal controversies: he is likely the only Baptist preacher to be acquitted of both arson (1912) and murder (1926)! Norris was charged with arson after his church's sanctuary burned to the ground. The circumstances were suspicious; Norris wanted to build a new sanctuary to accommodate his growing congregation, but his deacons prevented the move. Because of the fire, Norris was able to proceed with his plans for a new sanctuary. After a lengthy trial a jury acquitted Norris. The murder charge was an even more significant controversy. In 1926, Norris publicly criticized Fort Worth mayor H. C. Meacham for allegedly corrupt ties to the Catholic Church. When one of Meacham's friends, D. E. Chipps, confronted Norris in the latter's church office, Norris shot Chipps dead. Norris was indicted for murder but was acquitted in 1927. Norris claimed that Chipps had threatened him. Norris thought (incorrectly, it turns out) that Chipps had a gun, so he shot Chipps in self-defense. The jury agreed. Though Norris was acquitted, the media enjoyed painting the controversial pastor as a reckless and violent character. Journalists called him a "Shooting Salvationist" and fighting "gundamentalist."

Within the SBC, Norris attacked initiatives like the Seventy-Five Million Campaign and the Cooperative Program and criticized convention leaders, especially George Truett and L. R. Scarborough. His criticisms of Baylor University and Southwestern Seminary led to his church being excluded from the Tarrant County Baptist Association and the Baptist General Convention of Texas. In 1931, Norris withdrew his church from the SBC, though for years he led fundamentalist rallies that coincided with annual convention meetings. Beyond the SBC, Norris influenced the wider fundamentalist movement, especially among independent Baptists. He was involved in founding pan-fundamentalist groups such as the Baptist Bible Union and the Premillennial Missionary Baptist Fellowship. He became pastor of Temple Baptist Church in Detroit, Michigan, in 1935, which he led simultaneously with his Fort Worth congregation. He founded a Bible college in Fort Worth and edited a journal titled *The Fundamentalist*. Norris also mentored a number of younger ministers, most notably John R. Rice, an evangelist and longtime editor of the fundamentalist periodical *The Sword of the Lord*, who emerged as the leading independent Baptist in America following Norris's death.

In part because of criticism by Norris and other fundamentalists of Baptist schools that taught evolution, Southern Baptists adopted a confession of faith in 1925. The Baptist Faith and Message was a revision of the New Hampshire Confession drafted by a committee chaired by E. Y. Mullins. The president of Southern Seminary, Mullins was the leading Baptist theologian of his era. He wrote a widely adopted systematic theology textbook, *The Christian Religion in its Doctrinal Expression* (1917). He was a mediating theologian who was conservative enough to contribute to *The Fundamentals* but progressive enough to hire liberals like C. S. Gardner and W. O. Carver to teach at Southern. In his book *The Axioms of Religion* (1908), Mullins championed a

Edgar Young Mullins
(1860–1928)

E. Y. Mullins's Six "Axioms of Religion"

1. The theological axiom: The holy and loving God has a right to be sovereign.
2. The religious axiom: All souls have an equal right to direct access to God.
3. The ecclesiastical axiom: All believers have a right to equal privileges in the church.
4. The moral axiom: To be responsible, man must be free.
5. The religio-civic axiom: A free church in a free state.
6. The social axiom: Love your neighbor as yourself.

Excerpted from E. Y. Mullins, *The Axioms of Religion* (1908).

strongly individualist interpretation of Baptist identity that elevated liberty of conscience (called "soul competency") as the chief Baptist distinctive. He argued, "Observe then that the idea of the competency of the soul in religion excludes at once all human interference, such as episcopacy and infant baptism, and every form of religion by proxy. Religion is a personal matter between the soul and God." Mullins was also a leading Baptist statesman, serving as president of the SBC (1921–24) and the Baptist World Alliance (1923–28).

Adoption of the Baptist Faith and Message proved to be largely a symbolic gesture. Few churches adopted the statement as their doctrinal standard, and it had little to no effect on the employment practices of Baptist colleges and seminaries. Though the SBC did not adopt a confession of faith in 1845, Southern Baptists ironically were far more confessional at their founding than they were in 1925. Every one of the nearly 300 delegates present at the formation of the SBC represented a church that had adopted a version of the Philadelphia Confession or an abstract of that document. In later years many churches adopted the New Hampshire Confession. But by the 1920s, although virtually every church included a confession of faith in its constitution and bylaws, few congregations treated confessions as binding statements of their beliefs. It was rare for affirmation of a church's confession, or even familiarity with it, to be required of church members or ministers. Associations and state conventions also tended to ignore their confessional statements. Cooperation around common programs, especially the Cooperative Program, increasingly took precedent over cooperation around common doctrinal convictions. Confessions took a backseat in denominational life until the early 1960s.

Landmark Controversies

The Southwest had long been a stronghold for Landmark theology, which in the early decades of the twentieth century led to several schisms. In Texas, Samuel Hayden criticized non-Landmark Texas Baptists through his preaching and his periodical, the *Texas Baptist and Herald*. In 1897, the Baptist General Convention of Texas refused to seat him as a messenger. He retaliated by suing fifty Texas Baptist leaders, though the lawsuit was settled out of court. The Hayden Controversy galvanized Landmarkers, who formed the Baptist Missionary Association in 1900. In Arkansas, Landmarkers formed the General Association of Arkansas Baptists in 1902 as an alternative to the Arkansas Baptist State Convention. Ben Bogard, a pastor in Searcy, Arkansas, emerged as the group's major leader. In 1924, Bogard's group merged with Hayden's group, resulting in the American Baptist Association (ABA). ABA churches were similar to fundamentalist Baptist churches, though they also affirmed Landmarkism. In 1950, a schism in the ABA resulted in the Baptist Missionary Association of America.

Some Landmarkers remained within the SBC though they were suspicious of the convention's expanding bureaucracy. The leading Landmark church in the SBC was Ashland Avenue Baptist Church in Lexington, Kentucky. For many decades the church published J. M. Carroll's "The Trail of Blood" (1931), a widely distributed pamphlet that popularized the idea of an unbroken succession of Baptist churches since the time of the apostles. In 1950, Ashland Avenue established Lexington Baptist College. As mentioned in chapter 7, Landmark ideas spread through some denominational publications, especially J. M. Pendleton's *Baptist Church Manual* (1867), which remained in print through the Sunday School Board throughout the twentieth century. Though popular among some pastors, Landmark views had only nominal influence outside the Southwest and parts of Kentucky and Tennessee.

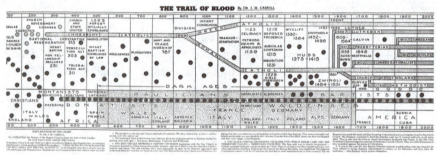

Famous chart depicting "The Trail of Blood" from Jesus to the present day.

World War II

The Second World War (1939–45) resulted in an estimated sixty million casualties, including at least forty million civilian deaths. Adolf Hitler's Nazi regime was responsible for at least eleven million deaths, including the executions of an estimated six million Jews. Hitler became German chancellor in 1933 and within weeks began consolidating his power over the government. The Nazi Party successfully infiltrated the state-sponsored Lutheran Church, and Jews found their rights restricted by Hitler's Third Reich, often with support from pro-Nazi clergy. The Confessing Church arose in 1934 in opposition to the anti-Semitism and borderline idolatrous worship of Hitler among many Protestants. Dietrich Bonhoeffer, Martin Niemöller, and Karl Barth were notable leaders in the Confessing Church, which adopted the

Barmen Declaration affirming traditional Protestantism in opposition to the Nazi-influenced German Christian movement.

The Baptist World Congress met in Berlin in August 1934, just weeks after the Confessing Church had been formed. German President Paul von Hindenberg died the day before the meeting began, and three days later Hitler declared himself to be the German *Führer*. During the Congress, Nazi propaganda claimed that Germany was a Christian nation, and many Baptists expressed pleasure with Hitler's crusade to rid Germany of pornographic literature and violent films. Some Baptists raised concerns about Nazi persecution of Jews while others were convinced that rumors of Jewish mistreatment were exaggerated. Regrettably, a large Nazi flag was prominently displayed behind the stage area throughout the Baptist World Congress.

Hitler attempted to unite Europe into a new German Empire, beginning with his invasion of Poland in September 1939. As with the Great War, Baptist responses to World War II varied. Reflecting the national mood, many Baptists in America initially advocated isolationism. Once the United States entered the war in December 1941, Baptists overwhelmingly supported the Allied cause. Pastors preached patriotic sermons, denominations passed prowar resolutions, and Baptist colleges offered their facilities to the military for training exercises. Some Baptists who had been pacifists, such as *Alabama Baptist* editor L. L. Gwaltney, became defenders of the war effort. Baptists generally agreed with President Franklin Roosevelt's argument that America entered the war to preserve "four freedoms": religious freedom, free speech, freedom from fear, and freedom from want. Of course Baptists were especially hopeful the war would preserve and spread religious freedom.

More than one million Baptist men served in the military during the war, with thousands of college-aged men rejecting educational deferments so they could enlist. Many Baptist clergymen served as chaplains. Northern Baptists endorsed 976 chaplains, the second most of any denomination behind the Methodists, while Southern Baptists endorsed more than 900. Clergy from smaller Baptist groups also served as chaplains, including four Seventh Day Baptist pastors. The Federal Council of Churches operated a General Commission on Army and Navy Chaplains to screen Protestant chaplaincy candidates. Due to concerns about ecumenism, Southern Baptists worked independently of the General Commission, endorsing chaplains through their Home Mission Board.

Like American women in general, Baptist women took on greater responsibilities in homes, churches, and the wider culture during the war. Many entered the workforce. With the absence of younger men, women served as Sunday school teachers, committee leaders, and music directors. The SBC's Woman's Missionary Union and the NBC's American Baptist Woman's

Missionary Society raised money for Russian refugees, urban missions, and evangelistic material for American servicemen. Though large numbers of men (and some women) served in the military, Baptist church attendance increased significantly during the war.

Despite widespread support for the war, some Baptists were conscientious objectors. Baptist papers in the South almost universally criticized conscientious objectors, and a few pacifist ministers lost their churches. Other Baptists defended the right of conscientious objection, including Southwestern Seminary ethicist T. B. Maston and the SBC's Social Service Commission. In 1940, Southern Baptists passed a resolution affirming the right of conscientious objection. Pacifists were encouraged to register their convictions with the SBC Executive Committee. More than 100 Southern Baptists applied for denominational recognition as pacifists and at least 52 received it. Among Northern Baptists an unofficial Baptist Pacifist Fellowship was formed in 1940. Around 150 Northern Baptist conscientious objectors served as noncombatants. Many worked in civilian public service camps that were overseen by Mennonites and other "Peace Churches."

Southern Baptist Resolution Defending the Rights of Conscientious Objection

Baptists have always believed in liberty of conscience and have honored men who were willing to brave adverse public opinion for the sake of conscientious scruples. A considerable number of members of churches of our Convention, through their interpretation of the moral teachings of Christ, have reached the position of a conscientious objection to war that prohibits them from bearing arms. . . .

Be it RESOLVED, That the Convention go on record as recognizing such right of a conscientious objection, and that the Convention instruct the Executive Committee to provide facilities for their registration with the denomination, in order that the Executive Committee may be able to make accurate certification to the government concerning them at any time it should be called for.

Annual of the Southern Baptist Convention (1940).

Baptists in America wanted President Roosevelt to use his wartime powers to advance moral causes they championed. The Twenty-first Amendment had been rescinded in 1933, but many Southern Baptists wanted a return to prohibition. For example, Florida Baptists urged President Roosevelt to ban alcohol among armed service personnel. The National Baptist Convention, Inc., asked Roosevelt to outlaw racial discrimination in the military. After Pearl Harbor, Northern Baptists protested the placement of Japanese-Americans in internment camps, including G. Pitt Beers, head of the ecumenical Home

Missions Council. Japanese-American Baptists engaged in evangelistic work within the camps, including Paul Nagano and Jitsuo Morikawa. The latter went on to pastor First Baptist Church of Chicago and become director of evangelism in the American (formerly Northern) Baptist Convention.

The war significantly disrupted Baptist foreign mission efforts. Mission work in Europe and the Middle East was virtually nonexistent due to combat. The Japanese imprisoned missionaries in China, and the occupation government shut down or took control of mission schools and hospitals. Some missionaries used their skills to aid the Allied cause, including Southern Baptists Edwin Dozier and John Birch. Dozier was a missionary to Japan who relocated to Hawaii to work with military intelligence as a Japanese code breaker. Birch was a missionary to China who worked for the United States Office of Strategic Services (forerunner of the Central Intelligence Agency) to collaborate with Chinese informants concerning Japanese troop movements. Later Birch was immortalized when the John Birch Society, a right-wing organization prone to antigovernment conspiracy theories, adopted their name in his honor. At least one Baptist missionary died as a result of the war: Rufus Gray of the Philippines perished in a Japanese labor camp.

The realities of war were pronounced for British Baptists. The Baptist Union sponsored several war-related committees, and more than 500 British Baptists served as chaplains. Baptist churches offered their facilities as emergency shelters, military dormitories, and feeding centers. Sixty British Baptist churches were destroyed and almost 700 damaged as a result of German bombing raids. The British government provided money to help rebuild church buildings, but it was difficult to raise all the funds needed to refurnish churches because members scattered during the war. As in America, some British Baptists were conscientious objectors and were assigned alternative means of service.

World War II ravaged Baptists in Northern and Central Europe. The Baptist movement was not strong in these regions, and the war contributed to the closing of hundreds of churches and seminaries. Thousands of Baptists were killed during the war, and others were left homeless. Numerous congregations lost their church buildings. In Germany alone around 5,000 Baptists died during the war, and another 40,000 were forced to flee their homes. Under the leadership of J. H. Rushbrooke, the BWA established a Relief Committee in 1943 to raise funds for Baptists on the continent. After the war the BWA aided many European Baptists, particularly German Baptists, in rebuilding church structures. The BWA also established a program to aid Baptist refugees in Europe who desired relocation to America. English-speaking Baptist denominations, especially Southern Baptists, sent missionaries to non-Soviet Europe in an effort to reestablish a Baptist witness on the continent.

Global Communism

In 1917, communists gained control of Russia, forming the Soviet Union in 1922. Following World War II, the Soviet Union emerged as a major global power. Eastern Europe was largely divided between Soviet-controlled nations and American allies, most notably Germany, which was carved up into capitalist West Germany and communist East Germany. Soviet efforts to expand their influence into Europe were met with stiff resistance from American president Harry Truman, who had been raised a Southern Baptist in Missouri. (While president, Truman nominally attended First Baptist Church of Washington, DC.) A "Cold War" ensued between the rival powers as each nation attempted to develop more advanced weapons and expand strategic alliances to hinder its opponent's influence. The Cold War dominated the world scene for almost fifty years.

Communists suppressed Baptists and many other religious groups. In the Soviet Union persecution began in the late 1920s and continued throughout the communist era. In Soviet-controlled European states, church buildings were confiscated, Christian schools were shut down, and local officials harassed pastors. In Czechoslovakia (modern-day Czech Republic), Baptists were persecuted more than any other group except Roman Catholics. In East Germany, Baptists worshiped in relative freedom, though their outreach efforts were stifled and they were cut off from Baptists in West Germany. In Poland, Baptists were socially ostracized and forbidden to distribute their literature. Following the Communist Revolution in China in 1949, all Christians were pressured to align with the Three-Self Patriotic Movement, a state-sponsored Protestant denomination. Other groups were declared illegal.

The Soviet Union and China exported communism to many parts of the globe, almost always oppressing Christians. Baptists declined numerically in nearly every nation where communism controlled the government and often lost elements of their distinctive identity as they merged with other denominations. Many Baptist churches met in secret, much like some of the earliest English Baptist churches in the seventeenth century. Communist authorities targeted pastors, and many were imprisoned, tortured, and even executed. Others were deported or voluntarily fled to Britain or North America. Many of the stories about Baptists under communist regimes remain to be told, though a rising generation of mostly European scholars is beginning to study this topic in depth.

One story that has been told is that of Josef Tson of Romania. Tson served as pastor of Second Baptist Church in Oradea, Romania, during the 1970s. In 1974, he was arrested by Romanian authorities and tortured for his convictions. In 1981, Tson was expelled from Romania and moved to the United States, where he founded the Romanian Missionary Society before returning to his homeland after the fall of communism. He helped found Emmanuel University in Oradea as an underground seminary in 1986; it is now the only accredited evangelical university in Europe. In recent years Tson has been disfellowshipped by Romanian Baptists for embracing Pentecostal views, but his testimony of faithfulness in the midst of persecution continues to inspire Baptists.

Global communism threatened Baptist mission work. Generally communist nations were "closed" to Western missionaries, most of whom were deported. Hundreds of missionaries were deported from China after Mao Zedong founded the People's Republic of China in 1949. Many of the exiled missionaries were Baptists from America, Canada, and the British Isles. North Korea was closed to missionaries after the Korean War, though missionaries worked closely with Baptists in South Korea. Free Will Baptist missionaries were forced out of Cuba in 1960 following that nation's communist revolution. By 1969, SBC missionaries had also left Cuba. Though Africa was largely untouched by communism, Baptist missionaries feared that postcolonial Africa would become communist; consequently, their presence there was minimal.

Missionaries who could work in communist lands provided Baptists in the West with firsthand accounts of persecution and other human rights violations. Southern Baptist missionaries in Southeast Asia were ardent supporters of America's war with Vietnam because of religious oppression by the communist North Vietnamese government. Some Baptist missionaries suffered death threats and even martyrdom at the hands of communists. When a communist coup in Indonesia was thwarted in 1965, a list of individuals to be "exterminated" was discovered that included many Baptist missionaries. Bill Wallace was perhaps the most famous missionary martyr

*Bill Wallace
(1908–1951)*

under communism. Wallace, a Southern Baptist, served as a medical missionary in China from 1935 to 1951 before being killed by local communist officials after refusing to leave the country. When the communist authorities accused Wallace and his coworkers of being spies, he responded, "We are what we seem to be. We are doctors and nurses and hospital staff engaged in healing the suffering and sick in the name of Jesus Christ. We are here for no other reason."

Billy Graham on Communism

The world is divided into two camps! On the one side we see Communism. On the other, we see so-called Western culture, and its fruit had its foundation in the Bible, the Word of God, and in the revivals of the seventeenth and eighteenth centuries. Communism, on the other hand, has declared war against God, against Christ, against the Bible, and against all religion!

This may be God's last great call! It was a dark hour when John Wesley and George Whitefield preached the gospel, but England had a great revival! That country was saved from the fate of the French Revolution. Unless the Western world has an old-fashioned revival, we cannot last!

Excerpted from Billy Graham, "Why God Allows Communism to Flourish," preached at his Greater Los Angeles Crusade (October 23, 1949).

In America, Baptists offered steady vocal opposition to communism, regularly denouncing it for stifling religious freedom. Southern Baptist evangelist Billy Graham, without doubt the most influential preacher in America during the second half of the twentieth century, regularly preached against "godless communism" at his evangelistic crusades. Some Baptists were caught up in anticommunist conspiracy theories. Independent Baptists such as J. Frank Norris and John R. Rice were convinced communists had infiltrated the government, schools, and even churches. In 1947, Norris accused SBC president Louie Newton of being a communist sympathizer after Newton visited Moscow and reported that Russian Baptists were not being persecuted. In 1960, a right-wing group accused more than 600 American (Northern) Baptist ministers of holding communist sympathies. Southern segregationists often (and incorrectly) accused Baptist civil rights leaders of being communists, especially Martin Luther King Jr.

The Baptist World Alliance offered a consistent witness against communism through its Human Rights Commission. Speakers at BWA Congresses regularly criticized communism and other threats to religious liberty. In 1949, the BWA helped form the European Baptist Federation (EBF) to promote Baptist growth in postwar Europe and to track statistics of Baptists in communist lands on behalf of the BWA. In 1956, the BWA invited five Russian Baptist leaders to visit America and speak at several denominational gatherings. Jacob Zhidkov, a Baptist pastor in Moscow and a future vice president of the BWA, led the delegation. Despite the BWA's anticommunist stands, fundamentalists frequently accused it of being soft on communism, largely because the group was global and advocated world peace rather than military defeat of communism.

Baptist Denominationalism in Midcentury America

Americans enjoyed considerable prosperity in the years following World War II. The wartime economic boom helped the United States fully recover from the Great Depression. After the war, with communism increasingly perceived as the biggest threat to American national security, the "military-industrial complex" (as Dwight Eisenhower called it) grew rapidly, creating thousands of jobs. Hundreds of thousands of American troops returned home from the war and enrolled in universities, funded through the G.I. Bill that was passed in 1944. In the mid-1950s the interstate highway system led to the proliferation of suburbs, shopping malls, and fast-food restaurants. The postwar years also proved prosperous for Baptists in America. It was an era of increased denominational expansion and competition between various Baptist groups.

Baptist Expansion and Competition

In 1894, the Fortress Monroe Conference resulted in a comity agreement between Southern Baptists and Northern Baptists intended to define each group's geographic boundaries. The agreement lasted less than two decades, and later comity conferences had little lasting effect either. The Illinois Baptist State Association separated from the Illinois Baptist State Convention in 1907 and affiliated with the SBC in 1910. In 1914, the Baptist General Convention of Oklahoma severed ties with Northern Baptists and aligned itself with the SBC. In 1919, the Missouri Baptist General Association voted to do the same. In 1928, the Arizona Southern Baptist Convention was formed and aligned with the SBC in 1929. In 1940, a Baptist General Convention of California was formed. It affiliated with Southern Baptists in 1942. In each case transplanted southerners comprised the majority of members in the churches forming the new SBC-related state conventions. Most had escaped the Depression-era South and relocated to northern cities or the West Coast.

In 1949, the SBC formed a committee to study the possibility of changing its name to the American Baptist Convention. Northern Baptists preempted

Southern Baptists and Intra-Baptist Cooperation

First: RESOLVED that, because local Baptist churches are independent in nature, they may be organized by Baptists anywhere with or without reference to griev-ances of other Baptist churches, or any other religious body. This liberty, of course, should never be used as a license to injure the work of other bodies.

Second: RESOLVED that, because of the voluntary principles that prevail, churches, associations, and state conventions of Baptists may cooperate with whomsoever they will, irrespective of geographical location.

Excerpted from the "Committee Report on Cooperation with Other Baptists,"
Annual of the Southern Baptist Convention (1949).

the SBC and adopted the name American Baptist Convention (ABC) in 1950. The ABC subsequently invited other Baptist bodies to merge with it under the new name; the Danish-Norwegian Baptist Conference was the only group to accept the offer (1957). Both the SBC and the ABC aspired to have a presence in every region of North America, though Southern Baptists proved more successful in their expansion efforts. By the mid-1960s, South-ern Baptists had established churches in all fifty states and had become the largest Protestant denomination in America. Southern Baptists were also rapidly expanding into Canada via migration, resulting in tensions with Canadian Baptist groups. By 1963, Southern Baptist churches in Canada had formed an association.

Baptists in America continued to prioritize foreign missions. Ameri-can Baptists maintained numerous schools and hospitals in foreign lands but increasingly encouraged churches on the mission field to become self-supporting and form indigenous Baptist associations and conventions. Southern Baptists also sponsored many schools and hospitals, though they continued to prioritize evangelism and church planting in foreign fields. Southern Baptist mission work outpaced American Baptist missions during this period, largely because SBC missionaries were far better funded. The Cooperative Program and the Lottie Moon Christmas Offering afforded Southern Baptist missionaries considerable financial freedom, removing the burden to return home to raise funds.

In home missions Southern Baptists remained committed primarily to evangelism, church planting, chaplaincy, and, beginning in the 1960s, disas-ter relief. The Home Mission Board, state conventions, and local associa-tions each engaged in home missions, resulting in both collaboration and competition. Southern Baptists did not cooperate with other denominations in home missions, reflecting both a sense of denominational self-sufficiency and the lingering influence of Landmarkism. American Baptists, influenced by the Social Gospel and ecumenism, regularly cooperated with other Protestants and enjoyed their greatest outreach success among immigrants who lived in northern urban centers. A key leader in American Baptist home missions was Jitsuo Morikawa, who advocated rethinking older proclamation-based evangelism strategies in light of justice concerns and interfaith dialogue.

Disaster relief remains a ministry priority for many Southern Baptist churches, associations, and state conventions.

African-American Baptists had focused on evangelism and church planting in Africa since the late-nineteenth century. By the 1920s many African-American women were serving as missionaries, often as teachers or nurses in African nations and on Caribbean islands. African-American Baptist missionaries cooperated with national believers and focused on turning over leadership of new churches to nationals as quickly as feasible. In addition to evangelism and church planting, African-American Baptists helped African Baptists build church edifices and championed economic development. Independent Baptist churches and other fundamentalist missionaries labored mostly in Central and South America, Australia, and Africa. Landmark Baptists such as the American Baptist Association focused on evangelism and church planting, mostly in Central and South America. Free Will Baptists expanded their mission efforts into Japan, South America, West Africa, and Western Europe.

The American Baptist Convention

American (formerly Northern) Baptist membership statistics remained relatively static during the mid-twentieth century, though American Baptists continued to expand their denominational ministries. Education remained a priority. Numerous seminaries and colleges were founded before World War II. In 1944, California Baptist Theological Seminary opened in Los Angeles. In 1968, the school merged with Berkley Baptist Divinity School to form the American Baptist Seminary of the West. Also in 1944, two ministries merged to form the Board of Education and Publication. The new ministry provided oversight to publishing efforts, Christian education initiatives, and the Baptist Youth Fellowship. That same year a retreat center opened in Green Lake, Wisconsin.

In 1950, the American Baptist Convention adopted a new denominational structure, creating the position of general secretary to lead the General Council, which had been formed in 1934 to represent the convention between annual sessions. Reuben E. Nelson served as the first general secretary. The General Council provided broad oversight of the ABC's national boards, each of which was led by a board of directors (elected by delegates to the annual meeting) and paid staff. The General Council also provided oversight of several smaller societies that worked in areas such as social concerns, ecumenical relations, men's and women's ministries, and historical preservation. A unified American Baptist Mission Budget allocated money to each ministry.

American Baptists remained active in pan-Baptist and ecumenical endeavors. American Baptists and Southern Baptists cooperated in the Baptist Joint Committee on Public Affairs, a religious liberty advocacy ministry founded by Southern Baptists in 1936. In 1947, the Baptist Joint Committee established an office in Washington DC, where Southern Baptist J. M. Dawson served as the first full-time executive director. Several other Baptist denominations became involved in the Baptist Joint Committee. The ABC also helped sponsor the Baptist Jubilee Advance (1959–64), a multiyear initiative involving many Baptist denominations that celebrated the sesquicentennial of the Triennial Convention's formation. The Baptist Jubilee Celebration was held in Atlantic City, New Jersey, in May 1964. Representatives attended the meeting from the ABC, the SBC, and several African-American Baptist groups. Speakers included Billy Graham and Martin Luther King Jr. The Baptist Jubilee Advance gave birth to the North American Baptist Fellowship (1964), which became a regional fellowship of the Baptist World Alliance.

American Baptists were founding members of the World Council of Churches in 1948 and remained active in the Federal Council of Churches, renamed the National Council of Churches of Christ in the USA (NCC) in 1950. Ecumenism lay at the center of a denominational controversy in 1958. ABC leaders wanted to relocate their headquarters to the Interchurch Center in New York City. The Interchurch Center housed the NCC's headquarters as well as offices for several mainline denominations and had been funded, in part, through financial gifts from John D. Rockefeller Jr. A slight majority of delegates voted to relocate to Chicago instead of New York. Valley Forge, Pennsylvania, emerged as a compromise choice. In 1960, the ABC opened its new headquarters in Valley Forge, though the Ministers and Missionaries Benefit Board rented space in the Interchurch Center. More than any other

Baptist group, midcentury American Baptists embraced the ethos of main-line Protestantism.

By the late-1960s, some American Baptists expressed concern that the trend toward denominational centralization undermined local church auton-omy. Others criticized how the General Council allocated mission money. In response ABC delegates appointed a Study Commission on Denominational Structure (SCODS) in 1968, which recommended the creation of a General Board of approximately 200 members. Three quarters of the General Board was elected through regional bodies. Annual meetings became biennial meet-ings as more day-to-day authority was invested in the General Board. The study commission further recommended a new name, the American Baptist Churches in the USA (ABC-USA), to reflect the emphasis on local represen-tation and the move away from annual meetings for decision making. The SCODS recommendations were approved in 1972 and implemented in 1973. Despite the emphasis on local representation, churches were less involved than before now that more power was invested in the General Board, and denominational business was increasingly downplayed at biennial meetings.

Southern Baptist Denominational Expansion

Southern Baptists enjoyed significant institutional growth during the post-war years. In 1950, Golden Gate Baptist Theological Seminary (established 1944) in San Francisco became part of the SBC, and Southeastern Baptist Theological Seminary was founded in Wake Forest, North Carolina. In 1957, Midwestern Baptist Theological Seminary was established in Kansas City, Missouri, following a governance dispute between Southern Baptist and American Baptist trustees of Central Baptist Theological Seminary. Cen-tral Seminary had been jointly operated by the two denominations since its founding in 1901. Also in 1957, the SBC took over the Carver School of Missions and Social Work in Louisville, Kentucky, formerly known as the WMU Training School. In 1963, the Carver School became affiliated with Southern Baptist Theological Seminary.

Nearly every denominational ministry expanded its programs, personnel, and infrastructure, a trend that also prevailed among Baptist state conven-tions. Expansion led to restructuring. In 1958, a denominational efficiency committee recommended expanding the Executive Committee staff and establishing a permanent headquarters, closer interagency coordination of programs, and greater emphasis on public relations and financial steward-ship. The consulting firm Booz, Allen, and Hamilton was contracted to guide the Executive Committee through the transitions. The Sunday School Board, Southern Seminary, and WMU also worked with Booz, Allen, and Hamilton during this period, demonstrating the growing influence of business models on denominational life. In 1963, a new headquarters was established in Nashville, Tennessee, to house the Executive Committee and several denominational commissions.

The SBC enjoyed steady growth in membership. In 1942, membership stood at just below 5.4 million. By 1963, the total membership had nearly doubled to 10.4 million. Baptisms increased steadily during this period, from 209,127 in 1942 to 355,325 in 1963. Sunday school played a central role in Southern Baptist outreach efforts. State convention personnel conducted training clinics to equip local church leaders to grow their churches through Sunday school membership enlistment and home visitation. The most well-known Sunday school initiative was "A Million More in '54," a campaign to enroll a million new Sunday school members in 1954. Though the program fell short of its goal, it did result in 597,361 new Sunday school members in 1954, more than double the number of new members added during the previous year. In many churches the Sunday school roll (which was open to any interested individual) became larger than the actual membership roll, which included only baptized believers.

"A Million More in '54" (1953)
by W. Hines Sims

A million more in fifty-four!
  Enrolled in Sunday School,
To hear the gospel, read the Word
  And learn the Golden Rule.
A million more in fifty-four,
  To leave the paths of sin;
To meet the Saviour, know His grace,
  And find new peace within.

A million more in fifty-four!
  The gospel will be sown
In hearts of women, boy and girls,
  And men who have not known
The saving pow'r of matchless grace
  Provided by God's Son

Who came and died on Calv'ry's tree
  To save them, ev'ry one.

A million more in fifty-four!
  Depends on workers true;
Our hearts, our strength, our wills, our
  time, We dedicate anew.
We each must visit, work, and pray
  In answer to God's call.
A work to honor Christ our King
  Demands our best, our all.

Chorus:
A million more in fifty-four,
  Enrolled in Sunday School;
A million more in fifty-four,
  Enrolled in Sunday School.

The Sunday School Board and state conventions promoted other influential programs. Vacation Bible School became an important outreach to children and families. Baptist Student Union provided fellowship, worship gatherings, and evangelism training for Baptist collegians. The WMU continued to sponsor RAs, GAs, and Acteens. In 1935, Baptist Young People's

Union, a discipleship ministry for teenagers, expanded into Baptist Training Union, which covered all ages. These programs provided remarkable homogeneity in a convention of autonomous churches increasingly dispersed all over the nation.

British Baptists

The Baptist Union also emphasized denominational efficiency and expansion during the mid-twentieth century. Denominational leaders frequently debated the best approaches to church efficiency and ministerial training, at times creating friction between theological colleges and local churches. Nevertheless, several colleges thrived. In 1928, Regent's Park College relocated from London to Oxford, where it grew steadily under principal H. Wheeler Robinson. In 1957, Regent's Park became formally affiliated with the University of Oxford. In 1938, Spurgeon's College affiliated with the Baptist Union. In 1946, the interdenomina-

Regent's Park College, Oxford University.

tional London Bible College was founded. Ernest Kevan, a Strict Baptist, was the founding principal. Many Baptist ministerial candidates chose to be educated at the new school.

Outreach and ecumenism remained important priorities. The Forward Movement, launched in 1936, focused on evangelism and church planting in close cooperation with other Free Churches. The Baptist Union participated in the Faith and Order Commission (1937) and served as a founding member of the World Council of Churches (1948). At the local church level, the relationship between outreach and ecumenism was reflected in the open membership policies adopted by many congregations, permitting some non-Baptists to join churches without being immersed as believers. Some British Baptists, though committed to outreach, were less ecumenical. Scottish Baptists also joined the World Council, though they withdrew their membership in 1955. Irish Baptists never joined the formal ecumenical movement.

Despite the emphases on ecumenism and expansion, Baptist Union membership declined from approximately 239,000 to 209,000 between 1900 and

1950. Baptists in Scotland and Wales also declined during this period, the latter by about 50 percent. These groups continued to shrink for the remainder of the century. Irish Baptists enjoyed steady, though moderate growth that continued through the twentieth century. Calvinistic Baptists, most of whom were independent of the British Baptist denominations, began to show signs of numeric growth during the postwar years, though most of their growth came between 1950 and 1980. Independent fundamentalist Baptist churches also continued to exist outside the Baptist Unions.

For Further Study

Ammerman, Nancy Tatom. *Baptist Battles: Social Change and Religious Conflict in the Southern Baptist Convention*, chapter 3. New Brunswick, NJ: Rutgers University Press, 1990.

Baptist History and Heritage 36, no. 3 (Summer-Fall 2001). Issue theme "Baptists and World War II."

Brackney, William H. *Baptists in North America*, chapter 6. Malden, MA: Wiley-Blackwell, 2006.

Early, Joseph, Jr. *A Texas Baptist Power Struggle: The Hayden Controversy*. Denton, TX: University of North Texas Press, 2005.

Fletcher, Jesse C. *The Southern Baptist Convention: A Sesquicentennial History*, chapter 6. Nashville, TN: B&H, 1994.

Glass, William R. *Strangers in Zion: Fundamentalists in the South, 1900–1950*. Macon, GA: Mercer University Press, 2001.

Green, Bernard. *European Baptists and the Third Reich*. Didcot, Oxfordshire, UK: 2008.

Hankins, Barry. *God's Rascal: J. Frank Norris and the Beginnings of Southern Fundamentalism*. Lexington, KY: University Press of Kentucky, 1996.

Harper, Keith. *The Quality of Mercy: Southern Baptists and Social Christianity, 1890–1920*. Tuscaloosa, AL: University of Alabama Press, 1996.

Jones, Keith G., and Ian M. Randall, eds. *Counter-Cultural Communities: Baptistic Life in Twentieth-Century Europe*. Bletchley, Milton Keynes, UK: Paternoster, 2008.

Marsden, George M. *Fundamentalism and American Culture*, new ed., chapters 16–21. New York: Oxford University Press, 2006.

Mathews, Mary Beth Swetnam. *Rethinking Zion: How the Print Media Placed Fundamentalism in the South*. Knoxville, TN: University of Tennessee Press, 2006.

Nettles, Tom J. "Southern Baptists: Regional to National Transition," in *Baptist History and Heritage* 16, no. 1 (January 1981): 13–23.

Randall, Ian M. *The English Baptists of the Twentieth Century, A History of the English Baptists*, vol. 4, chapters 5 and 6. Didcot, Oxfordshire, UK: The Baptist Historical Society, 2005.

Review & Expositor 96, no. 1 (Spring 1999). Issue theme "The [E. Y.] Mullins Legacy."

The Southern Baptist Journal of Theology 3, no. 4 (Winter 1999). Issue theme "E. Y. Mullins in Retrospect."

Stokes, David R. *The Shooting Salvationist: J. Frank Norris and the Murder Trial that Captivated America*. Hanover, NH: Steerforth Press, 2011.

Questions for Discussion

1. What precursors led to the Social Gospel? What new emphases did the Social Gospel bring about for Baptists? In what ways does the Social Gospel differ from the traditional gospel message as proclaimed by Baptists?

2. What comes to mind when you read the term *fundamentalism* as it applies to Baptists? What "fundamentals of the faith" were these Baptists seeking to preserve in light of modernism?

3. Who were some of the leading Baptist fundamentalists in America and Canada during this period? What distinguished the "denominational fundamentalists" from the "separatists fundamentalists" during this period?

4. Describe the situation leading up to the adoption of the Baptist Faith and Message in 1925. Compare and contrast the personalities of J. Frank Norris and E. Y. Mullins. Name any leading Baptist figures today that represent these differing approaches to denominational unity.

5 Discuss Landmark controversies among Baptists during this period. Why do you think a "sectarian reading of church history" through publications like "The Trail of Blood" appealed to Baptists in the early twentieth century?

6. Outline the various Baptist responses to World War II. In what ways did Baptists exhibit confusion regarding Hitler's agenda and claims of Jewish extermination early in the war? What impact did the war have on Baptist missions during this period? What impact did the aftermath of the war have on the Baptist movement in Europe?

7. Describe the impact of communism on various Baptist movements. How did the Baptist World Alliance respond? Why did fundamentalist Baptists consider their response to be inadequate? In what areas of the world today do Baptists face similar obstacles and threats?

8. In what ways did Baptists expand and compete with one another during this period? How did Northern Baptists preempt Southern Baptists regarding a change in name? Do you think denominational names are helped or hindered by including geographical modifiers like Northern, Southern, or American? Explain your answer.

9. What programs did Southern Baptists adopt during this period that led to their exponential growth? Do you have any of these programs in your church? If not, do you have similar programs in their place? What does the fact that Sunday school enrollment sometimes exceeded church membership suggest about Baptists and their understanding of the church during this period?

Chapter 11

CONTROVERSIES IN A CHANGING WORLD

Following World War II, Baptists in the English-speaking world became embroiled in several controversies. The quest by African-Americans for civil rights ushered in significant cultural change, especially in the southern states. Baptists were among both the key leaders and most vocal opponents of the civil rights movement. Baptists in many denominations also confronted the advance of progressive theology during this period. While some Baptist groups weathered theological changes with relatively little controversy, others experienced significant turmoil. During the final two decades of the twentieth century, Southern Baptists endured the most extensive (and widely reported) theological controversy of any major denomination in North America.

Baptists and the Civil Rights Movement

Following the American Civil War (1861–65), African-Americans were freed from slavery and given full citizenship rights with the passage of the Thirteenth (1865) and Fourteenth Amendments (1868) to the US Constitution. However, when Reconstruction ended in 1877, Southern states began to pass laws that undermined the civil rights of African-Americans. These so-called Jim Crow laws, named for a well-known black character in traveling minstrel shows, prohibited African-Americans from voting, thus rendering them politically impotent. The Supreme Court ruled in *Plessy vs. Ferguson* (1896) that racial segregation was legal as long as the segregated facilities were equally maintained—the famous "separate but equal" doctrine. As a result, for the first half of the twentieth century, the South was almost totally segregated, and African-Americans were mostly prevented from having leadership roles in the community beyond their local churches. With the exception of some early Pentecostal churches and underground music clubs in cities like Memphis, Tennessee, blacks and whites mixed socially in few venues. Vigilantism, including lynching, was often tolerated when whites felt African-Americans had committed a wrong, especially if the wrong was against a white woman.

The Civil Rights Movement: A Brief Overview

Several important precursors led up to the civil rights movement. In 1909, activists founded the National Association for the Advancement of Colored People (NAACP). Many African-Americans and some whites opposed segregation and other forms of racial discrimination through the NAACP and similar groups. Another important precursor was President Harry Truman's desegregation of the United States Armed Forces in 1948. In response to Truman's decision, fellow Democrat and Baptist Strom Thurmond, at the time the governor of South Carolina, led a temporary exodus of southern Democrats from the national party. Thurmond

*Harry S. Truman
(1884–1972)*

ran a third-party presidential campaign with the States' Rights Democratic Party, or the "Dixiecrats," as they were popularly known. But Truman was reelected, the Dixiecrats returned to the Democratic Party, and Thurmond was subsequently elected to the senate, where he served from 1954 to 2003.

By far the most important precursor to the civil rights movement was the landmark Supreme Court ruling *Brown v. Board of Education* (1954). *Brown* struck down the "separate but equal" doctrine as unconstitutional, paving the way for desegregation of public schools in the South and elsewhere. At the time of *Brown*, one of the associate justices of the Supreme Court was Hugo Black, a Southern Baptist and former senator from Alabama. During his long career on the bench (1937–71), Black was a vocal defender of desegregation in the South. He was also a leading proponent of the strict separation of church and state in America, writing several decisions to that effect, including the *Engel v. Vitale* (1962) decision that ruled teacher-led prayer in public schools to be unconstitutional.

The Montgomery Bus Boycott in Alabama (1955–56) marked a turn in the pursuit of civil rights. The boycott began when a woman named Rosa Parks refused to give up her seat in the front of a public bus to a white man, even though social custom dictated that blacks sat in the back of the bus when whites wished to sit in the front. Parks was a seamstress, an active member of the African Methodist Episcopal Church, and secretary of the Montgomery chapter of the NAACP. She was arrested and fined for her obstinacy. In response to her arrest, a new organization named the Montgomery Improvement Association (MIA) called upon all African-Americans to boycott public transportation in the city. The boycott lasted 381 days and resulted in the desegregation of public transportation in Montgomery. The boycott was led by two young African-American Baptist ministers in the city: Ralph David Abernathy called the organizational meeting of the MIA while Martin Luther King Jr. became the leader of and chief spokesman for the boycott.

The civil rights movement remained an influential force in America throughout the 1950s and 1960s. Several of the movement's key organizations were at least influenced by Christian principles, including the newly formed Southern Christian Leadership Conference (SCLC, 1957) and the Student Nonviolent Coordinating Committee (SNCC, 1960). King was the first president of SCLC while SNCC was comprised of mostly college-aged activists. Some older organizations influenced by Christianity and other religions also played a key role, including the NAACP, the ecumenical pacifist group the Fellowship of Reconciliation (1935), and the Congress of Racial Equality (CORE, 1942). Some key moments in the civil rights movement included the Freedom Rides in 1961, the March on Washington

*Martin Luther King Jr.
(1929–1968)*

in 1963, and the passage of the civil rights act in 1964. Numerous sit-ins, marches, and other forms of protest were also part of the civil rights movement. By the mid-1970s, the South was mostly desegregated; and racism, though present, was de facto rather than de jure.

African-American Baptists and the Civil Rights Movement

Several African-American Baptists emerged as key leaders in the civil rights movement, King (1929–68) being the most important. King was raised as a Baptist preacher's son in Atlanta and showed academic promise from a young age. He graduated from Baptist-related Morehouse College and Crozer Seminary before graduating in 1955 with a PhD in theology from Boston University. Along the way he was influenced by his evangelical roots in the National Baptist tradition, Social Gospel advocate Walter Rauschenbusch, neo-orthodox theologians Reinhold Niebuhr and Paul Tillich, an Anabaptist-like reading of the Sermon on the Mount, and Indian nonviolent resistance advocate Mohandas Gandhi. King embraced a curious mix of conservative and progressive views: he affirmed universal human depravity and the need for repentance and faith in Christ, but he harbored doubts about Jesus' divinity, his blood atonement, and the Second Coming. Though famous for his role as a civil rights leader, King was first a Baptist minister. He served as the pastor of Dexter Avenue Baptist Church in Montgomery from 1955 to 1960 and then co-pastor, with his father Martin Luther King Sr., of Ebenezer Baptist Church in Atlanta from 1960 to 1968.

Between 1955 and 1968, King was associated with numerous civil rights organizations and initiatives. He led the Montgomery Bus Boycott, was the founding president of SCLC, and was active in the Fellowship of

---

Martin Luther King Jr. Criticizes
White Racial Moderates

You deplore the demonstrations taking place in Birmingham. But your statement, I am sorry to say, fails to express a similar concern for the conditions that brought about the demonstrations. I am sure that none of you would want to rest content with the superficial kind of social analysis that deals merely with effects and does not grapple with underlying causes. It is unfortunate that demonstrations are taking place in Birmingham, but it is even more unfortunate that the city's white power structure left the Negro community with no alternative....

We know through painful experience that freedom is never voluntarily given by the oppressor; it must be demanded by the oppressed. Frankly, I have yet to engage in a direct action campaign that was "well timed" in the view of those who have not suffered unduly from the disease of segregation. For years now I have heard the word "Wait!" It rings in the ear of every Negro with piercing familiarity. This "Wait" has almost always meant "Never." We must come to see, with one of our distinguished jurists, that "justice too long delayed is justice denied."

Excerpted from Martin Luther King Jr., "Letter from a Birmingham Jail" (1963).

Reconciliation. He spoke widely on behalf of civil rights. He led famous marches on Washington, DC (1963), and Selma, Alabama (1964). At the March on Washington, King delivered his famous "I Have a Dream" oration, one of the most influential speeches (and sermons) in American history. In that speech King proclaimed, "When we let freedom ring, when we let it ring from every tenement and every hamlet, from every state and every city, we will be able to speed up that day when all of God's children, black men and white men, Jews and Gentiles, Protestants and Catholics, will be able to join hands and sing in the words of the old Negro spiritual, 'Free at last, free at last. Thank God Almighty, we are free at last.'"

King was arrested several times for his activism. In his widely read "Letter from a Birmingham Jail" (1963), he excoriated moderate white pastors who were sympathetic to the plight of blacks but were urging King to slow down and be less controversial. He famously argued, "Injustice anywhere is a threat to justice everywhere." King received numerous recognitions and awards for his activism, including the Nobel Peace Prize in 1964 and the *Pacem in Terris* Peace Award from the Vatican in 1965. In his later years King expanded his work to include activism to secure labor rights, improve the plight of the poor, and end the Vietnam War. Tragically, King was assassinated in Memphis in 1968 while speaking on behalf of striking sanitation workers.

Many other African-American Baptist ministers were important civil rights advocates as well. Some, like King, were located in the South. Ralph David Abernathy, who was King's closest friend, was instrumental in the Montgomery Boycott and the founding of SCLC. When King was shot in 1968, Abernathy, who by then was also a Baptist pastor in Atlanta, held King in his arms as the famous preacher-activist died. Fred Shuttlesworth, long-time pastor of Baptist churches in Birmingham, Alabama, and Cincinnati, Ohio, cofounded SCLC and helped organize the Freedom Rides in 1961. His fame spread during the Birmingham campaign of 1963, which brought national attention to the segregation in that city and the manner in which city officials often enforced segregation with violence. When four Ku Klux Klansmen responded to the Birmingham campaign by bombing Sixteenth Street Baptist Church, resulting in the death of four African-American girls, it marked a turning point in national perception of the civil rights movement. Other leaders pastored churches in the North. Adam Clayton Powell Jr. was pastor of the Abyssinian Baptist Church in Brooklyn, New York. In 1945, Powell became only the second African-American to be elected to Congress since Reconstruction. He was a key congressional ally of the civil rights movement until his death in 1972. Gardner Taylor, a native southerner, was pastor of the Concord Baptist Church of Christ in Brooklyn. Taylor was a vocal proponent of civil rights and was widely considered one of the best preachers in America during the second half of the twentieth century.

While all African-American Baptists wanted social equality, not all responded in the same way to the civil rights movement. In 1961 the National Baptist Convention, USA, Inc., the largest black Baptist denomination in America, split in part over how best to respond to the movement. Convention president Joseph Jackson wanted the denomination to be officially detached from the civil rights movement and believed some activists were too radical. Younger leaders like Martin Luther King Jr. and Gardner Taylor wanted the NBC to be more proactive. They also desired presidential term limits; Jackson had been serving since 1953. After Jackson defeated Taylor in the 1960 presidential election, a group that included King, Taylor, Abernathy, and

---

Southern Baptists Respond to the Civil Rights Movement

The Christ we serve, the opportunity we face, and the crisis we confront, compel us to action. We therefore declare our commitment, believing this to be right in the sight of God and our duty under the lordship of Christ.

We will respect every individual as a person possessing inherent dignity and worth growing out of his creation in the image of God.

We will strive to obtain and secure for every person equality of human and legal rights. We will undertake to secure opportunities in matters of citizenship, public services, education, employment, and personal habitation that every man may achieve his highest potential as a person.

We will accept and exercise our civic responsibility as Christians to defend people against injustice. We will strive to insure for all persons the full opportunity for achievement according to the endowments given by God.

We will refuse to be a party to any movement that fosters racism or violence or mob action.

We will personally accept every Christian as a brother beloved in the Lord and welcome to the fellowship of faith and worship every person irrespective of race or class.

We will strive to become well informed about public issues, social ills, and divisive movements that are damaging to human relationships. We will strive to resist prejudice and to combat forces that breed distrust and hostility.

We will recognize our involvement with other Christians and with all others of goodwill in the obligation to work for righteousness in public life and justice for all persons. We will strive to promote Christian brotherhood as a witness to the gospel of Christ.

Excerpted from "A Statement Concerning the Crisis in Our Nation" (1968).

Venchael Booth filed a lawsuit against Jackson. They lost and subsequently left the NBC to form the Progressive National Baptist Convention (PNBC) in 1961. The PNBC became the most theologically and socially progressive black Baptist denomination. It vocally advocated civil rights, passed resolutions against the Vietnam War, and eventually embraced the ordination of women.

White Baptists and the Civil Rights Movement

White Baptists also responded to the civil rights movement in several different ways. Some actively promoted civil rights. American Baptists, located mostly in the North, favored desegregation and supported the civil rights movement through resolutions and denominational literature. Many white Baptists in the ABC also lent material support to the cause. Martin England, whose roots were in the Southern Baptist Convention, used his position with the ABC's Ministers and Missionaries Benefits Board to aid black civil rights activists in the South. Edwin Dahlberg, a former president of the ABC and a committed pacifist, used his platform as a denominational leader and later president of the National Council of Churches to champion civil rights.

The situation was more complicated among Southern Baptists. Many convention leaders wanted equal rights for all regardless of ethnicity and led the SBC to endorse desegregation in official denominational pronouncements. For example, messengers passed a resolution praising *Brown v. Board of Education* at the 1954 SBC annual meeting. The SBC's Christian Life Commission (CLC) proposed the resolution. The CLC argued that racial equality was the most important moral issue facing Southern Baptists. Foy Valentine, who became executive secretary of the CLC in 1960, was a key proponent of civil rights in the SBC. He and others led the convention to adopt a document in 1968 titled "A Statement Concerning the Crisis in Our Nation." The statement denounced racism, affirmed the full spiritual and legal equality of all people, and emphasized a holistic approach to gospel proclamation that included cultural engagement.

Some Southern Baptists were particularly aggressive and overt in their promotion of civil rights. Will Campbell, an ordained Southern Baptist minister, became an activist who worked closely with civil rights leaders and participated in several marches. Progressive North Carolina pastors Carlyle Marney and W. W. Finlator were also controversial advocates of civil rights. Many Southern Baptist professors taught African-American ministerial students on nights and weekends in local churches or privately tutored black Baptist pastors. Clarence Jordan, author of the *Cotton Patch Gospel* (1968–73) and a PhD graduate in New Testament from Southern Seminary, founded Koinonia Farms in 1942, an intentionally racially integrated community near

Americus, Georgia, that caused a stir in the 1950s and 1960s. Southwestern Seminary ethicist T. B. Maston wrote three books on racial equality and regularly referenced the topic in his other writings. Maston argued, "If God is no respecter of persons, if he shows no partiality, our ultimate goal should be the elimination of all partiality, prejudice, and discrimination from our lives. All men should be considered as of infinite worth, created in the image of God, actual or potential children of God, and as members of the human race rather than of some division within that race."

In contrast to these racial progressives, many Southern Baptist pastors opposed desegregation, including denominational leaders such as Douglas Hudgins of First Baptist Church in Jackson, Mississippi, and W. A. Criswell of First Baptist Church in Dallas, Texas—though Criswell eventually changed his view. Some Baptist laypeople were militantly opposed to desegregation and active in groups like the White Citizens' Council and sometimes even the Ku Klux Klan. Many churches amended their constitutions and bylaws to preclude African Americans from their membership. Segregationists in the SBC were concerned that the denomination's leadership was too open to desegregation. When Martin Luther King Jr. spoke in chapel at Southern Seminary in 1961, segregationists in the SBC and beyond responded with a wave of criticism.

Southern Baptists Repent of Racism

Be it further RESOLVED, That we lament and repudiate historic acts of evil such as slavery from which we continue to reap a bitter harvest, and we recognize that the racism which yet plagues our culture today is inextricably tied to the past; and

Be it further RESOLVED, That we apologize to all African-Americans for condoning and/or perpetuating individual and systemic racism in our lifetime; and we genuinely repent of racism of which we have been guilty, whether consciously (Psalm 19:13) or unconsciously (Leviticus 4:27); and

Be it further RESOLVED, That we ask forgiveness from our African-American brothers and sisters, acknowledging that our own healing is at stake; and

Be it further RESOLVED, That we hereby commit ourselves to eradicate racism in all its forms from Southern Baptist life and ministry

Excerpted from "Resolution on Racial Reconciliation on the 150th Anniversary of the Southern Baptist Convention" (1995).

The Woman's Missionary Union and Foreign Mission Board missionaries to Africa proved to be some of the greatest champi-
ons of the Civil Rights movement among Southern Baptists. These missions-minded Baptists argued that it was inconsistent to preach the gospel to dark-skinned people in Africa but refuse to interact socially with dark-skinned people in the American South. With the exception of forward-thinking missionaries, as a general rule conservative Southern Baptists were opposed to, or at least lukewarm toward, civil rights while progressive Southern Baptists were more favorable to desegregation. By the 1970s, however, many theological conservatives were changing their views. Criswell was one of the first, leading First Baptist Dallas to open its membership to African-Americans in 1968. As discussed in chapter 6, in 1995 Southern

Fred Luter
(1956–present)

Baptists corporately repented of the racism that had characterized much of the convention's history and even contributed to its formation in 1845. In 2012, Southern Baptists elected Fred Luter of Franklin Avenue Baptist Church in New Orleans as the first African-American president of the convention.

Progressive Advance and Conservative Dissent

Around midcentury several Baptist groups, especially in North America and the British Isles, witnessed a surge of left-leaning theology within their ranks. This leftward trend renewed tensions between progressives and conservatives. The progressives who came of age after World War II were influenced by a number of traditions, including theological modernism, the Social Gospel, neo-orthodoxy, and eventually liberation theology. As in the fundamentalist-modernist controversies of an earlier generation, many progressives were professors in Baptist colleges and seminaries, denominational servants, and pastors of influential (especially older) congregations. Progressives advocated a variety of positions that put them at odds with the more conservative Baptists who were often in the majority. Like the earlier fundamentalists midcentury, conservatives dissented against progressives, leading to controversy and sometimes schism.

Progressive Trends

Baptist progressives and conservatives disagreed on a number of issues, including the nature of the Bible, the person and work of Christ, the role of women in ministry, and matters of war and peace. As a general rule Baptist progressives in North America were influenced by an individualistic interpretation of the doctrines of soul competency and liberty of conscience that they identified with Southern Baptist theologian E. Y. Mullins. Progressives often coupled individualism with neo-orthodox understandings of Scripture, denying biblical inerrancy and arguing the Bible merely "contained" God's revelation; Scripture is not a revelation from God in and of itself, they said. The tension between progressives and conservatives was somewhat less pronounced among American Baptists and Canadian Baptists because most fundamentalists had broken away from the large, leftward trending bodies prior to the mid-twentieth century and formed new denominations. Conservative groups that broke from American Baptists included the General Association of Regular Baptist Churches (1932) and the Conservative Baptist Association (1947). In Canada conservative splinter denominations included the Union of Regular Baptist Churches (1928) and the Fellowship of Independent Baptist Churches (1933), which merged to form the Fellowship of Evangelical Baptist Churches (1953).

Theological progressives and centrists who tolerated leftward drift led the American Baptist Churches in the USA after the 1920s. ABC-USA schools continued to move in a progressive direction in the postwar era while American Baptist missionaries focused more on social uplift than evangelism and church planting. Women's ordination became increasingly accepted after the 1960s, the ABC-USA remained heavily involved in the ecumenical movement, and the denomination actively supported the civil rights movement and criticized the Vietnam War. In part because of these emphases, the ABC-USA was identified with mainline Protestantism more than most other Baptist denominations in North America. Membership did not decline in the ABC-USA as much as it did in other mainline denominations, but the group was plateaued for most of the twentieth century.

Among Canadian Baptists increased secularization in Canadian culture and a decline in revivalism contributed to a progressive theological shift. Between World War II and the 1970s, several Canadian Baptist colleges closed due to declining enrollment. The leading Baptist institution, McMaster University in Toronto, became a private secular university in 1957, though McMaster Divinity School continued to be affiliated with the Canadian

Baptist Federation. Acadia University in Wolfville, Nova Scotia, made a similar transition in 1968, becoming a secular school and establishing Acadia Divinity College, which was affiliated with the Convention of Atlantic Baptist Churches. A progressive ethos characterized McMaster Divinity School and Acadia Divinity College while Carey Theological College in Vancouver (est. 1975) remained broadly evangelical. Mainline Canadian Baptists remained involved in the ecumenical movement, which led to growing calls for open membership and mutual recognition of baptism with pedobaptist groups.

McMaster Divinity College and Chapel, Hamilton, Ontario.

After World War II, Southern Baptists experienced far more tension over progressive theology than other Baptist groups. Since the denomination's identity centered on programs more than on theology, opportunity arose for the encroachment of liberalism even though most Southern Baptists were doctrinally conservative. Convention agencies focused on evangelism and missions, emphasized denominational loyalty, and avoided theological disputes as much as possible. Southern Baptists increasingly downplayed theology as they rallied around their programs rather than a confessional identity, despite their adoption of the Baptist Faith and Message in 1925. The robust theological vision of the nineteenth century was gone. As younger Southern Baptist scholars who were educated with postwar G.I. Bill funds began to push a leftward theological agenda in denominational colleges and seminaries, convention leadership began inching to the left as well. By the 1960s the youth counterculture was contributing to the progressive milieu in SBC-related colleges and seminaries.

The Christian Life Commission adopted a center-left social agenda that focused on advocating civil rights and critiquing American involvement in the Vietnam War. Convention programs that focused on youth and collegians, particularly Baptist Training Union in local churches and Baptist Student Union (BSU) in colleges, adopted a similar social agenda. *The Baptist Student*, the official publication of BSU, became a key means of promoting the progressive understanding of ethnicity, war and peace, and eventually theology among Baptist collegians. In 1968, BSU members in Raleigh-Durham,

North Carolina, formed Baptist Students Concerned as a grassroots movement to combat racism and the war in Vietnam. Foy Valentine hosted a panel
discussion with members of Baptist Students Concerned at the 1968 SBC
annual meeting.

Baptist Students Concerned stage a protest outside the 1968 SBC annual meeting.

Most of the overt theological controversy centered on schools because outspoken convention progressives tended to serve on the faculties of Baptist
colleges and seminaries. Few professors were classical theological liberals,
though higher criticism and neo-orthodox views of Scripture had influenced
many scholars. Theodore Clark and Frank Stagg were both accused of holding
liberal views at New Orleans Seminary during the mid-1950s. The former was
terminated while the latter was acquitted in a heresy trial. Both men denied
substitutionary atonement. At Southeastern Seminary conservatives accused
three New Testament professors of teaching Rudolf Bultmann's "demytholog-
ical" views of Scripture during the 1960s. None of the three were terminated
though all were encouraged to find new positions. In 1966, James McClendon was forced to resign from Golden Gate Seminary. McClendon's departure was precipitated by his vocal advocacy of the Civil Rights movement and
open opposition to the Vietnam War. In 1969, W. A. Criswell promoted biblical inerrancy in his *Why I Preach That the Bible Is Literally True*. He wrote
of inerrancy, "Let me speak directly to Southern Baptists. If our preachers,
evangelicals, pastors, churches, and institutions are true to that expression of
faith, we shall live. If we repudiate it, we shall die." The book was publicly

denounced by the National Association of Baptist Professors of Religion, which represented professors at Baptist colleges.

Several controversies centered on Southern Seminary. As early as the 1940s, Harold Tribble and W. O. Carver drew the attention of conservative critics. In 1947, the Congregationalist liberal theologian Nels F. S. Ferré was invited to lecture at Southern, provoking the ire of conservative Southern Baptists and Independent Baptists. In the 1950s Eric Rust was criticized for claiming the virgin birth was a myth while in the 1960s Dale Moody came under fire for advocating neo-orthodoxy and teaching that true believers can fall away from the faith. In 1970, New Testament professor Bill Hull preached a controversial sermon titled "Shall We Call the Bible Infallible?" that was subsequently published in *The Baptist Program*, the newsletter of the Executive Committee. Hull answered his own question in the negative: "Let us say, kindly but firmly, that here is not the decisive place for our denomination to take a stand, nor is this an issue worthy of splitting our ranks. There are many wonderfully unambiguous affirmations that we may all make about the Scriptures, but this is not one of them." Perhaps the most significant controversy at Southern during this period was the so-called Lexington Road Massacre of 1958, when the school's trustees terminated thirteen professors following a brief power struggle with seminary president Duke McCall. Most of the professors joined the faculties of Midwestern Seminary and Southeastern Seminary.

Women's ordination was another controversial issue. In 1964, Addie Davis became the first Southern Baptist woman to be ordained to the ministry at Watts Street Baptist Church in Durham, North Carolina. Two Southeastern Seminary professors, R. C. Briggs and Luther Copeland, participated in the ordination service. Davis was subsequently invited to pastor an American Baptist congregation in Vermont. The number of women in ordained ministry slowly grew during the 1970s and 1980s, though women's ordination remained uncommon in the generally conservative SBC. By the early 1980s, women were beginning to be hired as professors at Southern Baptist seminaries and in religion departments at Baptist colleges. In 1983, Southern Baptist Women in Ministry was formed to promote the ordination and placement of female ministers in Southern Baptist congregations.

By far the most important clashes between progressives and conservatives were two that concerned the biblical book of Genesis. In 1961, Midwestern Seminary professor Ralph Elliott published *The Message of Genesis* with Broadman Press. Elliott's book used the historical-critical method to question the historicity of Genesis 1–11 and suggest that Moses was not the author of the Pentateuch. In 1962, K. Owen White, pastor of First Baptist Church Houston, Texas, published a widely read essay criticizing Elliott titled "Death in the Pot." White wrote, "If the appeal is made for 'academic freedom,' let it be said that we gladly grant any man the right to believe what he wants to—but, we do not grant him the right to believe and express views in conflict with our historic position concerning the Bible as the Word of God while he is teaching in one of our schools, built and supported by Baptist funds." White was subsequently elected president of the SBC, serving 1963 to 1965.

In 1962, the convention adopted a motion criticizing heterodoxy in SBC seminaries and asking seminary trustees to deal with theological problems when they occurred. The motion was clearly directed at Elliott. The administration and trustees at Midwestern were supportive of Elliott, resolving that despite "disagreement with some of the interpretations" in *The Message of Genesis*, "we do affirm

K. Owen White
(1902–1985)

our confidence in him as a consecrated Christian, a promising scholar and teacher, a loyal servant of Southern Baptists, and a dedicated and warmly evangelistic preacher of the Gospel." The trustees informed Elliott that if he would not permit a second edition of his book to be published, all would be well. Elliott refused to acquiesce to the request and was fired for insubordination. He became an American Baptist pastor and later academic dean at Colgate-Rochester Divinity School. Elliott claimed that his beliefs were mainstream among Southern Baptist professors but that others used "doublespeak" to hide their true convictions while still sounding relatively conservative.

In the wake of the Elliott Controversy, the convention revised the Baptist Faith and Message in 1963. The revision committee was led by SBC president Herschel Hobbs, who was a theological conservative, though one who had been influenced by E. Y. Mullins's individualistic understanding of Baptist identity. Several articles in the revised confession were vague, including the article on Scripture, which both included a statement that the Bible contained "truth, without any mixture of error" and claimed that "the criterion by which the Bible is to be interpreted is Jesus Christ." Conservatives appreciated the former statement, which seemed to affirm biblical inerrancy, but

expressed hesitance at the latter, which they believed at least implicitly created a "canon within the canon." Many conservatives also balked at the claim
that Scripture is a "record of God's revelation" rather than a form of God's
revelation. Also troubling to some conservatives, the preamble exalted soul
competency to such a degree that it appeared the confession was not intended
to bind any convention employee.

Confessions and Soul Competency

Baptists are a people who profess a living faith. This faith is rooted and grounded in Jesus Christ who is "the same yesterday, and today, and forever." Therefore,
the sole authority for faith and practice among Baptists is Jesus Christ whose will
is revealed in the Holy Scriptures.

A living faith must experience a growing understanding of truth and must
be continually interpreted and related to the needs of each new generation.
Throughout their history Baptist bodies, both large and small, have issued statements of faith which comprise a consensus of their beliefs. Such statements have
never been regarded as complete, infallible statements of faith, nor as official
creeds carrying mandatory authority. Thus this generation of Southern Baptists
is in historic succession of intent and purpose as it endeavors to state for its time
and theological climate those articles of the Christian faith which are most surely
held among us.

Baptists emphasize the soul's competency before God, freedom in religion, and
the priesthood of the believer. However, this emphasis should not be interpreted
to mean that there is an absence of certain definite doctrines that Baptists believe,
cherish, and with which they have been and are now closely identified.

Excerpted from the preamble to the Baptist Faith and Message (1963).

A second Genesis controversy erupted less than a decade later. In 1969,
Broadman Press began to publish a new commentary series titled the Broadman Bible Commentary. G. Henton Davies, a British Baptist, was commissioned to write the commentary on Genesis. Davies was chosen because
Broadman did not want a Southern Baptist professor to come under scrutiny as had happened with Elliott. Davies's commentary argued for positions
similar to Elliott's, though Davies's work was written at a more scholarly
level than *The Message of Genesis*. Conservatives once again mobilized,
and in 1970 a motion was passed calling on the Sunday School Board to
cease production and sales of the commentary and have it rewritten from a
conservative perspective. However, the conservative victory was not total. A
motion requiring all SBC seminary professors to annually sign a statement
affirming biblical inerrancy was ruled out of order. Conservatives responded
by mobilizing in other ways over the next decade.

The Baptist Union of Great Britain was situated in a completely different context than Baptists in North America. Though Baptist fundamentalists were present in the UK, the British version of the fundamentalist controversy was the Downgrade Controversy, which reached its apex in the 1890s (see chap. 8). Since that time the Baptist Union had maintained a broadly evangelical identity that encompassed denominational fundamentalists, moderate evangelicals, and progressives. Many British Baptist pastors were committed to a Keswick understanding of holiness and an emphasis on personal evangelism but avoided the language of biblical inerrancy and downplayed premillennialism.

Throughout the twentieth century British Baptists became increasingly open to deaconesses and, by the 1960s, women ministers. The involvement of women in ordained ministry was a slow development, and there was little open opposition to women in ministry. The Baptist Union was involved in the ecumenical movement, which likely contributed to postwar interest in a more sacramental understanding of the Lord's Supper and baptism. Baptist sacramentalism proved more controversial than women in ministry, though a number of prominent theologians, including H. Wheeler Robinson and George Beasley-Murray, were sacramentalists. A handful of British Baptist scholars advocated radically progressive views. The most notable example was Michael Taylor, principal of Northern Baptist College, who denied the incarnation of Jesus Christ in a 1971 address to the Baptist Union Assembly. A subsequent effort to censure Taylor's views was blocked, though the Baptist Union publicly reaffirmed its commitment to orthodox Christology.

Conservative Dissent

As in the fundamentalist-modernist controversies, conservative dissenters pushed back against leftward trends among Baptists. Sometimes conservatives retained their denominational affiliation but identified more closely with evangelical parachurch ministries that reflected their theology. For example, some of the leading postwar evangelical theologians were American Baptists but identified most closely with the evangelical seminaries where they taught. That group included Carl F. H. Henry, Bernard Ramm,

*Carl F. H. Henry
(1913–2003)*

Harold Lindsell, and Roger Nicole. Each of these men also identified with Southern Baptists at various points in their lives. In general, these conservative scholars expressed dissent through their writings, with Henry's work proving to be the most influential. His treatise *The Uneasy Conscience of Modern Fundamentalism* (1947), which called for a wedding of evangelism and cultural engagement, helped launch the postwar evangelical movement. In later years his six-volume *God, Revelation, and Authority* (1976–83) helped clarify the doctrine of biblical inerrancy at a time when many evangelicals were experiencing controversy over that doctrine. Henry's views influenced many Southern Baptists when the SBC endured its own inerrancy-related controversy during the 1980s and 1990s, a topic we will discuss in the following section.

Some mainline Canadian Baptists also identified with evangelicalism, most notably Clark Pinnock. During his time on faculty at New Orleans Seminary in the late-1960s, Pinnock emerged as a vocal critic of progressive theology in the SBC, a champion of biblical inerrancy, and a mentor to conservative dissenters in the SBC. After relocating to McMaster Divinity School in 1977, Pinnock rejected inerrancy and moved in a more progressive direction. By the 1980s and 1990s, Pinnock was one of the most controversial evangelical theologians in North America, advocating inclusivism and open theism. Inclusivists argue that some unbelievers who never come in contact with the gospel will be saved based on their positive response to God's general revelation in nature. Open theists deny that God has exhaustive foreknowledge of all future events.

In most cases conservatives broke away from mainstream Baptist denominations. Some congregations in the ABC-USA affiliated with groups like the Conservative Baptist Association while Canadian conservatives sometimes joined the Fellowship of Evangelical Baptist Churches (FEBC) or, in some places, partnered with the SBC. Between 1953 and 1965, about a third of Canadian Baptists identified with the FEBC. More common in North America than joining a conservative group was for conservative churches to become independent Baptist congregations. Most separatists, whether part of a new denomination or independent, emphasized inerrancy, rejected ecumenism, and promoted a revivalistic ethos. The situation was similar among Baptists in the British Isles. In Scotland conservatives criticized the Baptist Theological College of Scotland in the 1940s; eventually many left the Baptist fold. In England most of the theological conservatives who broke with the Baptist Union were either Calvinistic, charismatic, or both.

Among Southern Baptists, midcentury conservative dissenters responded to progressive theology in a variety of ways. As with disgruntled conservative Baptists in other groups, many simply chose to leave the SBC in the 1950s and 1960s and become independent Baptists. In 1956, the Highland Park Baptist Church of Chattanooga, Tennessee, left the SBC after it was disfellowshipped from the Hamilton County Baptist Association. Highland Park had led the convention in baptisms every year between 1946 and 1955. Lee Roberson, the pastor of Highland Park, formed the Southwide Baptist Fellowship (1956) as a fraternal network for fundamentalist Baptists in the South. In 1959, Dallas pastor Jack Hyles left the convention to pastor the independent First Baptist Church of Hammond, Indiana, which pioneered bus outreach and built the largest Sunday school membership in America in the 1970s. Both Roberson and Hyles founded fundamentalist colleges to compete with denominational Baptist schools.

Some conservative dissenters chose to stay within the SBC and fight progressive advance. These denominational fundamentalists subscribed to periodicals like John R. Rice's *Sword of the Lord*, replaced convention programs like RAs and GAs with fundamentalist children's ministries like AWANAS (1950), and increasingly sent their collegians to independent Baptist colleges such as Piedmont Baptist College (1945) and Jerry Falwell's Lynchburg Baptist College (1971). Southern Baptist evangelists such as Jesse Hendley and Hyman Appleman networked closely with independent Baptists such as John R. Rice and Lee Roberson. Often, when preaching in SBC-related churches, these nominally Southern Baptist evangelists would denounce the Cooperative Program and the denominational compromise they believed it funded.

Conservative dissenters in the SBC often formed new institutions that competed with Cooperative Program-supported ministries. In 1962 conservative pastors in the Jacksonville Baptist Association in north Florida formed Luther Rice Bible College and Seminary. All Luther Rice professors were required to be Southern Baptists and affirm a statement of faith that endorsed biblical inerrancy, a literal six-day creation, and dispensational premillennialism. Luther Rice focused its efforts on educating nontraditional students already involved in ministry through correspondence courses.

W. A .Criswell (1909–2002)

In 1971, First Baptist Church of Dallas, led by W. A. Criswell, founded the

Criswell Institute for Biblical Studies, a Bible college that emphasized personal evangelism and verse-by-verse preaching. Also in 1971, Mid-America Baptist Theological Seminary began in Little Rock, Arkansas, as a conservative alternative to the SBC seminaries for Southern Baptist ministerial students. In 1975, the school relocated to Memphis, Tennessee, where it became the seminary of choice for many SBC conservatives.

In addition to forming new institutions, denominational fundamentalists also began to network together more deliberately, often for the purpose of trying to move the SBC to the right theologically. In response to the Broadman Bible Commentary, Bill Powell of the Home Mission Board formed a conservative coalition called the Baptist Faith and Message Fellowship (BFMF) in 1973. The BFMF published a periodical, *Southern Baptist Journal*, and advocated that conservative theology be taught in SBC-related colleges and seminaries. Conservative dissenters were further energized when *Christianity Today* editor Harold Lindsell wrote *The Battle for the Bible* in 1976. Lindsell's book provided documented evidence that SBC seminaries and state Baptist colleges had numerous professors who denied biblical inerrancy. By the mid-1970s, biblical inerrancy had become a key theological issue for Southern Baptists and would remain so during the final two decades of the twentieth century.

The Inerrancy Controversy and Its Aftermath

In the late 1970s Southern Baptist conservative dissenters began to mobilize in a way they had never mobilized before. The key leaders of this effort were Paige Patterson, president of the Criswell Institute and associate pastor of First Baptist Church of Dallas, and Paul Pressler, a Houston judge who had a special interest in teaching the Bible to teenagers in his church. These men were at the center of an activist conservative movement that developed a plan to take over the denominational machinery of the SBC by electing conservative presidents who would use their appointive powers to begin the process of populating trustee boards with fellow conservatives. Though conservatives

Paige Patterson
(1942–present)

had served as SBC presidents previously, including several who were vocal opponents of progressive trends, most did not know how the office could be used to help change the status quo.

The plan, originally suggested by Bill Powell, was to elect a string of conservative presidents, each of whom would appoint only movement conservatives to the Committee on Committees. The Committee on Committees would then nominate only conservatives to serve on the Committee on Boards, which would nominate a slate of prospective trustees—again, all conservatives—to fill vacancies at the various convention agencies and institutions. Messengers to the SBC annual meeting would then elect that slate of trustees. If successful, the plan would bring the board of every SBC entity under conservative control in about a decade. (The change would not be immediate because conservatives could elect fellow conservatives as trustees only as current trustees completed their terms of service.) While agency leaders often recommended potential trustees, the two committees involved in the nomination process were not obligated to accept those recommendations. This plan presented a constitutional path for conservatives to advance their agenda, assuming they had the votes to elect their presidential candidates and a viable pool of potential committee and board members who were committed to the conservative cause.

In addition to establishing their electoral strategy, conservative activists made two other key decisions in the late 1970s that proved instrumental to their success. They rejected the label *fundamentalist* in favor of the more benign *conservative*. While the two terms had often been used as synonyms, conservative activists knew that the former was problematic because of its association with J. Frank Norris, the King-James-Only position, strict ecclesiastical separation, and premillennial theology. This decision proved especially prescient after the Iranian Revolution in November 1979 led to the term *fundamentalist* being applied to militant Muslim revolutionaries.

More important, conservatives made biblical inerrancy the central issue of their movement. This proved helpful in at least three ways. First, it provided a unifying doctrine for conservatives that brought them together despite differences within the movement over eschatology, Calvinism, charismatic gifts, and (early on) women in pastoral ministry. Second, it established a starting point from which to discuss theological differences. Finally, it put progressives at a rhetorical disadvantage because they were forced to reject (or at least downplay) inerrancy while also arguing for a trustworthy Bible. Inerrancy emerged as the core doctrine for conservatives nervous about theological declension and an unwelcome shibboleth for those concerned that activist conservatives were making a mere power grab.

With their strategy in place, conservatives elected Adrian Rogers as president of the Southern Baptist Convention in 1979 on the first ballot with just over 50 percent of the vote. Rogers was one of the most popular preachers in the SBC and pastor of Bellevue Baptist Church in Memphis, Tennessee. He remained arguably the most influential Southern Baptist leader until his death in 2005, serving three one-year terms as president (1979–80, 1986–88). Some observers complained about alleged voting irregularities, the busing in of messengers, the use of skyboxes for strategy meetings, and the politicizing of the preconvention Pastors' Conference surrounding Rogers's election. Nevertheless, the conservative movement continued to surge as growing numbers of Southern Baptists attended the annual meetings and voted for conservative presidential candidates. Every SBC president since

Adrian Rogers
(1931–2005)

1979 has been a self-avowed inerrantist, and most have been closely identified with the Patterson-Pressler movement. Following Rogers's election, the resolutions adopted by the convention became more overtly conservative and increasingly addressed hot-button issues such as abortion and homosexuality, reflecting the shift in SBC leadership. Controversial resolutions rejected women in pastoral ministry (1984) and a progressive understanding of the priesthood of all believers (1988).

In 1980, a group of seventeen pastors met in Gatlinburg, Tennessee, to discuss ways to counteract the conservative movement. These pastors, led by Cecil Sherman of First Baptist Church Asheville, North Carolina, were convinced that conservatives were really power-hungry fundamentalists shaped more by right-wing secular politics than historic Baptist identity. The conservative resurgence among Southern Baptists coincided with a conservative resurgence in the Republican Party. Many SBC conservatives were supporters of Ronald Reagan and the New Religious Right that helped elect him president of the United States in 1980 over incumbent Jimmy Carter, a progressive Southern Baptist layman and Sunday school teacher from Georgia. The so-called Gatlinburg Gang believed that nonfundamentalist Southern Baptists needed to mobilize politically to prevent a fundamentalist takeover. While conservatives often referred to their opponents as "liberals," the pastors in Gatlinburg adopted the word *moderate* as the preferred descriptor of what they believed to be the mainstream Baptist tradition. The moderate coalition included theological centrists and progressives, as well as many denominational loyalists who were ambivalent about the theological issues but wished to preserve the pragmatic approach to cooperation that was in place for a generation prior to 1979.

The Inerrancy Controversy reached its apex between 1985 and 1987. More than 45,000 messengers attended the 1985 annual meeting in Dallas, Texas.

Cecil Sherman
(1927–2010)

Two Controversial Southern Baptist Convention Resolutions from the 1980s

Therefore, be it RESOLVED, That we not decide concerns of Christians [sic] doctrine and practice by modern cultural, sociological, and ecclesiastical trends or by emotional factors; that we remind ourselves of the dearly bought Baptist principle of the final authority of Scripture in matters of faith and conduct; and that we encourage the service of women in all aspects of church life and work other than pastoral functions and leadership roles entailing ordination.

Excerpted from "Resolution on Ordination and the Role of Women in Ministry" (1984).

Be it therefore RESOLVED, That the Southern Baptist Convention, meeting in San Antonio, Texas, June 14-16, 1988, affirm its belief in the biblical doctrine of the priesthood of the believer (1 Peter 2:9 and Revelation 1:6); and

Be it further RESOLVED, That we affirm that this doctrine in no way gives license to misinterpret, explain away, demythologize, or extrapolate out elements of the supernatural from the Bible; and

Be it further RESOLVED, That the doctrine of the priesthood of the believer in no way contradicts the biblical understanding of the role, responsibility, and authority of the pastor which is seen in the command to the local church in Hebrews 13:17, "Obey your leaders, and submit to them; for they keep watch over your souls, as those who will give an account;" and

Be finally RESOLVED, That we affirm the truth that elders, or pastors, are called of God to lead the local church (Acts 20:28).

Excerpted from "Resolution on the Priesthood of the Believer" (1988).

Convention president Charles Stanley of First Baptist Church Atlanta, Georgia, was sued over perceived abuse of parliamentary procedure. Eventually the lawsuit was dismissed because a court believed government interference in the SBC's internal affairs would violate church-state separation. Also in 1985, a Peace Committee was formed that represented conservative, moderate, and unaligned leaders. In 1986, the presidents of the six Southern Baptist seminaries ostensibly endorsed inerrancy in a document called the "Glorieta Statement." Conservatives griped that the presidents did not really believe the doctrine while moderates complained that the educators had capitulated to fundamentalist pressure. That same year conservative pastor William Crews became president of Golden Gate Baptist Theological Seminary without controversy. In 1987, the Peace Committee issued its findings, which stated that theological differences were at the root of the controversy. That same year SBC trustee boards began to come under conservative control, beginning with the Christian Life Commission and Southeastern Baptist Theological Seminary. Richard Land became president of the former in 1988, and Lewis Drummond became president of the latter that same year.

By the mid-1990s, every Southern Baptist entity had moved in a decisively conservative direction, often with controversy. In 1990, Al Shackleford and Dan Martin were terminated from their posts as vice president of public relations at the Executive Committee and editor of *Baptist Press*, respectively; many conservatives felt they wrote from a moderate bias. In 1992, following Lewis Drummond's retirement, Paige Patterson became president of Southeastern Seminary. The school experienced significant faculty turnover, but by 2000 Southeastern had grown from under 600 students to more than 2,100 students. Patterson remained among the most influential leaders within the SBC. He served as president of the Southern Baptist Convention from 1998 to 2000, during which time he initiated a major revision of the convention's confessional statement. In 2003, Patterson left Southeastern to become president of Southwestern Baptist Theological Seminary.

In 1993, R. Albert Mohler Jr. became president of Southern Baptist Theological Seminary. The seminary experienced ongoing controversy during the 1990s as Mohler emphasized confessional fidelity to the Abstract of Principles, biblical inerrancy, and a complementarian view of gender roles. However, by the early twenty-first century, Southern Seminary had become the largest SBC seminary. Mohler emerged as a key public theologian among Southern Baptists and the broader evangelical movement. In 1994, the trustees of Southwestern Baptist Theological Seminary terminated president Russell Dilday; Ken Hemphill became the new president. Midwestern Baptist Theological Seminary elected Mark Coppenger as president in 1995, and New Orleans Baptist Theological Seminary chose Chuck Kelley as president the following year. With the election of O. S. Hawkins as president of the Southern Baptist Annuity Board in 1997, a theological conservative sat at the helm of every SBC entity.

Theological Education in the SBC After the Inerrancy Controversy

As the presidents of your seminaries, we declare our unbending and fervent resolve to uphold all of these commitments. We will lead our institutions so that no harm shall come to your students and ministers; so that they will be rooted and grounded in the truth; so that they will be trained as faithful and effective preachers and teachers; so that they will bring honor to the church and not dishonor; and so that we shall be able to give a good answer and receive a good report when we shall face that stricter judgment which is to come.

Excerpted from "One Faith, One Task, One Sacred Trust" (1997).

Though contested presidential elections continued until 1990, moderates began gradually to disengage from the SBC during the mid-1980s. Some moderates became mainline Methodists, Presbyterians, and Episcopalians. In 1986, many among the more progressive wing of the moderate movement formed the Southern Baptist Alliance. Several moderate ministries were formed, including the periodical *SBC Today* (1982), The SBC Forum (1984), and Associated Baptist Press (1990). Moderate seminaries included the Baptist House at Duke University Divinity School (1989), Baptist Theological Seminary of Richmond (1991), Truett Seminary (1993), Campbell Divinity School (1995), McAfee School of Theology (1996), and Wake Forest School of Divinity (1999). By the early 1990s the controversy had shifted to the state conventions, where schools such as Baylor University, Stetson University, Wake Forest University, Furman University, and the University of Richmond either disaffiliated with their sponsoring convention or took steps to minimize denominational influence on the school.

One year after a preliminary gathering in 1990, centrist moderates under the leadership of former SBC presidential candidate Daniel Vestal formed the Cooperative Baptist Fellowship (CBF), which became the largest network of moderate Southern Baptists and former Southern Baptists. Cecil Sherman was the founding coordinator of CBF (1992–96), followed by Vestal (1996–2012). After the formation of CBF, moderates began to disengage from the SBC in earnest. By 2014, the Cooperative Baptist Fellowship included approximately 1,800 churches, most of which remained dually aligned but only nominally identified with the Southern Baptist Convention. The Southern Baptist Alliance changed its name to the Alliance of Baptists in 1992. The alliance remained smaller, more progressive, and more ecumenical than CBF. As of 2014, approximately 140 congregations affiliated with the alliance, including both moderate Baptist churches in the South and American Baptist congregations.

By the mid-1990s, SBC conservatives began to bring substantive changes to the culture of the convention. In 1997, the SBC was restructured, resulting in the consolidation of several ministries, the renaming of the mission boards, and a public recommitment by the seminaries to teach conservative theology. In 1998, the Baptist Faith and Message was amended to include an article on "The Family," which stated controversially, "A wife is to submit herself graciously to the servant leadership of her husband even as the church willingly submits to the headship of Christ." In 2000, the confession was revised to make it more consistently conservative than its 1963 predecessor. While moderates pointed out that the word *inerrancy* was not added to the confession, which for them confirmed the controversy was more about a power grab than a theological renovation, conservatives argued the addition was unnecessary since the statement had affirmed since 1925 that the Bible "has God for its author, salvation for its end, and truth, without any mixture of error, for its matter." Conservatives believed the Baptist Faith and Message had always affirmed the doctrine of inerrancy, even though it did not use the word. Southern Baptist seminary professors and missionaries were required to sign the revised confession, precipitating the final disengagement of most remaining moderates from SBC life. For all practical purposes the adoption of Baptist Faith and Message 2000 marked the end of the Inerrancy Controversy.

For Further Study

Ammerman, Nancy Tatom. *Baptist Battles: Social Change and Religious Conflict in the Southern Baptist Convention*. New Brunswick, NJ: Rutgers University Press, 1990.

Baptist History and Heritage 46, no. 1 (Spring 2011). Issue theme "The Progressive National Baptist Convention."

Flowers, Elizabeth H. *Into the Pulpit: Southern Baptist Women and Power Since World War II*. Chapel Hill, NC: University of North Carolina Press, 2012.

Hankins, Barry. *Uneasy in Babylon: Southern Baptist Conservatives and American Culture*. Tuscaloosa: University of Alabama Press, 2002.

Harvey, Paul. *Freedom's Coming: Religious Culture and the Shaping of the South from the Civil War Through the Civil Rights Era*. Chapel Hill, NC: University of North Carolina Press, 2007.

————. *Redeeming the South: Religious Cultures and Racial Identities Among Southern Baptists, 1865–1925*. Chapel Hill, NC: University of North Carolina Press, 1997.

Morgan, David T. *The New Crusades, the New Holy Land: Conflict in the Southern Baptist Convention, 1969–1991*. Tuscaloosa, AL: University of Alabama Press, 1996.

Newman, Mark. *Getting Right with God: Southern Baptists and Desegregation, 1945–1995*. Tuscaloosa, AL: University of Alabama Press, 2001.

Pressler, Paul. *A Hill on Which to Die: One Southern Baptist's Journey*. Nashville, TN: B&H, 1999.

Sherman, Cecil. *By My Own Reckoning*. Macon, GA: Smyth & Helwys, 2008.

Sutton, Jerry. *The Baptist Reformation: The Conservative Resurgence in the Southern Baptist Convention*. Nashville, TN: B&H Academic, 2000.

Willis, Alan Scot. *All According to God's Plan: Southern Baptist Missions and Race, 1945–1970*. Lexington, KY: University Press of Kentucky, 2004.

Wills, Gregory A. "Progressive Theology and Southern Baptist Controversies of the 1950s and 1960s." *Southern Baptist Journal of Theology* 7, no. 1 (Spring 2003): 12–31.

Questions for Discussion

1. What were the national issues that led to the civil rights movement in America? Did you know, prior to reading this chapter, that Martin Luther King Jr. was a Baptist minister? What does his involvement in the church and society suggest about his understanding of "separation of church and state"?

2. Summarize the contributions of other key African-American Baptist pastors involved in the civil rights movement. What issues led to the formation of the Progressive National Baptist Convention?

3. Summarize the contributions of key white Baptist leaders involved in the civil rights movement. What insights did Baptist missionaries in particular bring to this discussion?

4. Describe the core convictions of Baptist progressives during this period. Do you find these positions still held among Baptists today? Do you find these positions to be as controversial today as they were during this period? Explain your answer.

5. Describe the role played by the book of Genesis in Southern Baptist theological controversies during this period. What did Ralph Elliot mean when he used the word "doublespeak" to describe professors who shared his view? What ethical issues are raised when professors use "doublespeak"?

6. What issues did British Baptists encounter during this period? Why were the issues they faced somewhat different from those encountered by Baptists in America during this period?

7. Discuss the situation leading up to the adoption of the Baptist Faith and Message in 1963. What problems arose with the wording of the Baptist Faith and Message? Can you find any reasons in the preamble that would have caused concern for conservative Baptists?

8. Outline the conservative response to progressive theological trends. What institutions were formed by Baptists who left the convention? What was the strategy of conservatives who remained within the convention? What publications and periodicals arose as a result of their actions?

9. Discuss the Inerrancy Controversy in the Southern Baptist Convention. Who were the key leaders, and what were the main issues involved in the controversy? What was the aftermath for conservatives and moderates with respect to the convention and institutions that were founded?

Chapter 12

DEVELOPMENTS INTO THE TWENTY-FIRST CENTURY

The previous chapter focused on the American civil rights movement and controversies between theological conservatives and progressives among Baptists in the English-speaking world. These important themes often dominate discussions of Baptist history in the second half of the twentieth century. However, several additional topics deserve more attention than they sometimes receive. Developments in the geopolitical realm have brought many changes to Baptist life. Baptists in numerous countries have grown numerically, founded denominational bodies and related institutions, and developed indigenous leaders who are increasingly influential within the wider Baptist movement. Meanwhile, among the oldest Baptist groups, especially in the English-speaking world, a number of important trends emerged in the late twentieth and early twenty-first centuries. The extent to which these developments will affect Baptist identity and practices in the coming decades remains to be seen.

Global Baptist Developments

Most Baptists have been committed to foreign missions since at least the early decades of the nineteenth century. For a century and a half, missions primarily entailed North American and British Baptists sending missionaries to establish churches in Continental Europe, Asia, Africa, and Central and South America. By the time the Baptist World Alliance was formed in 1905, Baptists were beginning to establish denominational bodies outside the English-speaking world, though around 97 percent of all Baptists were still in North America and the British Isles. Despite two world wars and the threat of global communism, by the mid-twentieth century Baptists were increasingly becoming a global movement. Many of the oldest "mission fields" became home to thriving Baptist movements. At the same time missionaries began planting Baptist churches in new fields, often among "unreached people groups" with minimal Christian presence. The growth and maturation of Baptists worldwide is part of the story of the dramatic growth of evangelical Christianity in the Global South over the course of the twentieth century.

Baptists in Asia

Asia was the earliest Baptist foreign mission field, beginning with the work of William Carey and his colleagues in East India in 1793. Other early fields included modern-day Bangladesh (1795), Burma (1813), and Thailand (1833). By 1904, Baptists in Asia and Oceania combined numbered around 160,000. A century later Baptists in Asia alone had grown to 5.3 million, which was around seven times the number of Baptists in Europe, including the British Isles, where the Baptist tradition began. By the early twenty-first century, nearly half of all Asian Baptists (2.4 million) were located in India. However, these numbers should be viewed as conservative estimates since, in many Asian nations where Islam was the official religion, large numbers of "underground" Baptist churches existed outside of formal denominations. The same held true in communist China, which was discussed in chapter 10. China's vast network of underground churches made it difficult to tabulate the number of Baptists (or other Christian groups).

By 2011, three different Baptist denominations in India each had more than 400,000 members: the Nagaland Baptist Church Council (519,000), the Orissa Baptist Evangelistic Crusade (405,000), and the Samavesam of Telegu Baptist Churches (475,000). The dramatic growth among Indian Baptists coincided with the end of British colonialism in 1947. By mid-century many Western missionaries were pulling out of long-term mission stations, and nationals were taking greater ownership of outreach and education. Local Baptists joined Western missionaries in spreading the faith and establishing new churches in previously unreached parts of India and the rest of South Asia, including the predominantly Muslim nations of Pakistan and Bangladesh, which were part of British India until 1947. They then united as a single nation before a bitter civil war led to separation in 1971.

The greatest Baptist success story in all of Asia occurred in Nagaland, a state in northeast India. American (Northern) Baptist missionaries began working among the Nagas and other northern tribes in the 1830s. Baptist growth in the area became dramatic following World War I, in part due to a charismatic revival. Baptist missionaries oversaw education in the region on behalf of the British government, establishing local village schools, Bible schools, and a theological seminary. In 1950, the missionaries turned over control of their assets to a newly formed indigenous denominational body, the Council of Baptist Churches in North East India. The Council was made up of five constituent conventions, the largest of which was the Nagaland Baptist Church Council. Nagaland Baptists experienced another spiritual awakening in the late 1970s, leading to further numeric growth. By 2012, approximately 80 percent of the citizens of Nagaland were Baptists, which was the highest concentration of any state in the world.

Naga Translation of the Hymn "Jesus Loves Me"

Ili Jesuana Laishi,	*Pālaga I shitsanga*
Khikala jila, in a	*Ma, ili laishi*
Vare chiwui lāirikli,	*Lāirikli iya*

A second important Baptist mission field in Asia was Myanmar, known in the English-speaking world as Burma prior to 1989. Adoniram and Ann Judson initiated work in Burma in 1813 (see chap. 5). In 1865, Burmese Baptists formed the denominational body now known as the Myanmar Baptist Convention. The largest groups represented within the convention were the Karens and the Kachins, tribal minorities outside the mainstream of Burmese society. Myanmar remained an important mission field for American Baptists until the 1960s, when Western missionaries were expelled from the country by the communist government. Nevertheless, Baptists saw dramatic growth, especially among the Karens. Beginning in the late 1940s, Karen Baptists in Myanmar sent missionaries to work among Karen peoples in Thailand. The Myanmar Baptist Convention founded the Myanmar Institute of Theology in 1927, which remained the leading Protestant seminary in the region into the twenty-first century. As of 2011, the churches of the Myanmar Baptist Convention included more than 900,000 baptized members plus another half million unbaptized regular attendees. Like the American Baptists who first evangelized them, Myanmar Baptists remained strongly committed to the ecumenical movement.

Baptists have also enjoyed a strong presence in South Korea. Though Presbyterianism has always been the dominant form of Christianity in Korea, Baptists have been active in the Korean Peninsula since the 1890s. Prior to the late 1940s, Japanese occupation and then the Communist Party made life difficult for all Christians there. In 1948, the region was divided into North Korea and South Korea; the former was communist while the latter was democratic. The Communist Party virtually prohibited Christianity in North

Korea. In 1949, South Korean Baptists formed the Korean Baptist Convention. Growth was initially slow, due to both the Korean War (1950–53) and division among Baptists in the 1960s. By the 1970s, however, Korean Baptists began growing at a steady rate and developed a strong denomination with close ties to the Southern Baptist Convention. South Korean Baptists became key participants in the Baptist World Alliance in the latter years of the twentieth century. By 2012, South Korean Baptists were sending missionaries to numerous other nations, many of whom worked with Korean expatriates and emigrants. North Korea remained almost totally closed to Christianity.

Billy Kim was the key leader among South Korean Baptists for over five decades. In 1960, Kim became pastor of the Suwon Central Baptist Church, where he served until 2004. During his tenure the church grew from ten members to more than 12,000. Kim was converted and called to the ministry while an international student at Bob Jones University. Though not a fundamentalist, Kim was a theological conservative who emphasized personal evangelism and developed close ties with Baptists in America. In addition to his pastoral work, Kim founded numerous parachurch ministries, served as chairman of the missionary radio ministry called the Far East Broadcasting Company, and served

Billy Kim
(1934–present)

as the translator for Billy Graham's 1973 evangelistic crusade in Seoul. The latter was Graham's largest ever campaign, attracting more than 3 million people in three days. Kim also became a leader among global Baptists, serving as president of the Baptist World Alliance from 2000 to 2004. At the end of Kim's tenure as BWA president in 2004, the Southern Baptist Convention voted to defund the organization after the BWA received the Cooperative Baptist Fellowship into its membership the previous year. SBC leaders claimed the BWA tolerated liberal theology and was characterized by an anti-American attitude. Kim publicly expressed his disappointment with the decision of the SBC, a group with which he had long enjoyed a friendly relationship.

Baptists in Africa

Africa has been an important mission field for Baptists since the turn of the nineteenth century. The earliest Baptist strongholds were in West Africa and the southern part of the continent. Until the mid-twentieth century, missions were often intermingled with Western colonialism, periodically creating friction between missionaries and nationals. Between 1950 and 1980, most African nations became independent of colonial powers. Decolonization was peaceful and democratic in some nations while others experienced civil wars, coups, and violent revolutions. A new generation of missionaries, mostly from North America, went to previously unengaged nations in Africa throughout this period. African Baptists increasingly formed their own denominations during the latter half of the twentieth century. By 2011, the African continent was home to approximately 10.2 million Baptists in a wide variety of conventions, associations, and independent churches. Only North America had more Baptists (40 million) than Africa. The growth was remarkable; the total number of Baptists in Africa tripled between 1991 and 2011. Baptists were strongest numerically in Nigeria (3.5 million) and Uganda (1.5 million).

Southern Baptists initiated mission work in the British colony of Nigeria in 1850. Numeric growth was relatively slow for two generations, though a Nigerian Baptist Convention was formed in 1919. The convention remained the largest Baptist group in the nation. Nigerian Baptists began growing at a more rapid rate in the 1930s. After Nigeria gained its independence in 1960, the growth became even more pronounced. Nigerian Baptists worked closely with Southern Baptist missionaries in forming numerous institutions such as hospitals, colleges, a theological seminary, denominational programs, and an auxiliary Woman's Missionary Union. In addition to the Nigerian Baptist Convention and the smaller Mambilla Baptist Convention (26,000 members), Nigeria was home to many African Indigenous Churches with baptistic polity. African Indigenous Churches arose during the twentieth century among nationals, almost wholly independent of Western influences. As of 2011, Nigeria had more Baptists than any other nation in the world besides the United States.

Uganda, also a longtime British colony, experienced a series of revivals between the 1930s and the 1960s, mostly among the nation's Anglicans. Ugandan Baptists almost certainly benefited from the final years of the revivals. Conservative Baptists from America initiated Baptist mission work in Uganda in 1961, followed by Southern Baptists the next year. Uganda became an early stronghold among Baptists in East Africa, which had been mostly unengaged by Baptist missionaries during the colonial era. Ugandan Baptists faced significant persecution throughout the 1970s when dictator

Idi Amin, a Muslim, forced virtually all missionaries out of the country. But following Amin's ouster in 1979, Ugandan Baptists began to grow at a significant pace. Uganda Baptist Seminary, founded in 1988, retained close ties with Southern Baptists. As of 2011, Uganda had two different Baptist groups: the Baptist Union of Uganda (1972) and the Uganda Baptist Convention (1982).

Baptists in other parts of Africa had varied experiences, though Baptist movements grew in most parts of the continent. The one notable exception was North Africa, where Baptists and other Christians had virtually no presence due to the influence of Islam. West Africa was home to the earliest

Logo for the Baptist Theological Seminary of Zambia (est. 1967).

Baptist missionary work on the continent. War-torn nations such as Sierra Leone and Liberia have historically been the focus of African-American Baptist missionaries. Baptists grew in those areas but not at nearly the rate of Baptists elsewhere in Africa. Baptists in Cameroon, which was a historically British Baptist field, were strong, numbering around 175,000 by 2011. In the East the Kenya Baptist Convention included more than 800,000 Baptists. In the South, Baptists were strongest in Malawi and Zambia, with approximately 250,000 church members in each nation. Zambian Baptists operate a theological seminary.

In Central Africa, by the early twenty-first century the Democratic Republic of Congo (DRC), formerly Zaire, was home to almost 2 million Baptists in ten different denominational bodies. Baptist growth in the DRC was remarkable because the nation was devastated by two horrific civil wars. Central Africa was also home to one of the most significant African Indigenous Church movements, led by the controversial Baptist lay teacher and alleged healing prophet Simon Kimbangu (1887–1951). Based on his reading of John 14:15–17, Kimbangu believed he was the Holy Spirit in the flesh, a belief he passed on to his followers. Though Kimbangu died in prison and his followers were fiercely persecuted, in 1959 the Kimbanguist Church was legally recognized. As of 2011, it included approximately 3 million members. The leader of the Kimbanguist Church was Simon Kimbangu Kiangani, the grandson of the movement's founder.

Baptists in Latin America

Baptist missionaries became active in Latin America during the middle decades of the nineteenth century. Latin America includes Central America, South America, and the Caribbean Islands. Most of the region embraces Roman Catholicism, at least culturally, due to the work of monastic orders that accompanied Spanish and Portuguese conquistadors to the New World in the sixteenth century. The earliest Baptist fields were Mexico, Brazil, Argentina, and Chile. Often individual Baptists who relocated to these regions because of business interests pioneered mission work. Eventually denominational mission boards, especially those of Southern Baptists and Northern Baptists, became active in Latin America. Most Latino nations, with the exception of some of the Caribbean Islands, gained their independence between the early nineteenth and early twentieth centuries. As of 2011, Latin America had more than 2.8 million Baptists. By far the largest Baptist presence was in Brazil, which was home to nearly 2 million Baptists in three different conventions. No other Latin American nation had 100,000 Baptists, though Mexico, Cuba, Argentina, Venezuela, and Chile were each home to more than 50,000 Baptists.

Baptist work in Brazil began in 1871 when Southern Baptist ex-Confederates relocated to the nation and established a church. The expatriates appealed to the SBC Foreign Mission Board to send missionaries to Brazil. In 1882, the first Baptist church for Brazilian nationals was founded at Salvador, Bahia. In 1907, Baptists formed the Brazilian Baptist Convention (BBC). The BBC retained close ties to Southern Baptists and modeled its denominational structure after the SBC. The BBC formed foreign and domestic mission boards that together employed more than 500 missionaries by midcentury, many of whom served in surrounding Latin American nations. Brazilian Baptists also established numerous colleges and theological seminaries, though many of the former later became secular state colleges. By the 1960s Southern Baptist missionaries had turned over most of their evangelism and church planting work to Brazilian Baptists, though they continued to partner closely with the BBC in theological education; the presidents of Brazilian seminaries were normally SBC missionaries. In 1960, the Baptist World Congress met in Rio de Janeiro.

Brazilian Baptist life changed dramatically after the 1960s. Pentecostalism became a growing influence in the nation, leading to a split in the BBC. Baptists who embraced Pentecostal practices such as glossolalia, or "speaking in tongues," formed the National Baptist Convention of Brazil in 1967. Some Brazilian Baptists, especially in the BBC, began to embrace a more progressive outlook during the 1960s while others remained committed to more conservative theology. In the late-1990s, Southern Baptists shifted their missions strategy to focus on unreached people groups, embracing a trend that came to dominate evangelical missiology. In the ensuing years SBC missionaries largely left Brazil to focus on North Africa, the Middle East, and Asia. Theological education was turned over to Brazilian nationals, though some Baptist missionaries from America continued to raise their own support to serve as missionary professors. This general pattern was repeated across Latin America. Independent Baptist fundamentalists, who have long been active in Brazil, continued to focus on evangelism and church planting. Reformed Baptists engaged in church planting and theological education following the withdrawal of Southern Baptists. Richard Denham, a Reformed Baptist missionary, founded Editora FIEL (Faithful Publishers), which translated Calvinistic writings from English into Portuguese.

In Mexico the earliest Baptist work commenced in the 1840s in what is now Texas. In 1859, James Hickey, who worked for the American Bible Society, relocated from Missouri to Mexico to distribute Bibles. Hickey and his wife, another American expatriate named Thomas Westrup, and two Mexican nationals named José María and Arcadio Uranga planted the first Baptist church in modern Mexico in 1864. It was the first non-Catholic church there of any kind. By 1869, six more churches had been established. In 1870, Westrup became a missionary with the American Baptist Home Mission Society. Five years later, in 1875, Westrup's brother John Westrup Jr. became a missionary with the Southern Baptist Foreign Mission Board. In 1903, Baptists established the National Baptist Convention of Mexico (NBCM).

The Mexican Revolution, which lasted from 1910 to 1920, disrupted Baptist growth, but in the years following the NBCM began expanding its ministries. Mexican Baptists founded three universities and theological seminaries in Mexico City and Oaxaca. By the 1960s Mexican Baptists were growing numerically and expanding their infrastructure, though they still partnered closely with Southern Baptists. As in Brazil, that changed in the late-1990s with the implementation of a new strategy by the newly renamed International Mission Board of the SBC. Tensions between Southern Baptists and Mexican Baptists lingered into the early twenty-first century as a result of the SBC's removing its missionaries from Mexico. However, independent Baptists, Reformed Baptists, and Seventh Day Baptists continued to work in the nation. Beginning in the 1980s, Mexico emerged as a convenient place for Baptist churches and schools in America to send short-term mission teams.

In Cuba, Baptists began informal work in the 1860s; and by the 1880s both the Florida Baptist Convention and the SBC Home Mission Board had adopted Cuba as a mission field. The Spanish-American War between 1895 and 1898 interrupted this work, but by the turn of the twentieth century,

Cuba had become a key home mission field for Southern Baptists. An Eastern Baptist Convention and Western Baptist Convention were established in 1903 and 1905, respectively. The Cuban Revolution of 1959 and the transition to Marxism in 1961 significantly disrupted Cuban Baptist life for a season. Several dozen pastors and two SBC missionaries were arrested and sentenced to hard labor in 1965; all were released after a few years. Over time, restrictions were relaxed, and Cuban Baptists began to grow at a significant pace. Baptists from other nations, including America, were allowed to work with Cuban Baptists in short-term mission initiatives under the sponsorship of the Baptist World Alliance. By 2012, four denominations of Cuban Baptists had nearly 60,000 members. Beginning in the 1990s, moderate Baptists in the Cooperative Baptist Fellowship and the Alliance of Baptists partnered closely with many Baptists in Cuba while Southern Baptists, especially in the Florida Baptist Convention, focused on ministering to the nearly 900,000 Cuban-Americans who lived in south Florida.

In the 1960s some Latin American Christians, initially in the Roman Catholic Church, began to apply a Marxist social critique to their context and identify more closely with the poor and politically oppressed. The movement was given its name, liberation theology, following the publication of the influential book *A Theology of Liberation* (1971) by the Peruvian Catholic priest Gustavo Gutiérrez. While the best-known liberation theologians were Catholics, Latino Protestants, including Baptists, were affected by the movement. Latino Baptist theologians such as Orlando Costas of Puerto Rico, René Padilla of Ecuador, and Samuel Escobar of Peru attempted to appropriate insights from liberation theology without abandoning their evangelical heritage. They called their approach "integral mission" because it integrated evangelism and social justice. Each of these men was educated in North America or England, and Romero and Escobar taught in Ameri-

Samuel Escobar (1934–present)

can seminaries. Padilla and Escobar were speakers at the Lausanne Congress on World Evangelization in 1974, hosted by Billy Graham. At Lausanne they helped convince Anglican theologian John Stott, chairman of the committee

---

A Latino Baptist Theology of Mission

Summing up, then, mission as service in Jesus' name involves proclamation of the gospel of salvation; life in fellowship in the body, which is the church; worship and prayer in Jesus' name; and the multiplicity of tasks Jesus' disciples perform in response to human needs. . . . Today mission should consist of service—service both of the spiritual in proclaiming the Word and of the physical in meeting human needs, according to Jesus' model and in his name.

Excerpted from Samuel Escobar, *The New Global Mission: The Gospel from Everywhere to Everywhere* (2003).

---

drafting the Lausanne Covenant, to include the importance of social justice in the statement. When the Lausanne Covenant was adopted, it prioritized global evangelism, but it also stated: "We affirm that God is both the Creator and the Judge of all people. We therefore should share his concern for justice and reconciliation throughout human society and for the liberation of men and women from every kind of oppression."

Baptists in Oceania

Australia was claimed by England in 1770 and settled as a penal colony in 1788. Within a generation at least some Baptists were present on the continent. In the early 1830s John Saunders began serving in Australia on behalf of the Baptist Missionary Society, and in 1836 the oldest surviving Baptist church was established in Sydney. The congregation's present name is Central Baptist Church. Later that decade Scottish Baptists began to work in Australia. By the late nineteenth century, Thomas Spurgeon of Spurgeon's College (the famed preacher's son) had taken a special interest in Australia and was sending graduates of the school to become pastors of churches all over the continent. While German Baptist congregations and indigenous independent Baptist churches were also established, most Australian Baptists maintained close ties to the Baptist Union of Great Britain. The Baptist Union of Australia was formed in 1926. British Baptists began planting churches in New Zealand in 1851. The Baptist Union of New Zealand was established in 1882.

In the twentieth century Australian Baptists have focused their mission work on reaching aboriginal peoples in their nation. Foreign missionaries have been active in South Asian nations such as Bangladesh since the 1880s and, more recently, in Papua, New Guinea, since 1949. The Baptist Union in Australia sponsored five theological colleges while the Baptist Union of New Zealand sponsored two theological colleges, one of which served the Maori, the people group that is indigenous to the nation. Baptists in Oceania continued to foster close ties with British Baptists. Since the 1980s a growing number of independent fundamentalist Baptists and Reformed Baptists have planted churches in Australia and New Zealand. These congregations did not affiliate with the Baptist Unions. Baptists in Papua New Guinea formed a Baptist Union in 1977, which became the largest Baptist denomination in Oceania. As of 2010, Oceania had more than 165,000 Baptists, almost half of whom were part of the Baptist Union of Papua, New Guinea (approximately 80,000). The Baptist Union of Australia included around 62,000 members while the Baptist Union of New Zealand was home to approximately 23,500 members.

Key Trends, Threats, and Trajectories

In addition to the civil rights movement and theological battles between conservatives and progressives, Baptists were affected by several other important developments from the 1960s onward. Some Baptists viewed these trends as evidence of renewal while others considered them signs of declension. Some of these trends were outright threats to Baptist Christianity or even Christianity in general. This section briefly introduces some of the key developments that influenced Baptists into the twenty-first century, especially (but not exclusively) in the English-speaking world. These developments will influence how future historians recount the Baptist story.

"Miraculous" Gifts

In the first decade of the twentieth century, Christians in several nations began to argue that certain miraculous spiritual gifts that were practiced in the New Testament had been restored, particularly glossolalia, or "speaking in tongues." Known initially as Pentecostals, advocates of these gifts normally argued that speaking in tongues evidenced that a believer had been baptized in the Holy Spirit, a special empowering that occurred sometime after one's conversion. The Pentecostal movement in America, which is typically dated to the famous Azusa Street Revival in 1906, birthed a number of new denominations, though early on it had relatively little effect on Baptists. The Pentecostal Free Will Baptists, formed in North Carolina in 1959, were a noteworthy exception. Beginning in the 1960s, a growing number of non-Pentecostal Christians reported speaking in tongues and practicing other miraculous gifts. This new wave of miraculous gifts, known as the charismatic movement, provoked heated controversy in most denominations. "Continuationists" embraced the miraculous gifts to varying degrees while "cessationists" contended that such gifts ceased with the end of the apostolic era. Cessationists argued that speaking in tongues and prophesying were special apostolic gifts that demonstrated the authority of the men Jesus commissioned to establish the church and write the New Testament. These gifts were no longer necessary since the apostles were long dead and their authoritative word had been canonized in Scripture, cessationists said. Some cessationists believed that practicing the so-called miraculous gifts undermined the supreme authority of Scripture. Many Christians were unconvinced of cessationism but did not practice any miraculous gifts, remaining "open but cautious" toward the phenomena.

Baptists responded to the charismatic movement in different ways. In North America a number of Baptist churches, especially in larger denominations, embraced the miraculous gifts by the late 1970s. Canadian Baptist and charismatic theologian Clark Pinnock advocated the miraculous gifts in numerous writings throughout the 1970s and 1980s while several Southern Baptist professors offered a more cautious assessment in their books *Glossolalia: Tongue Speaking in Biblical, Historical, and Psychological Perspective* (1967) and *Speaking in Tongues* (1973). Charismatics in the ABC-USA formed the American Baptist Charismatic Fellowship in 1981 while Southern Baptist charismatics published *Fulness Magazine* and held an annual conference in Chattanooga, Tennessee.

Logo for the Full Gospel Baptist Church Fellowship (est. 1994).

Perhaps the most famous Baptist charismatic was Pat Robertson, an ordained Southern Baptist who founded the Christian Broadcasting Network (1960), ran for president of the United States (1988), and founded the Christian Coalition (1989). Many African-American Baptists embraced the charismatic movement, resulting in the formation of the Full Gospel Baptist Church Fellowship in 1994.

The charismatic movement proved controversial among Southern Baptists. In 1975, some proposed to exclude charismatic churches from the SBC. The effort failed. Nevertheless, Southern Baptists remained almost uniformly negative toward practices such as speaking in tongues, prophesying, and being "slain in the Spirit" (fainting under the apparent power of the Holy Spirit). Many Baptist associations disfellowshipped charismatic churches between the 1970s and 1990s, Southern Baptist seminaries did not employ professors who were openly charismatic, and the convention's two mission boards each enacted policies to prevent open charismatics from serving as missionaries. In 2005, the International Mission Board adopted a policy forbidding "private prayer languages," a devotional form of glossolalia, among its missionaries, provoking a significant controversy when a dissenting trustee began writing about his opposition to the policy on the Internet. Other groups that were predominantly cessationist included Free Will Baptists, Reformed Baptists, Landmark Baptists, and independent Baptists.

Southern Baptists of Texas Convention Reject Speaking in Tongues

RESOLVED, That the messengers to the Southern Baptists of Texas Convention meeting in Austin, Texas, November 13–14, 2006, declare that Southern Baptists in Texas typically believe that the modern practice of private prayer languages lacks a tangible foundation in Scripture; and be it further

RESOLVED, That we are opposed to unscriptural teaching relating to speaking in tongues, whether such speech be done in private or public; and be it further

RESOLVED, That we encourage the Southern Baptists of Texas Convention not knowingly to employ consultants and ministry staff who participate in or promote views or practices contrary to the position described herein; and be it further

RESOLVED, That we encourage all Southern Baptists to be patient, kind, and loving toward one another (1 Corinthians 13:4–8) regarding this ancillary theological issue, which ought not to constitute a test of fellowship; and be it finally

RESOLVED, That we encourage all Southern Baptists to refocus their attention upon the public and intelligible proclamation of the saving gospel of Jesus Christ, the Second Person of the divine Trinity, Who became a man, died on the cross, and arose from the dead, so that those who believe in Him may have eternal and abundant life.

Excerpted from "Resolution on *Glossolalia* and Private Prayer Languages" (2006).

Outside North America, Baptists tended to be more open to miraculous gifts. Many British Baptists embraced the charismatic movement. By the early twenty-first century, the two largest churches in the Baptist Union were multiethnic charismatic congregations pastored by immigrants from Africa. Kingsley Appiagyei, a native of Ghana who was elected president of the Baptist Union in 2009, established both congregations. In the Global South many Baptist groups were charismatic, reflecting larger trends. Many Australian and especially New Zealand Baptists were charismatic. In Brazil the National Baptist Convention was charismatic. Perhaps a majority of Baptists in Africa were charismatic, though some, such as the Zambian Reformed Baptist pastor Conrad Mbewe, remained vocal cessationists. In Asia many

Korean Baptist congregations and Chinese Baptist house churches embraced the charismatic gifts.

Evolving Worship Styles

One way the charismatic movement affected even noncharismatic Baptist churches was through the rise of "praise and worship" music. Praise and worship music was an offshoot of the contemporary Christian music (CCM) movement, which began in the 1960s with artists such as Larry Norman and 2nd Chapter of Acts. Many of the earliest CCM artists were charismatics who were converted through the Jesus People movement. As CCM became more popular in the 1970s and 1980s, a growing number of churches adopted a "contemporary" approach to their worship gatherings. Short praise choruses supplanted traditional hymns, guitars and drums replaced (or at least supplemented) pianos and organs, and dress became more casual in worship services. New Bible translations such as the Living Bible (1971) and the New International Version (1973) used updated language that resonated with many baby boomer Christians better than the older English of the King James Bible. While many, if not most, proponents of contemporary worship services did not advocate glossolalia, prophecy, or being slain in the Spirit, contemporary worshippers did adopt moderate charismatic practices such as raising their hands or dancing during congregational singing.

Many churches, including Baptist churches, experienced turmoil during the so-called worship wars of the 1980s and 1990s. Advocates of more traditional forms of worship, whether revivalistic or lightly liturgical, criticized contemporary worship as tasteless, trendy, or even irreverent while champions of the new approach argued that the new forms resonated with both younger Christians and the unchurched. For proponents of praise and worship music, content was more important than style. Many Baptist congregations lost members when pastors or music ministers introduced praise choruses, exchanged the organ for a guitar, or began reading from modern Bible translations. Many churches, especially larger congregations, avoided division by offering both traditional services and contemporary services to appeal to as many worshippers as possible. Denominational meetings and other conferences often tried to incorporate multiple styles of music for the same reason.

By the early 2000s many more traditional congregations had incorporated contemporary music, added a wider variety of instruments into their worship services, and gravitated toward a more casual style of dress. Music ministers were increasingly called "worship leaders" or "worship pastors," and many Baptist seminaries adapted their music programs to accommodate changing musical tastes in local churches. Some of the artists writing what were now

Open Road Community Church in Franklinton, North Carolina, is an example of a "biker church" that is reaching out to the motorcycle culture.

called "modern worship" songs were Baptists, particularly those associated with the Passion collegiate conference started by Southern Baptist minister Louis Giglio in 1997. Many churches, influenced by missiological strategies, adopted more contextual approaches to worship, with music, dress, and other elements of worship reflecting the cultural context. Members of "cowboy churches" dressed in spurs and baptized new converts in feeding troughs, members of "biker churches" wore Harley-Davidson Tshirts and heard sermon illustrations about motorcycle culture, and members of "hip-hop churches" wore baggy jeans and listened to soloists perform gospel-themed hip-hop songs.

The pendulum later swung again as some Baptists reacted to the trend toward contemporary worship by embracing a more liturgical approach. A growing number of Baptists, especially in the millennial generation (born since 1980), adopted practices such as liturgical Scripture readings, weekly celebration of the Lord's Supper, the reading of prayers, and the recitation of creedal statements such as the Nicene Creed and the Apostles' Creed. Baptists who identified with the "emerging church" movement sometimes added elements such as liturgical dance, iconography, painting, and sculpting during worship services. In 1997, a group of moderate former Southern Baptists drafted a document titled "Re-Envisioning Baptist Identity: A Manifesto for Baptist Communities in North America," often shortened to "The

Five Affirmations of "The Baptist Manifesto"

I.   We affirm Bible Study in reading communities rather than relying on private interpretation or supposed "scientific" objectivity.

II. We affirm following Jesus as a call to shared discipleship rather than invoking a theory of soul competency.

III. We affirm a free common life in Christ in gathered, reforming communities rather than withdrawn, self-chosen, or authoritarian ones.

IV. We affirm baptism, preaching, and the Lord's table as powerful signs that seal God's faithfulness in Christ and express our response of awed gratitude rather than as mechanical rituals or mere symbols.

V.   We affirm freedom and renounce coercion as a distinct people under God rather than relying on political theories, powers, or authorities.

Excerpted from "Re-envisioning Baptist Identity: A Manifesto for
Baptist Communities in North America" (1997).

Baptist Manifesto." Its signatories, who came to be called "Bapto-Catholics," advocated a postmodern approach to theology, liturgical worship, and a greater sense of ecumenism. Bapto-Catholics successfully convinced the centennial Baptist World Congress in 2004 to recite the Apostles' Creed at their meeting.

Ecclesiological Developments

Baptists have experienced significant ecclesiological developments in the past generation. During the 1980s many churches adopted a "seeker-sensitive" approach. The most famous seeker-sensitive church was the nondenominational Willow Creek Church in South Barrington, Illinois. In the seeker-sensitive model, a church's worship services function as outreach gatherings aimed primarily at converting non-Christians and reintegrating disaffected believers back into church participation. In many respects the seeker-sensitive movement was a post-revivalist strategy that was aimed at reaching middle-class suburbanites.

One of the most influential early seeker-sensitive churches in America was Saddleback Church in Lake Forest, California, which was planted by Rick Warren in 1980. Warren is best known for his book *The Purpose-Driven Life* (2002), which within five years had sold more than 30 million copies and become the best-selling nonfiction hardback in history. Saddleback Church was a Southern Baptist congregation, though the church did not use "Baptist" in its name and downplayed its denominational affiliation. By the early twenty-first century, many Baptist churches, especially newer congregations, did not include "Baptist" in their names. One denomination embraced this approach when the Baptist General Conference changed its name to Converge Worldwide in 2008. This trend reflected the postdenominational ethos of American Christianity.

Rick Warren
(1954–present)

A second ecclesiological development was the advent of multi-site congregations. In the late 1990s a growing number of churches, including Baptist churches, began to gather in more than one location. Some of the multi-site churches were long-established congregations such as Second Baptist Church of Houston, Texas, while others were new church plants. Proponents argued that a multi-site approach made it easier for a church to reach its community since the church was gathering in more than one loca-

Offering Spiritual Seekers a Life of Purpose

It's not about you.

The purpose of your life is far greater than your own personal fulfillment, your peace of mind, or even your happiness. It's far greater than your family, your career, or even your wildest dreams and ambitions. If you want to know why you were placed on this planet, you must begin with God. You were born *by* his purpose and *for* his purpose.

Excerpted from Rick Warren, *The Purpose-Driven Life* (2002).

tion. Many churches had already begun adopting home Bible studies, or "cell groups," often as a replacement for Sunday school, as early as the 1980s; in some cases additional church meeting sites evolved out of these groups. Some multi-site churches had live preaching by a "campus pastor" at every site while others used live video feeds or prerecorded sermons by their main preachers at satellite locations. Critics of multi-site churches questioned whether more than one location really constituted more than one church, queried whether a multi-site strategy was preferable to traditional church planting, and criticized the use of video sermons rather than live preaching. Some observers said multi-site strategies were compatible with connectional ecclesiologies such as Presbyterianism but incompatible, or at least in tension, with the traditional Baptist understanding of a gathered church.

A third ecclesiological development was the growing popularity of the multiple elders model of church governance in Baptist congregations. While some Baptist churches have had multiple elders off and on since the seventeenth century, this approach had never been widespread. Even in churches large enough to employ multiple staff members, often the "senior pastor" was the only minister considered to be an elder. That began to change in the 1990s. Multiple elder ecclesiology appeared in at least three different versions. Some churches, especially in the seeker-sensitive movement, treated elders as a church board. In this model the elders were typically unpaid laypeople with leadership skills. Others, especially some Reformed Baptist churches, adopted a semi-Presbyterian approach that differentiated, at least implicitly, between "teaching" elders and "ruling" elders. While the former were ministerial staff and sometimes other unpaid members with the ability to preach or teach, the latter were simply members who were good role models and strong leaders. Proponents of these versions of elder governance often expressed concerns about or even rejected congregational polity. The final version, popularized by Mark Dever of Capitol Hill Baptist Church in Washington, DC, made no distinction between teaching and ruling elders and strongly affirmed congregationalism. All elders were seen as pastors, all elders both led and taught, and all elders were required to meet the biblical qualifications spelled out in 1 Timothy 3:1–7 and Titus 1:5–9. Proponents of multiple elder models noted that the New Testament normally spoke of elders in the plural while opponents of these models countered that at least some versions were too Presbyterian and/or conflicted with congregational governance.

Resurgent Calvinism

The mid-twentieth century witnessed a revival of Calvinistic theology among many evangelicals. It began in Britain where some of the early pioneers were Martyn Lloyd-Jones and J. I. Packer. Lloyd-Jones spent his ministry in pedobaptist churches but personally rejected infant baptism and practiced believer's baptism by pouring while Packer was an evangelical Anglican. Lloyd-Jones's annual Puritan Conference provided a venue for Calvinists to gather while Banner of Truth Publications reprinted classic works in Reformed theology, especially by Puritans. Many Baptists were influenced by this trend, most notably Erroll Hulse of Leeds and Geoffrey Thomas of Wales. These Reformed Baptists, as they came to be known, rallied around the Second London Confession (1689), which was frequently reprinted during this era. They embraced a Baptist version of covenant theology, emphasized the regulative principle of worship, and viewed the Lord's Day (Sunday) as the Christian Sabbath. By the early twenty-first century, a growing number of Reformed Baptists in the British Isles combined Calvinism with a belief in the charismatic gifts. These same trends were evident to a lesser extent in Australia and New Zealand.

By the 1960s Calvinism was also influencing Baptists in North America. Early Reformed Baptist pioneers included Al Martin of New Jersey, Walter Chantry of Pennsylvania, and Bill Payne of Ontario, each of whom established informal fraternal ties with their British counterparts. Reformed Baptists tended to focus on church-based ministerial education rather than accredited seminaries and divinity schools. Many Reformed Baptists had close contact with Presbyterians, and often those Reformed Baptists who did seek a formal theological education did so in Presbyterian seminaries such as Westminster Theological Seminary in Philadelphia. By the early twenty-first century, Reformed Baptists had grown substantially, though it was difficult to know exact numbers since not everyone defined "Reformed Baptist" in the same way. The largest group of self-designated Reformed Baptists was the Association of Reformed Baptist Churches of America (ARBCA), established in 1997, which by 2013 included approximately eighty congregations in thirty states and Canada. ARBCA sponsored the Institute of Reformed Baptist Studies housed at Westminster Seminary California. In addition to ARBCA churches, many churches that affirmed the Second London Confession were either independent of any group or were part of a denomination, often the Southern Baptist Convention.

Not all Calvinistic Baptists identified as Reformed Baptists. As early as the mid-1950s, Calvinistic Baptists who tended to be dispensational rather than holding to covenant theology began to withdraw from the SBC, the ABC-USA, and the independent Baptist movement. These "Sovereign Grace Baptists" rallied around the annual Sovereign Grace Bible Conference, which was established in 1954 and hosted by Thirteenth Street Baptist Church in Ashland, Kentucky. The key leaders of the Sovereign Grace Baptists included Henry Mahan, pastor of Thirteenth Street Church, and evangelist Rolfe Barnard. D. J. Ward, who pastored churches in Tennessee and Kentucky, spearheaded a similar movement among African-American Baptists a generation later when he launched an annual Sovereign Grace Bible Conference in 1985.

In the early 1980s some erstwhile Reformed Baptists began to promote what they called "new covenant theology," a position that combined elements of both covenant theology and dispensationalism. Key early proponents of new covenant theology included evangelist John Reisinger, John Zens, publisher of the journal *Baptist Reformation Review*, and Georgia pastor Ron McKinney, who published a widely read magazine titled (in a nod to Spurgeon) *The Sword and the Trowel*. Churches that held to new covenant theology often adopted the First London Confession (1646) rather than the Second London Confession, claiming the former was more distinctively Baptist while the latter was a "baptized" version of covenant theology. Several new covenant churches formed the Continental Baptist Churches in 1983 while others remained independent of any formal association or network. By the turn of the twenty-first century, tension existed between the Reformed Baptists who affirmed covenant theology and those Calvinistic Baptists who affirmed new covenant theology. In addition to these two groups, some Baptist Calvinists, especially among independent Baptists, continued to advocate dispensationalism.

In the 1980s and 1990s, Calvinism began to become more controversial within Baptist denominations, especially the SBC, which for a century or more had occupied theological space somewhere between Calvinism and Arminianism. In 1983, Founders Ministries was established by Florida pastor Ernest Reisinger to promote Calvinism within the SBC. Founders Ministries was so named because many of the leading pastors and theologians in early Southern Baptist life were Calvinists. Founders hosted an annual conference, sponsored a quarterly journal, and published books and pamphlets related to Reformed theology. In 1993, Albert Mohler became the president of Southern Baptist Theological Seminary. Mohler identified with

John Piper
(1946–present)

the broadly Calvinistic theology of the Abstract of Principles; under his leadership Southern moved in a more Calvinistic direction, though not uniformly so. Mark Dever was identified with Calvinism as much as his ecclesiological views. Many SBC Calvinists looked to non-SBC Calvinistic theologians for inspiration, especially John Piper, whose church in Minneapolis was part of the Baptist General Conference, and R. C. Sproul, a Presbyterian scholar with a large following. In 2006, Mohler, Dever, and two non-Baptist Calvinists launched Together for the Gospel, a large biennial conference that promoted Reformed theology. Younger Southern Baptists increasingly embraced

Calvinism, though many opted for a more moderate "four-point" Calvinism that still affirmed general atonement. Calvinistic Southern Baptists were part of a larger "New Calvinism" movement that transcended denominations.

Southern Baptists Navigate Tensions over Calvinism

Cooperation

We affirm that Southern Baptists stand together in a commitment to cooperate in Great Commission ministries. We affirm that, from the very beginning of our denominational life, Calvinists and non-Calvinists have cooperated together. We affirm that these differences should not threaten our eager cooperation in Great Commission ministries.

We deny that the issues now discussed among us should in any way undermine or hamper our work together if we grant one another liberty and extend to one another charity in these differences. Neither those insisting that Calvinism should dominate Southern Baptist identity nor those who call for its elimination should set the course for our life together.

Confession

We affirm that *The Baptist Faith and Message,* as adopted by the Southern Baptist Convention in 2000, stands as a sufficient and truthful statement of those doctrines most certainly held among us. We affirm that this confession of faith is to serve as the doctrinal basis for our cooperation in Great Commission ministry.

We deny that any human statement stands above Holy Scripture as our authority. We also deny that *The Baptist Faith and Message* is insufficient as the doctrinal basis for our cooperation. Other Baptist Confessions are not to be lenses through which *The Baptist Faith and Message* is to be read. *The Baptist Faith and Message* alone is our expression of common belief.

Excerpted from "Truth, Trust and Testimony in a Time of Tension" (2012).

Calvinism led to conflict in many Southern Baptist churches and associations, especially when Calvinistic pastors were called to lead non-Calvinistic churches. In 2007, the Building Bridges Conference brought together Baptist Calvinists and non-Calvinists to discuss the disputed doctrines. In 2008, non-Calvinists hosted the John 3:16 Conference to critique Reformed theology. Both of these conferences resulted in books. Southern Baptist bloggers debated Calvinism on the Internet, and pastors published books on the topic. In 2012, a group of SBC non-Calvinists drafted a document titled "A Statement of the Traditional Baptist Understanding of God's Plan of Salvation." These "Traditionalists" distanced themselves from both Calvinism and Arminianism and claimed their views represented the majority of Southern Baptists. That same year Frank Page, president of the SBC Executive Committee, appointed a task force to make recommendations about how Calvinists and non-Calvinists could better cooperate in the SBC. The resulting document, titled "Truth, Trust and Testimony in a Time of Tension," focused on theological commonality and called for Southern Baptists on all sides of the debate to cooperate around the Baptist Faith and Message 2000 for the sake of the Great Commission.

Threats to Religious Liberty

Religious liberty has been a chief concern for Baptists since their earliest days. Beginning in the latter decades of the twentieth century, new threats presented new challenges and led to new partnerships. For Baptists world-wide the leading threat to religious liberty was either militant Islam or secu-larization, depending on context. For Baptists (and other Christians) in predominantly Muslim lands, persecution could be fierce when governments embraced a more radicalized version of Islam. Some Islamic nations passed laws discouraging or even outlawing conversion from Islam to Christianity. New converts in many nations were kidnapped, tortured, or even killed. In some Muslim lands the only evangelicals of any kind were Western diplo-mats and other expatriates. From time to time, even Western Baptist mission-aries were persecuted and martyred. For example, three Southern Baptist missionaries were murdered in Jibla, Yemen, in 2002. Two years later four International Mission Board missionaries were killed in Mosul, Iraq, includ-ing Larry and Jean Elliott, who served as Southern Baptist missionaries from 1978 until their deaths on March 15, 2004.

Larry and Jean Elliott, martyred Southern Baptist missionaries.

For Baptists in the West, secularization was a much greater threat. In America in the 1960s, Supreme Court decisions removed teacher-led prayer and Bible reading from public schools. Though most Baptists applauded these decisions at the time, by the 1980s some theologically conservative Baptists had come to see them as violations of the first amendment's guarantee of religious freedom. Even Baptists who were comfortable with the Supreme Court rulings pushed back against efforts to curb voluntary student religious clubs and moments of silence in public schools based on a secularist interpretation of the first amendment. Some Baptists were nervous about "faith-based initiatives," programs where federal and state governments offered funding to religious organizations that provided social services. Some Baptists balked at these programs because they considered them government sponsorship of religion. Others were concerned that organizations accepting government funds would be required to restrict their evangelistic outreach or institute hiring practices in conflict with their values.

In the first decade of the twenty-first century, homosexuality became increasingly accepted in Western nations. This trend presented several challenges to religious liberty. Same-sex marriage was legalized in several American states, beginning with Massachusetts in 2003. Canada legalized homosexual marriage in 2005 while Great Britain passed a law to that effect in 2013. Also in 2013, the US Supreme Court struck down the Defense of Marriage Act, opening the door for the federal government in America to legalize same-sex marriage in the coming years. Many Baptists in America were concerned that the legalization of same-sex marriage would lead to restrictions of religious freedom ranging from the loss of tax-exempt status to prosecution for refusing to perform or support wedding ceremonies for homosexual couples. In Canada, Baptists and other Christians feared that preaching against homosexuality could result in prosecution under that nation's hate-speech laws. In Sweden a Pentecostal pastor was prosecuted under a hate-speech law in 2003.

Abortion presented a different set of religious liberty challenges. When the US Supreme Court legalized abortion in 1973, many Baptists were ambivalent, though by the early 1980s most Baptists were pro-life opponents of abortion on demand. Theologically conservative Baptists especially believed that abortion was at least normally murder and violated the "sanctity of human life." The abortion issue was arguably the most important reason many Baptists identified with political conservatism during this period; the Republican Party's platform officially opposed abortion beginning in 1976. When Congress passed the Affordable Health Care Act in 2010 mandating universal health care in America, many Baptists and others were concerned that it forced Christian business owners to pay for, or delegate others to pay for, abortion procedures. Many Baptists also believed the new law mandated unjustly that business owners pay for contraception, which the Roman Catholic Church opposed for religious reasons. In 2012, the Southern Baptist owners of the retail chain Hobby Lobby sued the federal government, claiming the new law violated their religious liberty because it required the company to fund certain forms of contraception that cause abortions. In June 2014, the US Supreme Court ruled in favor of Hobby Lobby by a 5–4 majority. Several Baptist colleges also brought suit for similar reasons, winning their case in 2013. The Southern Baptist Ethics and Religious Liberty Commission (formerly the Christian Life Commission) supported the plaintiffs in each of these important lawsuits.

These threats led Baptists to work with others who shared their views on religious liberty, including other evangelicals, Roman Catholics, Orthodox Jews, and Mormons. This sometimes led to controversy. In 1994, Richard John Neuhaus and Charles Colson convened a group of Christian leaders who drafted a document titled "Evangelicals and Catholics Together." Neuhaus was a Catholic priest and editor of the journal *First Things*. Colson was a former political aide to President Richard Nixon who served a brief prison sentence for his role in the Watergate scandal. Colson converted to Christianity prior to his incarceration, joined a Southern Baptist church upon his parole, founded the ministry

*Charles Colson
(1931–2012)*

Prison Fellowship, and authored numerous books, including the best-selling spiritual autobiography *Born Again* (1976). Though "Evangelicals and Catholics Together" addressed cultural engagement, it also called for more ecumenical unity between evangelicals and Catholics. Southern Baptists Larry Lewis of the Foreign Mission Board and Richard Land of the Ethics and Religious Liberty Commission signed the document, though they later asked that their names be removed after receiving criticism.

In 2009, more than 150 religious leaders signed the "Manhattan Declaration: A Call of Christian Conscience," which called Catholics, Eastern Orthodox, and evangelicals to cooperate in defense of the sanctity of human life, traditional views of marriage, and freedom of conscience and religion. Colson, Southern Baptist theologian Timothy George, and Catholic legal scholar Robert George drafted the document. Numerous Southern Baptist leaders signed the "Manhattan Declaration," including several prominent pastors, theologians, and college and seminary administrators. As with "Evangelicals and Catholics Together," some criticized the "Manhattan Declaration" for promoting ecumenism between Roman Catholics and evangelicals. Nevertheless, the religious liberty threats posed by secularism increasingly led Baptists to build partnerships that once seemed unimaginable.

Possible Trajectories

By the second decade of the twenty-first century, it was unclear how these trends and threats might evolve into more settled trajectories. Many questions remained unanswered. What will Baptist identity mean in an increasingly postdenominational milieu? How closely will different Baptist groups cooperate with one another and with groups of other Christian traditions— including groups that once persecuted Baptists? How will Baptist worship and ecclesiology continue to evolve in various contexts? As Baptists become increasingly open to so-called miraculous gifts, will some Baptist groups be assimilated into the wider charismatic movement? Will future Baptists be more Calvinistic, more Arminian, or will most continue to try and carve out a position between these two points on the theological spectrum? Will Baptists in the majority world soon be sending missionaries to plant Baptist churches in secular Western nations? These and other questions demonstrate that the Baptist story will likely take many more interesting turns before it is completed.

For Further Study

Allen, David L., and Steve W. Lemke, eds. *Whosoever Will: A Biblical-Theological Critique of Five-Point Calvinism*. Nashville, TN: B&H Academic, 2010.

Anderson, Justice C. *An Evangelical Saga: Baptists and Their Precursors in Latin America*. Maitland, FL: Xulon Press, 2005.

Blumhofer, Edith L., Russell P. Spittler, and Grant A. Wacker, eds. *Pentecostal Currents in American Protestantism*, chapters 8 and 11. Champaign, IL: University of Illinois Press, 1999.

Dever, Mark E. *Nine Marks of a Healthy Church*, 3rd ed. Wheaton, IL: Crossway, 2013.

Hansen, Collin. *Young, Restless, Reformed: A Journalist's Journey with the New Calvinists*, chapters 1, 2, and 4. Wheaton, IL: Crossway, 2008.

Johnson, Robert E. *A Global Introduction to Baptist Churches*, chapters 5, 6, and 7. New York: Cambridge University Press, 2010.

Music, David W., and Paul Akers Richardson. *"I Will Sing the Wondrous Story": A History of Baptist Hymnody in North America*. Macon, GA: Mercer University Press, 2008.

Nettles, Thomas J. *By His Grace and for His Glory: A Historical, Theological, and Practical Study of the Doctrines of Grace in Baptist Life*, 2nd ed., chapter 11. Cape Coral, FL: Founders Press, 2006.

Waggoner, Brad J., and E. Ray Clendenen, eds. *Calvinism: A Southern Baptist Dialogue*. Nashville: B&H Academic, 2008.

Wardin, Albert W., ed. *Baptists Around the World: A Comprehensive Handbook*. Nashville, TN: B&H, 1995.

Watson, Edward. "A History of Influence: The Charismatic Movement and the SBC." *Criswell Theological Review* 4, no. 1 (Fall 2006): 15–30.

White, Thomas, Jason G. Duesing, and Malcolm B. Yarnell III, eds. *First Freedom: The Baptist Perspective on Religious Liberty*. Nashville, TN: B&H Academic, 2007.

Questions for Discussion

1. How has the Baptist movement developed in Asia? In what specific areas were Baptists most successful? Summarize the influence of Billy Kim among South Korean Baptists.

2. How has the Baptist movement developed in Africa? In what specific areas were Baptists most successful? What heretical teaching did Simon Kimbangu pass on to his followers?

3. How has the Baptist movement developed in Latin America? In what areas were Baptists most successful? What role did liberation theology and integration mission have among the people of Latin America?

4. How has the Baptist movement developed in Australia?

5. What is the distinction between continuationists and cessationists with respect to miraculous gifts? Describe the various ways Baptists responded to the charismatic movement. Which of these positions do you think presents the best argument from Scripture regarding miraculous gifts and speaking in tongues? Explain your answer.

6. Describe the changes in Baptist worship styles during this period. Which of these perspectives on or styles of worship best resembles what your church practices?

7. Identify three ecclesiological changes among Baptists since the 1960s. How did opponents of these changes challenge the changing ecclesiological tide? Do you have any reservations regarding any of these trends? Explain your answer.

8. Describe the resurgence of Calvinism among Baptists since the 1960s. How did this issue threaten Baptist cooperative efforts? What movements and conferences came about as a result of increased awareness of Southern Baptist Calvinists? What document did Frank Page call for Southern Baptists to rally around regardless of their perspective of Calvinism?

9. Provide examples of how persecution and secularization impacted the practice of religious liberty among Baptists and other Christian groups in the early twenty-first century. What current issues appear to limit the free expression of religion?

Section Four

BAPTIST BELIEFS

Chapter 13

IDENTITY AND DISTINCTIVES

The first twelve chapters of this book have focused on telling the Baptist story. We have tried to focus on the grand narrative of Baptists, giving particular emphasis to Baptists in the English-speaking world. We have concentrated our attention on key figures, movements, themes, and controversies. In this final chapter we want to discuss Baptist identity and priorities. While these topics have been referenced, and sometimes summarized, in past chapters, they have not been discussed in great detail. Since we are historians, our narrative has been primarily descriptive to this point. However, in this final chapter we want to be more prescriptive as we discuss the convictions and emphases of Baptist Christians in the early twenty-first century.

Baptist Identity

As with any denominational tradition, Christians who identify with the Baptists do so for a variety of reasons. One can find at least three different approaches to Baptist identity. Some people are Baptists by *conditioning* because their Christian experience has been mostly limited to Baptist churches. They may have been raised in a Baptist church, or they may have been converted through the ministry of a Baptist church, or they may have married a Baptist and joined his church. While the circumstances of becoming a Baptist may vary, those who have been conditioned as Baptists have what Gregory Wills calls a "tribal identity" because their commitment to being Baptist is rooted primarily in their family heritage or their long-term church participation. Often someone who is a Baptist by conditioning has always been a Baptist, so he has a hard time imagining being part of a

different Christian tradition. R. G. Lee, the famous twentieth-century Southern Baptist pastor, captured this approach with
a quip: "I'm Baptist born and Baptist bred,
and when I die I'll be Baptist dead."

Some people are Baptists by *convenience* because they presently attend
a Baptist church. Baptists by convenience have an institutional identity because their commitment to
being Baptist is rooted in their
local church membership or participation. Often someone who is
a Baptist by convenience could just
as easily be Methodist, Presbyterian, or Pentecostal, but because he
likes the Baptist church he is currently
a member of, he is a Baptist—for now.
This approach to Baptist identity is common in contexts where postdenomination-
alism has had significant influence. In many
communities people commonly move from
church to church based on preaching, music
styles, or programs without regard for denominational affiliation.

*Robert Green Lee
(1886–1978)*

Some people are Baptists by *conviction* because their beliefs and priorities
match those that have been historically identified with Baptist Christians. A
Baptist by conviction considers himself a Baptist ultimately because of what
he believes, which in turn influences his decision to join a congregation or
denomination that shares his beliefs. A Baptist by conviction would join a
different type of church only if he decided that the other church better represented his understanding of biblical truth. While we appreciate the first two
approaches to Baptist identity, we believe the third is the best option, even
for those who have been raised Baptist or who really appreciate their current
church membership in a Baptist congregation. What one believes about God,
the Bible, salvation, and the church is ultimately far more important than
one's heritage or preferences.

Since convictions matter in understanding religious identity, determining
the best sources for investigating Baptist convictions is important. Like all
Christian groups Baptists express their beliefs primarily through their sermons, prayers, and hymnody. Some of these sources are widely accessible
(hymnals) while others (sermons and prayers) are less so because they were
normally not published for most of Baptist history. From time to time,

Baptists have adopted catechisms for instructing their children in Christian doctrine. For example, in 1680 a London pastor named Hercules Collins published "An Orthodox Catechism," which was a Baptist revision of the influential Heidelberg Catechism of 1563. When available, catechisms are valuable windows into Baptist identity. Of course, many Baptists have published books, periodicals, and pamphlets, and these documents also help us understand Baptist identity.

Confessions, covenants, and ecclesiastical records are particularly fruitful sources for determining Baptist identity. These three sources demonstrate that Baptist identity has often been worked out in community. As this book has demonstrated, from the earliest days of the Baptist movement in the seventeenth century, Baptists have written confessions of faith that summarize their beliefs. For at least the past century, some Baptists have adopted a negative posture toward confessions. They suggest that any prescriptive use of confessions is "creedalism," or the elevation of a merely human standard above Scripture and an infringement on individual liberty of conscience. While this view is popular in some circles, it reflects a misunderstanding of Baptist history. As Timothy George argues, "The idea that voluntary, conscientious adherence to an explicit doctrinal standard is somehow foreign to the Baptist tradition is a peculiar notion not borne out by careful examination of our heritage."

> A N
> ## Orthodox Catechifm :
> Being the Sum of
> ## Chriftian Religion,
> Contained in the Law and Gofpel.
>
> *Publifhed*
>
> For preventing the Canker and Poifon of Herefy and Error.
>
> ─────────
>
> **By H. COLLINS.**
>
> ─────────
>
> *Search the Scriptures.* John 14. 39.
>
> *The Words that I have fpoken, the fame fhall judge you in the laft day.* John 12.48.
>
> ─────────
>
> *LONDON,*
>
> Printed in the Year, 1680.

"An Orthodox Catechism" *(1680)*.

Baptist confessions have been written by individuals, as with Thomas Helwys's Declaration of Faith of English People Remaining at Amsterdam in Holland (1611), and congregations, as with the confession adopted by First Baptist Church of Boston, Massachusetts (1665). Sometimes Baptist institutions have drafted confessions, as with Southern Baptist Theological Seminary's Abstract of Principles (1858) and the doctrinal statement of Uganda Baptist Seminary (2005). Often, however, confessions have been adopted by groups of Baptists from multiple churches, as with the Standard

Confession (1660), the Second London Confession (1689), and the Baptist Faith and Message (1925). Though Baptists have assigned varying levels of importance to confessionalism, confessions are often a good starting place for discussions of Baptist identity. As B. H. Carroll argues: "There was never a man in the world without a creed. A creed is what you believe. What is a confession? It is a declaration of what you believe." Confessions summarize many key beliefs of the Baptists who affirm them.

Local church covenants, which we discussed briefly in chapter 8, are a second important source for understanding Baptist identity. As Charles DeWeese argues, "Baptists worldwide have written and used hundreds, and perhaps thousands, of church covenants since initiating that development in England in the early 1600's. . . . Covenants deserve careful evaluation because they helped shape Baptist church membership standards and practices." As Timothy George notes, "Church covenants were the ethical counterparts to confessions of faith. Confessions dealt with what one believed; church covenants spoke about how one should live." The earliest English Baptists inherited a covenantal ecclesiology from the English Separatists, and like their forebears they made covenants central to their understanding of church membership. Even churches that were not constituted around covenants tended to adopt them later, as was the case with New Road Baptist Church in Oxford, which was founded in the 1650s but adopted a covenant in 1780. Many churches have written their own covenants while others have adopted generic church covenants. In America, New Hampshire pastor J. Newton Brown's covenant, which he published in his book *The Baptist Church Manual* (1853), was widely adopted by Baptist churches well into the mid-twentieth century. Many rural churches still display copies of "The Baptist Church Covenant" (Brown's covenant) on the walls of their sanctuaries or fellowship halls.

Ecclesiastical records constitute a third key source for understanding Baptist identity. From their earliest days, Baptist churches kept "minute books" of congregational meetings and sometimes deacons' meetings. These minute books frequently offer a helpful glimpse into Baptist identity in a given church or era. Associations, conventions, and Baptist institutions have also kept detailed records. Associational "circular letters"—short treatises that were written at the request of the association and circulated among member churches—provide valuable information about Baptist identity. For example, during the years of the American Civil War, the Sandy Creek Baptist Association in North Carolina made little reference to slavery in their associational letters, but they repeatedly argued the war was judgment for "Sabbath-breaking"—working or enjoying recreational pursuits on Sundays. Other valuable records include resolutions or position papers adopted by

J. Newton Brown's Church Covenant (1853)

Having been led, as we believe, by the Spirit of God to receive the Lord Jesus Christ as our Saviour; and, on the profession of our faith, having been baptized in the name of the Father, and of the Son, and of the Holy Ghost, we do now, in the presence of God, angels, and this assembly, most solemnly and joyfully enter into covenant with one another, as one body in Christ.

We engage, therefore, by the aid of the Holy Spirit, to walk together in Christian love; to strive for the advancement of this church, in knowledge, holiness, and comfort; to promote its prosperity and spirituality; to sustain its worship, ordinances, discipline, and doctrines; to contribute cheerfully and regularly to the support of the ministry, the expenses of the church, the relief of the poor, and the spread of the gospel through all nations.

We also engage to maintain family and secret devotion; to religiously educate our children; to seek the salvation of our kindred and acquaintances; to walk circumspectly in the world; to be just in our dealings, faithful in our engagements, and exemplary in our deportment; to avoid all tattling, backbiting, and excessive anger; to abstain from the sale and use of intoxicating drinks as a beverage, and to be zealous in our efforts to advance the kingdom of our Saviour.

We further engage to watch over one another in brotherly love; to remember each other in prayer; to aid each other in sickness and distress; to cultivate Christian sympathy in feeling and courtesy in speech; to be slow to take offense, but always ready for reconciliation, and mindful of the rules of our Saviour, to secure it without delay.

We moreover engage, that when we remove from this place, we will as soon as possible unite with some other church, where we can carry out the spirit of this covenant, and the principles of God's Word.

Baptist denominations, entities, and local churches. Whereas confessions focus on beliefs and covenants emphasize practices, ecclesiastical records often include valuable information pertaining to both.

When one examines all these sources, it becomes clear that Baptists hold the vast majority of their beliefs in common with other Christians. Like virtually every Christian tradition, Baptists have historically affirmed such foundational doctrines as the Trinity, the full deity and humanity of Christ, the virgin birth, God's direct creation of the universe, the inspiration of Scripture, the importance of Christian ethics, and the reality and eternality of heaven and hell. Like virtually every Protestant tradition, Baptists have normally believed in the supreme authority of Scripture, justification by faith alone, the priesthood of all believers, and the two ordinances (or sacraments) of baptism and the Lord's Supper. Like most evangelical Protestants, Baptists have historically affirmed the truthfulness and sufficiency of Scripture, the centrality of the atonement in securing salvation, the necessity of personal conversion, and the importance of Christian witness. In the case of the latter, Baptists have frequently been trailblazers among evangelicals in developing creative evangelism initiatives, participating in global missions, championing religious liberty, and advocating human rights.

In addition to these shared core beliefs, Baptists historically have also embraced certain beliefs they uniquely emphasize; we call these the "Baptist distinctives" or "Baptist principles." Most of the Baptist distinctives are ecclesiological in nature. Not every Baptist uses the same terminology for the distinctives, and not every church or denomination applies Baptist principles in exactly the same way, but nearly all Baptists affirm the same core beliefs as central to Baptist identity. Though none of these convictions is found only among Baptists, collectively they are defining convictions of Baptist Christianity. Wherever you find these distinctives affirmed, you find a "baptistic" church, even if that congregation does not self-identify as "capital B" Baptist, participates in diverse ministry networks with nonbaptistic churches, and even claims to be nondenominational. The remainder of this chapter will focus on historic Baptist distinctives.

Baptist Distinctives

All true Christians believe that Jesus Christ is Lord. Indeed, this is the foundational confession of New Testament Christianity: "If you confess with your mouth, 'Jesus is Lord,' and believe in your heart that God raised Him from the dead, you will be saved" (Rom 10:9). However, the free church tradition, of which Baptists are a part, has always placed unique emphasis on Christ's lordship by seeking to relate it to both individual discipleship and local church ecclesiology. Baptists believe Jesus exercises his sovereign, gracious, kingly rule over every individual believer and every local congregation. To be a Christian is to bow the knee to Christ's rule over your life through repentance and faith. To be a church is to strive to conform every aspect of congregational life to the will of Christ as it is revealed in the Bible. Baptists believe their distinctives reflect their submission to Christ's kingly rule over individuals and churches, closely following the practices of the New Testament churches, and reflect the gospel that Christ has commanded us to proclaim in word and embody in deed (Matt 28:18–20).

Regenerate Church Membership

Baptists believe that a local church's membership should be comprised only of individuals who provide credible evidence they have repented of their sins and trusted in Jesus Christ as their Lord and Savior. We refer to this ecclesiological distinctive as either the believer's church or, more commonly, regenerate ("born again") church membership. Many Baptist scholars agree that regenerate church membership is the foundational Baptist distinctive. For example, John Hammett calls regenerate church membership "the Baptist mark of the church." Regenerate church membership affirms that formal identification with the body of Christ is only for those who have acknowledged Christ's lordship over their lives by faith. This principle also closely relates the gospel to the church by making belief a prerequisite to membership.

The New Testament indicates that the earliest churches included only professing believers in their membership. The consistent pattern in the book of Acts is that conversion is prior to identification with the church (Acts 2:41–47; 4:4; 14:21). To Baptists biblical arguments for infant membership seem strained, frequently based more on tradition or a theological system than the practices of New Testament churches. One key promise of the new covenant prophesied in Jeremiah 31:31–34 is that all members of the covenant will "know" the Lord. Theologically, a believer's church is more consistent with the new covenant and the gospel it embodies than a church that grants any form of membership to non-Christians. Baptists, like all Christians, affirm the biblical command to raise their children in the "nurture and admonition of the Lord" (Eph 6:4 KJV). However, we do not believe this entails granting membership in Christ's new covenant community to the unconverted children of believers. To apply this principle to a current discussion among evangelicals, the gospel way and the New Testament pattern is that you must *believe* before you can *belong*.

Regenerate church membership was a core principle of the earliest Baptists that was clearly embodied in their confessional statements. Helwys's confession (1611) stated, "The church of Christ is a company of faithful people (1 Cor 1:2. Eph 1:1), separated from the world by the word and Spirit of God (2 Cor 6:17) being knit to the Lord, and one to another, by baptism (1 Cor 12:13) upon their own confession of the faith (Acts 8:37) and sins (Matt 3:6)." The First London Confession (1646) argues,

> Jesus Christ hath here on earth a spiritual kingdom, which is his church, whom he hath purchased and redeemed to himself as a peculiar inheritance; which church is a company of visible saints, called and separated from the world by the word and Spirit of God, to the visible profession of faith of the gospel, being baptized into that faith, and joined to the Lord, and each other, by mutual agreement in the practical enjoyment of the ordinances commanded by Christ their head and king.

Every major Baptist confession of faith up to the present day affirms regenerate church membership.

Historically, Baptists have employed two practices that aid in the pursuit of a believer's church. The first is the adoption of local church covenants, a topic mentioned earlier in this chapter. Charles DeWeese defines a church covenant as "a series of written pledges based on the Bible which church members voluntarily make to God and to one another regarding their basic moral and spiritual commitments and the practice of their faith." Until the early twentieth century, to join a Baptist church meant to voluntarily embrace the church's covenant as a general guide for life and godliness. Individually each member covenanted with the wider body. Corporately the whole body covenanted with Christ. While covenants were neglected for most of the twentieth century, the past couple of decades have seen renewed emphasis on covenantal church membership among both North American and British Baptists.

A second practice, often closely tied to church covenants, is redemptive church discipline. As we argued in chapter 8, Baptists historically have been committed to church discipline. John L. Dagg spoke for most Baptists when he wrote in 1858, "It has been remarked, that when discipline leaves the church, Christ goes with it." Church discipline safeguards regenerate church membership by protecting sound doctrine and promoting godly living. Church discipline is intended to bring about one of two results in the disciplined individual: conviction and repentance in the case of a rebellious but authentic believer or awakening to the gospel in the case of a false professor of Christianity. Church discipline is intended to be redemptive, not puni-

John L. Dagg (1794–1884) was a nineteenth-century champion of regenerate church membership and church discipline.

tive. For the wider church, discipline protects the purity of the congregation. Discipline communicates to the disciplined individual his need to repent and seek reconciliation with Christ and his church.

Church discipline declined for much of the twentieth century for a variety of reasons, including an emphasis on individualism (especially in North America), concerns about abusive applications of discipline, and an implicit prioritization of evangelism over discipleship in many churches. However, as with church covenants, greater emphasis has been given to church discipline in recent decades. For example, at their 2008 annual meeting in Indianapolis, Southern Baptists adopted a resolution titled "On Regenerate Church Membership and Church Member Restoration." Southern Baptists from a variety of theological and methodological perspectives came together and promoted the resolution. Regenerate church membership and practices that aid us in our pursuit of this principle are helpful points of unity for Baptist groups that are sometimes divided in other areas.

Southern Baptists Reaffirm a Believer's Church and Church Discipline

RESOLVED, That we humbly urge our churches to maintain accurate membership rolls for the purpose of fostering ministry and accountability among all members of the congregation; and be it further

RESOLVED, That we urge the churches of the Southern Baptist Convention to repent of the failure among us to live up to our professed commitment to regenerate church membership and any failure to obey Jesus Christ in the practice of lovingly correcting wayward church members (Matthew 18:15-18); and be it further

RESOLVED, That we humbly encourage denominational servants to support and encourage churches that seek to recover and implement our Savior's teachings on church discipline, even if such efforts result in the reduction in the number of members that are reported in those churches, and be it finally

RESOLVED, That we humbly urge the churches of the Southern Baptist Convention and their pastors to implement a plan to minister to, counsel, and restore wayward church members based upon the commands and principles given in Scripture (Matthew 18:15-35; 2 Thessalonians 3:6-15; Galatians 6:1; James 5:19-20).

Excerpted from "On Regenerate Church Membership and Church Member Restoration" (2008).

Believer's Baptism

Regenerate church membership may be the foundational Baptist distinctive, but believer's baptism is almost certainly the most well known. Believer's baptism is simply the idea that baptism should only be applied to individuals who give credible testimony of personal faith in Christ. The earliest Baptists practiced believer's baptism by affusion—pouring water over the head. The London General Baptist pastor Leonard Busher was the first

Baptist to advocate believer's baptism by immersion in his tract *Religious Peace; or, a Plea for Liberty of Conscience* (1614), though the practice was likely first implemented by Richard Blunt and the JLJ Church around 1641 (see chap. 1). Since that time Baptists have nearly universally practiced believer's baptism by immersion. Baptists argue believer's baptism by immersion was the New Testament practice because the Greek word *baptizo* literally means to immerse, dip, or submerge something in water. Furthermore, Baptists point out there is no evidence in the Bible of a *known* unbeliever being baptized. (Of course some professing Christians later turned out to be false believers.)

Baptists have often baptized converts outdoors as a public testimony before the watching world. This photograph was taken circa 1905.

When pedobaptists argue that believers and their children should be baptized, Baptists typically respond that any attempt to argue infant baptism from the New Testament amounts to eisegesis—reading convictions into the text rather than allowing convictions to arise from the text. Furthermore, pedobaptists cannot agree among themselves on a theology of infant baptism. Presbyterians, Lutherans, Roman Catholics, and the Eastern Orthodox disagree with one another on why infants should be baptized. To Baptists infant baptism seems like a practice in search of a theology to support it. By contrast, nearly all credobaptists—those who advocate believer's baptism—contend that believer's baptism by immersion is a symbolic depiction of the gospel, is an outward sign of the spiritual transformation within the life of the new believer, and marks the public identification of a believer with the body of Christ.

In the New Testament baptism is tied to the gospel in at least two different ways. First, baptism is tied to the *meaning* of the gospel. The key passage is Romans 6:3–5:

> Or are you unaware that all of us who were baptized into Christ Jesus were baptized into His death? Therefore we were buried with Him by baptism into death, in order that, just as Christ was raised from the dead by the glory of the Father, so we too may walk in a new way of life. For if we have been joined with Him in the likeness of His death, we will certainly also be in the likeness of His resurrection.

According to Paul, baptism symbolizes important gospel realities like union with Christ, the washing away of sin, regeneration, sanctification, and the resurrection from the dead. While some of these realities could be depicted through infant baptism, only the immersion of professing believers depicts all of them.

Baptism is also tied to the *proclamation* of the gospel. The key passage on this point is the Great Commission of Matthew 28:18–20: "Then Jesus came near and said to them, 'All authority has been given to Me in heaven and on earth. Go, therefore, and make disciples of all nations, baptizing them in the name of the Father and of the Son and of the Holy Spirit, teaching them to observe everything I have commanded you. And remember, I am with you always, to the end of the age.'" According to Jesus, part of what it means to evangelize the nations is to make disciples and baptize them. The goal is not a mere spiritual decision but a whole-life transformation that is evidenced in part through baptism.

Every Baptist confession affirms believer's baptism, and nearly every confession from the 1640s onward has specified immersion as the proper mode of baptism. For example, the First London Confession (1646) states,

> The way and manner of dispensing this ordinance [baptism], is dipping or plunging the body under water; it being a sign, must answer the things signified, which is, that interest the saints have in the death, burial, and resurrection of Christ: And that as certainly as the body is buried under water, and risen again, so certainly shall the bodies of the saints be raised by the power of Christ, in the day of the resurrection, to reign with Christ.

According to the Standard Confession (1660), "the right and only way, of gathering churches, (according to Christ's appointment, Matt 28:19–20) is first to teach, or preach the gospel, Mark 16:16, to the sons and daughters of men; and then to baptize (that is in English to dip) in the name of the Father, Son, and Holy Spirit, or in the name of the Lord Jesus Christ."

Though Baptists universally affirm believer's baptism, normally by immersion, in several chapters we have shown that Baptists have periodically debated the relationship between baptism, the Lord's Supper, and church membership. Historically, most Baptists considered baptism a prerequisite to both church membership and participation in communion. This view has been codified in most Baptist confessions, the one noteworthy exception being the Second London Confession (1689). However, not all Baptists have affirmed this view. As we discussed in chapter 7, Landmark Baptists sometimes restricted communion to members of their local churches, a practice they called "closed communion." However, the more common variation, which dates to the seventeenth century, is for some churches to practice an open membership by inviting pedobaptists to join the church and celebrate the Lord's Supper without first receiving believer's baptism. John Bunyan took this position in his debate with William Kiffen (chap. 2). Other early examples of open membership congregations include the Broadmead Baptist Church in Bristol and some Welsh Baptists in the eighteenth and nineteenth centuries. Many British Baptist churches have embraced open membership since the early twentieth century, though one also finds some examples of this practice in North America and Oceania.

A much larger number of churches have practiced open communion but maintained a closed membership; baptism is a prerequisite to church membership but not the Lord's Table. Robert Hall Jr. and Charles Spurgeon advocated this view in the nineteenth century (see chap. 5). Many Baptists in America gravitated to this position during the twentieth century. This has created tension in the Southern Baptist Convention because all three editions of the Baptist Faith and Message affirm baptism that, "being a church ordinance, it is prerequisite to the privileges of church membership and to the Lord's Supper." In the 1960s and 1970s, churches were sometimes disfellowshipped from local associations and even state conventions for practicing open communion. However, by the early twenty-first century, polls indicated that Southern Baptists were nearly evenly divided between open and closed communion churches, with the open communion congregations holding a slight majority. It remains to be seen whether closed communion will remain a common practice among Baptists, at least in the English-speaking world.

Congregational Polity

Polity refers to a church's basic structure and patterns of leadership. Congregational polity, or congregationalism, is the belief that local churches should be governed by their own membership. The Baptist Faith and Message

(2000) offers a concise summary of congregationalism: "Each congregation operates under the Lordship of Christ through democratic processes." Congregationalism can be contrasted with presbyterian polity, which invests final authority in church courts made up of elders, and episcopal polity, which affirms the final authority of a bishop or bishops. Congregationalism carried over into the Baptist movement from the English Separatists. Most Anabaptist groups also practiced congregationalism, which may have further influenced some of the early General Baptists.

A form of congregational polity is implied in several New Testament passages. In Matthew 18:15–20 and 1 Corinthians 5:1–13, two passages related to church discipline, the entire church is called upon to participate in excommunicating a wayward member. In Acts 6:1–6, the entire church at Jerusalem sets apart seven men to serve in a deacon role in the congregation. Assuming the epistles of Timothy and Titus were meant for a wider audience than simply the original recipients, in 1 Timothy 3:1–13 and Titus 1:5–9 churches are given specific qualifications by which to vet potential elders and deacons. Based on these passages, Baptists argue that, at minimum, the Bible suggests the entire church is responsible for maintaining its membership and selecting church officers. Prudentially, most Baptist churches also affirm the congregation's budget and approve major expenditures. The procedure for deciding other matters is contextual and varies from church to church.

Congregationalism is a corporate expression of the Reformation principle of the priesthood of all believers. In Exodus 19:6, the Lord refers to Israel as a "kingdom of priests," and in 1 Peter 2:9, Peter calls the church a "royal priesthood." Based on this the Reformers argued against the "sacerdotal" view of medieval Catholicism that affirmed a special class of priests who mediated God's grace to the laity through their administration of the sacraments. The Reformers argued for what might be called an "every-member ministry" that affirmed the dignity of all vocations as ways to glorify God, proclaim the gospel, and serve others. As Malcolm Yarnell has demonstrated, Anabaptists, English Separatists, and Baptists filtered their understanding of the believers' priesthood through Matthew 18:15–20, which they understood to point to congregational polity. In recent decades some Baptists have promoted a novel, more individualistic interpretation of this doctrine that they call the priesthood of *the* believer. This approach confuses individual liberty of conscience with the believers' priesthood. Furthermore, as Timothy George has argued, the idea of the priesthood of the believer has frequently been used to defend progressive understandings of biblical inspiration and authority, gender roles, and human sexuality. We advocate the older understanding of the royal priesthood, which we believe is more biblical and reflects the best of the Baptist tradition. For Baptists congregational polity is simply living out the priesthood of all believers in the context of the local church.

Sometimes Baptists use democratic language when they speak of congregationalism, but this can be misleading. Baptists argue that each local church is a "Christocracy" under the ultimate kingship of Jesus Christ and is to be comprised only of believers. Healthy congregationalism thus assumes a church is committed to the final lordship of Christ and is striving to maintain a regenerate membership. When these priorities are not affirmed, congregationalism can easily devolve into a mere democracy where various special-interest groups try to outvote one another in church member meetings. However, when congregationalism is practiced correctly, the church's regenerate members confirm to one another Christ's plan for their church as they seek to follow his will through submitting to his written Word. As J. L. Reynolds argued in 1849, "If churches are composed only of such as give credible evidence of having been taught by the Spirit of God, they may be safely entrusted with the management of their own interests."

When discussing church polity, we need to state an important caveat: congregationalism does not perfectly mirror New Testament polity. The polity of the earliest churches could best be described as a combination of congregationalism and the direct rule of the apostles; the specifics varied somewhat, depending on context. Congregationalism is an attempt to adapt the polity of the earliest churches to a world without authoritative apostles in the New Testament sense of that office. Baptists and other congregationalists believe their views represent a better adaptation than episcopal or presbyterian polities.

By the early twenty-first century, congregational polity had become perhaps the most controversial of the Baptist distinctives. One reason for this is a perceived incompatibility of congregational polity and pastoral authority. Scripture makes clear in 1 Thessalonians 5:12–13 and Hebrews 13:17 that Christians

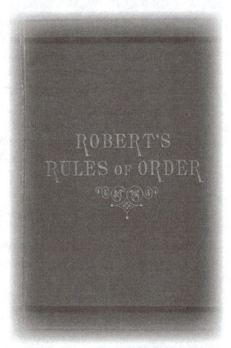

First edition of Robert's Rules of Order *(1876), which is used by many Baptist churches to order their membership meetings.*

are to honor and submit to their leaders. How can this be done when a pastor's employment is dependent on the will of the members? Another reason some Baptists downplay congregationalism is their experience with unhealthy expressions of congregationalism. Some have lived through combative church conferences where the congregation showed little love for Christ or for one another. Others have witnessed (or endured) mean-spirited votes of "no confidence" in a pastor or other staff members, often for unbiblical reasons. Still others have seen ineffective congregationalism where the whole church had a voice in even the most mundane decisions.

We are troubled by unhealthy versions of congregationalism, but we do not believe the answer is to abandon congregational polity. We are convinced congregationalism comes down to trust. The membership selects and holds accountable its pastors (also called elders), so in a sense the members have authority over their pastors. But it is also true that the members select pastors *to lead them*—pastors are not mere employees but are leaders who are called upon to "shepherd the flock of God," "oversee" the church, and "rule well" (see Acts 20:28; 1 Tim 5:17–19; 1 Pet 5:1–2). So in a sense, pastors also have authority over their members. The congregation trusts the pastor or pastors who lead them, and the pastors trust the members not to act in an unbiblical manner toward their leaders. A culture of trust, in the context of a regenerate membership, will help ensure that congregationalism is expressed in healthy ways that focus on kingdom priorities rather than pet agendas. To that end we suggest the following "organizational scheme" as embodying a healthy, Christ-centered congregationalism: each local church should be ruled by Jesus Christ, governed by its members, led by its pastors/elders, and served by its deacons.

Local Church Autonomy

Local church autonomy is a hallmark of the wider free church tradition and has been championed by Baptists since the inception of their movement. Local church autonomy is the idea that every church is free to determine its own agenda apart from any external ecclesiastical coercion. Baptists believe autonomy reflects the biblical pattern. As Stan Norman notes, "The Bible makes no reference to any entity exerting authority above or beyond the local church." Positively stated, churches have the freedom to follow the Lord's leading in their worship and witness. Put more negatively, no denomination or convention or association can force a church to do something it does not wish to do. Local church autonomy is closely related to the aforementioned Baptist distinctives: the whole congregation of regenerate saints takes ownership of the church's ministry with the understanding that Christ alone is Lord of the church and his will is the standard by which the church's faithfulness is measured.

Some Baptists, especially in North America, have argued that local church autonomy means every church is independent of other churches and that any ecclesial relationships beyond the local church are undertaken for purely pragmatic purposes. For example, one often hears Southern Baptists argue something like this: "The local church is primary, but we ought to cooperate in associations or state conventions or the Southern Baptist Convention because we can accomplish more for the kingdom when we work together than when we go it alone." We are not convinced this is the best way to think about autonomy. Historically, both General and Particular Baptists in England embraced a view of autonomy that valued congregational freedom but also affirmed a robust doctrine of the church universal and interchurch cooperation. The Second London Confession says of autonomy, "To each of these churches thus gathered, according to [Christ's] mind declared in his word, he hath given all that power and authority, which is in any way needful for their carrying on that order in worship and discipline, which he hath instituted for them to observe; with commands and rules for the due and right exerting, and executing of that power." This is a strong statement of the freedom of local churches to determine their own spiritual agendas.

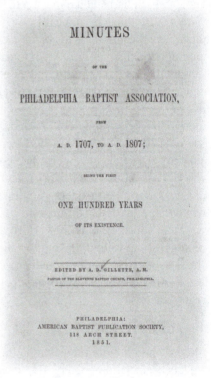

Inside cover of A. D. Gillette, ed.,
Minutes of the Philadelphia Baptist
Association, 1707–1807 *(1851).*

However, the same confession also claims the following concerning cooperation:

> As each church, and all the members of it, are bound to pray continually for the good and prosperity of all the churches of Christ, in all places, and upon all occasions to further every one within the bounds of their places and callings, in the exercise of their gifts and graces, so the churches, when planted by the providence of God, so as they may enjoy opportunity and advantage for it,

> ought to hold communion among themselves, for their peace,
> increase of love, and mutual edification.

The Baptists who adopted this confession affirmed the necessity of associational arrangements, not only based on pragmatic considerations but because cooperation is healthy and embodies the type of unity that will one day characterize Christ's church when it assembles at the marriage supper of the Lamb (Rev 19:6–10). Associational cooperation is as much about ecclesiology and eschatology as it is mission and fellowship. This view of ecclesiology carried over into colonial North America, especially New England and the Middle Colonies. The churches of the Philadelphia Association adopted a lightly amended version of the Second London Confession, including its affirmations of both autonomy and associationalism.

Many British Baptists continue to affirm the historic justification for associations, but during the nineteenth century a majority of American Baptists moved in a more independent direction, especially in the South and Southwest. This happened for many reasons. The American emphasis on freedom and individualism certainly played a role; these themes were frequently applied to both congregationalism and local church autonomy. Landmark sectarianism played a role as well, especially its frequent denial of the universal church. Both liberalism and fundamentalism contributed to the trend. While these movements differed greatly on doctrinal matters, both were thoroughly "modern" in that they prized individual and congregational freedom, albeit unto different ends. The tendency among Southern Baptists to equate cooperation with financial support of joint missions and ministry since the advent of the Cooperative Program in 1925 has furthered an overemphasis on independence and a mostly pragmatic understanding of cooperation.

Churches can and should cooperate with like-minded congregations so they can do more together than any one church can do alone, but this is not the only reason individual congregations should cooperate with one another. Local churches do not exist in isolation. In most places they are part of the wider body of Christ in a county, town, or city. Churches need one another, especially when they are of like faith and practice. We sharpen one another theologically. We come alongside one another when hurting churches have needs that can be met by sister congregations. We need to be humble enough to ask for help, selfless enough to serve sister churches, and biblical enough to heed the sound counsel of sister churches who lovingly point out errors and faults in our theology or methodology.

Historically most Baptists have agreed that autonomy must be balanced with accountability. Baptist associations and conventions have often chosen to cease cooperation with churches that embrace doctrines or practices that the majority judges aberrant. For example, in 1992 the Southern Baptist

Convention withdrew fellowship from two churches in North Carolina because one voted to bless the union of two homosexual males and the other voted to license a homosexual to the gospel ministry. Those churches were free to embrace that position, but they were also held accountable by sister congregations who determined their views to be unbiblical. Ultimately, of course, and most importantly, every church is accountable to Christ; he reveals his will for us in Scripture. He is the One to whom we will all one day give an account.

We believe autonomy is a means not to mere independence but to greater gospel freedom. Autonomy guarantees the freedom of individual churches to proclaim the gospel in whatever ways they believe the Lord is leading them. When Baptists are at our best, associations, state conventions, and national conventions help us cultivate this sort of gospel-centered cooperative autonomy. Autonomy should spur churches to greater faithfulness rather than tempting churches to strike out in their own directions—a move that too often leads to unbiblical compromise.

Religious Freedom

Baptists have always championed liberty of conscience for all people. Liberty of conscience is the belief that every person is free to follow his conscience in religious matters without any human coercion. The Abstract of Principles (1858) offers a good summary of this conviction: "God alone is Lord of the conscience; and He hath left it free from the doctrines and commandments of men, which are in anything contrary to His word, or not contained in it. Civil magistrates being ordained of God, subjection in all lawful things commanded by them ought to be yielded by us in the Lord, not only for wrath, but also for conscience sake." Baptists have sometimes called this principle by other names such as "religious freedom," "religious liberty," "soul competency," "soul freedom," and "soul liberty"; these terms are more or less synonymous. Liberty of conscience is not taught explicitly in a specific biblical passage but inferred from several biblical principles. As Stan Norman argues, religious freedom is among the "doctrinal corollaries" of "our convictions about and commitment to biblical authority, the lordship of Christ, and the nature and practice of a New Testament church."

Liberty of conscience functions on the personal level much like local-church autonomy functions on the corporate level. As such, it can be distorted into an overemphasis on freedom—in this case individual freedom. Some Baptists, especially E. Y. Mullins, have been accused of reading American individualism into the historic Baptist commitment to soul competency, resulting in a view of freedom that is at least potentially untethered from accountability. While it is debatable whether Mullins was too individualistic in his views—he was also a champion of congregational accountability—many Baptists have, without doubt, claimed his mantle in advancing highly personalized views of liberty of conscience. We believe liberty of conscience does not justify aberrant theology but rather provides the freedom for individual Christians to follow Christ's will as it is revealed in Scripture, remembering that one day we will each stand before him to give an account for our faith and practice.

John Leland Defends Liberty of Conscience

Government has no more to do with the religious opinions of men than it has with the principles of mathematics. Let every man speak freely without fear—maintain the principles that he believes—worship according to his own faith, either one God, three Gods, no God, or twenty Gods; and let government protect him in so doing, i.e., see that he meets with no personal abuse or loss of property for his religious opinions. Instead of discouraging him with proscriptions, fines, confiscation or death, let him be encouraged, as a free man, to bring forth his arguments and maintain his points with all boldness; then if his doctrine is false it will be confuted, and if it is true (though ever so novel) let others credit it.

Excerpted from John Leland, *The Rights of Conscience Inalienable, and Therefore, Religious Opinions Not Cognizable by the Law* (1791).

Historically Baptists have argued that the best way to preserve liberty of conscience is to promote a formal separation between church and state. Though many Baptists have lived in contexts where there was no church-state separation, Baptists have traditionally defended religious liberty for all people and advocated a free church in a free state. In fact, over the past four centuries, no other group of Christians has so consistently advocated religious liberty as a basic human right. This principle has been championed by Baptists all over the world and, alongside evangelism, is central to a distinctively Baptist approach to missions. As this book has made clear, numerous Baptists have defended religious freedom and church-state separation in treatises, tracts, sermons, and confessional statements. Thousands of Baptists have been fined, jailed, tortured, and even killed for their commitment to this principle. As the Baptist Faith and Message

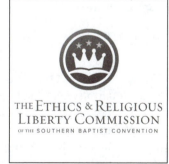

The Ethics and Religious Liberty Commission of the Southern Baptist Convention advocates for religious liberty in America.

(2000) says, "A free church in a free state is the Christian ideal, and this implies the right of free and unhindered access to God on the part of all men, and the right to form and propagate opinions in the sphere of religion without interference by the civil power."

In the past 200 years, and especially since the mid-twentieth century, many of the world's nations have come to embrace religious freedom as a fundamental human right. Often nations affirm a formal separation of church and state based on nonreligious theories of natural rights or broader pragmatic considerations. Historically, while Baptists have been willing to make cause with all people who defend religious freedom, we have argued for a free church in a free state for spiritual reasons. As Russell Moore argues, religious liberty is ultimately about the Great Commission. Church-state separation protects the freedom of Christians to proclaim Christ to non-Christians and make disciples from people of all nations.

As the West has become increasingly secularized, some have cited the separation of church and state to justify what Richard John Neuhaus calls a "naked public square" that is devoid of religious voices. This is not what Baptists advocate. Though not all Baptists apply the principle of church-state separation the same way, all Baptists agree that Christians have an obligation to be "salt" and "light" as we bear witness to the broader culture (Matt 5:13–16). For this reason most Baptists challenge secularist visions of church and state that seek to silence the voices of Christians or any other people of faith. Church-state separation is not an end in itself but is a strategy for allowing people of all faiths and no faith to live out their convictions without fear of coercion and persecution. As the previous chapter argued, Baptists have been willing to cooperate with other groups that value religious liberty and to defend the rights of all people to follow their consciences in spiritual matters.

Conclusion

We can think of no better place to end this chapter and this book. As we hope our narrative has made clear, the entire Baptist story consistently comes back to three key interrelated themes: promoting liberty of conscience, following Christ's will in our individual lives and churches, and proclaiming the gospel everywhere. Baptists have not always lived up to these ideals, but when we have been at our best, we have embodied them. As historians we appreciate these themes and the way they have been lived out by Baptists. As Baptist followers of Jesus Christ, we sincerely pray these three priorities will continue to be at the center of the Baptist vision in anticipation of that day when the Lord says to Baptists and all followers of Jesus Christ, "Well done, good and faithful servant. You have been faithful over a little; I will set you over much. Enter into the joy of your master" (Matt 25:23 ESV).

For Further Study

Allison, Gregg R. *Sojourners and Strangers: The Doctrine of the Church*. Wheaton, IL: Crossway, 2012.

Carroll, B. H. *Baptists and Their Doctrines*, The Library of Baptist Classics. Edited by Timothy George and Denise George. Nashville, TN: B&H, 1995.

Dever, Mark E. *The Church: The Gospel Made Visible*. Nashville, TN: B&H, 2012.

———. *Polity: Biblical Arguments on How to Conduct Church Life*. Washington, DC: Nine Marks Ministries, 2001.

Dockery, David S., ed. *Southern Baptist Identity: An Evangelical Denomination Faces the Future*. Wheaton, IL: Crossway, 2009.

George, Timothy. "The Priesthood of All Believers and the Quest for Theological Integrity." *Criswell Theological Review* (Spring 1989): 283–94.

George, Timothy, and Denise George, eds. *Baptist Confessions, Covenants, and Catechisms*, The Library of Baptist Classics. Nashville, TN: B&H, 1996.

Hammett, John S. *Biblical Foundations for Baptist Churches: A Contemporary Ecclesiology*. Grand Rapids, MI: Kregel Academic, 2005.

Harper, Keith, ed. *Through a Glass Darkly: Contested Notions of Baptist Identity*. Tuscaloosa, AL: University of Alabama Press, 2012.

Jewett, Paul K. *Infant Baptism and the Covenant of Grace*. Grand Rapids, MI: Eerdmans, 1978.

Norman, R. Stanton. *The Baptist Way: Distinctives of a Baptist Church*. Nashville, TN: B&H Academic, 2005.

———. *More Than Just a Name: Preserving Our Baptist Identity*. Nashville, TN: B&H Academic, 2001.

Schreiner, Thomas R., and Shawn D. Wright, eds. *Believer's Baptism: Sign of the New Covenant in Christ*. Nashville, TN: B&H Academic, 2007.

White, Thomas, Jason G. Duesing, and Malcolm B. Yarnell III, eds. *First Freedom: The Baptist Perspective on Religious Liberty*. Nashville, TN: B&H Academic, 2007.

———, eds. *Restoring Integrity in Baptist Churches*. Grand Rapids, MI: Kregel Academic, 2007.

———, eds. *Upon This Rock: The Baptist View of the Church*. Nashville, TN: B&H Academic, 2010.

Questions for Discussion

1. Describe the three approaches to Baptist identity. If you are a Baptist, which of these approaches best describes you? If you are not a Baptist, can you think of similar levels of belonging with respect to other religious traditions?

2. What are the three most important sources for studying Baptist identity? Has your church ever adopted a church covenant? If so, which one? What emphasis is placed on it, if any? Which items, if any, in J. Newton Brown's church covenant do you find helpful for church members? Which items, if any, in Brown's church covenant do you find unnecessary?

3. What biblical passages do Baptists point to in order to justify their understanding of regenerate church membership? In what ways is church membership affirmed in your church? Evaluate the statement, "You must believe before you can belong," as it relates to children of non-Christian parents.

4. On what basis do Baptists practice church discipline? Do you believe church discipline can have a redemptive purpose? Explain your answer.

5. Compare and contrast the credobaptist position on baptism with the pedo-baptist position. Which of these two positions seems most convincing? Explain your answer. If you were baptized as a believer, describe the experience. If you have not been baptized, have you ever witnessed a baptismal service? What do you remember most about it?

6. What is congregational polity? How does it differ from presbyterian and episcopal polity? In what way is congregational polity different from a mere democracy? What solutions are presented in this section with regard to unhealthy congregationalism? Can you think of more solutions? Explain your answer.

7. What do Baptists believe about local church autonomy? How did General and Particular Baptists affirm local church autonomy while promoting a form of connectionalism? Do you believe churches should be autonomous, independent, or have regulatory oversight by larger church bodies? Explain your answer.

8. Explain the difference between liberty of conscience and personal religious autonomy. Provide an example of each from earlier chapters in the textbook. Do you agree or disagree with the statement that "religious liberty is ultimately about the Great Commission"? Explain your answer.

9. Can you think of areas where Baptists might partner with non-Baptists in promoting religious liberty? What lines should be drawn and what limits should be observed when cooperating on a common cause with people from different denominational perspectives? Explain your answer.

NAME INDEX

SUBJECT INDEX

SCRIPTURE INDEX

John

3:16   *137, 315*
14:15–17   *300*

Acts

2:41–47   *331*
6:1–6   *337*
8:37   *18, 331*
17:26   *105*
20:28   *288, 339*

Romans

6:3–5   *335*
6:4   *23*
10:9   *330*
13   *91*

1 Corinthians

1:2   *331*
5   *197*
5:1–13   *337*
7:20–22   *155*
12:13   *331*
13:4–8   *307*
14:15   *52*
15:22   *48*

2 Corinthians

6:14–18   *98*
6:17   *245, 331*

Galatians

6:1   *333*

Ephesians

1:1   *331*
5:19   *53*
6:4   *331*
6:5   *154*

Colossians

2:12   *23*
3:16   *53*
3:22   *154*

1 Thessalonians

2:19   *108*
5:12–13   *338*

2 Thessalonians

3:6   *197, 333*

1 Timothy

3:1–7   *312*
3:1–13   *337*
5:17–19   *339*

Titus

1:5–9   *312, 337*
1:7   *201*
3:10   *197*

Philemon

12–16   *155*

Hebrews

6   *31*
13:17   *288, 338*

James

5:13   *53*
5:14–15   *98*
5:19   *333*

1 Peter

2:9   *288, 337*
5:1–2   *339*

1 John

10   *188*

Jude

3   *202*

Revelation

1:6   *288*
6:4   *88*
7:3   *12*
19:6–10   *341*

IMAGE CREDITS

B&H Publishing Group expresses deep gratitude to the following persons and institutions for use of the images in *The Baptist Story*. Our aim has been to properly credit every image in this volume. If we have failed to do that, please contact us at bhcustomerservice@lifeway.com. We will make the required correction at the next printing.

Band of Hope Review (1851): p. 197

Baptist Encyclopedia, The: p. 140

Baptist History Preservation Society, The: p. 33

Benge, Dustin: p. 243

Blackpast.org: p. 186 (no clear permission requirement)

Canadian Baptist Archives, McMaster Divinity College: p. 274

Chute, Anthony: p. 170

Desiring God Ministries: p. 310

Ethics and Religious Liberty Commission: p. 339

Finn, Nathan: p. 260

Haykin, Michael A. G.: pp. 13, 24, 27, 40, 41, 44, 46, 51, 62, 66, 71, 72, 82, 89, 94, 95, 98, 99, 100, 104, 105, 157, 199

John Carter Brown University: p. 80

Jones, Jonathan: p. 305

Jones, William, *Christ in the Camp* (p.d.): p. 172

Laboring in the Lord: p. 75

North Carolina Office of Archives and History: p. 77

Public domain: pp. 212, 256, 296, 328, 336